Tasks in Primary Mathematics Teacher Education

MATHEMATICS TEACHER EDUCATION

VOLUME 4

SCOPE

The *Mathematics Teacher Education* book series presents relevant research and innovative international developments with respect to the preparation and professional development of mathematics teachers. A better understanding of teachers' cognitions as well as knowledge about effective models for preservice and inservice teacher education is fundamental for mathematics education at the primary, secondary and tertiary level in the various contexts and cultures across the world. Therefore, considerable research is needed to understand what facilitates and impedes mathematics teachers' professional learning. The series aims to provide a significant resource for teachers, teacher educators and graduate students by introducing and critically reflecting new ideas, concepts and findings of research in teacher education.

For other titles published in this series, go to
http://www.springer.com/series/6327

Barbara Clarke • Barbro Grevholm
Richard Millman
Editors

Tasks in Primary Mathematics Teacher Education

Purpose, Use and Exemplars

 Springer

Editors

Barbara Clarke
Monash University
Faculty of Education
Wellington Road
Clayton VIC 3800
Australia
barbara.clarke@education.monash.edu.au

Richard S. Millman
Georgia Institute of Technology
Center for Education Integrating Science,
Mathematics & Computing (CEISMC)
Atlanta, GA 30332-0282
USA
millman@ms.uky.edu

Barbro Grevholm
University of Agder
Faculty of Engineering and Science
Department of Mathematical Sciences
NO-4604 Kristiansand
Norway
barbro.grevholm@uia.no

ISBN: 978-0-387-09668-1   e-ISBN: 978-0-387-09669-8
DOI: 10.1007/978-0-387-09669-8

Library of Congress Control Number: 2008938622

Printed on acid-free paper

springer.com

Preface

The idea for this book emerged from discussions at the Research Study Conference 15 organised by the International Commission for Mathematical Instruction. The study focused on professional education and development of teachers of mathematics and brought together invited participants from around the world. The authors in this book are a selection of presenters at that study conference, who subsequently contributed chapters with examples and elaborations of tasks used in primary mathematics teacher education. The authors first provided outlines that were subsequently reviewed by the editorial group and then after a second review process revised to produce the chapters you will find here.

This book is organised in three sections. The first section presents chapters with tasks for teachers and teacher educators that indicate the cyclic character of the work. The second section concerns tasks as a tool for developing mathematical knowledge for teaching. The third section is related to tasks as a tool for developing knowledge through and for practice. These three categories are of course overlapping but help to focus key aspects of the purpose of the tasks. Each section begins with an overview and the book ends with a concluding chapter.

The chapters in this book describe tasks that have been used successfully in mathematics teacher education for primary teachers in a range of contexts and countries. These tasks are often exemplars of broader categories of tasks or illustrative of techniques for developing particular understandings. While the tasks have a practical and experiential focus, a theoretical or research-based justification is included for each of them.

We do not see this as a book about how mathematics teacher education is conducted in a particular country or institution or about the policy for that but rather as a book about research-driven practices. The primary audience for this book will be mathematics teacher educators who focus on the preparation of elementary/primary teachers. The tasks are applicable across a range of contexts. While the tasks themselves are a useful resource, the rationales and discussions of the nature and purpose of such tasks can provide richer understanding of the role of tasks in primary mathematics teacher education – tasks as the meta-level focus.

We acknowledge with much thanks the work of Nike Prince whose careful attention to the final editing, thoughtful liaising with authors and organised management of the development of the manuscript made a very important contribution to this book.

Barbara Clarke, Barbro Grevholm, and Richard Millman

Contents

Contributors

Solange Amato, Lecturer, Faculty of Education, University of Braslia, Brasil

George Ashline, Professor of Mathematics, Saint Michaels College, Vermont, USA

Dan Canada, Associate Professor, Department of Mathematics, Eastern Washington University, USA

José Carrillo, Assistant Professor, Faculty of Educational Sciences, University of Huelva, Spain

Paulo Carvalho, Institute of Child Studies, University of Minho, Portugal

Valter Cebolo, Institute of Child Studies, University of Minho, Portugal

Barbara Clarke, Associate Professor and Associate Dean of Staff, Faculty of Education, Monash University, Australia

Nuria Climent, University of Huelva, Spain

Olimpia Figueras, Researcher, Mathematics Education Department of the Center for Research and Advanced Studies of the National Poly-technique Institute (Cinvestav), Mexico

George Gadanidis, Associate Professor, Faculty of Education, The University of Western Ontario, Canada

Mercedes García, Professor, Department of Didactic of Mathematics, University of Seville, Spain

Alexandra Gomes, Assistant Professor, Institute of Child Studies, University of Minho, Portugal

Theresa Grant, Professor, Department of Mathematics, Western Michigan University, USA

Barbro Grevholm, Professor of Mathematics Education, University of Agder, Norway

Joanne Lieberman, Assistant Professor, Mathematics and Statistics Department, California State University Monterey Bay, USA

Jane-Jane Lo, Associate Professor, Department of Mathematics, Western Michigan University, USA

Nicolina A. Malara, Professor, Department of Mathematics, Faculty of Science, University of Modena & Reggio Emilia, Italy

Richard Millman, Director, Center for Education Integrating Science, Mathematics and Computing, and Professor of the Practice of Mathematics, Georgia Institute of Technology, USA

Meg Moss, Associate Professor of Mathematics and Teacher Education Coordinator, Pellissippi State Technical Community College in Knoxville, TN, USA

Nitsa Movshovitz-Hadar, Emeritus Professor of Mathematics Education, Technion – Israel Institute of Technology, Israel

Immaculate Namukasa, Assistant Professor, Faculty of Education, University of Western Ontario, Canada

Giancarlo Navarra, Department of Mathematics, University of Modena & Reggio E, Italy

Pedro Palhares, Assistant Professor, Institute of Child Studies, University of Minho, Portugal

Andrea Peter-Koop, Professor of Mathematics Education, University of Oldenburg, Germany

Regina Quinn, Project Director and co-PI of the Vermont Mathematics Partnership, USA

Mariana Sáiz, Professor, Learning and Teaching of sciences, humanities and arts, Universidad Pedagógica Nacional México City, Mexico

Victoria Sánchez, Professor, Department of Didactic of Mathematics, University of Seville, Spain

Atara Shriki, Oranim – Academic College of Education, Israel

Rose Spanneberg, Director, Rhodes University Mathematics Education Project (RUMEP), South Africa

Kelly Svec, Student, University of Kentucky, USA

Anne Teppo, Independent scholar who collaborates with other mathematics educators around the world

Dana Williams, Graduate, University of Kentucky, USA

Function, Form and Focus: The Role of Tasks in Elementary Mathematics Teacher Education

Barbro Grevholm, Richard Millman, and Barbara Clarke

The choice of tasks and the associated pedagogies is a key aspect of teaching and learning mathematics (see, e.g., Brousseau, 1997; Christiansen & Walther, 1986). We argue that what students learn is largely defined by the tasks they are given. For example, we assume that tasks designed to prompt higher order thinking are more likely to produce such thinking than tasks designed to offer skills practice (see, e.g., Doyle, 1998; Hiebert & Wearne, 1997). We agree with Ames (1992) that tasks are more likely to be effective when students have meaningful reasons for engaging in the activity, when there is enough but not too much challenge, and that variety is important. This is equally true when the teachers are the learners of mathematics.

Ensor (2000) described the content of any preservice or inservice course as a *privileged repetoire*, because

> it involves a particular selection and combination of mathematics for the production of pedagogic tasks, a particular selection of pedagogic resources to facilitate this, and the arrangement of these tasks into sequences as lessons. The privileged repertoire also includes features of classroom arrangement, the regulation of teacher-pupil communication and the deployment of appropriate forms of assessment. (p. 235)

Clearly the tasks we choose and how we use them have an impact on the learning of teachers.

Tasks have function, form and focus. They have an aim in relation to the learning expected from student teachers, they are given a form to inspire, challenge and motivate students, and they have specific foci chosen by the constructors of the task.

B. Grevholm
Professor of Mathematics Education, University of Agder, Norway

R. Millman
Director, Center for Education Integrating Science, Mathematics and Computing, and Professor of the Practice of Mathematics, Georgia Institute of Technology, USA

B. Clarke
Associate Professor and Associate Dean of Staff, Faculty of Education, Monash University, Australia

B. Clarke, B. Grevholm, and R. Millman (eds.), *Tasks in Primary Mathematics Teacher Education: Purpose, Use and Exemplars,* Mathematics Teacher Education 4,
© Springer Science+Business Media LLC 2009

The function, form and focus of a task are key to the implementation of what the teacher educators choose to emphasise. In reading the chapters the intentions of the teacher educators become clear, particularly how they have reasoned during the design and redesign of the task. The theoretical foundations or research base for the development of the task are discussed by the teacher educators in the chapters in the book. Often research has been linked to the design and redesign of the task and the learning process of the teacher educator is revealed in some of the chapters.

The tasks are used to promote the development of specific competencies, properties or skills for mathematics teachers. There are different ways to perceive what is the goal of mathematics teacher education. A model for teacher education in mathematics (Grevholm, 2006) based on a longitudinal study of mathematics teacher education in Sweden helped to frame the structure of this book as well as the focus for editing and discussion. In the model, teacher education is seen as the development of a professional identity as a mathematics teacher. This identity development is complementing the private identity of the teacher and it is governed by social demands, culture and the national identity (Grevholm, Even, Szendrei, & Carillo, 2004). The model has five key components of the professional identity:

- A professional language
- A personal view on and beliefs about knowledge and learning
- Knowledge about classroom management, methods and material
- Competence to judge and diagnose pupils' learning in mathematics
- Knowledge in mathematics related to teaching.

All these five main elements are interrelated and closely linked to each other. The model (Fig. 1) also indicates the basis for the five main areas and the sources for the knowledge and competencies, and how they are interrelated in a complex system. Student teachers' experiences, earlier knowledge, observations, reflections, practice, research and theoretical studies during the education contribute to the development of the five aspects of the teacher identity.

Tasks have features with the potential to promote development across a range of components of the teachers' professional identity and particularly in relation to professional language. Other categorisations or components of teacher development required in both pre-service and in-service teacher education are given in work by Barbara Clarke and colleagues in the development of teacher professional standards in Australia (Clarke, 2005). There the focus is on teacher professional attributes, professional knowledge and professional practice. Using such categorisations as a basis provides a way to reflect on different tasks particularly on their function and their form but also importantly on their mathematical focus.

In order to illustrate how we see the tasks fitting into the categories of teacher competencies we will use a few of the tasks from the book. For example, the task proposed by Rose Spanneberg involves aspects of the development of a professional language. She discusses how she can identify the language of reflective writing for teachers on three levels: descriptive, dialogic and critical reflection. In the suggested task to create mathematics teaching portfolios, students are offered many different opportunities to develop their professional language in the writing of artefacts for the

Fig. 1 Concept map showing a model of mathematics teacher education seen as the development of a professional identity (Grevholm, 2006, p. 184)

portfolio. Focus for the portfolio is the teaching of mathematics and its development. The portfolio becomes a tool for professional growth and an instrument to improve classroom practices and links to two other aspects in the model above: classroom management and knowledge of mathematics related to teaching. Many of the tasks presented in the book have this quality to promote development related to several aspects of teachers' professional knowledge.

Two chapters use games as a mediating artefact in the learning process of students. Solange Amato exposes trading games for number work and Dan Canada uses The River Crossing Game to introduce a context for exploring the sum of two dice. Canada indicates that offering students opportunities to informally notice and describe the variability arising from the tasks will build a foundation for more robust conceptions of probability to develop in the future. The two authors use their knowledge about classroom material to create mathematical situations that offer powerful learning for students, which they can then offer to their prospective students. The situations that are created also open for student communication in different ways, again a link to the professional language of a teacher.

Many different aspects need to be considered in the selection of tasks for prospective teachers. Richard Millman, Kelly Svec and Dana Williams use the concept tasks with learning envelopes and set the following criteria for such tasks: they should establish a community of teachers; establish learning through research in future teachers; have a clear purpose that is not just doing a mathematical problem; develop mathematical intuition and the notion of surprise, and may have a social or mathematical environmental learning goal. A task with learning envelope is defined to be a complex activity carried out in a pre-service class, which has clearly defined learning goals and either can be modified and transported into a school classroom or is a meta-task/second order 'in school' exercise. The intention is that a task with a learning envelope should affect teachers directly through their future classroom activities. Prospective teachers should obtain an enriched knowledge of practice and content.

In many of the tasks the teacher educators show their competence to link theory and practice of mathematics teaching, thus being what Bergsten & Grevholm (2008) call knowledgeable teacher educators. The authors who have written the chapters in this book convince us that there is hardly any limitation for how the combined aims or purposes for teacher education can be achieved through the work with tasks. Teacher education must be seen as a life-long learning process and so these kinds of tasks can be used for in-service teachers as well as pre-service teachers and inspire them to use tasks in productive ways with their own students. We invite readers to enjoy the variation and richness in the suggested tasks for primary teachers.

We hope that the readers of this book will find many possibilities from the tasks in the following chapters, that they will see opportunities for the construction of alternative or extended tasks adjusted to the needs of each specific group of prospective teachers and possibly include them in their *privileged repertoire*.

References

Ames, C. (1992). Classrooms: Goals, structures and student motivation. *Journal of Educational Psychology, 84*(3), 261–271.

Bergsten, C., & Grevholm, B. (2008). Knowledgeable teacher educators and linking practices. In T. Wood & B. Jaworski (Eds.), *The mathematics teacher educator as a developing professional* (pp. 223–246). Rotterdam: Sense Publishers.

Brousseau, G. (1997). *Theory of didactical situations in mathematics*. Dordrecht: Kluwer Academic Publishers.

Christiansen, B., & Walther, G. (1986). Task and activity. In B. Christiansen, A. G. Howson, & M. Otte (Eds.), *Perspectives on mathematics education* (pp. 243–307). The Netherlands: Reidel.

Clarke, B. A. (2005). Assessing highly accomplished teachers of mathematics. In M. Coupland, J. Anderson, & T. Spencer (Eds.), *Making mathematics vital* (Proceedings of the 20th Biennial Conference of the Australian Association of Mathematics Teachers, pp. 87–92). Sydney: Australian Association of Mathematics Teachers.

Doyle, W. (1998). Classroom organisation and management. In M. C. Wittrock (Ed.), *Handbook of research on teaching* (pp. 392–431). New York: Macmillan.

Ensor, P. (2000). Recognizing and realizing "best practice" in initial mathematics teacher education and classroom teaching. In J. Bana & A. Chapman (Eds.), *Mathematics education beyond 2000* (Proceedings of the 23rd annual conference of the Mathematics Education Research Group of Australasia, pp. 235–242). Fremantle, Western Australia: MERGA.

Grevholm, B., Even, R., Szendrei, J., & Carillo, J. (2004). From a study of teaching practices to issues in teacher education. Thematic Working Group 12, CERME3. In M. A. Mariotti et al (Eds.), *Proceedings of CERME3*. Electronic publication. Pisa: University of Pisa.

Grevholm, B. (2006). Matematikdidaktikens möjligheter i en forskningsbaserad lärarutbildning. In S. Ongstad (Ed.), *Fag og didaktikk i lærerutdanning. Kunnskap i grenseland* (pp. 183–206). Oslo: Universitetsforlaget.

Hiebert, J., & Wearne, D. (1997). Instructional tasks, classroom discourse and student learning in second grade arithmetic. *American Educational Research Journal, 30*(2), 393–425.

Section A
Tasks as a Tool for Exploring the Cyclical Nature of Learning and Developing Reflection in the Teaching of Mathematics

Barbro Grevholm

This section of the book includes four chapters, all illustrating the cyclic character of work done by mathematics teachers or teacher educators. The lesson study cycle consists of the outline of a unit and a lesson, teaching the lesson, analysing the lesson and student thinking, and critical design and redesign of the lesson. This cycle is discussed in the first chapter by Joanne Lieberman. In the chapter by Theresa Grant and Jane-Jane Lo, the process of task creation, reflection on students' reactions to the tasks and task alteration creates a working cycle that helps the teacher educators and their students develop better understanding of the issues the classroom students face in solving the tasks. In chapter three Victoria Sánchez and Mercedes García explore three phases of their own work as teacher educators that are repeated in a cyclic way with different mathematical practices as content. In the chapter by Rose Spanneberg the cyclic character of a course in teacher education becomes visible through the portfolio that students create by collecting artefacts that illustrate their work from the beginning to the end of the course.

Lesson study is one of the central concepts in the chapter of Joanne Lieberman. She describes a lesson study cycle used to assist teachers in the critical design of tasks to make mathematics more meaningful for their students. The cycle begins with the outline of a unit and lesson. Teams of teachers produce a lesson plan which includes the goals of the lesson, where it is made visible what student behaviour the lesson is trying to foster, and what the students are expected to be able to do after the lesson. The second part is assessment and evaluation of the lesson and the third part about the progression of lesson to highlight students' learning activities. This part includes lesson introduction, main activities for the lesson, lesson closure and a short assessment. Based on this plan the lesson is taught and then collaboratively

B. Grevholm
Professor of Mathematics Education, University of Agder, Norway

B. Clarke, B. Grevholm, and R. Millman (eds.), *Tasks in Primary Mathematics Teacher Education: Purpose, Use and Exemplars,* Mathematics Teacher Education 4,
© Springer Science+Business Media LLC 2009

analyzed from the video by the teachers. They discuss student thinking during the lesson and how the lesson met its goals. Based on common reflections teachers then critically redesign the lesson and it is tried out again. Lieberman gives two concrete examples of the design of a lesson: 'Sum of angles in a triangle' and 'The division meaning of fractions'. She also exemplifies the transformation the team of teachers has undergone thanks to the work with lesson study. In the second year teachers have been asked to make student thinking visible in different types of lessons. A crucial element of designing tasks is to critically assess curricular materials or lessons and then be able to adapt them to better meet the students' needs. Lieberman claims that lesson study gives teachers permission to help them to focus on their students and their students' thinking.

The chapter by Theresa Grant and Jane-Jane Lo deals with reflections on the process of task adaptation and extension and they discuss the case of what they call computational starters. They point out that teachers must understand the basic mathematical ideas that underlie computational fluency and to use tasks in which students develop these ideas. The teachers must also recognize opportunities in students' work to focus on such ideas. One example they discuss is the situation where a student is supposed to work out 1004 minus 97. They call a starter an expression that is equivalent with the first expression but easier to solve. The student could for example figure out how many steps there are from 1007 to 100. An example given is a journal writing assignment for students, where they were asked to take their solution to a starter problem and come up with two different justifications of the procedure based on two interpretations of the subtraction observation. The starter problem was: Solve $1018 - 395 = $ ___ by using $1000 - 400$. Different answers from students are discussed in the chapter. The authors themselves have been helped by the process of task creation, reflection on students' reactions to the tasks and task alteration to better understand issues the students face as they work to learn mathematics with understanding. They claim that developing the tasks and the tasks themselves illustrate the importance of making connections among representations and the role it can play in developing flexible mathematical thinking.

Victoria Sánchez and Mercedes García in their chapter highlight the conceptualization and development of a primary mathematics teacher education programme. Thus it is the task of the teacher educator they are dealing with. Building on work by Llinares (2004) the authors identify systems of activity that enable teachers to solve the task in their profession: plan a lesson, assess, chose a textbook and instruction material and so on. The three systems they find in relation to this work are: to organize the mathematical content for teaching, to manage the mathematical content and discourse in the classroom, and to analyze and interpret mathematics students thinking. Thus, the systems refer to the pre-lesson, during lesson and after lesson activities by the teacher. These three phases are repeated again and again in a cyclic way in the work of teachers and teacher educators. As another dimension they see the actions teachers and students carry out in mathematics like defining, justifying, modelling, symbolizing and algorithmatizing. In a matrix with these two dimensions they find what they need to include in a mathematics methods course. Two concrete tasks the authors have used are included in the chapter and discussed. They claim that their practice and research have shown that the learning environment generated in primary school teacher training enabled some of the student teachers to identify individually and collectively the conceptual tools that were provided. If students also succeed in integrating the tools in their work the tasks are carried out differently and the students are more aware of and evaluated distinct feature that led to different decisions for the classroom work.

Rose Spanneberg writes about the use of teaching portfolios and sees them as a reflective tool for developing professional growth as well as improving classroom practices. Much of her discussion is based on the importance of the concept of reflection in teachers' professional work. To identify the language of reflective writing she uses the levels: descriptive reflection, dialogic reflection and critical reflection. Excerpts from students portfolios are given and discussed. A number of strong features in using teaching portfolios are mentioned: they enhance teacher professional development; they integrate all aspects of teaching; they support learning; they promote collegiality and social interaction among teachers, and they are reflective of a constructivist paradigm. The portfolios contain: lesson plans, analyses of own teaching, reflections on professional contact sessions at the university, reflections of learners work, a peer reflective report, and reflections on learners' reflections. The author describes how a teaching portfolio can be an effective task for mathematics educators to use both in initial training of students and for practising teachers of mathematics in primary schools.

Reference

Llinares, S. (2004). Building virtual learning communities and the learning of mathematics by student teachers. Regular lecture, ICME 10 Denmark. www.ICME10.dk.

Using Lesson Study to Develop an Appreciation of and Competence in Task Design

Joanne Lieberman

This chapter focuses on how lesson study can be used to assist teachers in the design of meaningful mathematical tasks for their students. It describes strategies in designing the lesson study process of "outline, teach, analyze, critically design" that support teachers' development of task design. The chapter explains how specifically using critical design after observing the original lesson and having teachers' focus on making student thinking visible can impact teachers approach to designing tasks. Participating in lesson study enables mathematics teachers to return to their original service ethic, and provides them with structures to focus on their students and students' thinking. Examples of specific tasks that were developed using this method are discussed, and how the method and prompts enabled teachers to challenge their students to think on their own, rather than simply following their teacher's thinking. The chapter is based on data collected from lesson study work with hundreds of teachers over a 6-year period.

Lesson study, a form of teacher professional development that is widely used in Japan, has been cited as a crucial element in the improvement of mathematics and science education in that country (Stigler & Hiebert, 1999). In recent years, lesson study has become increasingly popular in the United States with the hope that it can drastically improve the US educational system (Fernandez, 2002; Wang-Iverson & Yoshida, 2005). During the lesson study process teachers work in groups to develop a lesson plan that one of the teachers will teach and have others observe. After the teaching and observations, the group meets and analyzes the lesson's success in reaching its goals, and then makes revisions accordingly. Thus, a central element of lesson study is task design. The lesson study process can enable teachers to share and learn from each other ways to modify curriculum to engage students in meaningful mathematics.

Lesson study by its very nature has teachers actively making decisions about the curriculum and redesigning it. In the process, teachers first develop and adapt

J. Lieberman
Assistant Professor, Mathematics and Statistics Department, California State University Monterey Bay, USA

B. Clarke, B. Grevholm, and R. Millman (eds.), *Tasks in Primary Mathematics Teacher Education: Purpose, Use and Exemplars,* Mathematics Teacher Education 4,

curriculum based on their goals. They then collect data during the lesson to see if indeed their decisions resulted in the intended student learning. Lesson study can provide a structure for teachers to learn how to critically design – to critically assess and alter existing curricular materials.

Research has not been conducted to demonstrate lesson study's efficacy overall in improving mathematics instruction or student learning in the United States. At this stage, such general research would not be fruitful, given the variation in the way lesson study is conducted throughout the country (Lewis, Perry, & Murata, 2006). Even within one project trying to draw a causal link between teacher's participation in lesson study and improved student achievement would be difficult given that teachers often engage in other professional development as well and because nonparticipating teachers often gain some knowledge generated from lesson study by interacting with participating teachers. The purpose of this chapter is to contribute to needed lesson study research as described by Lewis et al. (2006) that provides "explication of the innovation mechanism" (p. 5). This chapter provides evidence that specific aspects of lesson study can change teachers' beliefs, goals, and strategies in designing meaningful tasks for students.

California State University Monterey Bay professors have been working with local teachers on lesson study for the past 7 years. Each year the number of participants has varied, with the most recent number being ~150 teachers from ten different school districts. While the logistics of team meetings varied from school to school, typically teams of teachers met for several days during the summer and a few times after school to plan their lesson, and were paid a stipend for their participation. Most teams took a day out of their classrooms to analyze and revise their lesson. This chapter is based on data collected over the 7-year period from lesson study planning meetings and debriefing sessions as well as from teacher interviews and focus groups of participating teachers. Draft and final lesson plans were analyzed to highlight types of changes made after teaching the lesson, and also to see how lessons changed as instructions to teachers changed in developing lessons over the years.

This chapter focuses on how my colleagues and I have designed tasks to assist teachers participating in our lesson study project in their design of meaningful mathematical tasks for their students. By *meaningful* we mean that it helps students makes sense of mathematics, connecting to, and building on prior knowledge (Ausubel, 1963; Novak, 2002). Students make sense of mathematics, seeing how and why it works, through their internal cognitive connections as well as through social interactions (Carpenter et al., 1997). When mathematics makes sense to students, they do not need to have the teacher judge the validity of their solutions, they convince themselves and others of it (Carpenter, Franke, & Levi 2003). I have summarized our approach as: *outline, teach, analyze, critically design* with an emphasis on making student thinking visible. This cycle is similar to the design cycle discussed by Gravemeijer and Cobb (2001) and Jaworski (2003). Gravemeijer (2004) describes the process as having a research team develop a preliminary design of instructional activities that are carried out in a classroom, then the process of students' mental activities are analyzed, and the activities are revised. I first describe our specific process and then discuss the focus on making student thinking visible, and how that emphasis has effected how teachers approach designing tasks. I describe examples of specific lessons that were developed using this method, and how the method and prompts enabled teacher learning.

1 Designing a Lesson Study Cycle to Assist Teachers in Critically Designing Tasks to Make Mathematics Meaningful for Students

Curriculum development and task design traditionally have not been part of American mathematics teachers' responsibilities and thus, pose challenges for them (Fernandez, Cannon, & Chokshi, 2003). Teachers typically are given a text and are required (or expected) to follow it. My colleagues and I originally asked teachers to fill out a detailed lesson plan template that asked for short and long term goals as well as predicting student responses to teachers' questions. These are standard prompts commonly used in lesson study (Wang-Iverson & Yoshida, 2005) and are consistent with a preliminary design phase in design research (Gravemeijer, 2004). Most of the teachers in our project struggled with this prediction. They were adept at recognizing lesson flaws when observing lessons or videos of the lessons, but could not predict those flaws in advance. Our lesson study cycle has thus evolved to shorten the original planning phase and lengthen the analysis and revision (critical design) phase. Our current lesson study cycle includes: outline, teach, analyze, critically design.

1.1 Description of the Process

1.1.1 Outline a Unit and Lesson

The lesson study process begins by having teams agree upon some shared beliefs about Mathematics instruction. Teams are provided a list of statements regarding specific classroom practices and about how students learn that the teachers rank from "strongly agree" to "strongly disagree". A few sample statements are: "Big, organizing ideas and inquiry questions are used when teaching content"; "Students spend more time involved in activities than listening to a teacher"; "Students have opportunities to teach and learn from each other".

From their individual responses, the team agrees upon two or three that they share and can modify to serve as their overarching goals. The purpose of the overarching goals is to have teachers think about, and focus on, broader goals they have for students. Instead of having them focus only on the content goals for the day, these overarching goals can redirect teachers to their original goals as professionals. When teachers enter the profession, they maintain a service ethic to serve their students (Yee, 1990). The technical culture of teaching mathematics to *cover topics* can overshadow teachers' original service ethic (Grossman & Stodolsky, 1994).

Professionals pledge their "first concern to the welfare of the clients" (Darling-Hammond, 1990, p. 25). This intention to serve all students is continually reaffirmed in lesson study as the primary purpose of teaching. By discussing their values and beliefs and incorporating these into their lessons, teachers reaffirm their professional purpose. They develop lessons that support this purpose to serve students, not just cover curriculum.

Grouped by grade level, teachers then choose an important problematic mathematics topic to research. They read through the California Mathematics Standards for their grade, and discuss topics that they believe are both important mathematically and are problematic for their students. Participants should not choose a topic just because they already know a *fun* activity for it. If the topic can be taught easily and does not relate to other areas in the curriculum or if students typically do not have trouble with it, then there is no reason to study that topic.

Teachers then develop a general unit plan and choose a lesson from the unit that they believe is key for the unit. Because these lessons usually require teachers to spend more time on the topic than usual, it is important for teams to choose a lesson topic that is at the core of the unit and will enable teachers to spend less time on other lessons because students will have a deeper conceptual knowledge that will assist them in making other mathematical connections. Teams use as a theoretical framework for designing their unit the five interwoven strands of mathematical proficiency described in the National Research Council's report (2001), *Adding It Up*. The strands are: conceptual understanding; procedural fluency; strategic competence; adaptive reasoning; and productive disposition. Teams may not be able to address each of the five in the single lesson, but they plan how the lesson fits into the development of the strands. The team then outlines a lesson plan that includes a description of the primary task in which students will engage. Teams respond to the questions found in Table 1 while writing their lesson plans.

1.1.2 Teach the Lesson

During this phase of the process at least one teacher from the team teaches the lesson in order for the team to analyze how the students interacted with the task. Other team members either watch it live as it is taught or watch it on videotape. In some cases, multiple teachers teach the lesson and the team compares students' responses. While teachers are observing, they are taking notes to provide evidence of student thinking.

1.1.3 Analyze the Lesson and Student Thinking

In this phase, teachers collaboratively observe and analyze the lesson or video, discussing student thinking during the lesson and how the lesson met its goals. University professors participate in these discussions as well, asking the team critical questions as the lesson progresses. The entire group discusses how well their goals and methods served students.

Table 1 Questions teachers address while planning their lesson

1. Goals of this lesson

   - What student actions and thinking is the lesson trying to foster (e.g. independent mathematical thinking, group cooperation)?
   - What are the mathematical goals for this lesson? What do you want students to come out of this lesson being able to know or do?

2. Assessment and evaluation

   - How will you determine by the end of the lesson if the lesson met each of its goals? (What problems or questions would you ask students?)
   - What evidence of learning will be observed or collected during the lesson to make student thinking visible? Examples of ways to make student thinking visible:
     - Many students explaining their reasoning in a class discussion;
     - Many students showing and explaining work at the board;
     - Students using hand-held white boards to show their work, not just answers;
     - Students explaining their thinking in small groups (with the teacher checking in frequently with groups and asking questions).
     - Students handing in a *quick write* (answering a conceptual question or showing their work/thinking for one or two problems)

3. Progression of lesson highlighting students' learning activities

   - Lesson Introduction: What will hook students into thinking about this lesson and connect to prior lessons?
   - Main activities for the lesson: What rich problem or activities will the lesson use to engage students, keeping them mentally active and thinking originally, whereby they develop their own strategies, not passively follow procedures? How does the lesson design make students' thinking visible to the teacher and observers? What strategies will make *mathematics meaningful* for all students? (Some examples include: using multiple representations, connecting to students' lives and prior knowledge, providing structures for communication).
   - Lesson Closure: How will you debrief the lesson, explicitly pulling out the important mathematical ideas of the lesson?
   - Short assessment if evidence has not been collected earlier in the lesson (e.g. a quick write or solving one problem).

1.1.4 Critically Design

After the lesson or video has been analyzed, teachers reflect on the discussion. The team is now prepared to carefully design the learning task. Design does not have to mean developing teaching materials from scratch. In fact, a crucial element of design is the ability to critically assess and alter existing curricular materials or lessons. I will, therefore, use the term critical design to refer to this active and critical role of planning. Teachers' original lessons can be designed from existing materials, and their revised lessons are designed from the original. They critically analyze existing plans to design their new lesson. By seeing how students interact with the original task, teachers now have insight into students' thinking about the concept. For the "Main Activities" section of the lesson plan, teachers add columns "anticipated

Table 2 Main activities of the lesson plan

Learning activities	Expected student responses	Points of evaluation

student responses" and "evaluation points". The teams re-write the main activities with more detail and with responses in the new columns (Table 2).

In addition, during the original planning phase, teachers often have difficulty uncovering the important mathematical concept underlying the mathematical goals they have set for their class. During the critical design phase, the team can now anticipate student responses to each part of the lesson, and when needed, redesign the lesson and its goals to focus more on the important underlying mathematical concept.

1.2 Examples of Insights Gained During Lesson Analyses

Below are specific examples of insights teachers gained when analyzing their lessons or videotapes, and how those insights influenced the final, more detailed lesson plan during the critical design phase of the process.

1.2.1 Surface Area of Cylinders

The purpose of this lesson was for 6th-grade students to learn how to find the surface area of a cylinder. The students used rulers to measure dimensions of a cylindrical can that was placed on their desk. The teachers expected the students to be able to see that the height of the can was the same as the width of a rectangle wrapped around the can, and that the circumference of the can was the same as the length of that rectangle. They expected the lesson to go smoothly, with students having little difficulty. Instead, students struggled to figure out what to measure. After teaching the lesson (and reviewing the video), teachers realized that the important and challenging aspect of this lesson was not having students simply develop a formula for surface area; it was having them visualize the 3-D lateral surface area in two dimensions and make the connection between height in 3-D and width in 2-D, as well as circumference in 3-D with length in 2-D. The planning phase of this lesson study cycle was not as fruitful as the analysis phase. During the analysis, the team discussed how they needed to spend more time with their class transforming 3-D objects to 2-D drawings. They needed to spend more time having their students deconstruct 3-D objects into flat objects. Activities such as breaking down a cereal box to see the 2-D figures from which it is composed or peeling off a rectangular label from a cylinder would help students visualize drawing nets from 3-D objects. Students had had some experience with these types of activities, but it was clear from the lesson that they needed a firmer grasp of this type of visualization. Without this background, students cannot successfully complete the task they were given.

1.2.2 Sum of Angles of Any Triangle Is 180 Degrees

In another lesson, the teachers' goal was for 5th grade students to understand that the sum of the angles of any triangle is 180 degrees. Students used protractors to measure the angles of several differently shaped and sized triangles. Students' data were often not accurate, and thus, incorrectly came to the conclusion that the sum of the angles of any triangle is not always 180 degrees. The team needed to revise the lesson, taking this into account. More importantly, though, the teachers learned that students do not understand the concept of angle measurement generally. The pre-knowledge necessary for this lesson was much greater than what teachers had expected. Teachers learned that the concept of angle measurement is much more complex than they had thought. Some students thought large triangles would have larger angles. They were sure they could make a very small triangle with the measure of each angle being 10 degrees. The teachers had not realized that the important mathematics necessary for this lesson was to understand what angles and their measurement mean. The teachers could not make this realization until they observed and listened to students.

1.2.3 Justifying Reasoning

The following task was designed by another group of teachers to have 4th and 5th grade students justify their reasoning while exploring the fractions in a novel way. The class had been working with fractions, but only looking at them as parts of a whole. The class was a 4th/5th grade combination, so they needed to use a problem that would be accessible for the 4th graders while also being challenging for the 5th graders.

Mr. Smith's brownie pan holds 20 brownies. Last night he baked three batches. He and his wife ate 3 brownies each for dessert. Mr. Smith ate an extra half a brownie as a midnight snack and another one for breakfast.

How many brownies did Mr. Smith bake?
How many does he have left to share with the thirty kids in his class?
How can you make sure that every person gets an equal share?
How much will each person get?

Be prepared to prove, present and explain your answer to the class using drawings, pictures, numbers, or words. You may create your own brownies out of construction paper to help you solve this problem.

Teachers did not know how students would go about solving the problem. They were surprised to find that most groups tried to solve the problem the same way, but had difficulty. When analyzing the video and student work teachers found the following issues. First, the wording was a little ambiguous. The last phrase of the last sentence says "and another one for breakfast". Some students interpreted the "one" as a whole brownie (as it was intended) and others interpreted it as another one half. That wording can be an easy change for the next version of the lesson.

More interestingly, the teachers were surprised that most students solved the problem by dividing up brownies, and then halves. Most students correctly multiplied 20 by 3 to get 60 original brownies. They then subtracted $7^1/_2$ brownies from 60 and got $52^1/_2$. At this point, students realized that each student in the class could have one whole brownie, so they subtracted 30 from $52^1/_2$ and got $22^1/_2$. This is where the problem became quite challenging for most students. Before teaching the lesson, the teachers were not able to anticipate student responses, and certainly did not expect so many groups to use the same method. Groups often doubled their numbers to see how many students they could feed if each ate a half. This allowed them to give an equal share to each of the 30 students. The groups kept track, that these shares were $^1/_2$ brownies, not full brownies. They doubled the $22^1/_2$ and got 45 shares. The 30 students each got a share (that was now a $^1/_2$ brownie), and they were left with 15 shares (halves). Some of the groups realized that when they doubled 15 they reached 30 again, and that each of these shares was now $^1/_4$ of brownie, so each student got $1 + ^1/_2 + ^1/_4$ brownie, or $1^3/_4$ brownie. Some groups subtracted incorrectly at the beginning of the problem and ended up with $6^1/_2$ brownies. They then divided the 6 brownies into fifths so that they could have 30 pieces, and simply dropped the $^1/_2$. Those groups gave an answer of $1 + ^1/_2 + 1/5 = 17/10$.

This lesson showed how the analysis phase provided the richest opportunity for the teachers' learning experience. At first students focused on finding an answer and wanted approval from the teacher. The teacher reminded them that the task was to prove their answer with drawings, pictures, numbers or words, at which time students re-engaged in order to justify their reasoning. The teachers learned how powerful this type of task can be for developing students' capacity for justification by generalization versus "appealing to authority" as described by Carpenter, Franke, & Levi (2003), and for developing the capacity of adaptive reasoning generally (National Research Council, NRC, 2001). The analysis phase of the lesson provided the teachers with information about how students approached the problem and justified their reasoning without instruction, and thus, what knowledge they brought to the situation and what they can learn that will help them.

2 Designing Key Prompts that Assist Teachers in Critically Designing Tasks to Make Mathematics Meaningful for Students

My colleagues and I have found that another key for enabling teachers to develop challenging tasks that provoke student thinking is to focus teachers on making students' thinking visible during the lesson study process. The Cognitively Guided Instruction (CGI) project has provided evidence that when students develop and communicate new mathematical understandings based on their own knowledge, they learn mathematics better (Carpenter, Fennema, Peterson, Chiang, & Loef, 1989;

Villasenor & Kepner, 1993). CGI recognizes that children have intuitive mathematical knowledge and that teachers can develop instruction that has students build on this knowledge without being told or shown how to do mathematics (Carpenter, Fennema, Franke, Empson, & Levi., 1999). Similarly, recent international studies have shown that a key feature of successful mathematics instruction is providing students with challenging tasks that provoke student thinking (Stigler & Hiebert, 1997; American Institutes for Research, 2005). The challenge is to assist American teachers in making that their priority and then assisting them in designing tasks that support the goal. Based on our work with hundreds of teachers in multiple school districts, a key for making this work is to focus teachers on making student's thinking visible during the Lesson Study process. As teachers develop lessons with the goal of making students' thinking visible, by definition, the lesson must make students think. Examples of strategies that are provided to teachers for making thinking visible are: having students show/discuss their methods in groups, having students show/discuss their method with the whole class, having students write out in words what they did and why they did it that way. When I use the term *visible* I also mean audible. The purpose is for the teacher and observers to be able to understand how the students are thinking about the mathematics during the lesson.

Lesson study provides permission to take risks. The purpose of developing, teaching, and analyzing the lesson is to learn about student learning. The lesson study team learns a great deal from both failure and successes; the purpose is not to develop a perfect lesson, it is for the team members to investigate how students think about the mathematics of the lesson. During the process teachers design lessons that often take them out of their comfort zone in order to produce evidence of student thinking that can be analyzed. Team members then have the opportunity to observe students learning math in ways that take some control away from the teacher. They are provided with a new vision for mathematics instruction and student learning. I will provide specific examples of teachers' shift in their design of tasks by describing some of their earlier and more recent tasks, and what caused them to make those shifts.

When my colleagues and I began our lesson study work, teachers tried to develop *the perfect lesson*. As one teacher says, she and her colleagues tried to make the lessons *student proof*. In other words, students could follow the task step by step and end up discovering what the teacher intended. Even at this school that has been diligently trying to improve mathematics instruction, teachers had not developed a need for pushing students' thinking. Teachers wanted to lead students to a discovery, but not have students do original thinking. They wanted students to understand why mathematics works the way it does, but they wanted to do so by having students follow the teacher's thinking. With the goal this year on making student thinking visible, their lesson did, indeed, require student to do original thinking. These teachers are now challenging themselves by working towards having students develop ideas themselves – think deeply about the ideas (not just *understand*). One of the teachers describes this transformation,

> The thing that I've really noticed the progression at Lincoln; when we first started doing Lesson Study we tried to make these lesson plans that were like student-proof, where we

just walked the kids right through; and I don't think we really had the understanding that we could get kids to do the stuff successfully but it didn't mean they were thinking about it at all. It could just be that they were following a recipe. It's almost like getting a MapQuest[1] to go to somewhere and you follow the MapQuest exactly, it doesn't mean you really know how to get there next time.... So this year, I think we really got the point of, we just want to see evidence of student thinking...let's think about student thinking.

An example of the transformation this team has gone through can be seen in two of the lesson study lessons. Two years ago, their lesson was about the sum of interior angles of a polygon. The team wanted their students to "discover" the formula that the sum is 180 times the quantity $n = 2$, where n is the number of sides of the polygon, and wanted them to understand where the formula came from. Students filled out a chart (Table 3) that had a column name of polygon, n-sides, number of triangles, number of degrees. At the bottom of the table there was a row for an n-gon. When filling out the chart, students could easily follow the pattern and get the correct answer without understanding why it worked the way it did (Table 3).

The teacher showed the class how to draw lines from one vertex to the other vertices, to create triangles within the polygon. The team realized later that students could go through this lesson, come up with the correct answer, and still not be able to re-create the formula. The students were able to fill out the table correctly, but did not do the thinking necessary to set up the table and develop the formula, and thus, would probably not be able to re-create the formula later.

This year, when teachers were given the prompt teachers to "make student thinking visible", the team developed a very different type of lesson. They developed their lesson with the goal of having students make connections between various representations of the same linear situation. They had students match cards with a *real life* situation (word problem), linear equation, t-table, graph, and ordered pairs. Students had to do the thinking in order to match the correct representations to each problem

Table 3 Sample template for "discovering" formula for sum of interior angles of a polygon

Name of polygon	Sketch	Number of sides (n)	Number of triangles formed	Number of degrees
Triangle				
Quadrilateral				
Pentagon				
Hexagon				
Heptagon				
n-gon				

---

[1] Electronic system that provides street-level detail and/or driving directions for a variety of countries (Wikipedia, http://en.wikipedia.org/wiki/MapQuest, accessed May 28, 2008).

situation. In addition, students had to justify their answers (in words, through work, or both). Below is an example of one of their situations:

> Fred and Ethel have been saving for many months in order to pay for their parents' 50th wedding anniversary. They have a total of US $5,000. Fred and Ethel now need to start paying for all of the food, music, flowers, hall rental and so forth. The bills work out to be a total of US $300 each month.

This team did not do a lot of revision after analyzing their lesson, but had a rich discussion based on their observations. They discussed questions students were asking each other in groups as they worked on the task, and which representations were causing the students the most difficulty. For example, they noticed that students had the most difficulty with the ordered pairs and they were not used to fitting an ordered pair with a situation. They also discussed the difficulty students had with one of the problems due to ambiguity in the wording. In contrast, with the polygon lesson, there was little evidence of student thinking to discuss. Teachers quickly came to the conclusion that the students *got it* – they got the correct formula.

Another example of how the instructions to "make students' thinking visible" for study lessons had the effect of teachers planning lessons that make students do original thinking was the "brownie problem" lesson described earlier. The teachers in this group have shifted their focus to having students develop concepts themselves, rather than be shown them. A key feature of the "brownie problem" lesson was that students had to convince each other (using their model) that they had the correct answer. This lesson was rich with evidence of student thinking. Students calculated answers and wanted to share them with the teacher. The teacher's response was that they must use a model to convince each other. Students went back to their groups realizing that they had a great deal more to do for the lesson. Developing the models forced more conversations and deeper conversations amongst group members.

A teacher in another lesson study group described how his experience of designing lessons for lesson study has changed the way he designs all mathematical tasks for his class. He gave the example of teaching 5th grade students to compare the relative size of fractions. He used to teach students the rule of multiplying the numerator of one by the denominator of the other. This method is a shortcut to finding an equivalent fraction with a common denominator. The result gives new numerators (with the same denominator), allowing the student to compare whole numerators only. When he taught this method, he taught it as a rule, without providing justification for why it works (or having students figure out why it works). This year he approached the same topic in a very different way. He put some unit fractions on the board and asked students to draw them. He then asked them what they noticed about the size of them. Students quickly noticed that fractions with a larger denominator were smaller pieces of the same whole. He then put up some fractions with the same denominator and different numerators and asked students to draw them. Students noticed that the larger numerators resulted in a larger fractional portion. This teacher provided these explorations as a foundation for comparing fractions. This example illustrates how a teacher thinks differently about designing lessons due to his experience of developing tasks for his involvement in lesson study.

3 Conclusions

While a central purpose of lesson study is for teachers to learn from engaging in the process, an additional benefit is that teachers can acquire a collection of key lessons that have been studied carefully. Teachers do not have time to conduct a lesson study cycle for every lesson, but this collection can build students' foundational conceptual knowledge for many of their curricular units enabling teachers to spend less time on other related lessons.

The lessons that teachers collect, though, are still not perfect. A crucial element of designing tasks is to critically assess existing curricular materials or lessons, and then adapt them to better meet the teacher's students' needs. As such, teachers continually adapt lessons based on their learning from the process of analyzing and discussing students' thinking about a topic, and based on their knowledge of the particular students they are teaching. In our project, teachers have been better able to critically design after they have seen a lesson taught, even if the revised lesson is going to be taught to a different group of students. After teachers have seen any group of students respond to the lesson, they are better able to predict what other groups of students, even different types, will do because they have a basis from which to predict and compare.

When they first teach the lesson, teachers often expect it to go as planned, and for students to think about the task the way the teachers think about it. After they have observed students interact with the lesson, they are better able to understand the important mathematical concepts underlying the lesson, as well as how students will think about the concept and task. Furthermore, the tasks teachers design are more mathematically meaningful if the teacher focuses on making student thinking visible. Because teachers typically do not see critical design as a part of their job – their job is to implement the curriculum laid out in textbooks – strategies need to be studied and shared about how to assist teachers in developing this skill. Similarly, US teachers are used to focusing lesson planning and observations on the teacher, rather than on the students (Fernandez, Cannon, & Chokshi, 2003). This chapter provided descriptions of the tasks my colleagues and I have used to assist teachers in learning how to design meaningful tasks that highlight student thinking.

Due to their participation in lesson study, teachers are now challenging their students to think on their own; not just follow the teacher's path to a particular discovery. This, in itself, requires more risk-taking by the teachers. They do not know where their students' thinking will go. In the past, most of the teachers in our project either showed students how to use skills or procedures to find an answer, or they guided students to discover a particular concept or formula, without having students do any of the thinking. Many of the teachers now see the value of developing tasks that will allow students to do original thinking. By having us ask teachers to make thinking *visible*, teachers have embedded formative assessment into their tasks. They (and other observers) are gaining knowledge about students' understandings and misconceptions while the lesson is being taught.

The tasks and processes described in this chapter demonstrate how lesson study can assist teachers in developing more meaningful mathematical tasks for their students, and how, they in turn, reaffirm their professional purpose – to serve students. US mathematics teachers maintain a specialized culture that is comprised of shared practices and beliefs about students, and mathematics teaching and learning. This technical culture is often strong and inhibits serving all students well due to the belief that mathematics is a sequential series of skills that teachers must cover, even if students are not learning them (Talbert & Perry, 1994). This technical culture for many teachers is given and signals, implicitly or explicitly, a tension between caring about students and maintaining the integrity of their subject or adhering to systemic requirements to cover material (Talbert & Perry, 1994). Lesson study gives teachers permission to return to their original service ethic, and assists them by providing structures to help them focus on their students and students' thinking.

References

American Institutes for Research. (2005). *What the United States can learn from Singapore's world class mathematics system*. Prepared for the United States Department of Education Policy and Program Studies Service.

Ausubel, D. P. (1963). *The psychology of meaningful verbal learning*. New York: Grune and Stratton.

Carpenter, T. P., Fennema, E., Franke, M. L., Empson, S. B., & Levi, L. W. (1999). *Children's mathematics: Cognitively guided instruction*. Portsmouth, NH: Heinemann.

Carpenter, T. P., Fennema, E., Peterson, P. L., Chiang, C., & Loef, M. (1989). Using knowledge of children's mathematics thinking in classroom teaching: An experimental study. *American Educational Research Journal, 26*(4), 499–531.

Carpenter, T. P., Franke, M. L., & Levi, L. (2003). *Thinking mathematically: Integrating arithmetic and algebra in elementary school*. Portsmouth, NH: Heinemann.

Carpenter, T. P., Hiebert, J., Fennema, E., Fuson, K. C., Wearne, D., & Murray, H. (1997). *Making sense: Teaching and learning mathematics with understanding*. Portsmouth, NH: Heinemann.

Darling-Hammond, L. (1990). Teacher professionalism: Why and how? In A. Lieberman (Ed.), *Schools as collaborative cultures: Creating the future now* (pp. 25–50). New York: Falmer Press.

Fernandez, C. (2002). Learning from Japanese approaches to professional development: The case of lesson study. *Journal of Teacher Education, 53*(5), 393–405.

Fernandez, C., Cannon, J., & Chokshi, S. (2003). A US-Japan lesson study collaboration reveals critical lenses for examining practice. *Teaching and Teacher Education, 19*(2), 171–185.

Gravemeijer K. (2004). Local instruction theories as means of support for teachers in reform mathematics education. *Mathematical Thinking and Learning, 6*(2), 105–128.

Gravemeijer K., & Cobb, P. (2001). *Designing classroom-learning environments that support mathematical learning*. Paper presented at the Conference of the American Educational Research Association, Seattle, WA.

Grossman P., & Stodolosky, S. (1994). Considerations of content and the circumstances of secondary school teaching. In L. Darling-Hammond (Ed.), *Review of research in education* (Vol. 20, pp. 179–221). Washington, DC: American Educational Research Association.

Jaworski, B. (2003). Research practice into/influencing mathematics teaching and learning development: Towards a theoretical framework based on co-learning partnerships. *Educational Studies in Mathematics, 54*(2–3), 249–282.

Lewis, C., Perry, R., & Murata A. (2006). How should research contribute to instructional improvement? The case of lesson study. *Education Researcher, 35*(3), 3–14.

National Research Council. (2001). Adding it up: Helping children learn mathematics. In J. Kilpatrick, J. Swafford, & B. Findell (Eds.), *Mathematics Learning Study Committee, Center for Education, Division of Behavioral and Social Sciences and Education*. Washington, DC: National Academy Press.

Novak, J. D. (2002). Meaningful learning: The essential factor for conceptual change in limited or inappropriate propositional hierarchies leading to empowerment of learners. *Science Education, 86*(4), 548–571.

Stigler, J., & Hiebert, J. (1999). *The teaching gap: Best ideas from the world's teachers for improving education in the classroom*. New York: The Free Press.

Stigler, J., & Hiebert, J. (1997). Understanding and improving mathematics instruction: An overview of the TIMSS Video Study. *Phi Delta Kappan, 79*(1), 14–21.

Talbert, J. E., & Perry, R. R. (1994). *How department communities mediate mathematics and science reforms*. Stanford, CA: Center for Research on the Context of Teaching, Stanford University.

Villasenor, A., & Kepner, H. S. (1993). Arithmetic from a problem-solving perspective: An urban implementation. *Journal for Research in Mathematics Education, 24*(1), 62–69.

Wang-Iverson, P., & Yoshida, M. (2005). *Building our understanding of lesson study*. Philadelphia: Research for Better Schools.

Yee, S. (1990). *Careers in the classroom: When teaching is more than a job*. New York: Teachers College Press.

Reflecting on the Process of Task Adaptation and Extension: The Case of Computational Starters

Theresa J. Grant and Jane-Jane Lo

For several years we have been designing materials to engage prospective elementary teachers in relearning computation with the kind of understanding necessary to support their work with future elementary students. Many of the tasks used for this purpose are extensions of the (numerical) starter problems from the elementary curriculum, *Investigations in Number, Data and Space* developed by TERC (1998), a non-profit educational organization in Boston. For example, consider the problem of evaluating $102 - 46$ by using one of the following numerical starters, or first steps: $46 + 50$, $102 - 50$, and $106 - 50$. In this chapter we discuss the issues that arose as we used these tasks with prospective teachers, and the additional adaptations that were developed over time in order to focus on these issues. Although our work focuses on the use of starters in the context of whole number computation, we conclude with a discussion of the more general advantages of such tasks by connecting our goals with the more general notion of mathematical proficiency, as defined by the National Research Council (2001).

1 Introduction

Teachers must understand the basic mathematical ideas that underlie computational fluency, use tasks in which students develop these ideas, and recognize opportunities in students' work to focus on these ideas. Many of us learned mathematics as a set of disconnected rules, facts, and procedures. As mathematics teachers, we then find it difficult to recognize the important mathematical principles and relationships underlying the mathematical work of our students. (Russell, 2000, p. 158)

Whole number computation has long been the mainstay of elementary mathematics curriculum; however recent recommendations in the United State suggest a different purpose for this focus. In *Developing computational fluency with whole*

T.J. Grant
Professor, Department of Mathematics, Western Michigan University, USA

J.-J. Lo
Associate Professor, Department of Mathematics, Western Michigan University, USA

B. Clarke, B. Grevholm, and R. Millman (eds.), *Tasks in Primary Mathematics Teacher Education: Purpose, Use and Exemplars,* Mathematics Teacher Education 4,
© Springer Science+Business Media LLC 2009

numbers, Russell (2000) explicates the goal of computational fluency put forth by the *Principles and Standards for School Mathematics* (National Council of Teachers of Mathematics, 2000). Students who can compute fluently: have efficient strategies for computation, are able to compute accurately, and have the flexibility to choose among strategies for solving problems (Russell, 2000, p. 154). Russell joins others (e.g., Bass, 2003; National Research Council, 2001) in contrasting the learning of computation for its own sake, to one in which whole number computation is seen as a key context through which students can learn to reason about numbers and the number system, and to deepen their understanding of interpretations and properties of the operations.

This view of the goal of mathematics learning in the area of whole number computation is consistent with a larger call for the development of mathematical proficiency, defined by the authors of *Adding it up* (National Research Council, 2001) as consisting of the following five interdependent strands:

- *conceptual understanding* – comprehension of mathematical concepts, operations, and relations
- *procedural fluency* – skill in carryout procedures flexibly, accurately, efficiently, and appropriately
- *strategic competence* – ability to formulate, represent, and solve mathematical problems
- *adaptive reasoning* – capacity for logical thought, reflection, explanation, and justification
- *productive disposition* – habitual inclination to see mathematics as sensible, useful, and worthwhile, coupled with a belief in diligence and one's own efficacy (p. 5).

This call for refocusing mathematics education in the United States is made with the recognition that it will require that teachers have the knowledge necessary to develop that proficiency in their students. However in our experience, prospective elementary teachers not only lack this kind of proficiency themselves, they have the disconnected and rule-based view of mathematics Russell refers to in the opening quote. In this chapter we reflect on our efforts to develop computational fluency in prospective teachers by adapting a particular mathematical task originally designed for use with elementary students. Careful analysis of the prospective teachers' responses to these adaptations suggest opportunities for developing additional key elements in general mathematical proficiency that could be applied beyond the realm of whole number computation. Issues and challenges for realizing these opportunities are illustrated and discussed.

2 Context

The authors have been participating in a curriculum development project to produce problem- and reasoning-based lessons and support materials to be used in college mathematics courses specially designed for prospective elementary teachers. In particular, we have been heavily involved in developing and piloting a whole number computation unit that seeks to enable prospective teachers to: (1) develop multiple ways of solving computation problems and (2) justify the validity of those strategies based on various interpretations of the operations. We consider these goals important for developing prospective elementary teachers' own computational fluency (Conference Board of the Mathematical Sciences, 2001) as well as their mathematics knowledge for teaching (Hill & Ball, 2004). Hill and Ball (2004) argue that teachers of mathematics need two kinds of knowledge: the *common* knowledge of mathematics (e.g., knowing how to solve a given mathematics problem) and the *specialized* knowledge of mathematics (e.g., why the method works, whether the method can be generalized to other problems).

In order to reflect on the kinds of specialized knowledge needed by teachers to facilitate the development of computational fluency in elementary students, we analyzed the whole number units of an innovative elementary curriculum: *Investigations in Number, Data and Space* (TERC, 1998). In analyzing this curriculum, we were struck by the potential of one particular type of task: the (numerical) *starter problem*. For example, consider the problem of evaluating $102 - 46$, and some possible numerical starters, or first steps: $46 + 50$, $102 - 50$, and $106 - 50$. Starters can encourage the development of alternative strategies, and bring out a particular interpretation of an operation. Those students who evaluate $102 - 46$ by starting with $46 + 50 = 96$ often recognize subtraction as the "inverse" of addition, and may think of the original computation as figuring out how many things do I need to add onto 46 to get to 102. Whereas a student who evaluates $102 - 46$ by starting with $102 - 50$ may think about the original problem as "I have 102 things, and need to take 46 things away." We saw great potential in using starter problems with prospective teachers, and hoped that by having them develop and justify various computational strategies, we would provide them with the opportunity to deepen and extend their understanding of mathematics and to begin to develop the kind of specialized knowledge of mathematics necessary for teaching.

In this chapter we share the ways in which we adapted the concept of the starter problem for use with prospective elementary teachers, and how these adaptations changed over several iterations of the cyclical process of task adaptation, implementation, analysis and revision. During this time, the first author had primary responsibility for writing the teacher notes for these lessons, and piloting this unit (along with other units). In order to reflect on this process, we reexamined those teacher notes, videotaped lessons, and student work. Finally, for the purposes of this chapter we focus on the beginning of the whole number computation unit, which focuses mainly on subtraction.

3 Initial Adaptations of the Computational Starter

In adapting the computational starters for prospective elementary teachers, our main focus was on how they could be used to enable prospective teachers to unpack their understanding of computation, for example, to consider what subtraction means.

Prior experience with practicing teachers highlighted a tendency to apply various mathematical "rules" in order to determine how to utilize a particular starter. Thus the beginning of the first unit on computation is as much about helping prospective teachers to confront the rule-based nature of their mathematical thinking, as it is about helping them to develop a better understanding of subtraction – the first operation in this unit. Consider, for example, the first task in this unit: determine the result of $1,004 - 97$ by using mental reasoning rather than using the algorithm that you learned as a child. This task allows us to: introduce the notion of the numerical starter, by discussing different students'[1] first steps; and highlight the rule-based nature of their thinking, by discussing the reasoning for their strategies – both correct and incorrect. Virtually every semester the following strategy arises: $1,004 - 100 = 904$, and $904 - 3 = 901$. The typical rationale offered for this erroneous strategy is that one must undo whatever has been done to the expression, that is, since 3 was added to 97 to get 100, we must subtract 3 in order to "even things out." In order for students to make sense of this error in a way will help them as future teachers, they need to consider what is meant by subtraction. The following dialogue illustrates the instructor's way of helping students move away from the rules of algebra and of positive and negative numbers, to considering what an elementary student might think about subtraction, in order to determine a reasonable next step of this strategy:

I: Tell me what this $(1,004 - 97)$ means in language that an elementary school kid could understand.
*S*1 : 1,004 take away 97.
I: 1,004 take away 97, is that reasonable? Can somebody use that way of thinking about subtraction and get away from algebra and get away from these rules that you're creating. And if I don't know positive and negative numbers, I just know that 1,004 take away 97 … how could I explain what's going on here? I'm supposed to do 1,004 take away 97. So what did I do instead?
*S*2 : Took away 100.
I: I took away 100. So …
*S*3 : You have to give 3 back.
I: So, so I took away 3 extra so I've got to put them back.

It is important to recognize that this shift from rules to meanings is not a simple one for prospective teachers, and one which emerges multiple times during this course. For further discussion of this, and other, challenges faced by prospective teachers and their instructors as they established new norms for doing mathematics in the context of relearning computation, see Grant, Lo, and Flowers, 2007).

In addition to engaging students in generating their own starters for problems and solving problems with particular starters, both of which are tasks that mirror those in the *Investigations* curriculum for elementary students, we developed several types of tasks that extend these ideas. These extensions were designed to further the focus on justification based on the meaning of the operations, and to support the

---

[1] Unless specified as elementary students, the term *students* is used to denote the prospective elementary teachers that were enrolled in our classes.

exploration of additional mathematical relationships. Our initial ideas for types of extensions included having students: analyze the strategy and/or justification of a peer, compare and contrast two different strategies within an operation, or compare and contrast similar strategies across different operations. For example, after students have had some experience working with subtraction, we ask them to consider how these strategies might be extended to addition. We have found it effective to do this in the context of considering a special case of a starter: one which is equivalent to the original expression, but is simpler to solve. Thus $1,004 - 97$ can be determined by considering the equivalent expression $1,007 - 100$. The extension task is then to consider whether one can use the "same strategy" for addition? Embedded in this task is the question of what it means to generalize this strategy to addition. Would it mean doing the exact same thing to the numbers in the expression: $1,004 + 97 = 1,007 + 100$? Or would it mean to accomplish the same underlying goal, that is, to create a starter that is equivalent to the original expression and yet is simpler to determine: $1,004 + 97 = 1,001 + 100$? In either case, why does the strategy work (or not work)?

Our hope was that these extensions to the elementary tasks would both enhance prospective elementary school teachers' understanding of number and operations, as well as their ability to justify their thinking beyond specific examples. While these extensions were somewhat successful in accomplishing these goals, we recognized the need to create additional adaptations that focused on some specific issues that arose in early piloting of these materials. In the following sections we discuss some of those issues, and the additional types of tasks that were developed over time in order to address them.

4 Broadening Our Thinking About Starters

One of the overarching goals of using starter problems was to focus students' attention on the multiple interpretations that could be made of the operations, and to learn to utilize these interpretations to reason about computation. For us, being able to think about one solution method through multiple interpretations is an important aspect of computational fluency and is critical to each teacher's future ability to encourage the same in their students. In the midst of implementing this unit for the first time, it became clear that some students developed a tendency to associate certain interpretation of an operation with certain solution strategies. With subtraction, the dominant interpretation among our students is the take-away interpretation. We considered this tendency to be related to their rule-based approach to mathematics, and thus there were two reasons for finding ways to confront this issue. First, we wanted students to be able to have a broader understanding of subtraction, and second, we wanted to facilitate a more *productive disposition* (National Research Council, 2001) towards mathematics as a subject involving reasoning, rather than disconnected rules. Therefore it was important to have students consider how to solve problems using starters that suggested a different interpretation. For example, determining $102 - 46$ by starting with $46 + 50 = 96$ is an example of a starter problem that often elicited a distance or missing addend interpretation of subtraction: how many things do I need to add onto 46 to get to 102, or what is the distance between 46 and 102. While some starters increased the likelihood of a particular interpretation arising, they were not a guarantee. In fact some students persisted in their efforts to always look at subtraction as take-away.

4.1 Focusing on Interpretations

To force students to think about subtraction in multiple ways, we created *interpretation-specific* starters. Figure 1 provides an example of such a task in which students were not only provided a numerical starter, but were also required to provide two distinct justifications of their strategy – one utilizing take-away (Sara's interpretation) and the other utilizing distance (James' interpretation).

In each justification, the student is expected to consistently utilize a particular interpretation of subtraction. Figure 2 provides an example student work that successfully accomplishes this. There are several things to notice about the different justifications provided by this particular student. For example, consider the different rationales for adding five in the third step of the strategy. In the take-away justification, the rationale for adding 5 is that you took away 5 too many things in the first step; in the distance justification, the rationale is that you had not yet accounted for the distance from 195 to 200.Also notice that the student is not only successful at keeping track of the relevant interpretation of subtraction, but is also careful to be explicit about the interpretation of addition being used in the second and third steps.

Not all students were successful at these kinds of tasks, and the work of several students indicated an inability to coordinate pictorial representations with particular solution strategies and/or particular interpretations of the operation. For many, this difficulty seemed to coincide with a resistance to viewing subtraction as distance. Consider one student's attempt to use the distance interpretation, and a number line

---

Two students were attempting to determine the result of $613 - 195$ by beginning with $600 - 200 = 400$. Each student had his/her own way of thinking about this problem. Sara was interpreting this problem as meaning *I have 613 things, and I take away 195 things, how many do I have left?* James was interpreting this problem as *I am trying to find out what the distance is between 195 and 613?*

a) There are several ways to evaluate $613 - 195$ by using the given starter ($600 - 200 = 400$). You must choose **one** such solution strategy that can be understood from both students' perspectives.

b) Provide two justifications for the solution strategy you provided for part a. One of these justifications must be written from Sara's perspective; the other justification must make sense from James' perspective.

Fig. 1 Interpretation-specific starter task

Solution Strategy:

1. $600 - 200 = 400$
2. $400 + 13 = 413$
3. $413 + 5 = 418$

Justification from Sara's perspective: She began solving the problem 613-195, by beginning with the starter problem $600 - 200 = 400$. From there she needs to combine 400 and 13, and this is because the original problem started with 613 things not 600 things ($613 - 600 = 13$). The next step for Sara was to take the 413 she has just gotten, and combine it with 5 more things because the original problem started with 195 things and she took out 200 things in the starter problem ($200 - 195 = 5$). Once 413 is combined with 5, she gets 418. Therefore, Sara knows when you begin with 613 things and you take away 195 things, there will be 418 things remaining.

Justification from James' perspective: He, like Sara, is solving the problem 613-195 with the starter problem of $600 - 200 = 400$. The starter problem showed James that there is a distance of 400 between 600 and 200. However, James needs to find the distance between 613 and 195. Therefore, James needs to find the distance between 600 and 613, which is 13. Then he needs to combine that with the 400 he has already, which is 413. Lastly, James needs to find the distance between 200 and 195, which is 5, and he needs to combine that with the 413, to give him 418. James now knows that there is a distance of 418 between 613 and 195.

Fig. 2 Consistent use of each interpretation

The problem is $613 - 195$ and we are using the starter of $600 - 200$. We are going to start with a number line to represent both the starter and the original problem.

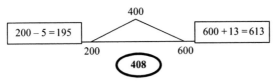

James wants to know what the distance is between 195 and 613. We are using the starter of 200 and the distance between 200 and 600 is 400. We did not add enough with our starter of 600 so we need to add an additional 13. We started with 5 too many at 195 so we need to deduct those by subtracting 5. When you combine our first answer of 400 plus the 13 and then remove the 5, you find the difference to be 408.

Fig. 3 Switching interpretations

drawing, to justify a strategy for determining $613 - 195$ by starting with $600 - 200$ (Fig. 3).Unlike the previous example of student work in which the student was able to consistently use one interpretation of the operation, this student switched interpretations mid-way through the work when explaining $200 - 5 = 195$.

While the picture matched the initial interpretation of 400 being the distance between 200 and 600, the student did not appear to extend this interpretation to the original problem. That is, the picture does not indicate the distance between 600 and 613, nor that between 195 and 200, nor the entire distance from 195 to 613. Furthermore the student's justification only refers to distance in the first two sentences, and eventually reverts to the take-away interpretation by the end. In this case, the student's inability to consistently utilize the distance interpretation likely contributed to his/her inability to determine the correct answer.

Although our teacher notes for the course indicate the importance of pictorial representations, like the number line, we did not anticipate the extent of the challenges the students would face in using them appropriately. We had naively assumed that prospective elementary teachers would have developed some basic competency with the use of number line representation through their pre-college schooling. Furthermore, we did not anticipate the tendency for students to assume a one-to-one correspondence between a pictorial representation and a particular interpretation of an operation. For example, some presumed that the number line could only be used with the distance interpretation of subtraction, when in fact the take-away interpretation can also be represented with a number line. This led to another variation of the starter task: combining numerical starters with pictorial starters.

4.2 Focusing on Pictorial Representations

The idea of the pictorial starter was initially prompted by students' tendency to view the number line as only being useful for the distance interpretation of subtraction. We experimented with this kind of task in both subtraction and multiplication. For subtraction, we sought to design a task that might enable our students to confront their difficulties with interpreting the number line in different ways. Thus we created the following task (Fig. 4) containing three pictorial representations – two of which involved a number line representation (only these two are shown) based on the most common number line representations generated by students from a previous semester. Our intention was that the pictorial representation on the left would encourage interpreting the starter (and the original problem) as take-away taking 400 away from 1,000 (mimicking the counting backward strategy a young child might

---

For the problem **1018 − 395** = __, three students began with the same starter: 1000 − 400 = 600. However they interpreted this starter differently, as is evidenced by their representations. Finish each student's work by solving the problem in a way that utilizes the given starter, and is consistent with their way of thinking about subtraction as indicated by their representation of the first step. Provide a written justification for each so-lution strategy along with representations for the remaining aspects of the strategy. Be explicit about how each student was thinking about the op-eration of subtraction.

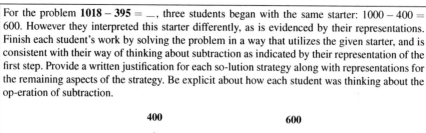

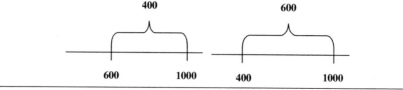

Fig. 4 Pictorial representations for the starter $1{,}000 - 400 = 600$

do when taking 4 away from 10: "9, 8, 7, and 6"). Whereas the picture on the right would encourage a distance interpretation: what is the distance between 400 and 1,000. We recognize that one does not have to interpret the representations in these specific ways, our goal was simply to raise the possibility of interpreting subtraction in two different ways, and allowing the notion that both interpretations could be represented using a number line to surface.

This task was somewhat productive in accomplishing our goals; however, inspection of the student work prompted us to alter the starter in future semesters. With the original starter ($1,000 - 400 = 600$), both numbers were changed from the original problem ($1,018 - 395$), the complexities of "getting back" to the original problem seemed to overshadow the issue of interpreting subtraction (as illustrated on the number line) in multiple ways. In our next iteration of this task we altered the starter for the problem so that only one number was different from the original problem (evaluate $1,018 - 395$ by utilizing the starter $1,018 - 400 = 618$). Our analysis of student writing assignment showed that this iteration of the task was more successful at pinpointing the issue we intended.

Students' ability to utilize the number line productively was further targeted by an exam item (Fig. 5) which combined two previously discussed ideas: creating an equivalent expression that is easier to compute than the original expression, and requiring students to use a particular picture (number line) to support their reasoning. In class discussion around why it makes sense to add the same quantity to both numbers in order to create an equivalent subtraction expression ($122 - 96 = 126 - 100$), students were typically more comfortable with interpreting subtraction as distance, and reasoning that when you add 4 to each number, you are keeping the distance (between 122 and 96) the same, but are simply shifting this distance 4 units to the left. Thus this task also increased the likelihood that a particular interpretation of the operation would emerge, for those students who chose the subtraction option. For those who chose the addition option, this task revealed the degree to which they were able to use the number line to represent addition (something which had received little attention up to this point).

Although most students were able to successfully demonstrate their understanding of how to use the number line, about 16% of the students (6 out of 38) could not do so on this task. Below are examples of two incorrect use of number line: one for the addition equivalent problem (Fig. 6a) and the other for the subtraction equivalent problem (Fig. 6b). Each example shows different misconceptions. Figure 6a demonstrates a basic understanding of the number line structure (the numbers are placed appropriately), but fails to represent $122 + 96$. Instead, the student is indicating

---

One solution strategy commonly used by elementary shcool students to solve an addition or a subtraction problem is to turn it into an equivalent problem. For example, one can evaluate $122 - 96$ by turning it into $126 - 100$, or evaluate $122 + 96$ by turning it into $118 + 100$. **Choose ONE** of these equivalent problem strategies (the addition <u>or</u> the subtraction) and use the number line model to explain <u>why</u> it works.

Fig. 5 Exam question requiring utilization of number-line model

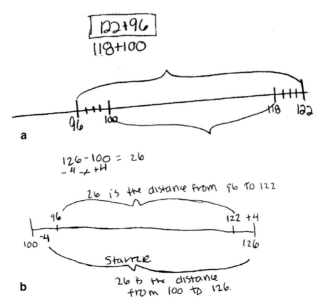

Fig. 6 Incorrect uses of number-line model. **a** Addition equivalent problem and **b** Subtraction equivalent problem

distances – that is, the distance between 122 and 96, and between 118 and 100. In our experience, this is appears to be a result of students attempting to translate their experience using distance to justify the equivalence of subtraction expressions directly the justification of equivalent addition expressions. In contrast, Fig. 6b shows an understanding of $122 - 96$ as finding the distance between 96 and 122, but a lack of understanding of the mathematical structure of the number line model. Without keeping 96 to the right of 100, the picture fails to demonstrate that the two distances, between $122 - 96$ and $126 - 100$, are equivalent.

Although the examples of tasks and student work discussed above are all in the context of subtraction, we created similar starter tasks for use with other operations and for doing computation with fractions and decimals. Some of the same issues arose in these other domains. For example, in working on whole number multiplication, our students were able to reason more flexibly when using the equal groups interpretation of multiplication (i.e., thinking about 31×97 as either 31 groups of 97 or 97 groups of 31), as opposed to the rectangular array/area interpretation. This is consistent with research showing that prospective elementary teachers in the United States do not have a well-developed concept of the relationship between multiplication and area (e.g., Simon & Blume, 1994). The use of interpretation and pictorial-specific starters was therefore just as critical in multiplication as it was in subtraction.

5 Discussion

We propose that forcing prospective teachers to "start" a problem in a particular way is productive in helping prospective teachers develop the kind of mathematical proficiency described by the National Research Council, (2001), and thus prepare future teachers to better understand their students' thinking. Our main mathematical goal in this unit has been to facilitate the development of computational fluency and the ability to justify strategies with tools accessible to elementary students such as multiple interpretations of operations embedded in everyday contexts and pictorial representations. This goal is most closely tied to three strands of mathematical proficiency: *conceptual understanding, procedural fluency, and adaptive reasoning*. Our experience using these tasks with prospective teachers also reveals their efficacy in fostering a more *productive disposition* towards mathematics (the fifth strand of mathematical proficiency). That is, moving away from rule-based learning to one based on reasoning about mathematics. The use of interpretation- and pictorial-specific starters was critical to this particular goal in that it enabled prospective teachers to broaden their understanding of the operations and allowed them to develop confidence in how to use this understanding to generate strategies based on reasoning. Finally, looking back we can see how these tasks have the potential to help them develop their proficiency in making sense and utilizing multiple representations in general, which is both an aspect of *strategic competence* and an essential foundation for algebraic reasoning (Brenner et al. 1997).

While we hope that we have made the case for the usefulness of the starter problems, we do not claim to have developed the perfect tasks to achieve our instructional goals. Furthermore, our experiences with designing and implementing these tasks suggest that the proposition is far from simple. In particular, the use of certain pictorial representations has created yet another tension between two different, though admittedly overlapping goals: learning particular mathematics content, and having a solid understanding of particular pictorial representations. In fact there is growing recognition of the importance of pictorial representations in mathematics teaching and learning. Diezmann and English 2001) define *diagram literacy* as "knowing about diagram use and being able to use that knowledge appropriately" (p. 77), and call for its development as one goal for mathematics instruction at all levels. It may be the case that students need more time to focus on a particular representation and its more general mathematical significance, in order to be able to effectively utilize that representation. This issue is of particular concern in the case of prospective elementary teachers, since many of the representations that we want them to utilize are ones that they have been exposed to for many years (e.g., number lines, area/array models), but about which they may have limited conceptual understanding.

The process of task creation, reflection on students' reaction to those tasks, and task alteration have allowed us – as curriculum designers and instructors – better understand the issues our students face as they work to learn mathematics with meaning. The challenge is to structure the tasks carefully so that they are open-ended enough to allow students to explore a particular mathematical idea through their own understanding, and yet focused enough to make sure that students are given opportunities to grapple with important issues. Although our work with the starter concept has been restricted to the area of computation, we see the potential of extending this concept to developing mathematical proficiency in other areas of mathematics.

References

Bass, H. (2003). Computational fluency, algorithms, and mathematical proficiency: One mathematician's perspective. *Teaching Children Mathematics, 9*, 322–327.

Brenner, M. E., Mayer, R. E., Moseley, B., Brar, T., Duran, R., Reed, B. S., et al. (1997). Learning by understanding: The role of multiple representations in learning algebra. *American Educational Research Journal, 34*, 663–689.

Conference Board of the Mathematical Sciences. (2001). *The mathematical education of teachers* (Vol. 11). Providence, RI: American Mathematical Society & Mathematical Association of America.

Diezmann, C. M., & English, L. D. (2001). Promoting the use of diagrams as tools for thinking. In A. A. Cuoco (Ed.), *The roles of representation in school mathematics* (pp. 77–89). Reston, VA: National Council of Teachers of Mathematics.

Grant, T. J., Lo, J., & Flowers, J. (2007). Shaping prospective teachers' justifications for computation: Challenges and opportunities. *Teaching Children Mathematics, 14*, 112–116.

Hill, H. C., & Ball, D. L. (2004). Learning mathematics for teaching: Results from California's mathematics professional development institutes. *Journal for Research in Mathematics Education, 35*, 330–351.

National Council of Teachers of Mathematics. (2000). *Principles and standards for school mathematics*. Reston, VA: Author.

National Research Council. (2001). *Adding it up: Helping children learn mathematics*. In J. Kilpatrick, J. Swafford, & B. Findell (Eds.), Mathematics Learning Study Committee, Center for Education, Division of Behavioral and Social Sciences and Education. Washington, DC: National Academy Press.

Russell, S. J. (2000). Developing computational fluency with whole numbers. *Teaching Children Mathematics, 7*(3), 154–159.

Simon, M. A., & Blume, G. W. (1994). Building and understanding multiplicative relationships: A study of prospective elementary school teachers. *Journal for Research in Mathematics Education, 25*, 472–494.

TERC. (1998). *Investigations in number, data and space*. Menlo Park, CA: Dale Seymour.

Tasks for Primary Student Teachers: A Task of Mathematics Teacher Educators

Victoria Sánchez and Mercedes García

This chapter is concerned with the tasks that mathematics teachers' educators pose in their classrooms. From our point of view, we cannot present these tasks without making explicit the theoretical perspective that underlies our decisions. This perspective has led us to choose what to teach and to decide how to teach. The identification of *systems of mathematics teachers' activity* and *mathematical practices* articulate the search of what to teach in a mathematics methods course. Its joint consideration provides us with a context in which the contents of the future primary teachers' curriculum are made explicit. From here, we present the process of designing two of the tasks that we implement in our classrooms.

1 Our Local Context

In order to contextualize this chapter, we start describing briefly our Primary Mathematics Teacher Education system at the moment. In Spain, Primary Education is taught by primary-school teachers who are responsible for all the areas at this level. They work with children aged 6–12. These teachers are trained at university. Three years of study are required to qualify as a primary teacher. In these 3 years the student teachers must obtain about 200 credits. The legal regulation on this degree establishes that 120 compulsory credits are common for all the Spanish universities. There are different specialties: Primary Education, Physical Education, Musical Education, Foreign Language, Nursery Education, Special Education, Audition and Language. Within the different subjects that form part of the curricula of these specialties, there are 9 credits devoted to Mathematics and its didactic for the specialty of Primary Education, and 4.5 credits in the specialties of Physical Education, Music

V. Sánchez
Professor, Department of Didactic of Mathematics, University of Seville, Spain

M. García
Professor, Department of Didactic of Mathematics, University of Seville, Spain

B. Clarke, B. Grevholm, and R. Millman (eds.), *Tasks in Primary Mathematics Teacher Education: Purpose, Use and Exemplars,* Mathematics Teacher Education 4,
© Springer Science+Business Media LLC 2009

and Foreign Language. In some universities these numbers of credits have increased a little. In the University of Seville, they have been increased from 3 to 5 credits, depending on the specialty.

When we planned the organization of these credits in our Primary Teacher Education program, we took into account that, in the future, Primary Teachers must use the mathematical ideas in the classroom from the perspective of mathematics and from their consideration as teaching/learning objects. Consequently, both perspectives must be taken into account in the pre-service education of those teachers. In our program, they are developed in two courses. The first one is a course of mathematics for teachers, situated in the first academic year. The second one is a mathematical methods course, developed in the second or third year, depending on the specialty. These courses share our theoretical framework, but their contents are different. Here we focus on the second course exclusively.

In the following sections, we will try to describe the tasks that we provide to our students in the mathematics methods course.

Before that, we want to emphasize a key idea from our point of view. We cannot make this description without making explicit the theoretical perspective that underlies our decisions. As teacher educators, this perspective has led us to choose the tasks and to decide how to implement them.

2 Mathematics Teachers' Systems of Activity

In the last decades, researchers such as Brown, Collins, and Duguid (1989), Cobb (1994), and Lave and Wenger (1991) have developed theoretical ideas that have been summarized by different authors (García, 2003, 2005; Putnam & Borko, 1997). These ideas enable us to understand the characteristics of cognition in an educational context. Our approach is rooted in some of them, in particular, the situative perspective that allows us to characterize the activity of teaching mathematics, the specific knowledge and skills that are needed for this activity, and the learning processes that allow student teachers to develop this knowledge. This involves defining the tasks implicit in the community of mathematics teachers from a theoretical perspective, identifying the systems of activity that enable the teachers to solve those tasks, and generating adequate learning environments. Following Llinares (2004), we consider such systems of activity to be

- The organization of the mathematical content for teaching. That includes being familiar with the mathematical contents as a teaching and learning object, using the knowledge of mathematics for designing, selecting and analysing worthwhile mathematical tasks, using the knowledge about the mathematical contents to design, analyze and select lessons and curricular resources.
- The management of the mathematical contents and discourse in the classroom. That includes being familiar with and identifying: (1) the phases and types of lessons of mathematics, (2) the characteristics of the mathematical interaction in the classroom, identifying the constraints and mechanisms which maintain the interactive course of mathematical communication in the classroom, and (3) the

characteristics of the management of debates as instruments for mathematical learning.

• The analysis and interpretation of mathematics students thinking. That includes becoming familiar with the theories for the learning and construction of mathematical knowledge, and the characteristics of the learning of mathematical concepts and procedures, using the prior knowledge for interpreting and analyzing the pupils' mathematical thinking.

Each system of activity can inform us about different aspects of a Mathematics Teacher Education program.

3 What to Teach in a Mathematics Methods Course

In addition to *systems of mathematics teachers' activity* that enable the teachers to solve their professional task – analogous to other grades, but with the additional characteristics specific to Primary school – in this course we need to consider the mathematical content as a teaching/learning object. Following Rasmussen, Zandieh, King, and Teppo (2005) defining, justifying and modelling, among others, are part of *'doing mathematics'* and underlie any mathematical content. They could be considered *mathematical practices*. Both *systems of mathematics teachers' activity* and *mathematical practices* articulate our ideas in the identification of what to teach in a mathematics methods course. The following table shows some of the different 'spaces' that must be considered from the Didactics of Mathematics (Table 1). The intersection of rows/columns (identified with an asterisk in the Table 1) provides us with a context in which the contents of the future primary teachers' curriculum are made explicit. The domains of mathematics teachers' professional knowledge (knowledge of and about mathematics, curricular knowledge, knowledge of learners and learning processes, instructional knowledge and knowledge about didactical-mathematics processes) are the background we consider to define these contents (García & Sánchez, 2002).

Table 1 Systems of mathematics teachers' activity and some mathematical practices

Systems of mathematics teachers' activity	To organize the mathematical content for teaching	To manage of mathematical contents and discourse in the classroom	To analyze and interpret what student teachers think/know
Mathematical practices			
Defining	*	*	*
Justifying	*	*	*
Modelling	*	*	*
Symbolizing	*	*	*
Others	*	*	*

4 How to Teach in a Mathematics Methods Course

In our classrooms, we try to create learning environments. We think that these learning environments may be generated by means of relevant tasks, active participation of the community members in the process of solving the tasks, working in small groups, taking into account previous knowledge and beliefs, and making explicit reasoning processes (García, 2000).

The use of conceptual tools enables the pre-service teachers to solve the proposed situation/task in such way that they become fit to participate fully in the mathematics teachers' community of practice (Lave & Wenger, 1991). Conceptual tools are understood as those concepts and theoretical constructs that have been generated from research in mathematics education leading to understanding and handling situations in which mathematics is taught and learned. They can be provided through videos, articles in mathematics education literature, or information provided for teacher educators. For us, as teacher educators, the generation of these environments has implied organizing our classroom along trajectories in which the above mentioned ideas are included (Fig. 1).

In these trajectories, the situation/task approaches the professional tasks of the mathematics teacher. In the following, we present an example of process that we have followed in the design of those tasks and the selection of conceptual tools that are going to be used in the corresponding trajectories.

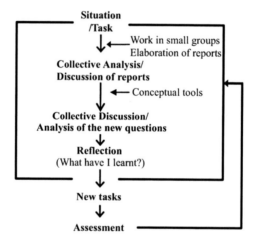

Fig. 1 Scheme of a teaching–learning trajectory (García, 2000, p. 63)

5 Designing Tasks

Identified spaces and trajectories, we were able to think in suitable tasks. We want to point out that both the design of the tasks and the choices of conceptual tools are 'open and dynamic' processes. Maintaining the trajectory as a consequence of our theoretical ideas, task and tools can change depending on the context (specific students, specialty ...) and our own personal development.

The tasks that we present here – Task A and Task B – are two of the tasks that we use in our mathematics methods course. Depending on the specialty, we include four or five tasks in an academic year.

5.1 Designing Task A

We start our work as teacher educators choosing the intersection rows/columns with which we want to work, as we can see in the following table (Table 2).

Table 2 Planning Task A using systems of mathematics teachers' activity and some mathematical practices

Systems of mathematics teachers' activity	To organize the mathematical content for teaching	To manage of mathematical contents and discourse in the classroom	To analyze and interpret what student teachers think/know
Mathematical practices			
Defining	–	–	–
Justifying	–	–	–
Modelling	*	–	–
Symbolizing	*	–	–
Others	–	–	–

In this case, we have situated in the intersection of the *Organization of the mathematical content for teaching* as a teachers' system of activity and *Modelling and Symbolizing* as mathematical practices (identified with an asterisk in the Table 2). This intersection is considered in the context of a mathematical content that appears in the curriculum of this level (Primary school). Here we focus on the multiplicative structure problems.

By considering together *Organizing the mathematical content for teaching/ Modelling and Symbolizing/arithmetic problems of multiplicative structure* we may choose into the space defined by rows/column some 'problematic spaces', understood as those fields/spaces of problems that the teacher educator wishes student teachers to think about in a certain moment.

In this occasion, some of these problematic spaces are:

- Type and structure of multiplicative arithmetic problems in mathematics elementary school curricula (6–12-year-old students)
- Different meanings associated to multiplication that appears in that curriculum (repeated addition, combinations ...)
- Different ways of considering how learners can solve those problems. What underlies the distinct solving strategies? What kind of difficulties can appear? How are these difficulties related to the types of problems?

- Role of the modes of representation as tools in the solving processes; relationships between symbols and meanings
- Mathematical modelling of real word situations
- Mathematical problems as teaching/learning objects
- Elements that a teacher needs to consider to work in different ways to organize the teaching of the multiplicative structure
- Elements that a teacher needs to work with in the classroom concerning different multiplicative problems and solving strategies. How can a lesson of problem solving be planned? How can it be managed? What are key elements in the process of assessing pupils' learning with respect to multiplicative structure problems?

These 'problematic spaces' lead us to go deep into aspects related to different teachers' domains of knowledge that, from our point of view, could be considered in this case. In the following table (Table 3), we make explicit some of these aspects.

Table 3 Aspects related to different teachers' domains of knowledge

School mathematics curriculum	• Arithmetic word problems in primary school curricula • MSAPs in primary school curricula • Criteria of analysis of MSAP • Classification of MSAP • Modes of representation in primary school curricula • Solving problem as a curricular content • Modelling as a curricular content • Mathematical language in primary school curricula
School mathematics learning processes	• Solving strategies of MSAP • Learning difficulties related to different types of MSAP problems • Analysis of the advantages and disadvantages of different modes of representation • Analysis of the advantages and disadvantages of MSAP for introducing the mathematical language
Teaching processes	• Design and selection processes of teaching tasks: elements that intervene, and application of specific tasks • Assessment of mathematical knowledge in primary school: characteristics, and teaching tasks as assessment tasks • Planning a problem solving lesson: study of the elements that intervene, and design of tasks • Assessment of problem solving The management of a problem solving lesson • Elements that intervene in the use and organization of word problems as a teaching object
Didactic-mathematical reasoning processes	• Comparing, assessing and selecting different ways of organizing a mathematical content for teaching • Comparing and assessing different strategies for solving a word problem • Different uses of word problems in primary school

MSAP multiplicative structure arithmetic problems

From here, we design a task that can involve as well as possible the above mentioned aspects. Here the task adopted the form of a case, which we show in the following picture.

Task A

You have just started at a new school. For the school year that is about to start, the staff has decided to change the textbooks and have asked your opinion on the choice. Which textbook would you recommend?

For our first steps in this professional task, we will settle for a given content, multiplicative structure arithmetic problems. In the booklet enclosed, we have selected all the information related to this type of problem found in two widely used primary-school textbooks.

- Start working with your group. Check the booklet carefully.
- Give and justify your assessment criteria.
- Let us suppose that some of those criteria are related to the elements involved in the teaching/learning of primary school multiplicative structure problems:

  ○ Indicate three of these elements that were useful in making your choice.
  ○ Do you agree with the contents? With their organization? With how they are presented?
  ○ What would you change (add or remove/leave as is), in each section?

As we show in the trajectory of teaching-learning (Fig. 1) the student teachers are provided with conceptual tools for the resolution of the task. These conceptual tools include information about the aspects related to different teachers' domains of knowledge that we have made explicit in Table 1. In particular, the articles, chapters of books, videos, which we selected in this case, are:

- Problem types, children's solution strategies and difficulties related to multiplication and division, (Carpenter, Fennema, Loef, Levi, & Empson, 1999, Chap. 4; Llinares & Sánchez, 1993; Nesher, 1992; Puig & Cerdán, 1989, Chap. 4; Quintero, 1986; Thompson & Hendrickson, 1986; Vergnaud, 1991)
- Curricular issues (National Council of Teachers of Mathematics, 2000)
- Problem solving as modelling (Carpenter et al., 1999, Chap. 5; Greer, 1997)
- Task design and planning (Cemen, 1989; Leblanc, Proudfit, & Putt, 1980; Quintero, 1986)

The teacher educator enlarges (or not) this information depending on the intention of highlighting or completing some ideas.

In the classroom, we start the teaching-learning trajectory providing students with a sheet with the case. After that, we follow the process indicated in Fig. 1.

Table 4 Planning Task B using systems of mathematics teachers' activity and some mathematical practices

Systems of mathematics teachers' activity	To organize the mathematical content for teaching	To manage of mathematical contents and discourse in the classroom	To analyze and interpret what student teachers think/know
Mathematical practices			
Defining	–	–	*
Justifying	–	–	*
Modelling	–	–	–
Symbolizing	–	–	–
Others	–	–	–

5.2 Designing Task B

In this case, we have chosen the intersection of *Analyze and interpret what student teachers think/know* as teachers' system of activity and *Defining/Justifying* as mathematical practices (identified with an asterisk in the Table 4). The context of mathematical content here is plane figures (Table 4).

Some of the problematic spaces that we may highlight in this case are the following:

- Geometrical elements in primary school curricula
- Plane figures in primary school curricula
- Modes of geometrical representation and their role in teaching/learning processes in those levels
- Ways of considering the definition in primary school curricula
- Ways of introducing geometrical justifications in primary school curricula
- Definitions and justifications as teaching/learning elements
- Different ways of considering geometry in primary levels from teaching and learning perspective. What models can help us in this analysis? What types of difficulties can arise?
- Elements that a teacher needs to consider in different ways of introducing the definitions of /justifications in figure planes for teaching
- Elements that a teacher needs to work with in the classroom concerning geometrical definitions/justifications. What are key elements in the process of assessing pupils' learning with respect to definitions/justifications?
- Tools of collecting information about mathematical learners' ideas/knowledge

These 'problematic spaces' lead to go deep into aspects related to different teachers' domains of knowledge, which we make explicit in the following table (Table 5):

From here, we elaborate the task. As the previous task (Task A), Task B adopts the form of a case:

Table 5 Aspects related to different teachers' domains of knowledge

School mathematics curriculum	• Geometric elements in primary school • Plane figures in primary school • Geometric modes of representation in primary school • Defining as a curricular content • Justifying as a curricular content
School mathematics learning processes	• Learning difficulties related to different geometric notions • Analysis of the advantages and disadvantages of different modes of representation in geometry • Analysis of the characteristics of spatial reasoning • Levels of geometric thinking (van Hiele) – what pupils learn/what pupils know • Learning difficulties related to defining and proving processes as a primary school content
Teaching processes	• Interview and questionnaire as tools in the teaching/learning process • Analysis of interview and questionnaire as a way of collecting information about pupils learning • Design and selection processes of teaching tasks: elements that intervene, and application of specific tasks • The process of assessment of mathematical knowledge in primary school: characteristics, and teaching tasks as assessment tasks • Elements that intervene in the organization of geometric contents as a teaching object
Didactic-mathematical reasoning processes	• Comparing and assessing different pupil's answers • Using pupil's answers in the planning process • Assessing and selecting different ways of organizing a geometric content for teaching

---

Task B

Juan has just joined the staff at a new primary school and in the stage he is assigned to he must teach mathematics. He has always thought that Geometry is an important part of school mathematics and that it is not given enough importance. In informal chats, his fellow teachers corroborate these ideas and he decides to suggest, if possible, collecting well-supported information based on more than just personal opinions, which could serve as a basis for evaluating the prior knowledge/ideas of the pupils about definitions and justifications in Geometry related to plane figures, and as a starting point for designing the geometry lessons.

The teachers suggest various alternatives concerning how this information should be collected. Some of them suggest interviewing certain students; others think a questionnaire with multiple-choice answers would be better.

The same thing happens concerning their interpretation of the data obtained. Some think their prior knowledge is sufficient to interpret the results, while others suggest a search on the Internet, or requesting information from experts that would allow a 'more scientific' interpretation.

In any case, they have to make basic decisions on the academic curriculum of the subjects they intend to collect the information for that will allow them to identify specific aspects related to the plane figures they want to consider.

- Which option would be the better, the interview or the questionnaire? Why? Base the answer on the characteristics of each option, pros and cons, examples of use.
- Following your choice, design a questionnaire or interview to collect the information required in one of the courses that corresponds to second or third stage.
- What do you think would be the key to seeing through the student responses?
- Once the student answers have been collected, how should they be classified? What criteria would be suitable? Choose the criteria, and establish the corresponding classification.
- What information does this classification contribute to your educational decisions?

In this task, the tools included information about the aspects related to different teachers' domains of knowledge that we have made explicit in Table 2. In particular, different information related to the characterization and analysis of geometrical reasoning and learning (Burger & Shaughnessy, 1986; Clements & Battista, 1992; Dickson, Brown, & Gibson, 1991, pp. 15–87; García & Llinares, 2001; Hershkowitz, 1990; Jaime & Gutiérrez, 1990; Vinner, 1991). As in the previous task, the teacher educator enlarge (or not) this information depending on the intention of highlighting or completing some ideas.

6 What Have Student Teachers Learnt?

From our theoretical references, we consider learning as the identification and use of conceptual tools in the process of handling a professional task. This consideration of learning has allowed us to identify in our research the following 'learning levels' (García, Sánchez, Escudero, & Llinares, 2006), shown in Table 6.

In our mathematics methods courses, we use these levels in the assessment of our students' knowledge in the different 'moments' of the learning processes. Our practice and research has shown that the learning environments generated in primary school teacher programs enabled some of these student teachers to identify individually and collectively the conceptual tools provided (Sánchez, García, & Escudero, 2006). Nevertheless, integration of these tools has been shown to be more complex. We have seen how, in situations in which such integration was achieved, the task was carried out differently, the students were aware of and evaluated distinct features that led to different decisions (e.g. to choose a

Table 6 Learning levels and their characteristics

Learning levels	Characteristics
Level 1	Conceptual tools not identified
Level 2	Tools identified, but not related to decisions
Level 3	Conceptual tools provided are identified and applied (used)
Level 4	Conceptual tools are identified, applied and integrated in a more general framework

different textbook or design different interviews/questionnaires). This shows the professional relevance of such integration and points out the need of advancing in this subject, extending this research agenda to both pre-service secondary mathematics teacher education and in-service programs at all levels.

Finally, we would like to get back to our practice. Research projects are not limited in time and scope. But the mathematics teacher educator practice is time-limited (an academic year), and has the main goal that student teachers become mathematics teachers. How many tasks are necessary to achieve this goal? What 'problematic spaces' and features of teacher's domains of knowledge should be considered? What tasks should be used? How about the diversity of student teachers? These are open questions that we would like to share with other teams, other colleagues, and other people.

References

Brown, J., Collins, A., & Duguid, P. (1989, January–February). Situated cognition and the culture of learning. *Educational Researcher, 18*(1), 32–42.

Burger, W., & Shaughnessy, M. (1986). Characterizing the van Hiele levels of development in geometry. *Journal for Research in Mathematics Education, 17*(1), 31–48.

Carpenter, T. P., Fennema, E., Loef, M., Levi, L., & Empson, S. B. (1999). *Children's mathematics. Cognitively guided instruction.* Portsmouth, NH: Heinemann.

Cemen, P. B. (1989). Developing a problem-solving lesson. *Arithmetic Teacher, 36*(2), 14–19.

Clements, M. A., & Battista, M. (1992). Geometry and spatial reasoning. In D. A. Grouws (Ed.), *Handbook of research on mathematics teaching and learning.* New York: Macmillan.

Cobb, P. (1994). Constructivism in mathematics and science education. *Educational Researcher, 23*(7), 4.

Dickson, L., Brown, M., & Gibson, O. (1991). *El aprendizaje de las matemáticas (Children learning mathematics).* Madrid: Labor.

García, M. (2000). El aprendizaje del estudiante para profesor de matemáticas desde la naturaleza situada de la cognición: Implicaciones para la formación inicial de maestros (Student teacher's learning from the situated nature of the cognition. Implications for prospective teachers). In C. Corral & E. Zurbano (Eds.), *Propuestas metodológicas y de evaluación en la formación inicial de los profesores del área de didáctica de las matemáticas (Methodological and evaluative proposals in the initial teachers' training from the didactic of the mathematics)* (pp. 55–79). Oviedo: Universidad de Oviedo.

García, M. (2003). A formaçao inicial de professores de matemática: Fundamentos para a definiçao de um currículo (Prospective mathematics teachers' training: Basis for the definition of a curricula). In D. Fiorentini (Ed.), *Formaçao de professores de matemática: Explorando novos caminhos com outros olhares (Mathematics teachers' training: Exploring new ways with others ways of seeing)* (pp. 51–86). Campinas: Mercado de Letras.

García, M. (2005). La formación de profesores de matemáticas. Un campo de estudio y preocupación (Mathematics teacher education. A field of study and concern). *Educación Matemática, 17*(2), 153–166.

García, M., & Llinares, S. (2001). Los procesos matemáticos como contenido: El caso de la prueba matemática (Mathematical processes as a content: The case of the mathematical proof). In E. Castro (Ed.), *Didáctica de la matemática en la educación primaria (Didactic of mathematics in primary education)* (pp. 105–122). Madrid: Síntesis.

García, M., & Sánchez, V. (2002). Una propuesta de formación de maestros desde la Educación Matemática: Adoptando una perspectiva situada (A proposal of teachers' training from mathematics education: Adopting a situative perspective). In L. C. Contreras & L. Blanco (Eds.), *Aportaciones a la formación inicial de maestros en el área de matemáticas: Una mirada a la práctica docente (Contributions to the prospective teachers' training in mathematics: A look to the educational practice)* (pp. 59–71). Badajoz: Servicio de Publicaciones, Universidad de Extremadura.

García, M., Sánchez, V., Escudero, I., & Llinares, S. (2006). The dialectic relationship between research and practice in mathematics teacher education. *Journal of Mathematics Teacher Education, 9*(2), 109–128.

Greer, B. (1997). Modelling reality in mathematics classroom: The case of word problems. *Learning and Instruction, 7*, 293–307.

Hershkowitz, R. (1990). Psychological aspects of learning geometry. In P. Nesher & J. Kilpatrick (Eds.), *Mathematics and Cognition* (pp. 70–95). New York: Cambridge University Press.

Jaime, A., & Gutiérrez, A. (1990). Una propuesta de fundamentación para la enseñanza de la geometría: el modelo de Van Hiele (A proposal of foundation for teaching geometry. The Van Hiele model). In S. Llenares & V. Sánchez (Eds.), *Teoría y práctica en educación matemática (Theory and practice in mathematics education)* (pp. 299–384). Sevilla: Alfar.

Lave, J., & Wenger, E. (1991). *Situated learning. Legitimate peripheral participation.* New York: Cambridge University Press.

Leblanc, J. F., Proudfit, L., & Putt, J. (1980). Teaching problem solving in the elementary school. In S. Krulick & R. Reys (Eds.), *Problem solving in school mathematics* (pp. 104–116). Reston, VA: NCTM.

Llinares, S. (2004). Building virtual learning communities and the learning of mathematics by student teachers. Regular lecture, ICME 10. Denmark: www.ICME10.dk.

Llinares, S., & Sánchez, V. (1993). La comprensión del significado del número. Resolución de problemas aritméticos elementales de estructura multiplicativa. (The understanding of number meaning. Solving word problems of multiplicative structure). *Serie: Elementos del conocimiento base para la enseñanza de las matemáticas. Conocimiento sobre el aprendizaje y los aprendices. Contenido aritmética. Nivel enseñanza primaria. Vídeo 5. (Series: Elements of base knowledge for teaching mathematics. Knowledge about learning and learners. Arithmetic content. Primary level).* Sevilla: Secretariado de Medios Audiovisuales de la Universidad de Sevilla.

NCTM. (2000). *Principles and standards for school mathematics.* Reston, VA: Author.

Nesher, P. (1992). Solving multiplication word problems. In G. Leinhardt, R. Putnan, & R. Hattrup (Eds.), *Analysis of arithmetic for mathematics teaching* (pp. 189–219). Hillsdale, NJ: Erlbaum.

Puig, L., & Cerdán, F. (1989). *Problemas aritméticos escolares (Arithmetic problems in the school).* Madrid: Síntesis.

Putnam, R. T., & Borko, H. (1997). Teacher learning: Implications of new views of cognition. In B. J. Biddle, T. L. Good, & I. F. Goodson (Eds.), *The international handbook of teachers and teaching* (Vol. 2, pp. 1223–1296). Dordrecht: Kluwer Academic Publishers.

Rasmussen, C., Zandieh, M., King, K., & Teppo, A. (2005). Advancing mathematical activity: A practice-oriented view of advanced mathematical thinking. *Mathematical Thinking and Learning, 7*(1), 51–73.

Quintero, A. (1986). Children's conceptual understanding of situations involving multiplication. *Arithmetic Teacher, 33*(5), 34–39.

Sánchez, V., García, M., & Escudero, I. (2006). Primary preservice teacher learning levels. In J. Novotná, H. Moraová, M. Krátká, & N. Stehlíková (Eds.), *Proceedings of the 30th Conference of the International group for the Psychology of Mathematics Education* (Vol. 5, pp. 33–40). Prague, Czech Republic: Faculty of Education, Charles University.

Thompson, C., & Hendrickson, H. (1986). Verbal addition and subtraction problems: Some difficulties and some solutions. *Arithmetic Teacher, 33*(7), 21–35.

Vergnaud, G. (1991). *El niño, las matemáticas y la realidad (The child, mathematics and reality).* Méjico: Trillas.

Vinner, S. (1991). The role of definitions in the teaching and learning of mathematics. In D. Tall (Ed.), *Advanced mathematical thinking* (pp. 65–81). Dordrecht: Kluwer Academic Publishers.

The Mathematics Teaching Portfolio: A Reflective Tool for Developing Professional Growth and Improving Classroom Practices

Rose Spanneberg

This chapter examines mathematics teacher portfolios as a powerful tool to promote reflection among teachers. The portfolio encourages teachers, through written reflective statements, to examine the teaching of mathematics in-depth and allow others to examine the thinking behind the teaching documented in the portfolio. The portfolio offers an excellent opportunity for teachers to think reflectively about teaching and at the same time provide evidence that could be used to guide practice. Teachers are encouraged to reflect on themselves as learners of mathematics and to reassess their role and classroom practices. Being exposed to reflective practice teachers learned the importance of documenting professional growth and expressing their beliefs about teaching and learning. Opportunities for collegial sharing and collaboration built into the portfolio construction allow the creators of the portfolios to share their concerns and anxieties about issues in mathematics. Teachers need to continually seek ways to improve their knowledge of mathematics in order to teach more effectively. If they opt to work collaboratively with colleagues the possibilities are much greater for them to define the best course of action for different situations than working in isolation.

1 Introduction

In South Africa as in many other parts of the world ongoing concern among mathematics educators is how can we improve and provide opportunity for effective change in the classroom. Recommendations for reform in mathematics education call for increased emphasis to assist teachers to make critically reflective judgements in the midst of action.

R. Spanneberg
Director, Rhodes University Mathematics Education Project (RUMEP), South Africa

B. Clarke, B. Grevholm, and R. Millman (eds.), *Tasks in Primary Mathematics Teacher Education: Purpose, Use and Exemplars,* Mathematics Teacher Education 4,
© Springer Science+Business Media LLC 2009

Bringing about such changes in the mathematics classroom is not easy. Hart (2002, p. 6) suggests that

> [T]eacher reflection is critical in teacher change. The act of reflecting on beliefs and behaviours allows teachers to make connections between their thought and actions and to recognize, expose, and confront contradictions and inconsistencies.

Teacher reflection has become a crucial concept in the professional growth of teachers. Since the thrust of this chapter is concerned with teaching portfolios as a reflective tool, the concept of reflective teaching should also be discussed: the potential of reflective practice, what it means and how it might impact on teaching.

In recent years reflection has become a crucial concept in the professional growth of teachers. A variety of definitions exist around reflection. Gilbert (1994) argues that reflection is not a new concept in education. John Dewey is acknowledged as a key originator of the concept of reflection, and his work is considered as a useful starting point for discussions about reflection. For Dewey (1933), reflection is both a meaning-making process and a disciplined way of thinking Freese (1999) drew on the work of Loughran & Corrigan (1995) and Schon (1983) defined reflection as the process of making sense of one's experiences deliberately, and actively examining one's thought and actions to arrive at new ways of understanding oneself as a teacher. I interpret reflection in the mathematics classroom as a process whereby teachers continuously examine, plan and revise their own practice.

The professional reflective practice in this chapter is linked to critical reflection. The purpose of this is to document, develop and change one's practice while continuously thinking about that practice. Critical reflection, according to Jay and Johnson (2002), often involves making a judgement. Through this judgement teachers question their own practice. They articulate their professional knowledge and reflect on what?, how?, and why? Wolf (1994) proposed that without reflections by the teacher on problems and successes, it is difficult to determine the depth of the teacher's understanding of the teaching and learning process.

2 Outcomes of the Portfolio Task

2.1 Teaching Portfolios as a Reflective Tool

Within the literature, teaching portfolios, have received growing recognition as a result of the benefits teachers and their students have derived from constructing a portfolio. Dana and Tippins (1998) describe science-teaching portfolios as a form of self-reflective inquiry undertaken to improve both the practice of teaching science and the teacher's understanding of teaching science. Zeichner and Wray (2001) stated that with the increased focus on preparing and developing teachers to be reflective and analytic about their work, teacher educators and staff developers have increasingly used teaching portfolios as one of a number of ways to stimulate greater reflection and analysis by teachers. My own experience in introducing practising teachers of mathematics to construct portfolios, support the belief that the writing of reflective statements by teachers provide evidence of teaching and learning in the classroom. In addition, written reflections allow teachers to examine their practice more deeply (Wolf, 1994). Similarly, De Rijdt, Tiquet, Dochy, and Devolder (2006) agree that a teacher is able to come to a deeper self understanding through reflection. In this way, a teaching portfolio can be seen as a vehicle for the growth of and the learning by teacher. Effective mathematics teaching requires what the learners know and how to assist them to better understand what they need to learn and then to support them to learn it well. Encouraging teachers to be reflective and analytical about their work will guide their professional judgment and activity in the classroom.

2.2 Language and Reflective Writing

During reflective writing teachers make use of language when they describe, report, express, articulate and explore reasons for and about their classroom practice. Various terms and phrases begin to appear in their writing as they experiment with the language special to their subject and practice. According to Goldsmith and Shifter (1997), teachers who seek to change their mathematics practice often find themselves in need of a different vocabulary and set of categories for thinking about teaching and learning. Their use of language itself helps them to reflect on specific classroom event. Both pre-service and in-service teachers would be guided by the language they engage in during the teaching sessions on the course that they are attending as well as the language borrowed from curriculum documents and academic readings.

To identify the language of reflective writing I will refer to Hatton and Smith's (1995, p. 41) levels of reflective writing:

Descriptive reflection: not only a description of events but some attempt to provide reason or justification for events or actions in a reportive or descriptive way.
Dialogic reflection: a form of discourse with oneself and exploration of possible events.
Critical reflection: involving reasons given for decisions or events that take account of the broader historical, and social and/ or political contexts.

The language of reflection that I have observed in my students' portfolios illustrated the above. When the purpose of reflection is to improve mathematics teaching and learning teachers must then examine their teaching to see what went well and what went wrong. In order for teachers to take action they first need to consider a number of possibilities and strategies that are appropriate to succeed or improve learning in the future. Teachers for example, report on lesson plans according to the new curriculum. At present, South African teachers are challenged by the three levels of planning (i.e. Learning programme; Work schedule and Lesson plan) in the new curriculum that they must implement at all phase levels. The entries below are examples of reflective writing on lesson plans:

> I find the repetitive writing of the three levels of planning frustrating.
>
> It is time consuming. I use a mind map and develop my work programme of what I intend to teach ...
>
> I have found it easier to work out the learning programme thereafter the work schedule and then the lesson plans. It became easier to plan the learning programme for the whole phase... I have found it difficult to adhere to the exact plan in presenting the lesson the reason was the frequent interruptions that hampered the application of the planned sequence.

Often teachers make use of language functions such as expressing feelings of success, articulating processes that were conducive to learning especially after they identified a problem and they then tried to improve the situation. The written reflections by teachers often express their beliefs about mathematics, mathematics teaching and learning. I consider teacher beliefs as the views, interpretations, own perceptions and judgement about their practice. What follows is an example of a mathematics teacher expressing a strong belief in the positive atmosphere that she tried to create in her mathematics classroom:

> I think the most important thing is for my learners to feel comfortable with me and with each other. I do think I handle discipline quite well, also I am not too strict with them. I really believe that this works well for me and helps me to work well with my learners... they don't feel threatened by me, they are comfortable doing the work.

Moreover, their written reflections revealed how individual teachers coped with situations in different contexts as well as the complexities of teaching. The next entry is on the difficulty with the use of English as a second language:

> The biggest problem for me is the issue of language. Most of the learners are struggling with English and they don't want to communicate in English. Because learners like to work in groups I allow them to use their mother tongue. In that way they are learning from each other.

Most teachers in our schools are experiencing the same problem. The reason for this is that the learners must learn mathematics through a second language, which is English. This language issue in learning and teaching reflects a typical situation occurring in most urban and rural schools in South Africa. Being an educator for inservice mathematics teachers for a number of years I support the view that teacher educators should foster the development of critical reflection so that teachers can become aware of the impact of their own actions upon the students that they teach (Hatton and Smith, 1995).

2.3 Teaching Portfolios Enhancing Teacher Professional Development and Growth

New paradigms for teacher development are beginning to emerge – one that challenges traditional forms of professional development. Traditionally teachers experienced professional development as a separate and distinct event. Teachers want opportunities that relate to their daily work. Some of these are: professional development that is directly related to teachers' classroom practices (which should also encourage teacher collaboration); teachers having a good understanding of the mathematics that they teach; and teachers reflecting critically on their learning experiences.

Teaching portfolios are often associated with the professional growth of teachers. For example, Green and Smyser (1996), writing about the teaching portfolio as a strategy for professional development and evaluation, in this sense a teaching portfolio allow teachers to make critical decisions about their practice through self-assessment. They can serve as a tool that teachers can use to inform and reshape their teaching.

The portfolio construction is a process more than a product. When teachers continuously reflect and carefully examine their practices, those practices are likely to improve. However, Green and Smyser (1996) explain that the professional development of a teacher is essentially a process of personal change. It is something that the teacher has to initiate and not something that is done to the teacher. Teachers themselves can only bring about change when they adopt new ideas and take responsibility to review their practice. Self-reflection, therefore, is the starting point for professional development. Naturally, it is the starting point for teaching portfolios as well. Consistent with this view is that of Ellsworth (2002) where she claims that portfolios can be used to help plan professional development for inservice teachers. She points out that the portfolio evidence can help practicing teachers see where they need to strengthen either own content knowledge in a particular area or their instruction of that content. It is therefore, fair to say that portfolios provide teachers with a professional tool to evaluate and improve their own development. My own experience in incorporating teaching portfolios into a mathematics course for inservice teachers supports this view. Being exposed to reflective practice in this way, teachers learned the importance of documenting professional growth and articulating their beliefs about teaching and learning. This was evident in a study I have conducted where interviews and analysis of reflective statements were considered. The teachers who participated in the study described the mathematics teaching portfolio construction as follows:

> The portfolio had made me realise that the teacher and learner cannot work in isolation from each other ... most importantly the portfolio gave me the opportunity to make mistakes, develop and progress, and to believe in myself as a teacher

Another teacher appreciated the value of the portfolios as a 'measurement tool'. He claimed that the reflective process helped him improve his teaching style and strategies.

> If learners had not understood a mathematical concept, it meant I could apply another strategy. The reflections helped me to see how the learners are progressing and where they experience problems or needed help. It also helped me to improve and refine my teaching skills, helping me to become a better teacher.

2.4 Teaching Portfolios Integrate all Aspects of Teaching

Reform in mathematics teaching is presently experiencing many challenges to change. Some of the demands are for teachers to assess the learners continuously and they must implement the use of alternative assessment strategies. Within new developments in teacher education, teachers are required to make use of teaching strategies very different to what they used in the past. Teachers need good knowledge of mathematics they can draw on to make learning more effective. They also need knowledge about how mathematical concepts and ideas can be represented in order to teach with understanding. Teachers should choose problem-solving tasks to introduce and teach mathematical concepts rather than the memorization of facts or procedures. Teachers must create environments conducive to learning. Effective mathematical tasks should be selected to encourage learners to be actively involved in their own learning. Teachers are required to engage in reflective practice to continuously try to improve and learn about their practice. One teacher in his reflection showed how he tried to improve the learners' understanding of prisms:

> I observed that learners were not able to calculate and identify parts of prisms. What I did to overcome this problem was to use other samples of prisms and gave each group a chance to identify the properties of at least one of the prisms we then shared the information with the whole class.

Many of the teachers in the inservice course revealed through their reflections how they tried to improve the learning and teaching in mathematics. They had to continuously revise their lesson plans and the way they teach.

2.5 Teaching Portfolios Support Learning

Having the portfolio task included in any of the mathematics courses is a result of the learning that teachers undergo in creating such a teaching portfolio. Loughran & Corrigan (1995, p. 565) make special reference to the learning advantages for prospective teachers.

> In preservice teacher education programs the teaching portfolio offers opportunities to student teachers' experiences, thoughts, actions, and subsequent learning about teaching to be documented.

Portfolios can greatly contribute to knowledge and reflection about own performance. The portfolio is seen first and foremost as a tool to support learning. It continuously offers the teacher an opportunity to gain new insights into the accomplishments in teaching. This is done when teachers carefully examine their own practices with the intention to improve that practice. Viewing teacher learning from the perspective of reflection and analysis, it is precisely the written reflective statements by mathematics teachers that are a vital tool in the learning process. Mathematics teachers have opportunity to learn to scrutinize their own performance, begin to understand what went well as well as what went wrong. The teachers can then consider strategies to improve success in future work and in this way take responsibility for their learning.

Teaching portfolios demonstrate how teachers help students learn as well as offering an opportunity for teachers to make a statement about their personal philosophy of teaching (Loughran & Corrigan, 1995). This was especially evident with my own students participating in a mathematics course. The examples that follow are portfolio reflection statements by practicing mathematics teachers:

Helen's reflection makes a statement about her perspective on assessment:

> I have now adopted the attitude that assessment is very important in the classroom, so I must make it work for myself and for the learners. Besides this, assessment most certainly guides my teaching I therefore depend on my learners' assessment and reflections as well as my own.

Another student, Anne, expressed a belief in the importance of preparing good questions in order to help learners to better understand the mathematics in the classroom:

> ... choose your questions very carefully so that you can focus on what you want learners to learn. If your questions are focussed and when you let the learners explain their ideas, if they do that, they will quickly see if they don't make sense.

Teaching portfolios can also highlight students' active exploration and selection of relevant information about their own strengths and weaknesses. This often leads to a person taking responsibility for further development (Tillema, 1998). Mark, reflecting on his lesson, reported how he could develop his lesson in future:

> I should develop investigative lessons to stimulate logical thinking and reasoning in my learners. I know what resources to use but need to plan detailed lessons properly ...

According to Wolf (1996) teaching portfolios allow teachers to retain examples of good teaching so they can examine them, talk about them, adapt them, and adopt them. Another reflection by Mark reveals the action he took after he adapted the teaching of mathematical patterns. He felt confident about his teaching and describes how he could help the learners:

> The learners really enjoyed the practical situations when building patterns with matchsticks and determining the rule for the patterns. I realised the importance of an open-ended approach in mathematics. The learners' mathematical writing ability developed whereby they wrote meaningful ideas on how they calculated the outcomes. The practical sessions enabled learners to explore and discover for themselves.

There is general agreement that teaching portfolios as a tool for reflecting on learning have much to offer teacher educators. Wolf (1994) points out that without reflections by the teachers on problems and successes, it is difficult to determine the depth of the teacher's understanding of the learning and teaching process.

2.6 Teaching Portfolios Promote Collegiality and Social Interaction Amongst Teachers

Collegial sharing and collaboration can be built into the portfolio process and can offer valuable opportunities for teachers to share and compare, support and advise each other. Tann (1993) suggested that the value of engaging in reflective activity is almost always enhanced if it can be carried out in association with other colleagues, as personal insecurities are reduced. For my purposes I engaged my students in portfolio conference sessions so that they shared the portfolios with each other. The students found this experience of sharing with others very helpful because they could share problems and concerns in mathematics with teachers of similar backgrounds. Barton and Collins (1993) reported that the collegial sharing and collaboration built into the portfolio help students to become more articulate. Students share their portfolio with each other for suggestion and support. Thus, teaching becomes a collaborative event, with discussion based on evidence collected in the portfolio. In recent years, research on the improvement in teachers' professional development programmes, promote collegiality among teachers as an important component. Silver (1996) cited in Smith (2001) suggested that professional development in mathematics should offer opportunities for teachers to work in collaboration with colleagues toward shared goals rather than working in isolation. Richert (1997) agrees that teachers require the presence of others in order to perform effectively. Similarly, Zeichner and Wray (2001) consider that the value of portfolios is greatly enhanced when teachers are given opportunities to interact with others on a regular basis in the construction of these goals. Shulman (1988) emphasised that a teaching portfolio should stimulate and facilitate professional interaction among teachers. Teacher educators today without doubt, accept that learning is a social process (Vygotsky, 1978). Wolf and Dietz (1998) propose that constructing a portfolio should be as well. Interaction with others should be part of the portfolio process as teachers set goals, carry out and document their work. It is important therefore, as mathematics educators, we consider the vital role teaching portfolios offer to improve not only teacher learning but also collaboration and interaction among teachers.

For the last two decades constructivism has emerged as the epistemological foundation for mathematics education, and a new vision developed of what it means to know and do mathematics (Hart, 2002, cited in Hoffman, 1989). How does the construction of a teaching portfolio fit into this theory of learning?

2.7 Teaching Portfolios is Reflective of a Constructivist Paradigm

Anderson and DeMeulle (1998) described the portfolio as an assessment tool reflective of a constructivist paradigm. It involves self-construction of knowledge within a social context, views assessment as ongoing and part of the learning process and includes active learning. From this point of view, teacher education programmes that supports this type of learning for their students, could find that the construction of teaching portfolios is an opportunity to develop constructivist thinking and learning. An important aspect for mathematics educators is for teachers to see the potential for their students to learn mathematics with understanding. There is a shift toward mathematical reasoning rather than memorizing procedures. Foote and Vermette (2001) explain that from a constructivist perspective to allow students to examine, reflect upon, and alter beliefs as they learn is compatible with portfolio evaluation. Many proponents of mathematics reform have advocated a constructivist perspective of teaching and learning (Cobb et al., 1989; Noddings, 1990; Simon, 1995). Constructivists recognise that reflection on practice, active learning, importance of prior knowledge and skills, collaboration and cooperation, participation in authentic activities are all important opportunities to enhance teaching and learning. From this perspective, portfolio construction matches a constructivist conception of learning.

3 Teaching Portfolios in Mathematics Teacher Education

Current world-wide reform in mathematics demands a shift from the traditional style of teaching and rote learning to more learner-centred instruction. The proposed changes of how mathematics should be taught and assessed require teachers to rethink their teaching practices. Such changes are not easy to accomplish, and therefore require appropriate professional development. Teachers' continuing professional development is being promoted to support instructional change in mathematics, new forms of professional development are needed for teachers (Clarke & Hollingsworth, 2002; Knight, 2002; Smith 2001). A number of alternative perspectives to support teacher change are identified in the literature. The concept of 'the reflective practitioner' and the idea that reflection in, on and for practice are seen as promising ways of improving practice. The need for monitoring teaching quality and professional development by means of portfolios has emerged (Kelchtermans, 1993; Smith and Tillema, 2001, cited in De Rijdt et al., 2006).

3.1 Teaching Portfolios Defined and Described

In order to provide a framework within which to present the portfolio process, I include some of the definitions and descriptions that have been identified by the authors of this topic.

De Rijdt et al. (2006) define the teaching portfolio as a purposeful collection of evidence, consisting of descriptions, documents and examples of what is good teaching for the teacher. Moreover, it contains reflections upon one's educational practices (p. 1,086). Wolf and Dietz (1998) suggest that the teaching portfolio is more than a collection of evidence. They offer the following definition:

A teaching portfolio is a structured collection of teacher and student work created across diverse context over time, framed by reflection and enriched through collaboration that has as its ultimate aim the advancement of teacher and student learning (p. 13).

Constructing a teaching portfolio can be seen as a vehicle for the growth of a teacher through self-assessment. The reflective analysis and artefacts (evidence) are seen as two major components of a teaching portfolio. It is therefore important for teacher educators in mathematics to create and foster a rich environment for effective reflection in order to enhance better understanding in teaching and learning in mathematics.

3.2 Suggestions in how to Design the Portfolio

Firstly, there is no 'one' right way of producing a portfolio. It helps to have a table of contents so that the portfolio developer can organise the content more clearly and it helps the reader better understand the content of the portfolio. Important, is to have a clear purpose of the task. Both the student and the educator should know the purpose right from the start of the process. The purposes will vary depending on the context in which the portfolio is constructed. De Rijdt et al. (2006) point out that creating a teaching portfolio is not an activity at one particular moment in time, but a process that should be extended over a period of time. It is often suggested that teachers articulate their educational philosophy as a first step in preparing a portfolio. A statement of philosophy is a written summary of professional beliefs concerning teaching.

The teaching portfolio should include documentation that supports teaching. These documents are often referred to in the literature as artefacts that programmes have asked their students to include. They can include: lesson plans, teaching journals, photographs, sample pupil assessment, and pupil work samples. Teachers can include a variety of their pupils' work to show the types of mathematical activities they use as teachers. All the evidence included into the portfolio should be accompanied by reflective statements. The reflective statements should tell the reader or reviewer what the teacher has learned about himself or herself and the practice of learning. According to Fernsten and Fernsten (2005) the reflection statements, a critical component of the portfolio, is a vital tool in the learning process. Through these writings the student gains clearer understanding of what they have accomplished, what was successful, and what improvement can be made in future.

The teaching portfolio that I have implemented in my mathematics education course included both Foundation and Intermediate Phase (elementary and middle school) teachers. In designing the teaching portfolio task, I attempted to achieve a balance between guidance for content and structure on the one hand, and flexibility and choice on the other. The focus of this task was on using portfolios with practicing teachers to encourage them to reflect on themselves as learners of mathematics and to reassess their beliefs and role as classroom teachers. The process of constructing the portfolio challenged teachers to display what they did in their classroom and to explore new instructional strategies they were exposed to during the course. Teachers collected various kinds of evidence reflective of what they taught in their classrooms.

The mathematics teaching portfolio consisted of the following items and includes examples of reflective statements by the students on the course:

- Lesson Plans: consisting of detailed descriptions of lesson plans, types of tasks recommended to implement the plan, assessment strategies, and accompanied by evidence of learners' work and reflective statements.

  > I need to build in a routine for at least one problem solving activity before each lesson I need to streamline my lesson plan and minimise content in a learning outcome. I need to make time after normal teaching time to help weaker learners...

- Analyses of own teaching: these insertions included observations the teacher made of his or her own teaching and the learning that took place over a period of time, and problems the teacher identified within the classroom and how these problems were addressed. This was an opportunity for the teacher to not only gain knowledge about their actions but also, to base actions on teacher's own classroom reflections.

  > During the course of my teaching I discovered that the learners have a serious problem as far as multiplication is concerned. I had to go back and teach multiplication again. I applied a new teaching strategy – a mathematical game. The one game I used was a dice game for find the product...

- Teachers' reflections on professional contact sessions at the university: the teachers had an opportunity to document their own professional growth. Their reflections also informed me how the course impacted on their teaching. Some of the difficulties some teachers experienced during their own learning at the university came to light.

  > In a short time he (lecturer) made a huge difference in my understanding of financial issues. The budget session was very useful because I am the treasurer at school with no formal accountancy education. I will use this knowledge that I have gained to teach and educate the finance committee at school...

- Reflection on learners' work: an opportunity was created here for teachers to learn about the understanding or misunderstanding of individuals in the classroom. It was an opportunity for the teacher to identify the needs of the learners and to plan his or her teaching accordingly. Strengths and weaknesses of certain learners could be identified and built on. The teacher could also determine what strategies worked or did not work. An account of what did not work well:

  > When the learners were working in groups, all the learners were not always actively involved. Also my instructions were not clear and learners did not understand what was expected of them. Too many objects were measured and learners lost concentration...

- Peer reflective report: A portfolio conference served as a checkpoint of the progress of the construction process. Furthermore, I sought to instil in the teachers an understanding that teaching portfolios are part of a process to become better teachers. Teachers who have often worked in isolation experienced an opportunity to discuss ideas with, and learn from, others engaged in the same process of documenting their instruction.

> I discovered a lot of things on which I can improve in my portfolio. During the conferencing session I gained a greater understanding of my partner's portfolio… 'Dabs' as we call her really inspired and lifted my spirits with her comments during the portfolio conference session.

- Reflections on learners' reflections: here teachers could learn a great deal about both their students and their teaching by reading what students said about their learning. A teacher wrote:

> Reading their reflections had me thinking about what I am doing, how I am teaching and whether I am allowing them to have meaningful experiences in their learning. I don't feel like a bad educator but I do realise I can't take for granted that because I feel good about what I am doing, the learners will also feel good about what they are learning. The learners' reflections helped me to keep my teaching and teaching strategies in perspective.

4 Disadvantages or Concerns in Constructing Teaching Portfolios

The time required for completion of the portfolio is often cited as a concern. Teachers do stress over the increased responsibility within an already heavy workload. This is especially the case for practicing teachers who have so many responsibilities. The fact that the key focus is on reflection they do not always find time to frequently write their classroom observations.

My own experience in working with teachers has shown that it takes a while for teachers to fully comprehend the requirements for such a task. Teachers are often confused regarding the purpose of the development of the portfolio as well as lack of clarity regarding required content. Working with teachers for whom English is a second language often finds it difficult to express themselves in English.

It also takes time for teachers to develop critical reflective skills. Teachers often confuse reflection with reporting. Rather than critically reflect on a lesson, teachers are more inclined to give a step-by-step report on what they did when they taught a specific mathematical concept. Ellsworth (2002) warns teacher educators not to assume that teachers know how to engage in productive reflection rather teach specific strategies for reflection to both preservice and inservice teachers. In my own mathematics education course I normally start with a structured reflective journal for the individual teacher. The journal includes reflective questions that guide teachers' thinking about their own professional growth during teaching contact sessions at the institution.

Reflecting on the learning that takes place in the classroom, the inservice teachers are able to identify what the problem, misconception or weakness is in the learning of mathematics, however, they often fail to clearly show what action to take to address the needs of the learners. Having checkpoints throughout the time of the portfolio construction process gives opportunity to highlight any issues that will be of value to the teachers.

It was also commented that without clear criteria for the construction and evaluation process it could negatively impact on teachers to meet the expectations set out in the portfolio task. Portfolios should not be seen as the ideal assessment tool for all teachers because some would perform better than others. It is important though that various assessment tools are used in conjunction with the portfolio.

5 Conclusion

In this chapter I have considered the teaching portfolio as a tool for teachers to reflect on their practice in terms of what they can do to improve teaching and learning of mathematics. In particular, I offer ways to address the portfolio task with a view to how it can be an effective task for mathematics educators to use with both initial training students and practicing teachers of mathematics in primary schools.

Within the broader field of education, the trend towards 'reflective practitioner' demands that teacher educators provide structures that support their students to explore their own as well as their learners' thinking about mathematics. By building shared understanding about ways to think about one's practice, both teacher educators and their students can collaboratively explore and investigate ways to co-reflect on opportunities to critically analyse and document teaching in everyday situations.

References

Anderson, R. S., & DeMeulle, L. (1998). Portfolio use in twenty-four teacher education programs. *Teacher Education Quarterly, 25*(1), 25–32.

Barton, J., & Collins, A. (1993). Portfolios in teacher education. *Journal of Teacher Education, 44*(3), 200–210.

Clarke, D., & Hollingsworth, H. (2002). Elaborating a model of teacher professional growth. *Teaching and Teacher Education, 18*(8), 947–967.

Cobb, P., Wood, T., Yackel, E., Wheatly, G., Merkel, G., McNeal, E., & Preston, M. (1989). *Problem-centered mathematics curriculum: Second grade*. West Lafayette, IN: School Mathematics and Science Center, Purdue University.

Dana, T., & Tippins, D. (1998). Portfolios, reflection an educating prospective for teachers of science. In B. J. Fraser & K. G. Tobin (Eds.), *International handbook of science education* (pp. 719–733). Dordrecht: Kluwer Academic Publishers.

De Rijdt, C., Tiquet, E., Dochy, F., & Devolder, M. (2006). Teaching portfolios in higher education and their effects: An explorative study. *Teaching and Teacher Education, 22*(8), 1084–1093.

Dewey, J. (1933). *How we think: A restatement of the relation of reflective thinking to the educative process*. Boston: DC Heath.

Ellsworth, J. Z. (2002). Using student portfolios to increase reflective practice among elementary teachers. *Journal of Teacher Education, 53*(4), 342–355.

Fernsten, L., & Fernsten, J. (2005). Portfolio assessment and reflection: Enhancing learning through effective practice. *Reflective Practice, 6*(2), 303–309.

Foote, C. J., & Vermette, P. J. (2001). Teaching portfolio 101: Implementing the teaching portfolio in introductory courses. *Journal of Instructional Psychology, 28*(1), 31–37.

Freese, A. R. (1999). The role of reflection on preservice teachers' development in the context of a professional development school. *Teaching and Teacher Education, 15*(1), 895–909.

Gilbert, J. (1994). The construction and reconstruction of the concept of reflective practitioner in the discourses of teacher professional development. *International Journal of Science Education, 16*(5), 511–522.

Goldsmith, L. T., & Shifter, D. (1997). Understanding teachers in transition: Characteristics of a model for the development of mathematics teaching. In E. Fennema & B. Scott Nelson (Eds.), *Mathematics teachers in transition*. Mahwah, NJ: Erlbaum.

Green, J., & Smyser, S. (1996). *The teacher portfolio: A strategy for professional development and evaluation*. Lancaster, PA: Technomic.

Hart, L. C. (2002). Preservice teachers' beliefs and practice after participating in an integrated content/methods course. *School Science and Mathematics, 102*(1), 4–14.

Hatton, N., & Smith, D. (1995). Reflection in teacher education: Towards definition and implementation. *Teaching and Teacher Education, 11*(1), 33–49.

Hoffman, K. (1989). *The science of patterns: A practical philosophy of mathematics education*. Paper presented at the annual meeting of the AERA Special Interest Group: Research in Mathematics Education, San Francisco, CA.

Jay, J. K., & Johnson, K. L. (2002). Capturing the complexity: A typology of reflective practice for teacher education. *Teaching and Teacher Education, 18*, 73–85.

Kelchtermans, G. (1993). Getting the story, understanding the lives: From career stories to teachers' professional development. *Teaching and Teacher Education, 9*(5/6), 443–456.

Knight, P. (2002). A systematic approach to professional development: Learning as practice. *Teaching and Teacher Education, 18*(3), 229–241.

Loughran, J., & Corrigan, D. (1995). Teaching portfolios: A strategy for developing learning and teaching in preservice education. *Teaching and Teacher Education, 11*(6), 565–577.

Noddings, N. (1990). Constructivism in mathematics education. In R. B. Maher & N. Noddings (Eds.), *Constructivist views on the teaching and learning of mathematics* (pp. 7–18). Reston, VA: NCTM.

Richert, A. E. (1997). Teaching teachers for the challenge of change. In J. Loughran & T. Russell (Eds.), *Teaching about teaching*. London: Falmer Press.

Schon, D. A. (1983). *The reflective practitioner: How professionals think in action*. New York: Basic Books.

Silver, E. A. (1996). Moving beyond learning alone and in silence: Observations from the QUASAR project concerning some challenges and possibilities of communication in mathematics classrooms. In L. Schauble & R. Glaser (Eds.), *Innovations in learning: New environments for education*. Mahwah, NJ: Erlbaum.

Simon, M. (1995). Reconstructing mathematics pedagogy from a constructivist perspective. *Journal of Research in Mathematics Education, 26*(2), 114–145.

Shulman, L. S. (1988). A union of insufficiencies: Strategies for teacher assessment in a period of education reform. *Educational Leadership, 46*, 36–41.

Smith, M. S. (2001). *Practice-based professional development for teachers of mathematics*. Virginia: NCTM.

Smith, K., & Tillema, H. (2001). Long-term influences of portfolios on professional development. *Scandinavian Journal of Educational Research, 45*, 183–203.

Tann, S. (1993). Eliciting student teachers' personal theories. In J. Calderhead & P. Gates (Eds.), *Conceptualizing reflection in teacher development*. London: Falmer Press.

Tillema, H. H. (1998). Design and validity of portfolio instrument for professional training. *Studies in Educational Evaluation, 24*(3), 263–278.

Vygotsky, L. S. (1978). *Mind in society*. Cambridge, Massachusetts: Harvard University Press.

Wolf, K. (1994). Teaching portfolios: Capturing the complexity of teaching. In L. Ingvarson & R. Chadbourne (Eds.), *Valuing teachers work: New directions in teacher appraisal.* Victoria: The Australian Council for Educational Research.

Wolf, K. (1996). Developing an effective teaching portfolio. *Educational Leadership, 53*(6), 34–37.

Wolf, K., & Dietz, M. (1998). Teaching portfolios: Purposes and possibilities. *Teacher Education Quarterly, 25*(1), 9–22.

Zeichner, K., & Wray, S. (2001). The teaching portfolio in US teacher education program: what we know and what we need to know. *Teaching and Teacher Education, 17,* 613–621.

Section B
Tasks as a Tool for Developing Mathematical Knowledge for Teaching

Richard Millman

This section describes tasks whose goal is to enrich the mathematical knowledge for teaching (MKT) of future and practising teachers and to help them realize that they must have a deeper conceptual understanding of the mathematics of the primary grades. MKT runs through all of the chapters of this section. The underlying threads of Sect. B are that tasks can be chosen to add to a conceptual understanding of mathematics through the use of a number of approaches which are usually not a part of a teacher education program. Thus the chapters involve enriching the classroom through video clips (Gadanidis/Namukasa and Millman/Svec/Williams), using games that show that intuition is an important part of learning mathematical content, for example, the notion of variability in statistics (Canada), viewing children's literature (such as *Alice in Wonderland*) as a way to provide content focus for future primary teachers and the study of mathematical logic (Movshovitz-Hadar/Shriki), modelling real-world tasks for fourth graders (Peter-Koop) through the use of Fermi problems, and "math therapy" in which poetry is used (Gadanidis/Namukasa). Furthermore, four of the chapters have suitably adopted some tasks for children and practising teachers (Canada, Gadanidis/Namukasa, Millman/Svec/Williams and Peter-Koop) which add a special depth to these tasks.

The chapter by Canada approaches the role of variability through the use of three tasks. These tasks provide a foundation for an intuitive basis of concepts in probability and statistics. Here the emphasis is on variability as a way of seeing that phenomena differ rather than looking more formally towards variability in terms of the definition of standard deviation. Through the use of the River Crossing Game, the author gives a task by which future teachers and primary school students (grades 6 and 7) will add to their intuition about what kind of variation one might expect. Through the "Known Mixture" task, the students are led to see the difference be-

R. Millman
Director, Center for Education Integrating Science, Professor of the Practice of Mathematics, Mathematics and Computing, Georgia Institute of Technology, USA

B. Clarke, B. Grevholm, and R. Millman (eds.), *Tasks in Primary Mathematics Teacher Education: Purpose, Use and Exemplars,* Mathematics Teacher Education 4,

tween an event having probability (of being yellow) of .7 and every sample of 10 objects having exactly 7 yellow chips. The combination of the "Known mixture" and "Unknown mixture" tasks demonstrate the differences between the concepts of probability, prediction, variability, and measures of central tendency.

The chapter by Movshovitz-Hadar and Shriki deals with the use of the famous *Alice's Adventures in Wonderland* by Lewis Carroll as a vehicle for a logic course which follows another one semester content course. The authors of this chapter provide a theoretical foundation for their approach to the difficulties of understanding logical inferences which are encountered by students and future teachers. Their intervention strategy is a series of lessons plans for potential discussions of logic which start with quotes from *Alice's Adventures*. They categorize these quotes as logic, mathematics, general issues, or science and prepare tasks for the future teachers. Their analysis of their students' response to the intervention is contained in their conclusion. The appendices contain a number of such tasks which would be valuable to those who wish to follow their strategy.

The chapter by Millman, Svec and Williams gives a set of tasks for future primary school teachers by using a collection of video clips to show them why they must have a conceptual understanding of the mathematics of primary school in order to strengthen their knowledge and provide a deep learning experience for their students. In addition, there is a video clip task that has, as a goal, the increase in the confidence of the future teachers to learn some new mathematics by working in small groups and presenting to their peers. The authors describe two video clips from the collection, one of a second grader doing two-digit subtraction in three ways (two of them correct and conceptual and the other procedural and incorrect) and one of a fourth grader who divides fractions without the use of paper or pencil. In the third task, the relationship between perimeter and area of a rectangle was explored in a student presentation which used a video clip of a child. The use of presentations by future teachers resulted in an increase in the level of their mathematical confidence. The authors conclude that the use of video clips of children doing mathematics can show the need for MKT, the recognition that children will invent their own ways of solving mathematical problems, the necessity for a conceptual understanding, and the benefit of an overlap of "content" and "methods" courses in the preparation of future teachers.

The chapter by Gadanidis and Namukasa presents two geometric and two algebraic tasks which involve significant mathematical problems. These tasks, which are given to both present and future primary school teachers, focus on offering them opportunities to experience the joy of mathematical insight in order to change their view of what mathematicians do and how students learn mathematics (called "math therapy.") The approach of the authors includes employing a number of applets including a music video of poetry. The data collection of their project consists of participant reflections, online discussions, and mathematics essays, all of which are analyzed using qualitative methods. They present results of the math therapy approach which deal with issues of frustration, attention, collaboration, and the complexity of mathematics, attitudes, beliefs and practice.

The chapter by Peter-Koop deals with Fermi problems. These tasks deal with real-world problem solving which demand the construction of a mathematical model, a procedure to find the unknown quantity, and a transfer of the mathematical result to the real-world situation. The greatest difficulty in solving the Fermi tasks is the modelling. The results of this chapter come from a 4-year study involving future teachers and within the context of teaching experiments in grades 3 and 4 in Germany. The author gives a theoretical framework around modelling processes. She then describes her results that there is a multicyclic process represented in the work of the children, that even problems with a high level of complexity can be solved appropriately by the children, and that the modelling activity serves as a conceptual tool.

Based on the literature surrounding the concept of volume, the chapter by Sáiz and Figueras deals with tasks in a workshop for present teachers. One of the tasks, using cylinders or silos, explores whether two figures which have the same surface area needed to have the same volume. A second one shows that changing the linear dimensions of an object does not have a linear effect on its volume. This concept is sometimes called the "similarity principle" or "homothecy." The last task deals with the equivalencies between units of capacity and units of volume. These rich tasks give depth to the knowledge of the inservice teachers in their workshop. The authors believe that their approach also is applicable to future teachers.

The chapter by Teppo uses task-based lessons as the organizing principle for a mathematics content course for future primary teachers. Teppo points out that a course constructed in this manner must pay careful attention to the selection and sequencing of the tasks and the research base that supports these decisions. The purpose of each of the tasks is to add to the scaffolding of the MKT of the future teacher, be grounded in a real-world basis, include an interpretation of the question, and be both open-entry and open-process. This approach is motivated in part by Japanese-style lesson study. A set of six word problems about proportion illustrate the author's approach.

Pushing Probability and Statistics Tasks in a New Direction

Dan Canada

Along with the increased emphasis on probability and statistics in the school curricula of countries across the world has come increased research on how primary and secondary students reason about these topics. Slower to emerge has been research aimed at what preservice teachers know about probability and statistics, and how best to develop their conceptions of key aspects of these content strands. Specifically, while attention is often paid to notions of randomness, graph sense, and the meaning of an average, less attention is paid to developing the critical notion of variation, or variability in data and chance. Therefore, the activities and tasks profiled in this chapter, while embracing several contexts in the realm of probability and statistics, are based on recommendations from emerging research suggesting that a focus be put on variability.

1 Introduction

This chapter highlights three tasks that recent research along with in-class experience suggests are useful for promoting an increased awareness and understanding of the role of variability in probability and statistics among primary schoolchildren and their prospective teachers.

Certainly there has been increased curricular emphasis on probability and statistics around the world, as examples from Spain, Great Britain, Australia, New Zealand, America, and other countries attest (Batanero, Godino, Valecillos, Green & Holmes, 1994; Shaughnessy, Garfield, & Greer, 1996; Watson & Moritz, 2000). Within those curricular strands, research and practice has begun to focus on student thinking in several areas, such as notions of randomness, graph sense, or the meaning of an average value. However, variability – beginning with intuitive notions of

D. Canada
Associate Professor, Department of Mathematics, Eastern Washington University Eastern Washington University, USA

B. Clarke, B. Grevholm, and R. Millman (eds.), *Tasks in Primary Mathematics Teacher Education: Purpose, Use and Exemplars,* Mathematics Teacher Education 4,

how results or observations differ from one another – has emerged as a foundational concept to reasoning about both probability and statistics (Cobb & Moore, 1997; Wild & Pfannkuch, 1999; Shaughnessy, Ciancetta, & Canada, 2004).

Variability, as suggested above, is not being used here as a reference for standard deviation or other more formal definitions, but rather as a reference for the fundamental way that phenomenon differs. For example, the amount of change in your pocket may differ from day-to-day, as might the time you take brushing your teeth each night. The number of heads you might get in ten flips of a fair coin will likely vary from one set of ten flips to another. If twenty different students with meter sticks take turns measuring the same distance (of the length of a hallway, for instance), those twenty measurements will unlikely be identical – they'll vary to some extent. The number of red lights you encounter on your drive to school varies. We live in a world filled with variation, yet much of the standard curriculum at the primary grades focuses more on simply finding probabilities, graphing data, or finding descriptive measures such as a mean, median, or mode (Shaughnessy, 1997). What has been needed yet typically is lacking in the curricula, many educators have noted, is more attention to the role of variability in reasoning about probability and statistics.

The tasks and extensions that follow are composed of in-class activities, discussion prompts, and written questions, and are all based on traditional types of manipulatives (such as tossing dice, drawing samples of chips from a bag, or using spinners). These tasks push in a new direction by focusing on the variability inherent in the situation and the implications for making probabilistic statements about predicted outcomes. Students' response exemplars are drawn from experience in doing these tasks and extensions in classrooms for grades 6 and 7, as well in university teacher-preparation classes. Since many of the preservice teacher responses were quite similar in spirit to those of school children, both groups of participants are referred to as "students" in this chapter unless additional distinctions are warranted.

2 The River Crossing Game

Using tosses of two dice is a common way of discussing independent events, and many curricular materials focus on the distribution of the sum of two dice with questions such as "What are the chances that the sum is a 7?" However, the *River Crossing Game* (discussed below) offers a deeper and richer context for looking at the sum of two dice, again with a focus on variability.

Credit for this activity goes to the *Math and the Mind's Eye* curriculum (Shaughnessy & Arcidiacono, 1993). Using two players, each player gets 12 chips to place on their side of a "river," along spaces marked 1 through 12 (Fig. 1). After configuring their chips into their initial arrangements such as those shown in Fig. 1, players took turns tossing a pair of dice. If either player had any chips on the space showing the total for the dice, one chip could "cross the river" and be removed from the board. The winning player was the first one to remove all the chips on his or her side.

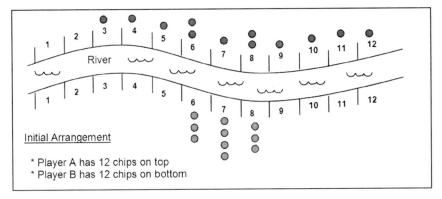

Fig. 1 Initial strategies for River Crossing Game

Fig. 2 Cumulative frequency chart (Dotplot) for sums of dice

For instance, in Fig. 1, if the dice resulted in a sum of 10, Player A on top could remove one chip. If the dice showed 8, Players A and B could each remove one chip. The question motivating the game is: What's the best initial arrangement for the 12 chips? Experience suggests that it is unlikely two players come up with the same arrangement (which would imply a tie game), but if that does occur then one opponent or the other may choose to make a change in their arrangement, in light of what arrangement their opponent is choosing to play. Teams of students can then play several games, keeping track of the results of each toss of the dice for all games on a dotplot: Sums are given along the horizontal axis, and students can just make a mark showing the sum obtained from every toss (Fig. 2). The purpose of the Dotplot for Sums is to obtain cumulative results for the sums of two dice resulting from experimental data. They can also keep track of which two initial arrangements are played in each game, and which arrangements beat other arrangements.

In our experience, students' initial arrangements changed from game to game. For example, if students saw from their dotplots that sums of 6, 7 and 8 tended to occur more than other sums, some students chose to put most of their chips on those spaces. Other students continued to spread out their chips, feeling that in the course of tossing the dice, they would get sums such as 2 or 12 (they quickly realize that the sum of 1 is impossible). After letting students play a few games, we collected all the papers that recorded what two initial arrangements were used in each game (and which arrangements won), and also all the cumulative dotplots for showing sums for all the rolls of the dice for all games.

We first put up in front of the class the sheets showing examples of the different initial arrangements used and which were winners, and launched a discussion about what they as a class thought was the best strategy as far as initial arrangements. Comments ranged from those who favored putting all their chips "closer together around the 7," suggesting tighter variation, to those who wanted "kind of an even amount" on each sum, suggesting wider variation. Our experience shows that some people in class eventually steer the conversation to the topic of what is most likely to occur for the sum of two dice, at which point we also put up in front of class all of the cumulative dotplots.

It's typical for each dotplot to show well over one hundred tosses of the dice, since the dotplots were meant to record tosses of the dice for all games (and some games can take quite a large number of tosses to finish). As students look across all the dotplots, it's useful to focus attention on the variability in areas such as the shape of the graph, how many rolls were at the lowest sum of 2 or the highest sum of 12, or seeing which sum had the highest frequency of rolls. Even if students know what the theoretical distribution looks like (which is symmetrical around 7, as shown in Fig. 3), the dotplots are unlikely to mirror such a perfect distribution.

As an example of one class discussion, as students were discussing the dotplots they noted quickly that some graphs had the mode at 7 but most did not. Even for the students who knew that 7 was the most likely sum, there was a distinction between that knowledge of the theoretical probability and the varied results of the experimental data gathered by the class. It did seem to the class that sums of 6 or 7 or 8 were more likely than any of the other sums, but they agreed that in one hundred tosses of the dice even the mode could vary. Other students noticed how the shapes of the graphs were different in the sense that they "went up and down" in different places (more fives followed by less sixes, for examples), but there were some similarities in the sense that most graphs showed less results on the extremes of 2 and 12 than elsewhere. As one student put it, "there are trends, but there's still a lot of variation from group to group."

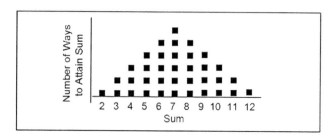

Fig. 3 Theoretical distribution for sum of two dice

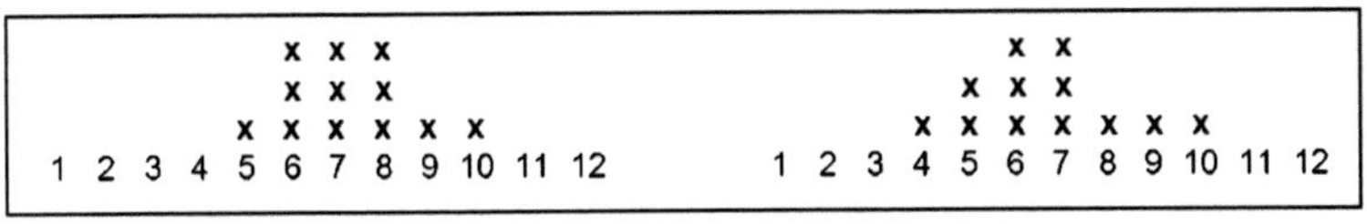

```
            x  x  x                           x  x
            x  x  x                        x  x  x
            x  x  x  x  x                 x  x  x  x  x  x
   1  2  3  4  5  6  7  8  9  10 11 12     1  2  3  4  5  6  7  8  9  10 11 12
```

Fig. 4 Experienced strategies for River Crossing Game

After discussing what was considered most likely to occur as a sum for tossing two dice, we returned to the question of what might be an optimum initial arrangement for playing the River Crossing Game. An example of two strategies, informed by having now had experience playing and by looking at the theoretical distribution, are given in Fig. 4. A question might arise as to why people don't just put all their chips on 7, since that sum is most likely to occur in a single toss of two dice. Such a question is a good opportunity to bring out the connection that putting all the chips of 7 is making a statement of expectation of no variation. Yet in reality, even though a sum of 7 has the highest probability of all other sums for a single toss of two dice, variation is unavoidable.

The real question in the *River Crossing Game*, therefore, is: What kind of variation is reasonable to expect? If putting all the chips on the 7 is anticipating too little variation, then so too would spreading the chips out evenly from 2 to 12 also be anticipating too much variation. Negotiating that middle ground, between too little and too much variation, is a key part of this activity. Ultimately, between looking at the dotplots showing cumulative sums of the dice and also the various strategies for initial arrangements, the *River Crossing Game* affords a rich context to focus attention on variation versus expectation.

3 Known and Unknown Mixtures

Another common activity is to have students draw objects like colored chips from a bag. If we know what chips are in the bag ahead of time, these types of activities mimic other random devices like drawing cards from a deck or throwing dice or using spinners. For example, having a total of ten chips (two blue and eight red), we can ask the probability of reaching in the bag and drawing out a blue chip. The activity described next extends these ideas to arrive at a wonderful context for discussing multiple ideas in probability and statistics with a focus on variability.

With *Known Mixture*, have students work in teams of two of three. Give each team a bag containing 70 yellow chips and 30 green chips. Tell them ahead of time what is in the bag, and make it clear they are focusing on the number of yellows in a handful of ten chips drawn at random from the bag. In fact, a trial will be defined as taking thirty handfuls (with replacement), each of size ten, and writing down the number of yellows in each handful. Have students make predictions about how many yellows they'll get in each of their thirty handfuls, and put these predictions on a poster. An example from a team in one class is shown in Fig. 5.

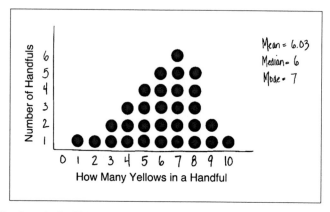

Fig. 5 Predicted results for 30 handfuls

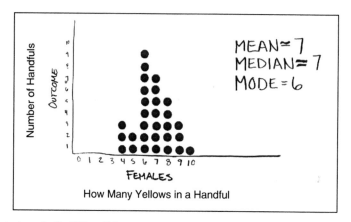

Fig. 6 Actual results for 30 handfuls

In discussing similarities and differences in the predictions, it is common for teams to put the highest numbers of yellows between 6 and 8, with a mode for the posters often being at 7 (which corresponds to the proportion $7/10 = 70/100$). Also, many posters may have some results at 10 yellows, and some may have predicted results all the way down at 0 yellows. It is interesting that even though "7 Yellows" may seem like the most likely result for a handful of ten chips drawn from such a *Known Mixture*, students often intuitively realize they will be getting results other than 7 even before actually doing the experiment.

After discussing the predictions, have the teams draw the thirty handfuls (with replacement), recording the results as they proceed. The results can again be put on posters and put up in front of class. We found it useful to have a row of the "Predicted Results" posters with another row of "Actual Results" immediately below the predictions (keeping each teams' predictions aligned with their actual results). The actual results for the team from Fig. 5 are now shown in Fig. 6.

Once all of the "Actual Results" posters are up in front of the class, next to their respective "Predicted Results" posters for each team, one good starting point for discussion is simply to ask students what they notice, or what seems surprising. In our experiences with this activity, students tend to notice how all of the "Predicted Results" posters seem more alike to each other than to the "Actual Results" posters. For instance, in one class, most of the predictions had a mode at 7, while most the actual results had modes somewhere other than 7. Also, the range for the predicted results was typically wider than for actual results. In particular, students often predicted results at the lower extremes (from 0 to 2) which did not occur in actual results. Ultimately, there was a consensus in class that the actual results were more varied than anticipated.

Having a sense of what kind of variation arises from samples drawn from a known mixture, students are then well-positioned to consider the case of the *Unknown Mixture*. When we did this part of the activity, we gave to each group of students an identical jar containing the same mix of yellow and green chips. The mix was not announced to the students (it was actually 550 yellows and 450 greens, although the activity will still work wonderfully with fewer total chips). In their groups, the students first had to decide what sample size they wanted to use (we imposed an upper limit of size twenty for all groups) and how many samples they wanted to draw. Then they had to carry out their plans, do the sampling, graph the results, and make some conjecture about the true mixture in the jar.

As an example of one group's results and reasoning, the group who made the poster shown in Fig. 7 used samples of size ten, and they drew 40 samples. However, they obtained their "guesstimate" of 57% by looking to their mean of 5.47 yellow and also their mode and median of 6 yellow, and finding a value that they felt was somewhat close to both 5.47 and 6, namely, 5.7. Then they used the ratio of sample size to population and determined that 570 yellow chips out of 1,000 total chips would correspond to 57%.

They added the informal "margin of error" because they knew that plus-or-minus three percentage points would cover their mean, median, and mode. Other groups

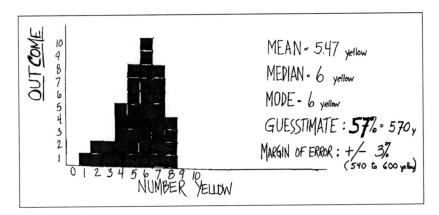

Fig. 7 Poster for the unknown mixture

selected sample sizes that went as low as 6 and as high as 200, and after discussing the different estimates we decided to try for a class consensus. This is a good time to informally introduce the idea of confidence by relating the idea to what was shown in the posters. For example, the group for the poster in Fig. 7 was not confident of the point estimate of exactly 570 yellow, but was fairly confident that the true value was somewhere in the interval from 540 to 600 yellow.

Comparisons across all the posters showed that the sample sizes for ranged from 6 to 20, and the numbers of trials ranged from 20 to 70. Predictions ranged from 500 to 600 yellows, with a couple of groups offering an interval. In discussion, we asked the class as a whole what would or would not be surprising to them, and the class expressed no surprise if the true value was 520 yellow, or 580 yellow. The class eventually came to a consensus on an interval as small as 540 yellow to 570 yellow. The big idea here was that an unknown mixture (or any other realistic sampling situation) does not mean that nothing can be said with any confidence about the mixture. For example, the class was overwhelmingly confident that there were more yellows than greens, but not as high a ratio as 650 to 350. Despite attempts to have the students accept that in real life sampling investigations, having some degree of confidence in an interval is the best that can be hoped for or expected, students still wanted to know the exact percentage, which was revealed at the end.

4 Cereal Box Stickers

This final activity involves the use of a Five-spinner (one that has five numbered regions of equal area) to simulate the following situation: Suppose there are five types of stickers you want to collect, but each box of cereal only contains one sticker. Assuming there is an equal chance of getting any given type of sticker in a box of cereal, how many boxes would you expect to have to open to collect all five types of sticker? What would be a typical number of boxes a person might expect to open? Making a few other appropriate assumptions, this situation can be investigated by finding out how many times a student would have to spin the Five-spinner in order to have the pointer land on all the numbers (Shaughnessy & Arcidiacono, 1993).

When we do this with our classes, again the first thing we do is have students make intuitive predictions. Some students realize that the shortest number of spins would be five, and they'll comment that such a result would be "very lucky." But there are also usually some extremely high estimates also (up into the thousands), because some students stress that "you just never know" or that you could be very unlucky, waiting for that last number to occur. The important thing is to focus on the variation in the initial predictions, along with the notion that in the absence of any data, most people really have no idea about how many spins would be typical to expect in to order to achieve all five numbers on a Five-spinner.

To then begin the activity of gathering some data, define a *trial* as follows: Using the Five-spinner, make a spin and keep track of what number the pointer lands on. Keep making spins until all five numbers have been landed upon, then stop and

			x															
			x															
	x		x		x													
	x		x		x		x				x							
x	x		x	x	x		x				x		x			x	x	
05	06	07	08	09	10	11	12	13	14	15	16	17	18	19	20	21	22	23

Fig. 8 Dotplot showing how many spins for each of 20 trials

count how many spins you did. The idea is to record on a dotplot how many spins each trial takes. We usually start by having each pair of students complete 20 trials, and then have them post their dotplot up in front of the class. Results such as those illustrated in Fig. 8 are typical.

As Fig. 8 shows, results for twenty trials typically are quite spread out, and gaining a sense of "What's Typical" from such a graph is not at all obvious. Once there are plenty of dotplots for twenty trials up in front of class, a discussion similar to those for the previous activities can take place, which again would focus on the variation shown in each graph. We found that students are really quick to pick up on how diverse the results for twenty trials are, and they notice how all of the standard measures of centre – mean, median, and mode – typically jump around quite a bit from graph to graph. Whereas the mode might be 8 in one poster (as in Fig. 8), it might be 12 or 14 in another.

Despite the variation in results, however, once again we found that students were quick to speak about how "more of the marks" were "clustered" or "grouped" more toward the lower numbers (such as from 8 to 12) than in the higher number of spins. When we asked for any modification on their prediction for the number of cereal boxes they would expect to have to open (that is, how many spins would they expect to have to make to get all five numbers), none of the students thought that it should typically take above 15 spins.

As class discussion moves towards gaining a better picture of "What's Typical?" for the Cereal Box investigation, often the notion of gaining more data is mentioned by students. Groups of students can either conduct more trials, or (as we have done with our classes) the class can aggregate the data from the different dotplots. One such graph of aggregate class data, using six groups' data (for a total of 120 trials), is shown in Fig. 9.

The data shown in Fig. 9 are interesting because even though they still present a varied picture to many students (many of whom will claim the mode of 7 as "what they'd expect"), the median for the data is 10 spins and the mean is 11.2 spins. The true expected value for the Cereal Box investigation, while not a calculation that is generally taught in precollege mathematics, is close to 11.5. Thus, aggregating data in this situation still provides a mean value very close to a reasonable answer for how many boxes a person might have to open, yet also illustrates the variation that is inherent in probabilistic situations.

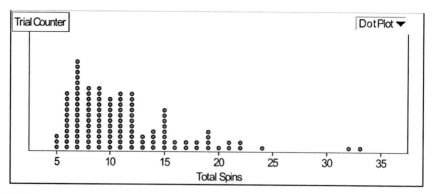

Fig. 9 Example of class aggregate data for 120 trials

In our classes, once we had obtained a graph of class aggregate data such as Fig. 9, we focused on questions that necessitated a consideration of variation. For example, we asked if students would be surprised if they obtained 15 spins or more for the outcome of a trial. Using the graph to find that about 20% of all the class data was at 15 spins or more, some students thought they'd be "not too surprised." Many in class felt that the outcome for any trial would much likelier be under 15 spins than over, but "it could happen." Even knowing that the mean for a huge number of trials is between 11 and 12 spins, our students were seen to be developing an awareness of and appreciation for the variability in results.

5 Discussion

Variability is at the heart of statistical inquiry, and it is quite appropriate to begin turning attention to intuitive notions of variation when discussing any type of probabilistic or data gathering activities. Yet, this kind of attention is often missing from the way probability and statistics is typically approached. As an example, consider the sampling ten chips from *Known Mixture* (70 yellows and 30 greens). Once students are taught the standard notion (using proportional thinking) that "The probability of drawing a yellow chip is 0.7," research shows this ratio is powerful anchor for their thinking (Canada, 2004). Thus, when students consider "How many of their ten chips will be yellow?" they will gladly say seven yellow chips. So powerful is the anchor of ratio thinking, however, that when some students consider drawing several handfuls of ten chips with replacement, they'll also give the number of yellows in each handful as "7,7,7,7…" The reasoning goes that if 7 is the most likely occurrence for one handful (a true statement), then 7 is the most likely for every handful. Thus, predicting a string of ten 7s for ten handfuls seems perfectly reasonable for those students who aren't aware of the reality that variation makes a string of ten 7s extremely unlikely (Canada, 2006; Shaughnessy et al.,, 2004).

As research has begun to show, a great model for attenuating students to variability in probabilistic situations can be distilled down the following three components: First, have students make predictions concerning the situation. Have them talk about *what* they expect and *why*. Discuss predictions made by the class in terms of what was similar or different. Second, have them actually gather data about the situation, creating a variety of visual displays. Although simple dotplots were profiled in this chapter, other types of graphs are also relevant and useful in terms of the way they emphasize or disguise variability. Third, discuss the results gathered by the class not only in terms of how the results compared from one group to another, but also how the results compared to the predictions.

Some useful extensions to the activities described in this chapter revolve around a "Real-or-Fake?" format. That is, after the activities have been done in class and discussed, show some results that supposedly arose from the activity and ask if the class thinks the results are real or fake. An example of such a "Real-or-Fake?" task for the *Known Mixture* situation is presented in Fig. 10. Having done the activity and seen many graphs for true results for thirty handfuls, it is no surprise that most students in our experience express a high degree of mistrust for the supposed results shown in Fig. 10. Having done the activity and seen many graphs for true results

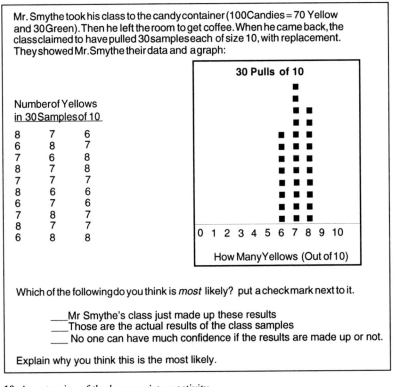

Fig. 10 An extension of the *known mixture* activity

for thirty handfuls, it is no surprise that most students in our experience express a high degree of mistrust for the supposed results shown in Fig. 10. It is in fact highly unlikely that thirty handfuls would have the tight spread shown in the graph. So, despite the contention of some students that such results "could happen," the main consensus pointed to an awareness that the variability in such a situation would likely not produce the results shown. Interestingly, not many of our students chose the third option in Fig. 10 (suggesting that one could not have much confidence in determining if the results were real or fake), and instead held strong opinions, mostly in favor of rejecting the results as unrealistic.

Similarly, a "Real-or-Fake?" task extension for the *Cereal Box* activity offers two graphs, one of which results from genuine data and one of which is contrived (see Fig. 11). Students who have actually done the activity and graphed the results of twenty or thirty trials are quick to note that the top graph (for Class A) looks "too perfect" and therefore unrealistic. In fact, the lower graph (for Class B) more accurately reflects the kind of variation students get in the graphs for their own data.

What's important to attend to in "Real-or-Fake?" type questions such as the one presented in Fig. 11 is the language that students use in their explanations, and what

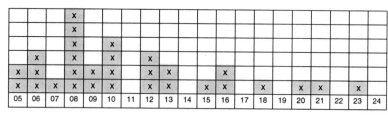

Fig. 11 An extension of the *cereal box stickers* activity

kinds of conceptions they are trying to convey. For example, students might refer to the graph for Class A as "too clustered" or "evenly grouped" to connote the idea of less variation; the graph for Class B might be described as being "more spread" or having "clumps" of data in different places to connote the idea of more variation.

6 Conclusion

Informal descriptions of variability are important building blocks to a more robust understanding of probabilistic and statistical thinking (Makar & Canada, 2005; Canada and Makar, 2006). The activities and extensions described in this chapter help move traditional contexts for probability and statistics investigations in a direction that develops elementary students' intuitive awareness of and appreciation for variability in these contexts.

The standard probability and statistics curricula in some schools places attention on doing activities, gathering and graphing data, and describing data using measures of centre such as mean, median and mode. Such attention is warranted, yet the danger is that students can develop an understanding of chance and data that is unduly tied to expected values and measures of centre without a sense of what variation to expect. Yet, any meaningful lines of statistical inquiry that students might engage in during their subsequent schooling will always be about managing, explaining, or otherwise describing and accounting for variation.

An understanding of variation for elementary students "does not mean understanding of 'standard deviation' but of something more fundamental – the underlying change from expectation that occurs when measurements are made or events occur" (Watson, Kelly, Callingham & Shaughnessy, 2003, p. 2). Torok and Watson conducted a study of conceptions of variation with sixteen students from grades 4 through 10 and found "this study successfully explored students' understanding of variation without ever employing the phrase 'standard deviation'" (2000, p. 166).

Thus, offering students opportunities to informally notice and describe the variability arising from the tasks described in this chapter will plants seeds of variation that can grow into more robust conceptions of probability and statistics in the future.

References

Batanero, C., Godino, J., Valecillos, A., Green, D., & Holmes, P. (1994). Errors and difficulties in understanding elementary statistical concepts. *International Journal of Mathematical Education in Science and Technology*, 25(4), 527–547.

Canada, D. (2004). *Elementary preservice teachers' understanding of variation*. Unpublished doctoral dissertation, Portland State University, Portland, OR. (Online: www.stat.auckland.ac.nz/~iase/publications/dissertations/dissertations.php)

Canada, D. (2006). *Variability in a probability context: Developing preservice teachers' under-standing*. In Proceedings of the 30th Conference of the International Group for the Psychology of Mathematics Education, Prague, Czechoslovakia.

Canada, D., & Makar, K. (2006). *Preservice teachers' informal descriptions of variation*. Paper delivered at the 2006 annual meeting of the American Education Research Association, San Francisco, CA.

Cobb, G., & Moore, D. (1997). Mathematics, statistics, and teaching. *American Mathematics Monthly, 104*(9), 801–824.

Makar, K., & Canada, D. (2005). *Preservice teachers' conceptions of variation*. In Proceedings of the 29th Conference of the International Group for the Psychology of Mathematics Education, Melbourne, Australia.

Shaughnessy, J. (1997). Missed opportunities in research on the teaching and learning of data and chance. In F. Bidduch & K. Carr (Eds.), *Proceedings of the 20th Annual Conference of the Mathematics Education Research Group of Australasia* (pp. 6–22). Rotorua, NZ: MERGA.

Shaughnessy, M., & Arcidiacono, M. (1993). *Visual encounters with chance (Unit VIII, Math and the Mind's Eye)*. Salem, OR: The Math Learning Centre.

Shaughnessy, J. M., Ciancetta, M., & Canada, D. (2004). *Types of student reasoning on sampling tasks*. In Proceedings of the 28th Conference of the International Group for the Psychology of Mathematics Education, Bergen, Norway.

Shaughnessy, J., Garfield, J., & Greer, B. (1996). Data handling. In A. Bishop, K. Clements, C. Keitel, J. Kilpatrick, & C. Laborde (Eds.), *International handbook of mathematics education (Part 1)* (pp. 205–237). Dordrecht, The Netherlands: Kluwer.

Torok, R., & Watson, J. (2000). Development of the concept of statistical variation: An exploratory study. *Mathematical Education Research Journal, 12*(2), 147–169.

Watson, J., Kelly, B., Callingham, R., & Shaughnessy, J. (2003). The measurement of school students' understanding of statistical variation. *The International Journal of Mathematical Education in Science and Technology, 34*(1), 1–29.

Watson, J., & Moritz, J. (2000). Developing concepts of sampling.*Journal for Research in Mathematics Education, 31*(1), 44–70.

Wild, C., & Pfannkuch, M. (1999). Statistical thinking in empirical enquiry. *International Statistical Review, 67*, 233–265.

Logic in Wonderland: *Alice's Adventures in Wonderland* as the Context of a Course in Logic for Future Elementary Teachers

Nitsa Movshovitz-Hadar and Atara Shriki

The teaching experiment described in this chapter assumes at the outset that children's literature can be a useful context for teaching elementary ideas of logic while bridging the gap between the abstractness of formal logic and its expression in a real world context. Alice's Adventures in Wonderland, by Lewis Carroll (a unique combination of a logician and a story teller) was chosen for this purpose, based upon a careful examination of its potential. Inspired by The Annotated Alice (Carroll 2000), over 75 additional annotations to Carroll's book were developed, having in mind their employment in an introductory course in logic for prospective elementary school teachers specializing in mathematics. These annotations are in four categories: Logic, Mathematics, General education, and Science. Sample annotations are included. This chapter describes the tasks and activities developed for the course. Data collection instruments were interwoven in the teaching materials development. A sample is included as well. Several results are reported and discussed.

1 The Problem

The importance of connectivity and of making mathematics relevant to the learner as vehicles for improving learner's understanding and motivation to delve into more depth in mathematics, are emphasized in many major documents (e.g. NCTM 2000). If this is true of any area in mathematics, it must be true for formal logic, which, from our experience with prospective teachers, is among the least favorite topics in teachers colleges. This topic is perceived as not useful, dry, uninteresting, and definitely not directly applicable to the school curricula. Nevertheless, an introductory one-semester course in logic follows an elementary course in set theory, and both

N. Movshovitz-Hadar
Emeritus Professor of Mathematics Education, Technion – Israel Institute of Technology, Israel

A. Shriki
Oranim – Academic College of Education, Israel

B. Clarke, B. Grevholm, and R. Millman (eds.), *Tasks in Primary Mathematics Teacher Education: Purpose, Use and Exemplars,* Mathematics Teacher Education 4,
© Springer Science+Business Media LLC 2009

are mandatory for accreditation, in Israel. It should be noted that in various other countries an elementary course in formal logic is not compulsory at college level, yet many of them engage students with topics that are related to logic, such as quantifiers, producing proofs and inferring from statements (Dubinsky & Yiparaki, 2000; Selden & Selden, 1995; Moore, 1994).

How can the teaching of logic for prospective teachers be made more "juicy"? Is there an intriguing way to expose students to "the game" of drawing conclusions? – These were the questions we struggled with as we started preparing for the new academic year. It occurred to us that it might be useful to employ Lewis Carroll's masterpiece for this purpose. Would students benefit from it? Enjoy it? That remained to be seen. To find out, we set up an empirical intervention study that is described in this chapter.

2 A Brief Theoretical Background

2.1 Difficulties of Students in Reasoning and Inferring Logically

Promoting children's reasoning abilities has been widely recognized as one of the pillars of mathematics education, for many years (e.g. Gregory & Osborne, 1975). Clearly, teachers cannot be expected to promote their students' reasoning properly, unless they themselves understand logical implications and are able to employ them reliably. Teachers colleges requiring an introductory course in logic and set-theory assume these courses to serve the purpose of constituting the foundation for developing future-teachers' logical thinking, or at least their ability to distinguish between valid and fallacious inferences.

Nonetheless, research points to various difficulties students encounter while requested to infer logically. Dubinsky and Yiparaki (2000) studied difficulties students have with mathematical statements that involve quantifiers. They believe that it is not reasonable to expect undergraduate students to learn much mathematics if they do not know how to read and interpret the language of mathematics. They argue that in order to understand a complex statement there is a need to analyze the statement based on the syntax of the language in which the statement is given. These researchers showed that university students meet various difficulties when they are requested to relate to logical statements involving quantifiers and that they are much more capable of handling the natural language statements than mathematics statements. Moore (1994) found that undergraduate mathematics majors have difficulties in producing even apparently trivial proofs. The students in Selden and Selden's (1995) study could not reliably determine the logical structure of common mathematical statements, and had difficulties in determining the correctness of their proofs. In addition, the students had trouble with transforming informally written mathematical statements into equivalent formal versions using symbols. Many students have difficulties in producing formal arguments and manipulating symbols in a formal way without having a deeper understanding of what the symbols really mean (e.g. Schoenfeld, 1991).

Part of these difficulties can be attributed to the traditional approaches to teaching logic, in particular to the language that is used within these courses (Epp, 2003), and to the manner in which the various aspects of logic are presented in textbooks (Alibert & Thomas, 1991). In the vast majority of students' textbooks, statements are not written in formal language but in "natural" language (Dubinsky & Yiparaki, 2000). Moreover, Dreyfus (1999) believes that students are unable to give satisfactory explanations and answers because most of them had never learned what counts as a mathematical argument.

Logic, by its nature, is abstract, and the manner in which words and statements are used in the spoken everyday language is not always consistent with their meaning in the context of logic. Furthermore, students have difficulties in managing logical statements in both contexts (Dubinsky & Yiparaki, 2000).

Cheng, Holyoak, Nisbett, and Oliver (1986) found that integrating concrete examples into logic courses and explaining logical principles by referring to analogies in everyday life improve students' ability to reason.

This suggests that a possible way to overcome the difficulties is teaching logic through children's literature. Indeed, Cotti and Schiro (2004) view the use of children's literature as *"one of the powerful tools available to help in teaching mathematics"*, as it provides *"a rich, meaningful, real world or fantasy context that can stimulate and motivate children's learning"* (p. 339).

2.2 Using Children's Literature as a Means for Teaching Mathematics

The use of children's literature presents *"a natural way to connect language and mathematics"* (Midkiff & Cramer, 1993, p. 303). Integrating children's literature in mathematics lessons enables students to be actively engaged with the learning materials (Conaway & Midkiff, 1994), and provides a base for establishing understanding of concepts (Midkiff & Cramer, 1993). It can also serve as an important vehicle for exploring mathematical ideas, as the natural context and the fact that mathematics is naturally embedded in familiar situations offer opportunities for discussing and highlighting mathematical ideas (Whitin, 1994). Moreover, *"Stories can help students understand the meaningful contexts that support mathematical thinking. They will see mathematics not as a prescribed set of algorithms to master, but as a way of thinking about their world. Children's literature presents a nonthreatening avenue to test out current notions about important mathematical concepts"* (Whitin & Gary, 1994, p. 394). *"And, most important"* Whitin (1994) claims *"children's literature powerfully demonstrates that mathematics is a way of thinking. For these reasons children's literature deserves a prominent role in the mathematics curriculum for all learners"* (p. 441). Furthermore, Whitin and Gary (1994) perceive the use of children's literature as an open invitation for students to connect their own interests and experiences to various mathematical concepts. In this way mathematics is no longer regarded as limited to workbooks, but becomes a purposeful tool for solving problems and making decisions.

Considering the above, we believe that for teaching elementary ideas of logic, the use of children's literature in general, and *Alice* in particular, can bridge between the abstractness of logic and its expression in everyday life. In addition, it might also help to reject the belief of many mathematics educators as to the fact that logic is too dry to capture students' interest (Epp, 2003). Teaching and learning logic through *Alice* convey an educational message too. Assuming that future teachers have no previous experience with learning or teaching in that style, it provides them with an opportunity to become familiar with this method and recognize its benefits for their future students. This is in accord with Cotti and Schiro's (2004) findings that most mathematics teachers are in favor of using children's books during mathematics instruction, believing that it might help in creating situations in which children can construct their own mathematical meanings.

Encouraged by these findings, and inspired by *The Annotated Alice* (Carroll, 2000) we developed additional annotations to this book, having in mind its implementation in training prospective elementary school teachers in general, and in particular those specializing in mathematics. These annotations are in four categories: Logic, Mathematics, General education, and Science.

The rest of this chapter details the strategy for integrating *Alice's Adventures in Wonderland*, with our annotations as mentioned above, in the learning environment for an introductory logic course for prospective elementary school teachers.

It also discusses the sequencing of a series of appropriate tasks, and the underlying rationale for their design, as the backbone of the empirical course, illustrated by a sample of task-worksheets.

In addition this chapter presents the research method and instruments employed to collect data pertaining to the impact of this empirical course, as interwoven in the teaching-learning process to minimize interference between the two.

Several results related to students' achievements and motivation are also discussed within space limitation.

3 The Process

We developed a series of 90 minutes lesson-plans based upon reading quotes from *Alice's Adventures in Wonderland*, and discussing them with our students. The lesson plans include handouts for independent study and group work. Designing the learning environment took five steps:

a. The first step was a careful examination of Lewis Carroll's text, highlighting quotes that have a potential for becoming starters for our students' activities or discussions. We found 75 quotes and annotated them. These annotated quotes were classified into four categories: (i) Logic (ii) Mathematics, (iii) General issues of education, and (iv) Science. Here are a few examples in each category.

 i. Logic. E.g. *It was all very well to say 'Drink me,' but the wise little Alice was not going to do that in a hurry. 'No, I'll look first,' she said, 'and see whether it's marked "poison" or not'; for she had read several nice little histories... such as,* *that a red-hot poker will burn you if you hold it too long; and that if you cut your finger very deeply with a knife, it usually bleeds; and she had never forgotten that, if you drink much from a bottle marked 'poison,' it is almost certain to disagree with you, sooner or later.*

However, this bottle was not marked 'poison,' so Alice ventured to taste it, and finding it very nice, (it had, in fact, a sort of mixed flavour of cherry-tart, custard, pine-apple, roast turkey, toffee, and hot buttered toast,) she very soon finished it off (Carroll 2000, Page 17, top half).

Discuss with students the sentence – it's marked "poison" or not – in particular the meaning of the word "or". Is there a third alternative?

Discuss with students the "if…then…" statements in this paragraph, as well as their corresponding inverse, converse and contra-positive. Could Alice be sure that the bottle was safe to drink? (See also Appendix 1, example ii.)

ii. Mathematics. E.g. *'What a curious feeling!' said Alice; 'I must be shutting up like a telescope.' And so it was indeed: she was now only ten inches high, and her face brightened up at the thought that she was now the right size for going through the little door into that lovely garden'* (Carroll 2000, Page 17, lines 9–10 from bottom).

Discuss with students – measurement of length: ideas such as various units, measurement tools, comparison, estimation – show by hands how long is 10 inches;

iii. General issues of education. E.g. *What an ignorant little girl she'll think me for asking…* (Carroll 2000, Page 14, lines 7–9).

Discuss with students – the issue of refraining from asking "stupid" questions. Should we hurry to ask every question? Should we try and figure out things for ourselves first? Or look for a written reference (as in a scientific enquiry), or some posted information (as in finding your way in a new place).

iv. Science. E.g. *First, however, she waited for a few minutes to see if she was going to shrink any further: she felt a little nervous about this; 'for it might end, you know,' said Alice to herself, 'in my going out altogether, like a candle. I wonder what I should be like then?' And she tried to fancy what the flame of a candle is like after the candle is blown out, for she could not remember ever having seen such a thing* (Carroll 2000, Page 17, line 12 from bottom).

Discuss with students – the three states of aggregation and the law of conservation of material

The annotations revealed that an opportunity to discuss a specific subject in logic, such as *exclusive and inclusive "or"*, occurred more than once in the text, obviously. It also revealed that the first chapter is the richest in resources (22 annotations of total of 75) for raising logic issues. This had an impact on the next steps in our work.

b. The second step was to compare the essence of these annotations with the syllabus of a traditional introductory course in logic for future-teachers, and to examine the prospect of covering the syllabus. The results showed that the first chapter is not only the richest, but includes pointers to everything we intended to employ in the syllabus. Namely, Logic and everyday language: A simple sentence and the truth value.

Negation. A compound sentence. Binary sentential connectives and their truth tables: Conjunction and "and"; Disjunction and inclusive/exclusive "or"; De Morgan's Laws; Implication and conditional sentences; Necessary and sufficient conditions; Equivalence and biconditional sentences. Inference rules: Affirming the Antecedent (Modus Ponendo Ponens) and Denying the Consequent (Modus Tollendo Tollens); Tautologies and equivalence; Quantifiers: Existential and Universal ones. Proof: Direct and indirect (by negation), by exhaustion, by counterexample.

c. At this point we faced **a dilemma**: which of the two lesson-plan sequencing options is more effective? The two options with conflicting rationale being (i) Sequencing along the logic syllabus and integrating suitable quotes from *Alice*, vs. (ii) Re-sequencing the logic syllabus along page by page reading of *Alice*, namely stopping at suitable quotes for raising issues from the syllabus in the order they occur. The former seemed right from the mathematics teaching aspect we were accustomed to, giving it a new spark, on the account of breaking the flow of the story into somewhat disconnected pieces. The latter seemed more revolutionary, as it implied breaking the commonly accepted order of teaching the subject matter, due to constraints imposed by the literal context. Having considered the pro and cons, we decided to face the challenge and struggle with re-sequencing our logic syllabus as dictated by the flow of the story. Because the first chapter was found to be the richest (as mentioned in the first step above) we naturally focused the exposition on the first chapter from *Alice*, and hence decided to use the rest of the story as resource for practice activities. At the end of this chapter we return to this dilemma and look into our decision in retrospect to examine its justification in view of the result.

d. We then proceeded **by outlining a series of fourteen 90-min lesson-plans** based upon reading through the text of *Alice's Adventures in Wonderland* (Carroll 2000), designating the stops at certain quotes to be used as a leverage for discussing certain themes in logic, mathematics (mostly set-theory), or sometimes science or general issues of education. These lesson-plans served as the backbone for the course.

e. Finally, we prepared a detailed design of tasks for each of the 14 lessons. Our approach took into consideration our desire to collect data for this empirical study. However, we strictly adhered to our top priority of the course, namely providing students with a series of learning experiences leading to an understanding of the main themes of the course. This was the guideline we adopted as we designed the learning activities and tasks as instruments for data collection, integrated into the teaching-learning process. The next section gives the details of the task development.

4 Activities and Tasks Development

The general rule we followed in the lesson-plan detailed design was a variation on the old maxim: *First tell them what you are going to tell them, then tell them, then tell them what you have told them.* Rather than "tell them", we took the constructivists' approach and attempted to provide the students with learning activities.

To this end, the framework for material development for each lesson included the following eight stages:

(1) Individual activity (handout): A short opening question–answer activity, through which students initially wonder about their elementary concepts and pre-conceptions related to the major themes of that lesson. This activity sets up the stage for teaching and clarifying the concepts and the ideas (see stages 3 and 6 below). Follow up on this activity is deferred (see stage 8 below).

(2) Whole class activity: Reading aloud a section from *Alice* (Chapter 1), followed by, when relevant, a short whole class discussion of educational/mathematical/scientific issues triggered by the section just read.

(3) Individual activity (handout): A guided study of selected quotes from the section of *Alice* just read, aimed at introducing a theme in logic. This activity makes students work on the connection between the use of the concepts in the text and their intuitive pre-concepts as revealed in the initial activity (see stage 1 above). This handout is revisited later (see stage 6 below.) Two sample handouts appear in Appendix 1.

(4) Small-group/whole class activity: Discussion of the individual ideas surfaced through the previous individual activity, giving time for students, exchange of their ideas, attempting to convince one another in case of disagreements.

(5) Expository teacher action: Course instructor presents the concepts and the ideas coherently, resolving any misunderstandings that may have occurred previously.

(6) Whole class discussion: Students take a second look at their writings in the handout of stage 3 resolving any points that remained unclear.

(7) Practice and take-home assignment (handout): This handout is based upon quotes from chapters other than the first one in *Alice*, quotes which bring up the topics in logic, discussed in class. Two sample handouts appear in Appendix 2.

(8) Individual activity (handout): A second attempt to address the questions in the opening handout (stage 1). This activity intends to make students aware of their knowledge development and bring up yet unclear issues. A sample handout appears in Appendix 3.

Materials developed were revised twice. Once after the first experimental implementation of the course, and again at the end of the second semester. The full range of materials is included in Shriki and Movshovitz (2008).

5 The Study

Our study took the nature of action-research using the following as data collecting instruments:

a. Students' response to the lesson-opening handouts. (see section 4 "Activities and Task Development", stage 1 above, and a sample handout in Appendix 3);

b. Students' response to the lesson-end handouts. (see section 4 "Activities and Task Development", stage 8 above, and a sample handout in Appendix 3);

c. Students' work on selected homework assignment handouts. (see section 4 "Activities and Task Development", stage 7 above, and sample handouts in Appendix 2)

d. Informal 5–7 minute individual conversational interviews with 2–3 students conducted on the way out of each lesson; the affective domain was at the focus of these conversations, hence students' feelings about the knowledge gained through the lesson that had just ended were probed.

e. Written lesson reports documenting the implementation of each lesson-plan and detailing critical events and the informal interviews; Reports were written in an accumulative diary immediately after the end of each lesson; (Due to the lack of sufficient funding for this project it was impossible to videotape the sessions, so instead we used these records as evidence for analysis of the outcome.)

f. Students' response to end-of-term evaluation in two parts: (*i*) Final 120 minute ordinary end-of course written exam based upon the syllabus (A sample test-item appears in Appendix 4.) *(ii)* Essay writing: Students were asked to reflect upon the development of their personal knowledge within the particular set up of the course and to discuss pro and cons for integrating children's literature in school mathematics and in teachers college mathematics.

6 Results and Discussion

The results obtained by administering the instruments mentioned in section 5 above, served as a data base for analyzing student's progress and attitudes as well as for revising the materials.

At the beginning of the first lesson we distributed copies of *Alice*, telling the prospective teachers that it was going to be our textbook for the logic course. Many students turned the pages of the book and expressed a slight embarrassment, wondering how it would be possible for "*a book with no numbers and no formulas*" to serve as a textbook.

Eighteen students participated in the second experimental implementation of the course. Comparing their final grades using instrument $f(i)$ with previous years groups of students who took this course without *Alice*, yielded no significant difference.

Due to space limitations we focus in the rest of this section on the results yielded by the Essay Writing instrument *f(ii)*.

As will be detailed below, students' written reflections referred mainly to their benefits from the entire learning environment that encompassed reading from *Alice* and working on the activities and the tasks. They also related to possible implications of their course experience to their future school teaching. A few students pointed to some disadvantages of learning logic through *Alice* or any other subject through children's books. Here are a few excerpts from their essays.[1]

---

[1] The excerpts are translated from Hebrew, as it is the tongue in which teaching took place.

6.1 Benefits from Learning Through Reading Alice

Referring to the benefits of learning logic through *Alice*, most of the students described their experience using affective as well as cognitive expressions:

> ... reading Alice made me realize that logic is not merely a 'mathematical matter', but also relates to one of the most amazing children's book on which I was raised, and probably to many others too...;
>
> ...Alice is a book full of imagination and humor. It deals with 'children's matter' in children's language. It is most enjoyable to learn logic, which appears to be boring, in that manner. It made me feel very special...;
>
> Like Wonderland, logic also seems to me as fantasy. Thus it was fascinating to learn logic through Alice.
>
> The topics in logic are very complex. I believe that reading Alice changed the entire atmosphere that might have been created in the lessons otherwise. I suppose it made me and the other students more relaxed;

A few students mentioned that reading from *Alice* helped them understand some specific topic:

> ...for example, the empty set. The story discusses the subject in a very concrete manner;
>
> It was interesting to learn topics like 'if...,then...', 'for all' through reading the story.
>
> I suddenly found myself looking for conditional sentences or quantifiers in other texts like the news paper as well.

6.2 The Learning Environment

Integrating *Alice* in the logic course established a new and untried learning environment for the students. They expressed it as follows:

> Using the book of Alice for teaching logic enabled us to experience different learning environment, an enjoyable one.
>
> No more books full of formulas, no more conventional exercises and other standard teaching aids that are used in other math courses. It was really a new and satisfying experience for me;
>
> Learning through Alice urged me to attend the lessons. I don't remember feeling like that before, actually I tend to miss many lessons and learn from books. I enjoyed the lessons very much. There was one lesson I could not attend, but I was very curious to know what parts of the book you read that day and what issue came out of it;
>
> Reflecting on my experience with this original learning environment, I realize that reading Alice motivated me to learn logic not just because I was forced to, but mainly because I enjoyed it.

6.3 Implication for School Teaching

Part of the students related not only to their own new experience with the new environment, but also to its potential for implementation in school teaching:

We all know that children don't read much these days. They prefer watching television and chatting through the computer. I believe that as educators we should strive to find ways to show them how fun reading is. Teaching mathematics through children's books can serve both purposes – enjoying reading books and enjoying the learning of mathematics.

I love the idea of teaching mathematics using children books. It is very interesting. It made me more attentive. I even implemented the method (using Five Balloons) in one of the classes in which I am practicing my math teaching, and I felt that it was easier for the children to learn the subject as I connected it to their own world;

It is most advisable for teachers to integrate children's books in mathematics lessons or any other lessons. In this way we, the adults, can enter the children's life, speak their language, and actually experience being a child again;

I think it is a great way to teach children. Stories help attract their attention, and the children would wait for the next lesson to hear the rest of the story, like I did.

Teaching logic based on Alice showed me that there are other ways to teach mathematics, moving away from the routine. I believe teachers should be able to implement various teaching methods. They should learn how to surprise their students; otherwise the students might get bored;

Integrating Alice or other children's books in mathematics lessons provides an unusual stimulus to learn the subject matter. It motivates the students and inspires their learning. From my experience with Alice, I believe that enjoyment encourages learning;

Children, especially the young ones, cannot concentrate during the entire lesson period. They need frequent breaks. Reading stories that are relevant to the topic of the lesson, can be used for 'letting the mind rest', and enable the children to be more attentive.

6.4 Disadvantages of Learning Through Alice or Other Children's Book

Four of the eighteen students referred to the difficulties they experienced with learning logic through *Alice* and commented also about the possible limitations of integrating children's books in mathematics lessons:

There were times that reading the book disturbed be. Although the sentences and the described situations seemed strange to me, I insisted on considering them as 'normal', namely-things that might happened in my everyday life. It distracted my mind from the lesson;

Many times I found myself confused. I could not decide whether I should refer to the sentence in its logical sense or to its meaning in the context of the story;

Alice's story is a fairy tale, and is not relevant to our topic. You could provide us other examples, not from the book, using much more simple words, and consequently we could have used more time for learning logic;

Using children literature might also be 'dangerous'. The story may possibly distract the students' attention, and they would be busy with the plot instead of the subject matter.

In summary, it appears that most of the prospective teachers' utterances refer to affective aspects and to their satisfaction from the learning environment. Additional research is needed in order to be able to determine whether prospective teachers who experience learning logic through *Alice* perceive and understand the various topics differently or better than those who learn it in a more traditional manner.

7 Concluding Remarks

Reflecting upon the teaching experiment we conducted, we feel that the bold move of breaking the common order of an introductory course in logic had a justifiable payoff. Students as well as us came out of the course with a sense of fulfillment, having coped with challenging tasks that had meaning, and appreciating the power of logic as putting language matters in order. Nevertheless, further in-depth analysis of the data collected is needed in order to reveal the subtleties of students under-standing of logic gained through such a different course and possibly their ability to cope with a higher level course in logic following such an introduction. It would be interesting also to attempt *logic in wonderland* method in school and examine its impact on school students' language and reasoning ability.

Appendices

Note: The framed segments are quotes from Carroll (2000). The Appendices include sample materials translated from Shriki and Movshovitz (2008).

Appendix 1

This appendix includes two samples of the individual activity handouts based upon our convention of reading from *Alice* Chap. 1. (see above section 4 "Activities and Task Development" stage 3). These handouts intentionally did *not* have a title so as not to disclose their focus to the students too early, before it is explicitly discussed.

   (i) Handout related to the "or" connective.

   Based upon the following quote from *Alice*, answer the questions below:

> **Alice follows the White Rabbit**
> But when the Rabbit actually took a watch out of its waistcoat-pocket, and looked at it, and then hurried on, Alice started to her feet, for it flashed across her mind that she had never before seen a rabbit with either a waistcoat-pocket, or a watch to take out of it, and burning with curiosity, she ran across the field after it, and was just in time to see it pop down a large rabbit-hole under the hedge.
> **Lewis Carroll, *Alice's Adventures in Wonderland*, p. 12**

1. Did the White Rabbit have a watch? How do you know?
2. Did the White Rabbit have a pocket in his waistcoat? How do you know?
3. Is it true to say: "The White Rabbit had a watch and a pocket in his waistcoat"? Why?
4. Is it possible to replace the statement: "... she had never before seen a rabbit with **either** a waistcoat-pocket, **or** a watch to take out of it..." with the statement: "...she had never before seen a rabbit with a waistcoat-pocket **and** a watch to take out of it..." without changing the meaning of the original statement? Why?

5. If your answer to the previous question was positive, do you believe that "or" and "and" have the same meaning?

Now, we go on reading: "In another moment down went Alice after it, never once considering how in the world she was to get out again".

Based upon the following quote from *Alice*, answer the questions below:

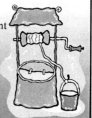

Alice is falling into the well
The rabbit-hole went straight on like a tunnel for some way, and then dipped suddenly down, so suddenly that Alice had not a moment to think about stopping herself before she found herself falling down what seemed to be a very deep well.
Either the well was very deep, or she fell very slowly, for she had plenty of time as she went down to look about her and to wonder what was going to happen next.
Lewis Carroll, *Alice's Adventures in Wonderland*, p. 12-13

In questions 6, 7 chose the answer that appears to you to be correct

6. Assume the well was very deep. Can you conclude from the above quote that Alice fell very slowly?

   a. Obviously yes b. Obviously not c. It is impossible to tell

7. Assume that Alice fell very slowly. Can you conclude from the above quote that the well was very deep?

   a. Obviously yes b. Obviously not c. It is impossible to tell

8. Consider the last two quotes. Is there any difference between the meaning of "either...or..." in the two quotes? Explain.

(ii) Handout related to the conditional connective
   Based upon the following quote from *Alice*, answer the questions below:

Alice is pondering
It was all very well to say "Drink me," but the wise little Alice was not going to do *that* in a hurry. "No, I'll look first," she said, "and see whether it's marked '*poison*' or not"; for she had read several nice little' stories about children who had got burnt, and eaten up by wild beasts, and other unpleasant things, all because they *would* not remember the simple rules their friends had taught them: such as, that a red-hot poker will burn you if you hold it too long; and that, if you cut your finger *very* deeply with a knife, it usually bleeds; and she had never

1. List all the expressions in the text that describe a stipulation. Do they have a common structure?
2. Consider Alice's decision to drink from the bottle. What was it based upon? Would you approve of it? Why?

Appendix 2

This appendix includes two samples of the practice and take-home assignment based upon reading from Alice Chap. 2 on. (see above section 4 "Activities and Task Development" stage 7). These handouts intentionally have a title so as to connect their focus to earlier class work.

(i) Practice and take-home assignment related to the connective "and".

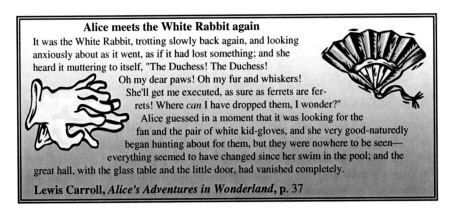

Alice meets the White Rabbit again
It was the White Rabbit, trotting slowly back again, and looking anxiously about as it went, as if it had lost something; and she heard it muttering to itself, "The Duchess! The Duchess! Oh my dear paws! Oh my fur and whiskers! She'll get me executed, as sure as ferrets are ferrets! Where *can* I have dropped them, I wonder?" Alice guessed in a moment that it was looking for the fan and the pair of white kid-gloves, and she very good-naturedly began hunting about for them, but they were nowhere to be seen— everything seemed to have changed since her swim in the pool; and the great hall, with the glass table and the little door, had vanished completely.

Lewis Carroll, *Alice's Adventures in Wonderland*, p. 37

In each of the following paragraphs two statements are given with their truth value. They are followed by a question. Mark the correct answer and give your reasons, based on the data.

1. a. In *Wonderland* the following statement is false:
   "The White Rabbit was looking for the pair of white kid-gloves and the White Rabbit was looking for his shoes".

   b. In *Wonderland* the following statement is true:

   "The White Rabbit was looking for the pair of white kid-gloves".
   Which of the following is correct?

   – "The White Rabbit was looking for his shoes" is a True statement;
   – "The White Rabbit was looking for his shoes" is a False statement;
   – Parts a and b contradict each other;
   – There is not enough information to determine whether the White Rabbit was looking for his shoes or not.

   Your reasons:

2. In *Wonderland* the following two statements are true:

   a. "The White Rabbit was trotting slowly back again, and the White Rabbit was looking anxiously about as it went";
   b. "The White Rabbit was looking anxiously about as it went"

Which of the following is correct?

- "The White Rabbit was trotting slowly back again" is a True statement;
- "The White Rabbit was trotting slowly back again" is a False statement;
- Parts a and b contradict each other;
- There is not enough information to determine whether the White Rabbit was trotting slowly back again or not.

Your reasons:

3. In *Wonderland* the following two statements are false:

   a. "Alice was looking for the Duchess, and the White Rabbit was looking for the fan";
   b. "Alice was looking for the Duchess"

Which of the following is correct?

- "The White Rabbit was looking for the fan" is a True statement;
- "The White Rabbit was looking for the fan" is a False statement;
- Parts a and b contradict each other;
- There is not enough information for determine whether the White Rabbit was looking for the fan or not.

Your reasons:

4. a. In *Wonderland* the following statement is true:
"The White Rabbit was looking for the pair of white kid gloves and the White Rabbit likes the Duchess".

[b.] In *Wonderland* the following statement is false:
"The White Rabbit likes the Duchess".

Which of the following is correct?

- "The White Rabbit was looking for the pair of white kid gloves" is a True statement;
- "The White Rabbit was looking for the pair of white kid gloves" is a False statement;
- Parts a and b contradict each other;
- There is not enough information for determine whether the White Rabbit was looking for the pair of white kid gloves or not.

Your reasons:

(ii) *Practice and take-home assignment related to the inferences from statements including the words "All" and "Only", relating them to necessary and sufficient conditions.*

During her walk in Wonderland Alice met a cat. Alice asked for the cat's assistance. The following is a part of their conversation:

Based upon the following quote from *Alice*, answer the questions below:

Alice's conversation with the Cat

"Would you tell me, please, which way I ought to go from here?"

"That depends a good deal on where you want to get to," said the Cat.

"I don't much care where —" said Alice.

"Then it doesn't matter which way you go,'" said the Cat.

"—so long as I get *somewhere*," Alice added as an explanation.

"Oh, you're sure to do that," said the Cat, "if you only walk long enough."

Alice felt that this could not be denied, so she tried another question. "What sort of people live about here?"

"In *that* direction," the Cat said, waving its right paw round, "lives a Hatter: and in *that* direction," waving the other paw, "lives a March Hare. Visit either you like: they're both mad." "But I don't want to go among mad people," Alice remarked.

"Oh, you can't help that," said the Cat: "we're all mad here. I'm mad. You're mad."

"How do you know I'm mad?" said Alice.

"You must be," said the Cat, "or you wouldn't have come here."

Lewis Carroll, *Alice's Adventures in Wonderland*, p. 65-6

1. In each row in the table below two statements appear followed by a conclusion. You are to determine whether the conclusion is true, false, or may be the statements do not provide enough information in order to reach the conclusion. Justify your choice.

	Statements	Conclusion	The conclusion is … Choose: True/False/Not enough data to decide, and justify your choice
a.	All those who come to *Wonderland* are mad; *Alice* doesn't come to *Wonderland*	*Alice* is not mad	True/False/Not enough data to decide
b.	Only those who come to *Wonderland* are mad; *Alice* comes to *Wonderland*	*Alice* is mad	True/False/Not enough data to decide
c.	All those who come to *Wonderland* are mad; *Alice* comes to *Wonderland*	*Alice* is not mad	True/False/Not enough data to decide
d.	Only those who come to *Wonderland* are mad; *Alice* doesn't come to *Wonderland*	*Alice* is mad	True/False/Not enough data to decide
e.	All those who come to *Wonderland* are mad; *Alice* doesn't come to *Wonderland*	*Alice* is mad	True/False/Not enough data to decide
f.	Only those who come to *Wonderland* are mad; *Alice* comes to *Wonderland*	*Alice* is not mad	True/False/Not enough data to decide
g.	All those who come to *Wonderland* are mad; *Alice* comes to *Wonderland*	*Alice* is mad	True/False/Not enough data to decide
h.	Only those who come to *Wonderland* are mad; *Alice* doesn't come to *Wonderland*	*Alice* is not mad	True/False/Not enough data to decide

2. Which of the eight rows in the table above describes the conversation between Alice and the Cat?

3. Consider again the conversation between Alice and the Cat. Which of the following statements summarizes the Cat's claim:

   - In order to be mad, it is necessary to come to Wonderland;
   - In order to be mad, it is sufficient to come to Wonderland;
   - In order to come to Wonderland, it is necessary to be mad;
   - In order to come to Wonderland, it is sufficient to be mad.

Appendix 3

This appendix includes a sample of the opening handout revisited at the end of each topic. (see above section 4 "Activities and Task Development" stages 1 and 8).

An opening and lesson-end handout related to quantifiers.

On top of each table below there is a true statement followed by several possible conclusions in the body of the table. Consider the suggested conclusion in each entry then mark by "x" the decision you believe to be right and justify your choice:

T – The suggested conclusion is true, as it follows from the statement.

NN – The suggested conclusion does not necessarily follow from the statement.

F – The suggested conclusion is false as its contrary follows from the statement.

1. The true statement: Every girl named Alice likes books with picture.

	Suggested conclusion	T	NN	F	Your justification
a.	The girl named Alice Smith does not like books with pictures				
b.	Every girl named Alice does not like journals with pictures				
c.	Grandmother Alice does not like books with pictures				
d.	Every girl named Alice likes books with no picture				
e.	There exist a girl named Alice who does not like books with pictures				
f.	There does not exist a girl named Alice who does not like books with pictures				
g.	Dinah is a girl who likes books with pictures				
h.	Every girl whose name is not Alice does not like books with pictures				
i.	Not every girl named Alice likes books with pictures				
j.	The girl named Alice Johns likes books with pictures				

2. The true statement: In Wonderland there exist white rabbits that can speak

	Suggested conclusion	T	NN	F	Your justification
a.	In Wonderland there exist no white rabbits that can sing				
b.	In Wonderland there exist white rabbits that cannot speak				
c.	In Wonderland every white rabbit can speak				
d.	In Wonderland there does not exist a white rabbit that cannot speak				
e.	In Wonderland every animal that is not a white rabbit cannot speak				
f.	In Wonderland there is at least one white rabbit that can speak				
g.	In Wonderland there does not exist a white rabbit that can speak				
h.	In Wonderland there exist white rabbits that can speak				
i.	In Wonderland there exist cats that can speak				

3. The true statement: There are no cats that do not eat carrot

	Suggested conclusion	T	NN	F	Your justification
a.	There exist cats that eat carrot				
b.	There exist cats that do not eat carrot				
c.	There exist dogs that eat carrot				
d.	All cats eat carrot				
e.	There are no cats that eat mice				
f.	There exist cats that eat bread				
g.	There exist cats tat do not eat cabbage				
h.	All cats drink milk				
i.	Street cats do not eat carrot				

Appendix 4

This appendix includes a sample item from the final exam (see above section 5 "The Study" part f).

After Alice ate a piece of mushroom that grew in Wonderland, her neck grew so much that she was able to reach the treetops. She could easily bend her long neck in any direction and curve it like a snake. In one of the treetop Alice met a large pigeon that was hatching her eggs and watching them from snakes. The pigeon was convinced that Alice was a snake, while Alice was trying to persuade the pigeon that she was only a little girl. The following is a part of the conversation that took place between Alice and the pigeon.

Alice's conversation with the Pigeon

"But I'm not a serpent, I tell you!" said Alice. "I'm a—I'm a—"

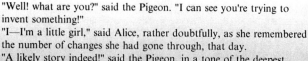

"Well! what are you?" said the Pigeon. "I can see you're trying to invent something!"

"I—I'm a little girl," said Alice, rather doubtfully, as she remembered the number of changes she had gone through, that day.

"A likely story indeed!" said the Pigeon, in a tone of the deepest contempt. "I've seen a good many little girls in my time, but never *one* with such a neck as that! No, no! You're a serpent; and there's no use denying it. I suppose you'll be telling me next that you never tasted an egg!"

"I have tasted eggs, certainly," said Alice, who was a very truthful child; "but little girls eat eggs quite as much as serpents do, you know."

"I don't believe it," said the Pigeon; "but if they do, why, then they're a kind of serpent: that's all I can say."

Lewis Carroll, *Alice's Adventures in Wonderland*, p. 55-6

---

1. What arguments is the pigeon using to prove that Alice is not a little girl? Are these arguments valid (correct in a logical sense)?
2. What arguments is the pigeon using to prove that Alice is a snake? Are these arguments valid (correct in a logical sense)?

References

Alibert, R., & Thomas, M. (1991). Research on mathematical proof. In D. Tall (Ed.), *Advanced mathematical thinking* (pp. 215–230). Dordrecht: Kluwer Academic Publishers.

Carroll, L. (2000). *The Annotated Alice*, the Definitive Edition, with introduction and notes by Martin Gardner W.W. Norton and Company, Inc., NY.

Cheng, P. W., Holyoak, K. J., Nisbett, R. E., & Oliver, L. M. (1986). Pragmatic versus syntactic approaches to training deductive reasoning. *Cognitive Psychology*, 18, 293–328.

Conaway, B., & Midkiff, R. B. (1994). Connecting literature, language and fractions. *Arithmetic Teacher*, 41(8), 430–433.

Cotti, R., & Schiro M. (2004). Connecting teacher beliefs to the use of children's literature in the teaching of mathematics. *Journal of Mathematics Teacher Education, 7*, 329–356.

Dreyfus, T. (1999). Why Johnny can't prove. *Educational Studies in Mathematics, 38*(1), 85–109.

Dubinsky, E., & Yiparaki, O. (2000). On student understanding of AE and EA quantification. In E. Dubinsky, A. H. Schoenfeld, and J. Kaput (Eds.), *Issues in mathematics education: Vol. 8 research in collegiate mathematics education, IV* (pp. 239–289). Providence, RI: American Mathematical Society.

Epp, S. S. (2003). The role of logic in teaching proof. *American Mathematical Monthly,* 110(10), 886–899.

Gregory, J. W., & Osborne, A. R. (1975). Logical reasoning ability and teacher verbal behavior within the mathematics classroom. *Journal for Research in Mathematics Education,* 6(1), 26–36.

Midkiff, R. B., & Cramer M. M. (1993). Stepping stones to mathematical understanding. *Arithmetic Teacher,* 40, 303–305.

Moore, R. C. (1994). Making the transition to formal proof. *Educational Studies in Mathematics,* 27(3), 249–266.

NCTM (National Council of Teachers of Mathematics) (2000). *Principles and standards for school mathematics.* Reston, VA: NCTM.

Schoenfeld, A. H. (1991). On mathematics as sense-making: An informal attack on the unfortunate divorce of formal and informal mathematics. In J. F. Voss, D. N. Perkins, & J. W. Segal (Eds.), *Informal reasoning and education* (pp. 311–343). Hillsdale, NJ: Erlbaum.

Selden, J., & Selden, A. (1995). Unpacking the logic of mathematical statements, *Educational Studies in Mathematics,*29(2), 123–151.

Shriki, A., & Movshovitz-Hadar, N. (2008). (In Hebrew) *Logic in Wonderland*: *A textbook for prospective teachers.* Accepted for publication by MOFET publishing house, Israel.

Whitin, D. J. (1994). Exploring estimation through children's literature, *Arithmetic Teacher,* 41(8), 436–441.

Whitin, D. J., & Gary, C. C. (1994). Promoting mathematical explorations through children's literature. *Arithmetic Teacher,* 41(7), 394–399.

Tasks using Video Clips of Children in a Content Mathematics Course for Future Elementary School Teachers

Richard Millman, Kelly Svec, and Dana Williams

One of the major problems in the mathematical education of future primary teachers is the need to convince them that they will need a deep, conceptual understanding of the mathematics of primary school in order to give all of their students a quality education. This chapter argues that the brief use of video clips of children in a content mathematics course can address issues of attitude, the need for understanding the mathematical knowledge for teaching, and the recognition that children will invent their own ways of doing mathematics. The tasks discussed here are structured around the use of video clips in student presentations.

Tasks involving video clips of children in mathematics content courses for future teachers are a useful and effective way to introduce and address questions such as why future teachers need such mathematics courses and why a conceptual understanding of mathematics is so important for their success and that of their students. Video clips that involve children working through mathematical problems affect the attitudes of future teachers. In this chapter, we will first present the effects that video clips have on future teachers and how, after watching and discussing the clips, their attitudes change. We will then describe a classroom presentation that involved a video clip of a child. The clip emphasized content knowledge and the "mathematical habit of the mind" that enriches mathematical teaching. In both cases, we will describe the future teachers' reactions to the clips in terms of attitude and approach to content knowledge.

In the United States, mathematicians, rather than mathematics educators, are usually the instructors in the first courses dealing with the content needed to teach the mathematics of elementary and middle school. They are confronted with four initial

R. Millman
Director, Center for Education Integrating Science, Mathematics and Computing, and Professor of the Practice of Mathematics, Georgia Institute of Technology, USA

K. Svec
Student, University of Kentucky, USA

D. Williams
Graduate, University of Kentucky, USA

B. Clarke, B. Grevholm, and R. Millman (eds.), *Tasks in Primary Mathematics Teacher Education: Purpose, Use and Exemplars,* Mathematics Teacher Education 4,
© Springer Science+Business Media LLC 2009

and substantive student attitudinal issues as listed below. We will describe a task, which approaches the first three through the use of video clips of children doing mathematics. We will then report on the response of the future teachers in terms of their assessment of the need for mathematical content knowledge at the K-5 level. The issues addressed are:

- How to convince the future teachers that they will need a deep understanding of mathematics in order to teach it at the K-5 level.
- How to convince the future teachers that a true "understanding" of the material does not mean merely how to do procedures but rather depends on thorough understanding of the concepts, that is, conceptual understanding of the material.
- How to persuade the future teachers that all children are capable of learning mathematics and that the use of different learning strategies is important (a fundamental idea which is embodied in the Standards of the National Council of Teachers of Mathematics (NCTM, 1995) as the Equity Principle.
- How to persuade the future teachers themselves that they are capable of teaching mathematics with conceptual understanding.

The content mathematics courses at the University of Kentucky are a two-semester sequence, which precedes the methods course. The courses are taught by graduate students, part-time instructors, and a faculty member, all in the Mathematics Department. The courses are coordinated by the outreach professor of mathematics (the first author). There are 16 sections taught between the two semester-long courses during the year. The syllabus for the courses is uniform and covers Chaps. 1 through 13 from a standard content book (Long & DeTemple, 2006). The responses of the future teachers that are presented in this article are those observed across the sections during the two academic years 2004–2005 and 2005–2006.

Video tapes and video clips are used for many educational purposes but generally appear later in a prospective teacher's educational coursework. In this chapter, we will show the advantages of introducing video tapes of children to the future teachers during their first semester of the mathematics content course. Video clips were used twice in each section of the first course. Additionally, in designing their required presentation to the class, two of the students in one section (the second and third authors of this article) prepared and made use of a video tape of a fifth grader dealing with the geometric problem from Ma (1999). It is this presentation that illustrates some insights into the fourth bullet above. The role of presentations in addressing the fourth bullet and, more generally, integrating assessment in a mathematics content course, is described in Millman and Ma (2006).

There has been a general recognition these days that elementary school teachers need to have a deep conceptual knowledge of the mathematics of elementary school and that just a procedural one will not suffice. Ball and Bass (2003) discuss the Mathematical Knowledge for Teaching (MKT) as differentiated from the notion of "Pedagogical Knowledge for Teaching" of Shulman (1986). Ma (1999) talks about the concept of a "Profound Understanding of Fundamental Mathematics", for example. Bass, an eminent research mathematician and former president of the American

Mathematical Society, takes the view that the mathematics of teaching should be thought of as one thinks of branches of applied mathematics – "[the mathematician should] … understand sensitively the domain of application, the nature of its mathematical problems, and the forms of mathematical knowledge that are useful and usable in the this domain" (Bass, 2005, p. 418). The Bass article is extremely useful for all mathematicians who teach the content mathematics course for future teachers.

A goal of our approach is to help the students recognize the need for a content mathematics course and allow them to discover for themselves (through assessing video clips) that a thorough understanding of the Bass/Ball concept of MKT is needed in order for them to be successful. Future teachers will see, as a result, that it is necessary to have multiple views of the content of elementary school mathematics, to connect those to the standards of the National Council of Teachers of Mathematics (NCTM), and the state in which they teach, and to integrate their content knowledge with what they will learn in their methods courses later.

In the first semester, we showed some video clips (using the IMAP – Integrating Mathematics and Pedagogy – videos from San Diego State University), (Philipp and Cabral, 2005) which demonstrate clearly that children will invent their own ways of doing problems, sometimes correctly and sometimes not. The video clips seen by the classes dealt with subtraction (and the role of place value) viewed in three ways (Gretchen in video clip 3), and a child's division of fractions in his head (Elliot in video clip 16). The total amount of time spent watching and discussing the video clips was under 90 min so this approach does not reduce the class time spent on mathematics in any significant way.

We will now discuss the effect these two clips had on the future teachers in detail. The task for the instructor is to select, set the stage, and show the video clips. The task for the future teachers is to think about the reaction of the children to mathematics and the implications of those reactions from the viewpoint of the content preparation of future teachers.

Video clip 3 shows a second grader, Gretchen, doing a two-digit subtraction problem (70 - 43) in three different ways. The first is procedural and, because she remembers the procedure incorrectly, her answer is wrong. The second is with strips and singles and the third with a hundreds chart. These two approaches are conceptual and both are done correctly; however, she insists that the procedural way is the correct way and that its answer (in spite of the fact that the other two methods agree) is the right one. This video clip task gives the future teachers a chance to view, in the context of school children, the difference between procedural and conceptual approaches, to see how easy it is for procedures to be "mis-remembered", and to view different approaches which appeal to different learning styles to the same (subtraction) problem. In all of the sections of the course, the Gretchen video clip brought home the points in the first three bullets from the beginning of this chapter.

The video clip of the fourth grader, Elliot, who divides fractions in his head, has a striking effect on future teachers. In most sections, one of the future teachers will say, "Would you play that again?" while another will inevitably ask, "Will we have students like that?" The answers, of course, are "Yes". The first question allows the instructor to discuss the need for thoroughly understanding the mathematics (in this case, division of fractions). Because Elliot solves the second fraction division problem (also in his head, although incorrectly) using the result of the first one, the future teachers need to have a conceptual understanding of this topic. The second question gives the opportunity for the instructor to discuss the Equity Principle of the NCTM to emphasize that mathematics is for all students, from those who are struggling to those, like Elliot, who are quite proficient.

There is, of course, much pressure on practising teachers to have their students perform well in the standardized exams such as the Kentucky Core Content Test (KCCT) of the CATS (Commonwealth Accountability Testing System). Because of these end of year tests in the schools and the high stakes that they involve, it is important that curricular changes in university content or methods courses be correlated with the KCCT or standard exams in other states. We were, therefore, led to include in our examination of video clip tasks how the video clips reflect the Commonwealth of Kentucky standards. The completed assessment forms for the video clips that were reviewed are contained in Millman, Svec, and Williams (2005). We found that the IMAP tasks are well aligned with the KCCT and CATS. The form itself consisted of five questions and is given below.

Evaluation Form for Clips:
Clip #_____Grade Level_____

Question 1: What is the mathematics content?
Question 2: What is the level of conceptual understanding of the student? Where do the topics appear in the "Kentucky Core Content for Mathematics Assessment"?
Question 3: What PUFM (Profound Understanding of Fundamental Mathematics) should the watcher have to be able to decide whether the student is correct?
Question 4: What PUFM should the watcher have to be able to help the student?
Question 5: What is a one or two sentence question for the MA 201 instructors to be able to guide the discussion of the MA 201 students?

Because we believe in the philosophy that it is important to ground the content course in the practice, these evaluation forms were reviewed by a fourth grade teacher (Angela Gonzales, Northern Elementary School, Lexington, KY) and we thank her for her valuable comments.

We will now describe one of the classroom presentations in which two of the future teachers (Svec and Williams) used, at their own initiative, a video clip to introduce their problem. Presentations in the content mathematics course by future teachers are described more fully in Millman and Ma (2006). Student presentations are required in both semesters of the course in all of the sections. Svec and Williams decided to include a videotape of a child to set the scene for the "perimeter versus area of a rectangle" conjecture of Liping Ma's Chap. 4 (1999). We will discuss how this clip added extra life to that presentation and to the content course by the reactions of the students.

The classroom presentation focused on the mathematical concepts of area and perimeter of closed shapes, specifically rectangles. To begin, a conjecture on area and perimeter following a scenario by Ma (1999) was presented to the class by the two students. Their purpose was to provide the future teachers with a better conceptual understanding of the two concepts (area and perimeter). The scenario from Chap. 4 was presented in the terms that follow:

> Imagine that one of your students comes to class very excited. She tells you that she has figured out a theory that you never told the class. She explains that she has discovered that as the perimeter of a closed figure increases, the area also increases.

To help the class visualize the conjecture, a video clip of a 5th grade student (age 11) demonstrating the theory was presented. The video clip was staged where the student was asked to present a scenario similar to the one described by Ma. The student told of a recent experience she had at home while helping to install an electric fence for her dog. She explained that the dimensions of the fence in the front yard were 9 yd by 5 yd. Therefore, the perimeter of the front yard fence was 28 yd and the area was 45 sq yd. The dimensions of the fence in the back yard were 9 yd by 6 yd. The perimeter of the back yard fence was 30 yd and its area was 54 sq yd. Therefore, the student concluded that, as the perimeter of the yard increased the area also increased. The example the student presented was as follows:

Showing this clip immediately got the attention of the class, for it allowed them to see a real student demonstrate the mathematical concept we were focusing on. After showing the clip, the future teachers were asked to raise their hands if they agreed with the student's theory. About one half of the future teachers in the class raised their hands, agreeing that as the perimeter of a rectangle increases, the area also increases. The results of this poll were similar to the findings of Ma in her research on how U.S. teachers reacted to this same scenario. Most US teachers either agreed or were not sure about the claim. Though it is common for teachers to agree with what seems to be a logical theory, the presentation stressed the importance of not assuming a theory which sounds logical (or poetic) to be correct without first examining it.

The presentation began by trying to prove or disprove the conjecture made by the student. As a teacher might begin with his or her own 5th graders, the presentation opened up with a review of the definitions of perimeter and area and reminded them that perimeter (P) is the measurement of the distance around the rectangle and area (A) is the measurement of the space within the rectangle. The equations for each are:

$$P = 2L + 2W$$
$$A = LW$$

L is length and W is width.

It was felt within the team that it would be engaging to work with the students in the class to get to a conclusion. This was started by making a chart on the board, representing length, width, perimeter, and area. Getting the class further involved, the team let the class give dimensions of certain rectangles, determine the area and perimeter, and, then, have them increase the rectangle's perimeter and give the new dimensions, and calculate area. This was done with a couple of numbers and all seemed to support the child's theory. A geoboard was also used to show this idea more visually. Svec and Williams had already determined that the theory was false, but, just in case the student's numbers did not go in the direction the team had intended, the team had other numbers prepared.

L	W	P	A
4	4	16	16
8	1	18	8

At this point, the presentation had disproved the child's theory because it only takes one counterexample to disprove it, which is an important lesson for future teachers.

However, delving deeper, another conjecture was examined. The class was asked "Could two different rectangles have the same area?" and "What happened to the perimeter in this case?"

L	W	P	A
9	4	26	36
3	12	30	36

As the perimeter increased, the area stayed the same; it did not increase, so this disproved the theory as well.

This task provided the presenters a chance to demonstrate to a class of college students the notion of a "Mathematical Habit of the Mind" which is interpreted as looking to see where there might be a kernel of truth in a child's theory. What part, then, of the child's theory is true? If one variable of the rectangle stays the same and only the other is changed (say length is constant and width varies), then as perimeter increases, so will the area.

An important point was made to the class that there was a difference between the student in the staged clip and the student from Ma's scenario. The student in the clip was told to illustrate a theory, but the 5th grade student in Ma's scenario actually discovered this theory on her own. Therefore, she was very excited to tell her teacher about her theory. The point was made to the class on how important it is for teachers to take advantage of these types of situations as they arise in the classroom. The lesson of this part of the task is that when students are excited and enthusiastic, they are more receptive to learning and will more than likely do a better job of retaining and internalizing the information that they have discovered. A mathematical habit of the mind will reinforce the student's enthusiasm and insights. The child in the video clip produced a totally teachable moment. The conjecture became a time to either drop the plan for the day and move on to something else or rearrange the next day to tackle the question.

During the work with video clips, it became clear that the video clips played a key role in a future classroom for the following reasons:

- They give a future teacher a hint at the amazing ways children's minds can work and the theories and methods they can come up with. During these teachable moments, it really becomes clear that a detailed understanding of content is the key to helping a child or class decide if they are doing a problem incorrectly or correctly.
- It is important to be able to think on one's feet and a shallow knowledge of content and the reasons behind the method will not only inhibit the learning of the children in the classroom, but might also turn them away from mathematics as their own logic is ignored.
- Children capture the attention of an audience of future teachers. In a class of future teachers, all the students have an interest in children. Using video clips containing children takes advantage of this to motivate these future teachers to increase the depth of their understanding of mathematics.

There is also another issue dealing with the attitude of students at the beginning of the content course but it is easily remedied. We include this topic because the mathematicians who teach the course may not realize that it is present as "background noise" in the classroom. Students generally do not know that this mathematics course is not about; for example, classroom management, how to work with special needs students, or the use of manipulatives. They believe that the mathematics sequence is about how to teach because they do not realize that there are a number of methods and other education courses beyond the mathematics courses. It is very useful to let the students know at the beginning of the content course that there are many more classes to come and that this two-semester sequence one is focused on the mathematical content, not mathematics methods.

In conclusion, the use of video clips addresses some important issues of attitude, the need for MKT, the recognition by the future teachers that children will invent their own ways (sometimes right and sometimes wrong) of doing mathematics, the blurring of the notion of a "content" and a "methods" course, and the need for depth of mathematical understanding for the teaching of elementary school children.

Acknowledgments This work is funded by Title II grant P336A020006-04 CFDA #84.336A from the Educational Professional Standards Board of Kentucky. The opinions of this chapter are those of the authors.

References

Ball, D., & Bass, H. (2003). Toward a practice-based theory of mathematical knowledge for teaching. In B. Davis & E. Simmt (Eds.), *Proceedings of the 2002 Annual Meeting of the Canadian Mathematical Education Study Group* (pp. 3–14). Edmonton, AB: CMESG/GCEDM.

Bass, H. (2005). Mathematics, mathematicians, and mathematics education. *Bulletin of the American Mathematical Society, 42*(4), 417–430.

Long, C. T., & DeTemple, D. W. (2006). *Mathematical reasoning for elementary teachers* (4th ed.). Boston: Pearson, Addison-Wesley.

Ma, L. (1999). *Knowing and teaching elementary mathematics*. Mahwah, NJ: Erlbaum.

Millman, R., & Ma, X. (2006). The design of a mathematics content course to integrate the assessment principle: Recent results. *Proceedings of the 4th Annual Hawaii International Conference on Education* (pp. 4552–4558). Honolulu: HICE.

Millman, R., Svec, K., & Williams, D. (2005). *Assessment of IMAP video clips of children for a content mathematics course for future elementary school teachers*. Paper presented at the First Conference of the Appalachian Association of Mathematics Teacher Educators. *Proceedings of the Appalachian Association of Mathematics Teacher Educators*. Lexington, KY:

National Council of Teachers of Mathematics. (1995). *Assessment standards for school mathematics*. Reston, VA: NCTM.

Philipp, R., & Cabral, C. (2005). *IMAP: Integrating mathematics and pedagogy to illustrate children's reasoning*. Pearson, NY: Merrill Prentice-Hall.

Shulman, L. (1986). Those who understand: Knowledge growth in teaching. *Educational Researcher, 15*(2), 4–14.

Teacher Tasks for Mathematical Insight and Reorganization of What it Means to Learn Mathematics

George Gadanidis and Immaculate Namukasa

The mathematics-for-teachers tasks we discuss in this chapter have two qualities: (1) they offer teachers opportunities to experience the pleasure of mathematical insight; and (2) they aim to disrupt and reorganize teachers' views of what it means to do and learn mathematics. Given that many future and inservice elementary teachers fear and dislike mathematics, it is perhaps not too far-fetched to suggest that there is a need for "math therapy." We believe that a form of mathematics therapy may involve new and different experiences with mathematics. Such experiences, considered broadly to include questions or prompts for mathematical exploration, draw attention to deep mathematical ideas and offer the potential of experiencing the pleasure of significant mathematical insight. In our work with teachers we have developed and used a variety of mathematics tasks as opportunities for experiential therapy. The tasks aim to challenge some of the mathematical myths that future teachers believe to be true and are typically assumed by them in mathematics classrooms. The tasks have potential to disrupt teachers' view of mathematics, and to start the process for reorganizing their thinking about what mathematics is and what it means to do and learn mathematics.

In this chapter we describe and discuss four of the mathematics tasks which involve non-routine mathematics problems that we use in our mathematics-for-teachers program. This program is offered annually to our 440 future elementary school (K-8) teachers, who generally lack confidence in mathematics and often fear and/or dislike the subject. It is also offered to inservice teachers through a series of mathematics-for-teachers courses. A student response summarizes the effects of our approach.

> I felt lost at first as I struggled to remember math concepts from childhood and adolescence. I felt confused. What did a poem have to do with math? I was perplexed. Was there not only one answer to a mathematical question? I felt apprehensive. How would I discuss a

G. Gadanidis
Associate Professor, Faculty of Education, The University of Western Ontario, Canada

I. Namukasa
Assistant Professor, Faculty of Education, University of Western Ontario, Canada

B. Clarke, B. Grevholm, and R. Millman (eds.), *Tasks in Primary Mathematics Teacher Education: Purpose, Use and Exemplars,* Mathematics Teacher Education 4,
© Springer Science+Business Media LLC 2009

mathematical concept that I did not fully understand? Then as I got into the swing of things, I felt more confident with my opinions, my answers and most importantly myself. I felt cheerful that I was experiencing math as a student and that I would hopefully be able to empathize with my future students. I felt happy that math instruction could be made to be engaging. Finally, I was giddy that I was thinking about math, actually thinking about math and not doing everything else to avoid it.

1 Mathematics for Teachers

It's not surprising to meet people who wear their view that "I'm not a math person" as a badge of honor. It concerns many mathematics teacher educators that this is also the case among future mathematics teachers. Recently, at an orientation assembly, we asked our in-coming group of 440 elementary teachers how they felt about mathematics. When asked to raise their hands if they loved mathematics, 15–20 hands went up. When asked to raise their hands if they hated mathematics, a sea of hands filled the auditorium. Most elementary teachers have narrow views of what mathematics is and what it means to do mathematics (Fosnot & Dolk, 2001; McGowen & Davis, 2001). Given this mathematics education predicament, this not-uncommon perception of mathematics as an abhorrent subject, we suggest that there is a need for "math therapy," which involves new and different experiences with mathematics.

Our mathematics-for-teachers tasks have two qualities: (1) they offer teachers opportunities to experience the pleasure of mathematical insight; and (2) they aim to disrupt and reorganize teachers' views of what it means to do and learn mathematics.

1.1 The Pleasure of Mathematical Insight

The tasks are content oriented and are designed to motivate teachers to attend deeply to mathematics and to relationships among concepts. Davey (1999) argues that attention is aesthetic in nature. Whenever we bring consciousness to bear upon a topic, either individually or communally, we engage it in emotional and imaginative ways. We use attention to gain insight, to learn and extend ourselves, to incorporate a new thing, whether that is a new way of solving an old problem or finding new ways to express an idea. We extend our understanding, we become more complex, and this feels good (Gadanidis & Hoogland, 2004). Dissanakye (1992) talks about an "aesthetic sensibility" that "acts as one of our primary meaning-making capacities in all domains" (p. 25). Attention is our way of gaining beauty and meaning from experience.

Our tasks, considered broadly to include questions or prompts for mathematical exploration, draw attention to deep mathematical ideas and offer the potential of experiencing the pleasure of significant mathematical insight (Gadanidis, 2004). Moments of significant insight fix the experience in one's consciousness, enriched by a strong sense of accomplishment and confidence (Burton, 1999). Insight leads to a feeling of satisfaction, a sense of great clarity, and is accompanied by a positive emotional response. There is a sense of "authorship" of the ideas, which provides an important element of self-affirmation and confidence (Barnes, 2000). Such moments are inspiring. They are moments of deeper understanding, they have the power to transform attitudes and beliefs about what is mathematics and they inspire teachers to seek more of these moments (Liljedahl, 2002).

To Hadamard (1996/1945), for an individual, during such moments "ideas pop up with brevity, suddenness and immediate certainty, after an incubation period, from the unconscious to the conscious" (p. 14). To Davis and Hersh (1981) such moments indicate "that something has been brought forth which is genuinely new… a new understanding for the individual; a new concept placed before the community" (p. 283). Such moments involve a shift in an entire mathematical world. In topological terms, learning, gaining insight, forming abstract concepts and observing general categories and other such radical shifts are equivalent to a cataclysmic adjustments of a space and landscape – an earthquake or an eruption. Such shifts are not simply a question of deepening or smoothening existing valleys or hills: they are about reconfiguration of the overall territory. The dynamics that might have been resetting, widening or deepening part-by-part, basin by basin at aha moments of insight, intellectual evolutions, cultural revolutions or paradigm shifts do reset all-at-once. Disrupting and re-organizing experiences does require shifts in understanding (Sumara, 2002) akin to a geographical landscape formation. Future teachers who fear mathematics may need shifts akin to therapy. Our mathematics-for-teachers program seeks to evoke changes that afford preservice teachers to move beyond their mathematics horizon, beyond their familiar mathematical world through the use of content based tasks.

1.2 Disrupting and Reorganizing Teachers' Views

The tasks we use in our mathematics-for-teachers program help improve and deepen teachers' mathematical knowledge. However, our primary goal is not to increase teachers' mathematical content knowledge, but to offer "experiential therapy." In light of our experiential therapy goal, tasks are chosen based on their potential to disrupt teachers' view of mathematics, and to start the process for reorganizing their thinking about what mathematics is and what it means to do and learn mathematics. The tasks that we develop and use aim to challenge some of the mathematical myths that future teachers believe to be true and are typically assumed by them in mathematics classrooms, which we discuss below.

Myth 1: Mathematics is a cold science – rather than an aesthetic, human experience (Gadanidis & Hoogland, 2004). We select tasks that promote a degree of comfort or enjoyment with doing mathematics and at the same time broaden views about mathematics. We provide opportunities for teachers to reflect on their work on the tasks by writing about what they learned and what they felt while engaged in the task. These reflections are then summarized and organized based on the themes that emerge and then they are given back to the teachers to read and discuss. This provides an opportunity for teachers to see what others are thinking and feeling, to find affirmation in similar experiences of others and to rethink their own experiences in light of contrasting experiences. This also provides opportunities for discussing aesthetic qualities of the mathematics experience.

Myth 2: Mathematics is about learning procedures for getting correct answers – rather than attending to and gaining insights about the complexity of mathematical ideas (Gadanidis, 2004). An integral component of the experiential therapy is the culminating assessment, where teachers are asked to write a "math essay" on a randomly chosen task that we have worked on. Associating mathematics assessment with writing an essay shifts the focus from learning methods for answering questions to exploring more complex mathematical relationships. In writing the mathematics essay (on a maximum of two pages, in 30 min), teachers choose to discuss such issues as: different strategies of solving the problem, varied mathematical connections the problem evokes, moments of insight or even frustration with the problems, extensions to the problem or related mathematical problems, and pedagogical implications. In the online discussion component of our program, teachers are encouraged to collaborate in preparing possible essay responses. The mathematics essay takes away the pressure of standard assessments where the focus is on being able to answer test questions, and offers teachers an opportunity to reflect on (to retell and rethink) their experience doing and learning mathematics based on one of the mathematics-for-teachers tasks.

Myth 3: A good teacher makes learning easy – rather than creating situations where students have to think hard (Jonassen, 2000). The tasks we design and use create situations where teachers have to explore complex mathematical relationships and attend to doing mathematics deeply and for extended periods of time. Teachers need to have such experiences first hand, to build up their mathematical confidence and increase their expectation of what they (and their students) are capable of accomplishing mathematically. Ginsburg (2002), who has studied young children doing mathematics, suggests that, although mathematics is "big," children's minds are bigger. He argues that "children possess greater competence and interest in mathematics than we ordinarily recognize" and we should aim to develop a curriculum for them in which they are challenged to understand big mathematical ideas and have opportunities to "achieve the fulfillment and enjoyment of their intellectual interest" (p. 7).

Myth 4: Teaching should start with what a child already knows and understands – rather than also with what a child can imagine (Egan, 1997). The online applets that accompany the tasks often use poetry to introduce the task. Peacock (1999) suggests, poetry is screen-sized. A poem is compact enough and cohesive enough to be held in one's mind as a whole. Poetry also makes use of image and metaphor, both of which help the reader sense deeper relationships to be explored and engage the imagination (Zwicky, 2003). We also use mathematical literature as a starting point for doing mathematics, such as Lewis Carroll's (1885) *A Serpent with Corners*, which is discussed in Task 2. Some of the poems have also been set to music and are offered as music videos in the applets.

2 Mathematics-for-Teachers Tasks

In this section we share four of the mathematics-for-teachers tasks that we have designed and used. The first two tasks deal with geometry concepts and the last two tasks deal with algebra concepts.

2.1 Task 1: I See it, it's Invisible!

It's amazing how exciting geometry has become for me. I never thought that as a person in my 20s that I would be excited to look for geometric shapes in everyday life and to also try and imagine shapes in unorthodox places. This is "shaping" up to be one of the most fun university classes that I've taken.

One of the first prompts in this task asks teachers to "Use your finger to draw an invisible circle in mid-air. Now hold it at the ends of its diameter, and flick it, making it spin. What three-dimensional figure did you cut out of space?" Prompts such as these are also in the poem that is part of the applet shown in Fig. 1. The applet also contains a music video of the poem, along with a number of annotations that offer extensions to the mathematics offered in the poem. Such applets are part of the online component of our mathematics-for-teachers program. One teacher commented, "I started to enjoy math and poems, in fact, I am trying to write one poem right now! This module made me see everything around me with a new lens!"

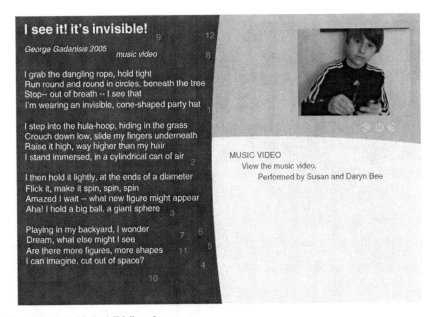

Fig. 1 "I see it, it's invisible" applet

When we used this task in a fully online mathematics-for-teachers course, teachers used the drawing feature of our discussion board to create and post drawings that illustrated the figures they imagined being cut out of space. Figure 2 shows a curve and triangle that could be formed using one's body. "While doing my physio today I realized that by stretching into a bridge, my body makes a half-moon shape. It also helps to stretch my glutes! My physio also helped me see triangles while doing leg stretches." Figure 3 shows figures that can be created using the movement of a swing. "I used to play on a swing hanging on a big tree! But instead of swinging back and forward, I used to play twisting it so it would spin until the ropes become parallel again! I guess for few seconds I was inside a cone! It did make me feel dizzy but I liked it!" Figure 4 shows a figure skating movement to help others imagine what might be cut out of space when the triangle formed as the skater's legs twirl. Figure 5 shows an imaginary sphere formed by two cupped hands. "I was also thinking what kind of shape I could make with my hands, and after a while, I could see an invisible sphere in my hands! Yes, just imagine yourself making a snow ball!"

This task helps teachers see mathematics all around them and engage with mathematical ideas in ways that can be discussed outside of the classroom setting. As one

Fig. 2 Body shapes

Fig. 3 A swing

Fig. 4 Figure skating

Fig. 5 A sphere

teacher commented, "I learned that math can be discussed with your family and friends just like you would a favorite book or new movie." Another teacher commented, "The world around us is full with geometric shapes we've never 'seen' before, just taken them as granted. I understand your feeling perfectly about the sensation of 'having new glasses' when looking around!" The task also helped teachers see a creative side of mathematics. "It is the first time that I have realized/felt that math isn't just BLACK & WHITE and can cause quite creative outcomes/discussions" (Capitals in original).

Teachers also made pedagogical connections. "I learned in this module that asking for examples from everyday life to students makes them think, discuss with each other, form opinions, learn more deeply, and remember more about that lesson. In this way math lessons can be serious and fun in the same time, and every student in the class is engaged in discussion." "I realize that it is another way of teaching math, not boring and strict how I had in school when I was younger, but funny, inspirational, imaginative; a pleasure to listen to everyone's opinions and make your own opinion about the subject. I feel that this course will remain deeply in my memory, and it will make me think twice when wanting to teach a stereotypical lesson."

2.2 Task 2: A Serpent with Corners

This task uses an excerpt from *A Serpent with Corners* (see below), from Lewis Carroll's (1885) *A Tangled Tale*. We selected it based on "its length (short enough given our time constraints) and due to its high mathematical potential" (Gadanidis, Simmt, Sterenberg & Tumanov, 2004). Gadanidis et al. (2004, p. 64) note that: "As we read and discussed the story, we noticed that the flow of the story was interrupted at places. For example, the description of the rectangle as being 'oblong' caused us to question whether this referred to a rectangular shape with length greater than width, or whether is also referred to elliptical shapes. It seemed to us that such an interruption, such an ambiguity, was desirable, as it caused us to imagine alternatives and to wonder about a variety of contexts for the problem stated by Balbus in the story."

"A friend of mine has a flower-garden – a very pretty one, though no great size – How big is it?" said Hugh.

"That's what you have to find out!" Balbus gaily replied. "All I tell you is that it is oblong in shape – just half a yard longer than its width – and that a gravelwalk, one yard wide, begins at one corner and runs all around it."

"Joining onto itself?" said Hugh.

"Not joining onto itself, young man. Just before doing that, it turns a corner, and runs around the garden again, alongside of the first portion, and then inside that again, winding in and in, and each lap touching the last one, till it has used up the whole of the area."

"Like a serpent with corners?" said Lambert.

"Exactly so. And if you walk the whole length of it, to the last inch, keeping in the centre of the path, it's exactly two miles and half a furlong. Now, while you find out the length and breadth of the garden, I'll see if I can think out that sea-water puzzle."

"You said it was a flower-garden?" Hugh inquired as Balbus was leaving the room.

"I did," said Balbus.

"Where do the flowers grow?" said Hugh. But Balbus thought it best not to hear the question. He left the boys to their problem, and, in the silence of his own room, set himself to unravel Hugh's mechanical paradox.

This task is also presented as an applet (shown in Fig. 6) where variations of the problem may be explored. This usually a difficult task for many teachers, requiring sustained attention to mathematical processes and an exploration of multiple solution strategies. The task lends itself to algebraic and geometric solution processes, as well as a trial-and-error approach. The geometric solution typically has a significant aesthetic effect on teachers, due its simplicity and beauty. The geometric solution relates the length of the path to the area of the garden. For example, for a $5\,m \times 6\,m$ garden (see Fig. 7), the area is $30\,m^2$ and the length of the path is $30\,m$, which makes sense in retrospect as the path has to travel through all of the "squares" of the garden.

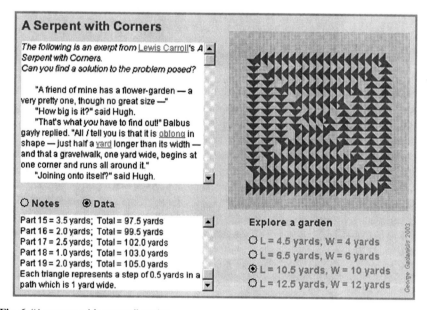

Fig. 6 "A serpent with corners" applet

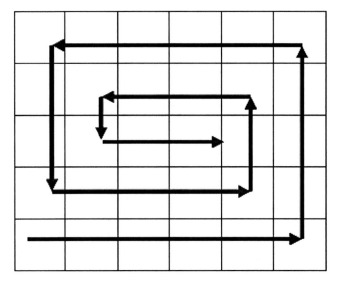

Fig. 7 The path

2.3 Task 3: Growing Patterns

This task has recently been developed and has been used in an inservice teacher education setting. The task starts off quite harmlessly with an exploration of the growing pattern shown in Fig. 8.

The following questions are considered:

- What changes (or remains the same) as the pattern grows?
- How can we develop a rule for finding the 20th iteration without drawing the diagrams that precede it?

As teachers work on the problem, the instructor circulates and asks the questions proposed by Blanton and Kaput (2003):

- Tell me what you were thinking?
- Did you solve this a different way?
- How do you know this is true?
- Does this always work?

Blanton and Kaput (2003) suggest that "These questions not only reveal students' thinking but also prompt students to justify, explain, and build arguments – processes that lie at the heart of algebraic reasoning" (p. 73). These questions work at two levels for the teachers: at the level of modelling metacognitive thinking and at the level of modelling a pedagogy they could employ in their own classroom.

The task is then extended by asking "How many square tiles are needed to build the first 20 iterations?" Teachers quickly realize a few ways of finding the number of tiles needed for the 20 iterations. A few teachers focus on what changes (and

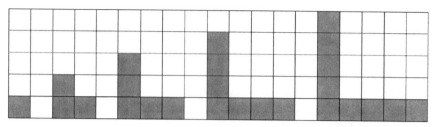

Fig. 8 A growing pattern

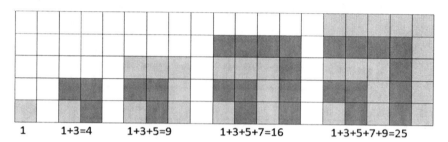

| 1 | 1+3=4 | 1+3+5=9 | 1+3+5+7=16 | 1+3+5+7+9=25 |

Fig. 9 Noticing that the sum of the first N odd numbers is $N \times N$ or $N2$

what remains the same) in the diagram, others on what changes in the total number of tiles at each iteration and yet others at what changes from the previous iteration to the next. Those who focus on the patterns in the diagram, say that the corner tile is constant while the vertical and horizontal arms are of equal length, a length that begins at the second step and increases by one tile. These teachers come up with the observation that for the 20th iteration, $1 + 2(20 - 1)$ tiles will be needed. This focus stresses what a constant and what $n - 1$ in a function might mean geometrically.

When teachers focus on the changes in the iterations they soon see that the number of tiles needed for the 20 iterations is the sum of the first 20 odd numbers. In finding the sum, teachers look for patterns and try to generalize. They attend to the number patterns. They notice that odd numbers can be paired up so that $1 + 39 = 40$, $3 + 37 = 40$, $5 + 35 = 40$, and so forth. This leads to solution and to a pattern that can be generalized and expressed algebraically. When they discover that the number of tiles needed for 20 iterations is 400, they notice that $20^2 = 400$. This leads to further explorations where they notice that 4 tiles are needed for 2 iterations, 9 tiles for 3 iterations, 16 tiles for 4 iterations, and so forth. They discover that the sum of the first n odd numbers is n^2. Using tiles of different colors they represent this visually, as shown in Fig. 9.

When we look at the pattern in Fig. 9 we experience a sense of aesthetic fit, a sense of mathematical pleasure. The image of the Ls fitting together draws our attention; it says, "look at me"; to use Heidegger' (1927–1964) phrasing, it calls us to think. We sense the pleasure of seeing the connection between the odd numbers, their geometric representations as Ls, the visual proof that the sum of the first ten odd numbers is 10^2, and the general solution of finding the sum of the first n odd numbers. Experiences such as these help us appreciate the beauty of mathematics and the pleasure of mathematical thinking and insight. It is such experiences that teachers need in order to develop an understanding and an appreciation of mathematics.

Teachers also begin to use the geometry of data and numbers to think about algebraic and general expressions. Their thinking is re-organized to include visual proofs. If this type of visual proof works for finding the sum of odd numbers, teachers wonder whether there is a visual proof for finding the sum of the natural numbers (i.e., $1 + 2 + 3 + 4 + 5 + 6 + \ldots$). Figure 10 shows a visual representation of the sum of the first ten natural numbers. If they draw the diagonal line shown in Fig. 10, they can see that the sum (or the number of tiles needed to represent the first ten natural numbers) is a little more than the half the area of the 10×10 square. Then they consider how they might express this algebraically.

Engaging elementary school teachers with algebra is necessary, as algebra remains an Achilles heel of mathematics education. Some research indicates that the teaching and learning of algebra typically focuses on symbolic algebra over other representations (Borba & Confrey, 1996; Kieran, 1992; Kieran & Sfard, 1999; Nathan & Koedinger, 2000). Consequently, though they learn to manipulate algebraic expressions, students do not seem to be able to use them as tools for meaningful mathematical communication (Kieran & Sfard, 1999). The majority of students do not acquire any real sense of algebra and, early on in their learning of algebra, give up trying to understand algebra and resort to memorizing rules and

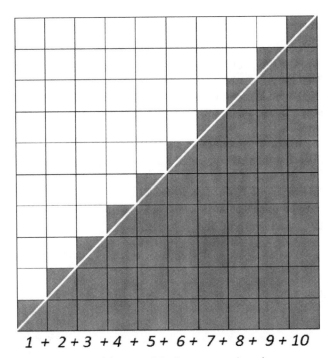

$1 + 2 + 3 + 4 + 5 + 6 + 7 + 8 + 9 + 10$

Fig. 10 A visual representation of the sum of the first ten natural numbers

procedures (Kieran, 1992:, Kieran & Sfard, 1999). Kieran & Sfard (1999) suggest that the rules of algebra may appear arbitrary to many students because "all too often they are unable to see the mathematical objects to which these rules are supposed to refer" (p. 2). Suggestions for providing students with meaningful experiences in algebra learning include student exploration of multiple representations of algebra concepts (Borba & Confrey, 1996, pp. 319–320; Kieran & Sfard, 1999, p. 3). It is also suggested that the traditional approach to teaching algebra, which typically starts with symbolic representation and decontextualized manipulation and later moves to visual and graphical representation and problem-based contexts, should be reversed (Borba & Confrey, 1996, pp. 319–320). Graphs, and other visual representations, which are often treated as a mere add-on to algebra could become the foundation of algebra teaching and learning (Kieran & Sfard, 1999, p. 3).

2.4 Task 4: Making 10

One of the skills that students develop in the elementary grades is that of finding missing numbers (adapted from Gadanidis (2004)). For example, they learn and practice finding missing numbers in equations such as the following:

- $\_ + 4 = 15$
- $12 - Y = 5$
- $3 \times \_ = 45$
- $\_ \div 5 = 3$

Although it's important for students to practice and learn the skill of finding missing numbers in equations, the concept on its own is not a big idea in junior grade mathematics, as variables are portrayed as only representing an unknown. One way to make the learning of this skill more meaningful mathematically is to relate it to bigger ideas about equations and variables, where variables represent changing quantities.

In this task, teachers explore the equation $\_ + \_ = 10$. They roll a die to get the first number and then they calculate the second number. They write the pairs of numbers in table and in ordered pair form (see Fig. 11), and plot the ordered pairs on a grid (see Fig. 12). Then they repeat this for $\_ + \_ = 6$ and $\_ + \_ = 4$. Teachers express surprise that the ordered pairs line up (see Fig. 12). "I had the 'aha'

Equation	Ordered Pair
1 + 9 = 10	(1,9)
2 + 8 = 10	(2,8)
3 + 7 = 10	(3,7)
4 + 6 = 10	(4,6)
5 + 5 = 10	(5,5)

Fig. 11 Ordered pairs

Fig. 12 Graphs

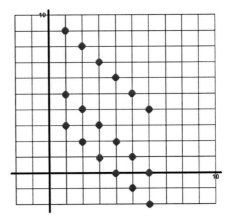

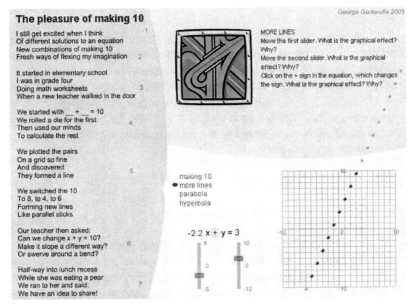

Fig. 13 The pleasure of making ten

feeling when I saw the diagonal line pattern on the graph. That was my favorite part." Teachers also notice that the graph of $\_ + \_ = 4$ could be used as a visual proof of $6 + -2 = 4$ and $5 + -1 = 4$. That is, $(6, -2)$ and $(5, -1)$ line up with $(4,0)$, $(3,1)$, $(2,2)$ and $(1,3)$. They also explore equations whose graphs are not parallel to the ones in Fig. 12 and whose graphs were not straight lines. Such mathematical connections appear to be pleasing to teachers. "I loved the adding/graphing we did and how you could take problems and branch out … it really makes something in my mind click."

The applet version of the task (see Fig. 13) starts with a poem that tells the story of the task from a student's point of view. It also offers opportunities to change the coefficients in linear, parabolic and hyperbolic functions and notice the dynamic effect on the graph.

This task draws teacher attention to the difference between a variable as a place holder and a variable as a changing quantity. In a typical missing number exercise, like $B + 3 = 12$, the variable is a place holder for the missing number. In an equation like $X + Y = 10$, there is a situation of co-variation, where the variable is not only expected to change, but the change in the value of one of the variables also affects the value of the second variable.

3 Math Therapy

As we offer our mathematics-for-teachers program for inservice and preservice teachers, we also collect data from the learned/felt reflections done at the end of each session, the online discussions that follow sessions, and from the math essays they write at the end of the course. We conduct multi-layered, structured content analysis of the data, with the content analysis adhering to the "stage model of qualitative content analysis" defined by Berg (2004, p. 286). We do not have the space to report in detail on the method and on the findings. However, we can report some of the themes that are emerging.

3.1 Frustration

Many of the mathematics activities were novel experiences for the teachers. Unlike typical mathematics teaching where the teacher seeks to make learning easier by organizing classroom experiences in small, bite-sized pieces, the tasks we used sought to create opportunities for teachers to problem solve and pose new questions as well as to think in mathematical ways. However, solving non-routine mathematical problems and drawing resources from one's conceptual understanding (rather than solely from one's practiced procedures) in a mathematics setting, especially for people with little experience doing so, can be a frustrating experience. Teachers expressed a level of frustration, especially with early course experiences, as reflected in the comments below.

> I'm still frustrated by my inability to see the conclusion or the point. I can't seem to push my thinking beyond the exercise to the solution, on my own.
>
> As they work through more tasks, teachers' frustration seems to dissipate.
>
> My feelings of frustration are gradually turning into curiosity as I begin to think about new ways of approaching math.

3.2 Attention and Insight

As teachers engage with the mathematics tasks, they began to experience moments of insight. These were pleasurable moments that served as "remuneration" for the effort and attention that they gave to the problems.

> ... it really makes something in my mind click.
> I had a lot of moments where things just popped!
> When a student in our class made a discovery, our discussion reached its most enthusiastic and exciting points.

3.3 Collaboration

Although at times teachers were asked to think about a problem individually before attempting it as a group, the pervasive atmosphere was one of collaboration. Being able to work with others helped reduce stress with doing mathematics and exposed teachers to the mathematical thinking and problems solving strategies of others.

> I felt really comfortable working in my group. It is easy to experiment with different things with other people versus working alone, and more ideas seem to come out.
> The most important thing I learned so far is how important it is to share ideas/experience with others! In this course, I thought I would learn from ONE professor, but instead of one, I learned from many.

3.4 Time

Teachers were given ample class time to work on problems in a low stress atmosphere. In fact, most of the problem solving was done in class, and take-home assignments mostly consisted of course readings rather than mathematics problems.

> I liked that we were asked what other methods can we come up with to test right-handedness/left etc. Then we were given time in class to go through and actually try ideas – it's been so long since I've had an experience like that in school. It was relaxing.

3.5 The Complexity of Mathematics

Most elementary mathematics teachers view mathematics as a subject of procedures for getting correct answers. As they worked through the mathematics-for-teachers tasks, many teachers started expressing more elaborate views of mathematics.

> Mathematics is a very complex subject that can be looked at from various angles.
> Infinity can be negative? What? I have never heard of a discussion of infinity or anything else "mysterious" in a math class (except this one).

Things have recently all come together for me regarding math. I see connections in and to math everywhere. Math has started to consume my thoughts.

Math is looked upon as a very dry subject, because there is the idea that there is no creativity in it, unlike English, or drama. On the contrary thanks to this course we have been shown that this is not the case.

3.6 Teaching Mathematics

At the beginning of the mathematics-for-teachers program, teachers expressed apprehensions about mathematics and a lack of desire to teach it. As the course progressed, preservice teachers started expressing an excitement for teaching mathematics.

It was so interesting to see how attitudes towards teaching mathematics and mathematics in general changed from the first class to the end of the term. Initially, there were numerous concerns about one's ability to teach math and fears about adequacy. However, many of these concerns often changed to feelings of excitement.

I faced my "math demons" and actually grew to enjoy a subject I thought would be my nemesis forever.

3.7 Beliefs and Practice

Although teachers expressed perceptions of mathematics and of teaching and learning mathematics changed significantly as the course progressed, these new perceptions were also accompanied with apprehensions that they would be able to put them into practice.

This class has completely shattered my understanding of math and how to teach math. It makes me feel that teaching math is going to be difficult – or at least more challenging than I previously thought. There are so many ideas – I feel overwhelmed.

Teachers in the mathematics-for-teachers program overwhelmingly expressed that experiencing the course helped change their view of mathematics and of teaching and learning mathematics. In fact, the concept of doing mathematics as a therapeutic experience came from the first offering of the program. By the middle of the first course offering, students started referring to our problem solving sessions as "math therapy." However, we do not expect that a single course experience can create comprehensive or permanent changes in teachers' perceptions of mathematics and mathematics teaching. Neither can we assume that such an experience will significantly affect teachers' classroom practice; teaching is also greatly affected by accepted teaching practices in the wider school community (Buzeika, 1999; Ensor, 1998) and by conflicting priorities (Skott, 1999). However, our research indicates that such mathematics-for-teachers experiences are important starting points for change in teachers' perceptions and classroom practice.

References

Barnes, M. (2000). Magical moments in mathematics: Insights into the process of coming to know. *For the Learning of Mathematics, 20*(1), 33–43.

Berg, B. L. (2004). *Qualitative research methods for the social sciences.* New York: Pearson.

Blanton, L. M., & Kaput, J. J. (2003). Developing elementary teachers algebra eyes and ears. *Teaching Children Mathematics, 10*(2), 70–77.

Borba, M. C., & Confrey, J. (1996). A student's construction of transformations of functions in a multiple representational environment. *Educational Studies in Mathematics, 31*, 319–337.

Burton, L. (1999). Why is intuition so important to mathematicians but missing from mathematics education? *For the Learning of Mathematics, 19*(November), 27–32.

Buzeika, A. (1999). Teachers' doubts about invented algorithms. In O. Zaslavsky (Ed.), *Proceedings of the 23rd Conference of the International Group for the Psychology of Mathematics Education* (Vol. 2, pp. 161–168). Haifa, Israel: PME.

Carroll, L. (1885). *A tangled tale.* Accessed April 20, 2008, from, http://etext.library.adelaide. edu.au/c/carroll/lewis/tangled/tangled.html.

Davey, N. (1999). The hermeneutics of seeing. In I. Heywood & B. Sandywell (Eds.), *Interpreting visual culture: Explorations in the hermeneutics of the visual* (pp. 3–29). New York: Routledge.

Davis, P. J., & Hersh, R. (1981). *The mathematical experience.* Boston: Birkhäuser.

Dissanakye, E. (1992). *Homo aestheticus.* New York: Free Press.

Egan, K. (1997). The arts as the basics of education. *Childhood Education, 73*(6), 341–345.

Ensor, P. (1998). Teachers' beliefs and the problem of the social. In A. Olivier & K. Newstead (Eds.), *Proceedings of the 22nd Conference of the International Group for the Psychology of Mathematics Education* (pp. 280–287). Stellenbosch, South Africa: PME.

Fosnot, C. T., & Dolk, M. (2001). *Young mathematicians at work. Constructing multiplication and division.* Portsmouth, NH: Heinemann.

Gadanidis, G. (2004). The pleasure of attention and insight. *Mathematics Teaching, 186*(1), 10–13.

Gadanidis, G., & Hoogland, C. (2004). Mathematics as story. In G. Gadanidis, C. Hoogland, & C. Sedig (Eds.), *Mathematics as story: Mathematics through the lenses of art & technology* (pp. 128–135). Toronto, ON: Fields Institute for Research in Mathematical Sciences.

Gadanidis, G., Simmt, E., Sterenberg, G., & Tumanov, V. (2004). Mathematics as story. In G. Gadanidis, C. Hoogland, & C. Sedig (Eds.), *Mathematics as story: Mathematics through the lenses of art & technology* (pp. 62–65). Toronto, ON: Fields Institute for Research in Mathematical Sciences.

Ginsburg, H. G. (2002). Little children, big mathematics: Learning and teaching in the pre-school. *Proceedings of the 26th Conference of the International Group for the Psychology of Mathematics Education* (Vol. 1, pp. 3–14). University of East Anglia.

Hadamard, J. (1996/1945). *The mathematician's mind: The psychology of invention in the mathematical field.* Princeton, NJ: Princeton University.

Heidegger, M. (1927–1964). *Basic writings.* In D. F. Krell (Ed.), *Revised & expanded edition.* New York: Harper Collins.

Jonassen, D. H. (2000). *Computers as mindtools for schools. Engaging critical thinking* (2nd ed.). Upper Saddle River, NJ: Merrill/Prentice-Hall.

Kieran, C. (1992). The learning and teaching of school algebra. In D. A. Grouws (Ed.), *Handbook of research on mathematics teaching and learning* (pp. 390–419). New York: MacMillan.

Kieran, C., & Sfard, A. (1999). Seeing through symbols: The case of equivalent expressions. *Focus on Learning Problems in Mathematics, 21*(1), 1–17.

Liljedahl, P. (2002). The 'aha moment: Students' insight into the learning of mathematics. *Proceedings of the 24th Annual Meeting of the North American Chapter of the International Group for the Psychology of Mathematics Education* (pp. 887–896). University of Georgia.

McGowen, M. A., & Davis, G. E. (2001). What mathematics knowledge do preservice elementary teachers value and remember? In R. Speiser, C. A. Maher, & C. N. Walter (Eds.), *Proceedings of* the 23rd Annual Meeting, North American Chapter of International Group for the Psychology of Mathematics Education (pp. 875–884). Snowbird, Utah.

Nathan, M. J., & Koedinger, K. R. (2000). An investigation of teachers' beliefs of students' algebra development. *Cognition and Instruction 18*(2), 209–237.

Peacock, M. (1999). *How to read a poem ... and start a poetry circle*. Toronto, ON: McClelland and Stewart.

Skott, J. (1999). The multiple motives of teaching activity and the role of the teacher's school mathematical images. In O. Zaslavsky (Ed.), *Proceedings of the 23rd Conference of the International Group for the Psychology of Mathematics Education* (Vol. 4, pp. 209–216). Haifa, Israel: PME.

Sumara, D. (2002). *Why reading literature in schools still matters: Imagination, interpretation, insight*. Mahwah, NJ: L. Erlbaum.

Zwicky, J. (2003). *Wisdom & metaphor*. Kentville, Nova Scotia: Gaspereau Press.

Teaching and Understanding Mathematical Modelling through Fermi-Problems

Andrea Peter-Koop

While there is a large body of research on mathematical problem solving and modelling at primary school level, the mathematical modelling process itself has not been given much attention in research. In order to support and identify mathematical modelling processes, Fermi problems have been used in a classroom based study with third and fourth graders. In contrast to standard word problems that frequently just require the application of one or two simple algorithms and therefore do not provide information on how to find a mathematical model, Fermi problems provide the necessary complexity for studying authentic mathematical modelling. Videotapes of small group work in a grade four classroom provided the data basis. The analysis of the classroom data suggests that word problems with a high level of complexity can be solved in sensible and appropriate ways by third and fourth graders. The Fermi problems in this context served as "model-eliciting tasks", because the required modelling process necessitates multiple modelling cycles with multiple ways of thinking about givens, goals, and solution paths.

1 Introduction

Numerous studies in the last two decades have highlighted the difficulties students (and teachers) experience when dealing with real-world related word problems (e.g. see de Lange, 1998; Reed, 1999; Verschaffel, Greer, & De Corte, 2000). In this context, it is important to acknowledge that mathematical applications in real-world situations are by no means trivial – the contrary is the case. Frequently it is the complexity of the real world situation that provides various challenges for the solution process. A team of future teachers were utterly surprised when encountering the difficulties that fourth graders experienced when asked to solve a "rather easy" problem from the text book that asked them to calculate the amount and cost of wallpaper needed to decorate a child's bedroom while a drawing of the room including the

A. Peter-Koop
Professor of Mathematics Education, University of Oldenburg, Germany

B. Clarke, B. Grevholm, and R. Millman (eds.), *Tasks in Primary Mathematics Teacher Education: Purpose, Use and Exemplars,* Mathematics Teacher Education 4,

dimensions of the walls, windows, door and the price of the wallpaper per roll was provided. Several children failed because they did not realise that wallpaper comes in rolls and has a standard width and length per roll. Others forgot to subtract the areas of the windows and door or failed to work out the corresponding relationship between the area in the room and the rolls of wallpaper required.

However, children's difficulties in solving real-world related word problems are not only related to complex, non-routine problems but already occur with respect to so called "routine problems" that involve the application of a simple algorithm. Due to difficulties with the comprehension of the text and the identification of the "mathematical core" of the problem, primary school children frequently engage in a rather arbitrary and random operational combination of the numbers given in the text (e.g. see Bauersfeld, 1991; Verschaffel, De Corte, & Lasure, 1994). In doing so, they fail to acknowledge the relationship between the given data and the real-world context. Failure in solving these word problems is obviously not related to a lack of practice. In a quantitative study, Renkl and Stern (1994) who analysed the data of 568 students from a total of 33 German primary classrooms found that the success rate in solving traditional word problems is not significantly improved by repeated practice. But what makes even rather simple real-world related problems so difficult?

Real-world problem solving involves the "mathematisation" of a non-mathematical situation, that is:

- the construction of a mathematical model with respect to the real-world situation,
- the finding (calculation) of the unknown, and
- the transfer of the mathematical result derived from the mathematical model to the real-world situation.

Many teachers find and also research suggests (e.g. see Winter, 1994) that the greatest difficulty in this process relates to the identification of an appropriate mathematical model, which requires context knowledge of the real-world situation as well as creativity

However, the last stage of this modelling process, the transfer of the (arithmetical) result to the real-world situation, also presents children with unexpected problems. Verschaffel and De Corte (1997) for example found that fifth graders frequently believe that "37.5 jeeps" is the correct answer to the following problem: "300 soldiers have to be transported by jeep to their training site. Each jeep can hold 8 soldiers. How many jeeps are needed?" This answer (the arithmetically correct result of the division 300/8) is furthermore resistant to correction, because children tend to persist with this answer, even when they are questioned about its sense. Checking the result of the division $300/8 = 37.5$ confirms their understanding that the answer "37.5 jeeps are needed for transportation" is the arithmetically correct result, and hence the right answer. In this context, Freudenthal (1984) points out the construction of a "magical compatibility" with respect to word problems. Because students frequently fail to relate the fictive content of the word problem to their real-life experiences, from their point of view the solution of a word problem does not need to match reality (Verschaffel, De Corte, & Lasure, 1999).

The majority of previous publications on word problem solving in primary mathematics either focus on the quantitative analysis of teaching and learning difficulties or the description of problem types, their level of difficulty and/or their potential for the teaching and learning of mathematical modelling (e.g. Silver, 1995). The mathematical modelling process itself however has not been given much attention. Pehkonen (1991) pointed out the need for the investigation of problem solving strategies and modelling processes in primary mathematics classrooms in order to complement our scientific knowledge which is currently mainly based on clinical investigations.

This chapter draws on the results of a 4-year-study involving future teachers that was initiated with the concern that little is known about primary students' real world problem solving strategies and modelling processes as related to the dynamics of group problem solving in an authentic classroom setting considering mixed abilities of the students as well as the variety of their socio-cultural experiences. Fermi-problems provided the context for the teaching experiment in grade 3 and grade 4 classrooms. However, before details of this teaching experiment, its specific tasks and its results are introduced, it is important to reflect our understanding of the modelling process.

2 Models of the Modelling Process

Heymann (2003) portrays the concept of mathematical modelling in his book on the role of mathematics for general education as follows:

"The concept of modelling can describe the applicability of mathematics and its relation to the "real" world in a very general and, at the same time, quite elementary way. Whenever mathematics is applied to describe and clarify objective situations and to solve real problems, a mathematical model is constructed (or, recourse is taken to an already existing model). Assertions about the relevant situation or solutions to the problem under examination resulting from the use of the model are not valid in isolation from the model. They are in need of interpretation and must be checked for their appropriateness" (p. 130).

With respect to the need for interpretation of the solution, the dominance of its arithmetical correctness for primary students has been outlined above.

In order to help students with respect to solving word problems, mathematics teachers often promote a systematic three-step-approach: find the question – do the calculation – give the answer (Fig. 1). This scheme is closely related to the four stages of the mathematical problem solving process described by Pólya (1957, pp. 5–16): (1) Understanding the problem, (2) Devising a plan, (3) Carrying out the plan, and (4) Looking back. Based on Pólya's distinction, in German curriculum documents the modelling process is frequently modelled itself in the following rather simplified way. The processes represented by the three arrows (modelling, data processing in the model, interpretation) correspond to the stages 2 to 4.

In order to understand why many students experience difficulties with traditional word problems that often "only" require the application of a taught procedure or

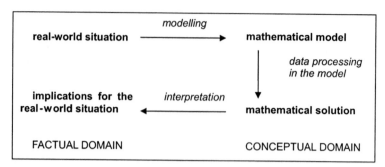

Fig. 1 Structure of the modelling process

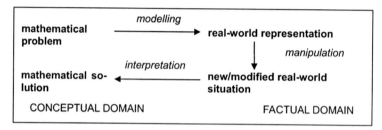

Fig. 2 Structure of the visualisation/illustration process

algorithm, it may be helpful to investigate on which basis and experiential background primary school children develop mathematical models.

In early childhood mathematics, students frequently do not experience mathematics as a tool to solve real-world problems; mathematics itself is visualised by representing sets of various objects (marbles, teddies etc.) by numbers. Hence, the structure of the modelling process (Fig. 1) can also be modelled in the reverse direction as a visualisation/ illustration process (Fig. 2).

Simple addition problems such as $3 + 4$ for example, are frequently illustrated with a little story: Anna has 3 marbles and Peter has 4. How many marbles do they have together? In the classroom situation, Anna's 3 marbles and Peter's 4 marbles are combined and counted. The combining of the two sets with 3 and 4 objects to one set with a total of 7 objects, i.e. the manipulation of a real-world situation in order to create a new or modified real-world situation, illustrates the addition process. Thus, objects, not numbers, are represented first. In this context, mathematical modelling can be understood as a reverse procedure to trusted and subconscious processes of visualisation/illustration developed in junior primary mathematics. Traditional word problems hence may not be the best context for developing mathematical modelling skills, because often the particular wording of the problem already suggests the choice of operation to be connected with the given numbers, thus the relationship between the real-world context and mathematics does not need to be explored. In order to foster and highlight cooperative mathematical modelling processes Fermi problems have been used in the classroom based study.

3 Teaching and Learning Mathematical Problem Solving

This section describes how Fermi problems provided the context for the study as well as the methodological and organisational details of the teaching experiment conducted in a grade 4 classroom in an urban schools in a city in north-western Germany. Furthermore, different student solutions will be introduced and analysed.

3.1 Fermi Problems: Context for Developing Mathematical Modelling Skills

Enrico Fermi (1901–1954), who in 1938 won the Nobel Prize for physics for his work on nuclear processes, was known by his students for posing open problems that could only be solved by giving a reasonable estimate. Fermi problems such as "How many piano tuners are there in Chicago?" share the characteristic that the initial response of the problem solver is that the problem could not possibly be solved without recourse to further reference material. However, while individuals frequently reject these problems as too difficult, Clarke and McDonough (1989) pointed out that "pupils, working in cooperative groups, come to see that the knowledge and processes to solve the problem already reside within the group" (p. 22). The following criteria guided the development/choice of problems used in the research project:

- the problems should present challenges and intrinsically motivate cooperation and interaction with peers,
- the wording of the problems should not contain numbers in order to avoid that the children immediately start calculating without first analysing the context of the given situation, and to challenge students to engage in estimation and rough calculation and/or the collection of relevant data,
- the problems should be based on a selection of real-world related situations that include reference contexts for third and fourth graders, and
- the problems should be open-beginning as well as open-ended real-world related tasks that require decision making with respect to the modelling process.

Overall ten such problems were either selected from the literature or developed by future teachers in a methods course and then trialled in a pilot study. The following four problems met the above criteria best and provoked mathematically rich solutions. Therefore they were chosen for the main study and posed in grade 3 and grade 4 mathematics classes during the teaching experiments:

- How much paper does your school use in 1 month?
- How many children are as heavy as a polar bear? (van den Heuvel-Panhuizen, (1996)
- Your class is planning a trip to visit the Cologne Cathedral. Is it better to travel by bus or by train?

- There is a 3 km tailback on the A1 motorway between Muenster and Bremen. How many vehicles are caught in this traffic jam?

The traffic problem which was taped from the radio traffic announcements one morning fascinated the students most and stimulated heated discussions and impressive mathematical thinking. It was therefore selected for discussion in this chapter.

3.2 The Classroom-Based Study

This section focuses on the conduction of the teaching experiment in a grade 4 classroom and offers a detailed description of the students' solutions to this problem.

3.2.1 Introducing the Problem

The lessons conducted as part of the study all followed the same procedure: After the presentation the problem a brief round of discussion was allowed in order to make sure that all students had understood the task. The class then was split into small groups of four or five children. In this particular grade 4 class the students were invited to form their own groups which led to a group formation primarily based on friendship, gender and similar ability. The members of two of these groups (one male, one female) were also so called "low achievers".

Equipment and literature for the data collection (such as scales, information on bus/train fares, books on animals, measuring tapes etc.) were held available for immediate use according to specific requests by the students. Each lesson took 90 min. Up to 60 min were allowed for the group work (half of this time was frequently needed for the data collection and background research) and the remaining time was used for the introduction and discussion of the group's solution. It was made clear to the groups that their work would be presented to the whole class and that each group member was expected to be able to describe and explain the group's solution. A worksheet was provided for the groups to write down their work and overhead copies of these worksheets helped the students to explain their work as well as to relate to the results and strategies of the other groups during the strategy conferences (see 3.2.3) following the group work. The students were encouraged to generate tables, make drawings (see Fig. 3), or do little experiments in order to foster their solution processes.

3.2.2 Data Collection and Analysis

While solving the problem, each group was videotaped. In order to ensure sufficient audio quality, the groups were working in different rooms supervised by two future teachers – one being responsible for the audio and video recording, the other acted in the teacher's role observing and supporting the group with material requested and organisational advise while not interfering with their solution process. Small group

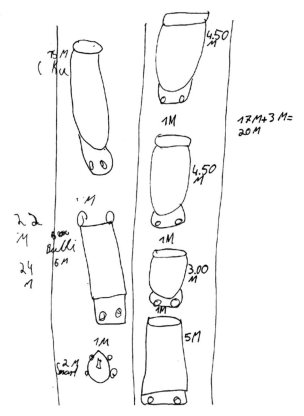

Fig. 3 Drawing of group B showing 1 m separation of vehicles

work was chosen for two reasons: (1) Fermi problems are often rejected when posed for individual work because they are perceived to be too difficult, and (2) the audio recordings of the group discussions allow insight into the process of the solution in addition to studying the product, i.e. the work sheets with the different groups' solutions which will be introduced in the following subsection (for a detailed analysis of the interaction patterns displayed in the group work see Peter-Koop, 2002).

The methodological framework of the project was based on the interpretative research paradigm (Bauersfeld, Krummheuer, & Voigt, 1988). Researchers conducting interpretative classroom research seek to investigate typical structures by analysing single cases which are regarded as exemplary. Their focus is the "universal in the special case" and the goal of the interpretation is to comprehensively perceive and understand the (inter)actions of the observed individuals. The significance of the interpretative research paradigm is related to an international change from content-based and individual-psychological approaches towards interpersonal human relations in (mathematics) education. The data collection and interpretation involved future teachers as teacher-researchers (Peter-Koop, 2001) following a strict analytical procedure (for details regarding this procedure see Peter-Koop & Wollring, 2001).

3.2.3 Strategy Conferences and Assessment

For the presentation and discussion of the groups' results, the whole class came back together in their maths room for strategy conferences at the end of the lesson. These strategy conferences were also videotaped and subsequently analysed.

It is interesting to note that young children obviously prefer what seems to be an unstructured approach which often only during the presentation of their work to the whole class becomes systematic (Peschel, 1996). Hence, the strategy conferences lessons provided substantial opportunity for the students to reflect on and compare their work with other approaches. In this context, the fact that there was always more than one reasonable and acceptable solution only initially presented the children with irritation and led to controversial discussions. After that, they demonstrated increasing confidence and enjoyment with respect to the challenges set by the different problems.

While, traditionally, the assessment if the problem solution is seen as the responsibility of the teacher, the strategy conferences also provide a suitable forum for peer assessment. In this context each student has two roles: on the one hand as a group member he/she shares responsibility regarding the appropriate solution of the given task and its presentation. On the other hand, each student also acts as a critical and informed evaluator with respect to the work of the other groups and hence has to argue from both perspectives. In our observations, this led to friendly and constructive criticism while successful solutions and innovative approaches were honoured with praise.

3.2.4 Results of the Group Work in a Grade 4 Class

Immediately after the video recordings of the group work episodes, the future teachers involved expressed the impression that the work in the groups was "rather chaotic" and "haphazard". However, the groups' working sheets suggest, that most groups – including the low achievers – were highly successful in finding an appropriate solution to the question of how many cars would be caught in the 3 km traffic jam. While the future teachers were clearly impressed with the accuracy of the children's estimates, at the same time most of them were doubtful as to whether the group members would be able to present and explain their solution to the whole class. As it turned out, with the exception of one mixed-ability group, all groups from this grade 4 class managed to explain their solution process. Interestingly enough, it was the group (group B) who illustrated the situation in a drawing (see Fig. 3) of their understanding of a traffic jam acknowledging a one metre separation gap between the vehicles.

Figure 4 in contrast shows the work sheet of group C. The solution of this four supposedly low achieving boys clearly reflects the ideas and strategies they have developed. The first part of the group work was dedicated to measuring the length of different vehicles in the school car park and the direct school neighbourhood. In our experience most groups preferred to work with authentic data rather than basing their work on estimations.

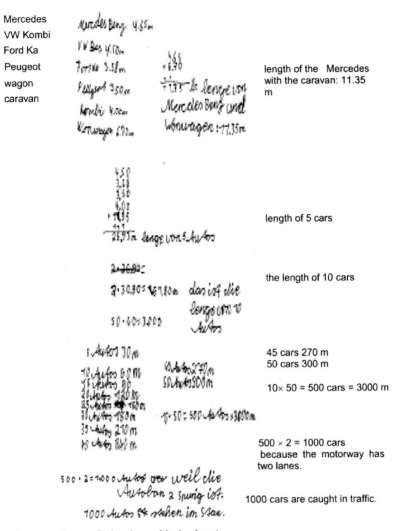

Mercedes		
VW Kombi		
Ford Ka		
Peugeot		length of the Mercedes with the caravan: 11.35 m
wagon		
caravan		

length of 5 cars

the length of 10 cars

45 cars 270 m
50 cars 300 m

$10 \times 50 = 500$ cars = 3000 m

$500 \times 2 = 1000$ cars because the motorway has two lanes.

1000 cars are caught in traffic.

Fig. 4 Solution of group C (four low-achieving boys)

After initial difficulties rounding the calculated 26.93 m length of five cars to a more manageable number they struggled for some time to understand the proportional relationship between the number of cars and their added lengths. The derived number of cars (500) they finally multiplied by two because they thought the motorway in the section between the two cities had two lanes.

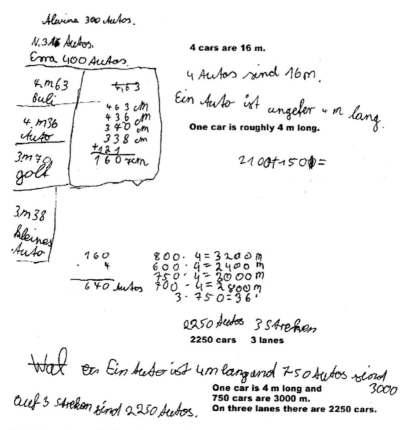

Fig. 5 Solution of group D (four low-achieving girls)

The four low-achieving girls in group D started their group work by the recording of their individual estimates of the cars caught in the 3 km traffic jam (see Fig. 5). However, they realised the need to mathematically validate these estimates in order to find out which is most accurate. Like the other groups they collected data by measuring different vehicles in the school car park. When adding their length they realise that their total length was about 16 m and conclude that one vehicle is roughly 4 m long. Having established an estimate of the length of one car they then tried to find a number that multiplied with 4 equals 3,000. Based on their knowledge of times tables they attempted to determine that number – first trying 800 which was too big, then 600 which turned out to be too little, then 700 and finally 750. One girl insisted that the motorway between Muenster and Bremen had 3 lanes, hence they multiplied 750 by 3 and arrive at the answer 2,250 cars.

While groups B and C managed to mathematically model the given situation I a way that lead to plausible – yet still not perfect solutions as the discussions during the strategy conference suggested – the three boys and two girls of group A (a mixed ability group) did not manage to find such a solution and were quite aware of that fact. Their answer was 51 cars – a number they realised to be definitely too small. However, several reviews of their solution process including some stimulus from the future teacher looking after this group did not lead them to realise the mistake in their mathematical model (see Fig. 6). They started by repeatedly adding the lengths of different vehicles they had measured and found that this was not an optimal approach when they found the length of 17 cars to be roughly 115 m. Through multiplication they then tried to reach 3,000 m – firstly multiplying by 9 (2,035 m) and then by 3 (3,105 m). However, while they were multiplying the metres, unlike group C they did not recognise the proportional relationship between the total length and number of the vehicles. Hence, they considered 17 cars to be the number of cars in one lane and multiply that by 3 which gives them a total of 51 cars, because they know that the stretch of motorway has three lanes.

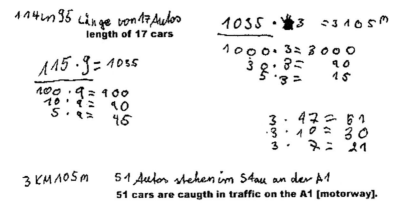

length of 17 cars

51 cars are caugth in traffic on the A1 [motorway].

Fig. 6 Calculation of group A (a mixed ability group of three boys and two girls)

In order to solve the traffic problem in a satisfactory way for the whole class, the strategy conference was of crucial importance. During the introduction and discussion of the different solutions by the four groups several aspects became clear: When being confronted with the group C's solution the members of group A realised their mistake, while the boys of group C learned from group A and group D that the respective motorway stretch has three lanes. Group D was confronted with the criticism that their data sample did not include trucks or caravans and therefore would not authentically model the types of vehicles using a motorway. Furthermore, all three groups realised the potential for improvement of their solutions when they saw the drawing of group B (see Fig. 3) that suggested to add 1 m to each vehicle to acknowledge the distance between the vehicles in the model.

The depth and quality of the classroom discussion and the structured and well explained introduction of the solutions by the groups came as surprise for the future teachers involved in the study. After the completion of the group work they expressed their perception of the group work to a large extent as "chaotic, unstructured and erratic" and their doubts as to whether the group members would be able to present and explain their solutions and critically assess the solution processes of their peers. The opposite held true.

4 Understanding the Modelling Process

The interpretative analyses to a large degree confirm the future teachers initial impressions. In general, the sequential analyses of the transcripts reveal a rather aimless and unstructured approach. Most groups did not develop and then execute a solution plan as suggested by Pólya (1957). Hence, the modelling processes did not match the strategy taught in class (question–calculation–answer). However, understanding the problem (the first stage described by Pólya) obviously played an important role in the solution, because extensive discussions of the real-word situation and related personal experiences generally preceded the mathematical modelling process. Furthermore, the analyses frequently identified a slowly developing process in which hypotheses were generated, tested, confirmed or neglected while arithmetic results were interpreted leading to the development of further solution ideas. The literature, however, suggests only one modelling cycle (see Fig. 1). The interpretative analyses in contrast suggested an interweaving of the factual and the conceptual domain. But the transcripts of the group work turned out to be too detailed to enable identification of the underlying general structure of the students' modelling processes. Therefore, the transcripts were condensed in the format of episode plans (see Fig. 8 on the following page) in order to highlight the stages characterising the mathematical modelling approach. These episode plans indicate that the different stages outlined in the literature are revisited several times. Figure 7 shows the modelling process demonstrated by group C which is representative of the analysis of other group work episodes.

The analysis of the classroom based data suggests that word problems with a high level of complexity (such as Fermi problems) can be solved in sensible and appropriate ways by third and fourth graders. While in traditional problem solving at primary school level only one modelling cycle is needed, Fermi problems can serve as "model-eliciting tasks" (Lesh & Doerr, 2000), because the required modelling process extends beyond the application of a standard algorithm and necessitates multiple modelling cycles with multiple ways of thinking about givens, goals, and solution paths (Bell, 1993). Lesh and Doerr point out that model development is learning. In this context, the group work data shown above indicates that the outcome of the modelling activity is a conceptual tool that exceeds the solution of a specific problem. During their solution process, the four fourth graders of group C (supposedly low achievers) developed new mathematical knowledge. Their working (see Fig. 4) as well as the interpretations of the group work documents that they have discovered the concept of proportionality in using proportional calculation in order

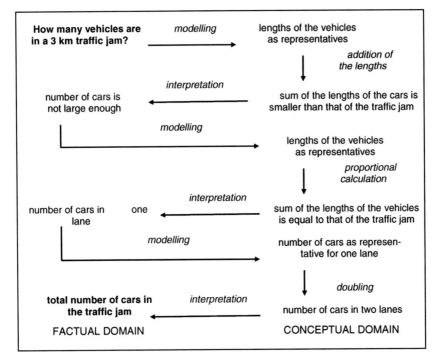

Fig. 7 Graphical representation of the modelling process of group C

to determine the number of cars in a 3 km tailback based on their estimate that five cars occupy ∼30 m. In addition, the four girls in group D who were also considered as low achievers by their teacher, discovered the concept of mean, which to that point had not been taught, when reflecting the result of the addition of the length of four different vehicles.

The results of this study agree with the findings from the analyses of secondary students' modelling processes by Lesh and Doerr (2000) who highlighted "the need for teachers to examine students' developing models in order to assess student knowledge and understanding and to foster continued model development in ways that evolve as the student models evolve" (p. 375). Qualitative analyses of the future teachers' learning processes document that they had profoundly underestimated primary students' mathematical modelling competencies. In addition, this study revealed multi-cyclic modelling processes in contrast to a single modelling cycle as suggested in the literature. Hence, it can be concluded that mathematical modelling processes should be given more attention in mathematics teacher education as well as mathematics education research.

Episode Plan "Traffic-Problem"
Preparation Phase
André reads out the problem again and the group decides to measure some cars in the school car park. After returning to the classroom the lengths of different cars are noted on the worksheet.
1st Idea Phase
David and Peter argue, that the caravan can not be considered by itself – it needs a large car pulling it.
1st Calculation Phase
The lengths of the Mercedes and the caravan are added (11.35 m).
2nd Idea Phase
The children collect ideas as to what needs to be calculated and what other information could be relevant for solving the problem. They decide to start by adding the measured lengths of the cars in the car park.
2nd Calculation Phase
The lengths of the 4 cars and the Mercedes and caravan together are added (26.93 m).
1st Reflection/Recording Phase
The future teacher helps the children to deter-mine the number of the vehicles (5)
3rd Idea Phase
The students think about how the arithmetic result can be related to the total length of the traffic jam.
2nd Reflection/Recording Phase
The total length of the 5 vehicles is noted.
3rd Calculation Phase
The students want to round the result (26.93 m). David suggests to round it up to 30.90 m
4th Idea Phase
Once again the students try to make a relation to the length of the traffic jam.
3rd Reflection/Recording Phase
The future teacher summarises their thinking and the according interim results so far.
5th Idea Phase
David suggests to double the determined length of 5 cars and to round this result.
4th Calculation Phase
David and Ralf calculate 2 x 30.90 m.
4th Reflection/Recording Phase
They decide to write down that the total length of 10 cars is 61.80 m.
6th Idea Phase
The students try to find out how to get to 3000 m based on the 60 m that they have calculated so far.
5th Reflection/Recording Phase
The future teacher repeats that the total length of 5 cars is 30 metres and that of 10 cars 60 metres.
5th Calculation Phase
They continue to calculate the total length of 15 cars (90 m) ... 50 cars (300 m) and call out the results.
7th Idea Phase
David suggests to multiply the last result by 10, because he realised that 10 x 300 is 3000.
6th Calculation Phase
Together they multiply 10 times 50.
6th Reflection/Recording Phase
Prompted by the future teacher they write down their calculation (10 x 50 = 500 cars = 3000 m).
8th Idea Phase
André points out that the motorway has 2 lanes.
7th Calculation Phase
They multiply their result (500 cars) by 2.
7th Reflection/Recording Phase
David summarises again why they doubled their result and writes the answer sentence.

Fig. 8 Episode plan based on the transcript of the group work episode of group C

References

Bauersfeld, H. (1991). Sachaufgaben! – Nichts als Ärger!? *Grundschulzeitschrift*, *42*, 8–10.

Bauersfeld, H., Krummheuer, G., & Voigt, J. (1988). Interactional theory of learning and teaching mathematics and related mircroethnographical studies. In H.-G. Steiner & A. Vermandel (Eds.), *Foundations and methodology of the discipline mathematics education* (pp. 174–188). Bielefeld: Bielefeld University, IDM.

Bell, M. (1993). Modelling and applications of mathematics in the primary curriculum. In T. Breiteig, I. Huntley, & G. Kaiser-Messmer (Eds.), *Teaching and learning mathematics in context* (pp. 71–80). London: Ellis Horwood.

Clarke, D. J., & McDonough, A. (1989). The problems of the problem-solving classroom. *The Australian Mathematics Teacher*, *45*(2), 20–24.

de Lange, J. (1998). Real problems with real world mathematics. In C. Alsina, J. Alvarez, M. Niss, A. Pérez, L. Rico, & A. Sfard (Eds.), *Proceedings of the 8th International Congress on Mathematical Education* (pp. 83–110). Seville: SAEM Thales.

Freudenthal, H. (1984). Wie alt ist der Kapitän? *Mathematik lehren*, 5, 38–39.

Heymann, H. W. (2003). *Why teach mathematics? A focus on general education.* Dordrecht: Kluwer.

Lesh, R., & Doerr, H. (2000). Symbolizing, communicating and mathematizing: Key components of models and modelling. In P. Cobb, E. Yackel, & K. McClain (Eds.), *Symbolizing and communicating in mathematics classrooms* (pp. 361–383). Mahwah, NJ: Erlbaum.

Pehkonen, E. (1991). Developments in the understanding of problem solving. *Zentralblatt für Mathematikdidaktik*, *23*(2), 46–50.

Peschel, F. (1996). *Offener Unterricht am Ende – oder erst am Anfang?* Projekt OASE Bericht No. 2, FB2 der Universität Gesamthochschule Siegen.

Peter-Koop, A. (2001). From "teachers researchers" to "student teacher researchers": Diagnostically enriched didactics. In M. van den Heuvel-Panhuizen (Ed.), *Proceedings of the 25th conference of the International Group for the Psychology of Mathematics Education* (Vol. 1, pp. 72–79). Utrecht University.

Peter-Koop, A. (2002). Real-world problem solving in small groups: Interaction patterns of third and fourth graders. In B. Barton, C. Irwin, M. Pfannkuch, & M. O. J. Thomas (Eds.), *Mathematics education in the south pacific* (Proceedings of the 25th annual conference of the Mathematics Education Research Group of Australasia, Auckland, pp. 559–566). Sydney: MERGA.

Peter-Koop, A., & Wollring, B. (2001). Student teacher participation in interpretative classroom research projects. *Mathematics Teacher Education and Development*, 3, 4–15.

Pólya, G. (1957). *How to solve it. A new aspect of mathematical method.* Princeton, NJ: Princeton University Press.

Reed, S. K. (1999). *Word problems. Research and curriculum reform.* Mahwah, NJ: Erlbaum.

Renkl, A., & Stern, E. (1994). Die Bedeutung von kognitiven Eingangsvoraussetzungen und schulischen Lerngelegenheiten für das Lösen von einfachen und komplexen Textaufgaben. *Zeitschrift für Pädagogische Psychologie*, *8*(1), 27–39.

Silver, E. A. (1995). The nature and use of open problems in mathematics education: Mathematical and pedagogical perspectives. *Zentralblatt für Didaktik der Mathematik*, *27*(2), 67–72.

van den Heuvel-Panhuizen, M. (1996). *Assessment and realistic mathematics education.* Utrecht: CD-B Press, Utrecht University.

Verschaffel, L., & De Corte, E. (1997). Teaching realistic mathematical modelling and problem solving in the elementary school. A teaching experiment with fifth graders. *Journal for Research in Mathematics Education*, *28*(5), 577–601.

Verschaffel, L., De Corte, E., & Lasure, S. (1994). Realistic considerations in mathematical modelling of school arithmetic word problems. *Learning and Instruction*, 4, 273–294.

Verschaffel, L., De Corte, E., & Lasure, S. (1999). Children's conceptions about the role of real-world knowledge in mathematical modelling of school word problems. In W. Schnotz, S. Vosniadou, M. Carretero (Eds.), *New perspectives on conceptual change* (pp. 175–189). Oxford, UK: Elsevier Science.

Verschaffel, L., Greer, B., and de Corte, E. (2000). *Making sense of word problems*. Lisse: Svets Zeitlinger.

Winter, H. (1994). Modelle als Konstrukte zwischen lebensweltlichen Situationen und arithmetischen Begriffen. *Grundschule, 26*(3), 10–13.

A Research-Based Workshop Design for Volume Tasks

Mariana Sáiz and Olimpia Figueras

Three tasks related to the concept of volume that are suitable for workshops designed for inservice and preservice primary school teachers are described; in some cases, they are useful for secondary school teachers as well. The tasks have been selected in order to serve as a means to confront specific common errors and misconceptions related to the concept of volume reported in the research literature on mathematics education, and to support teachers in a process of rethinking about their knowledge of this concept. For each one of the tasks an explanation of why it was selected is included and the difficulties that can be brought to discussion and the competencies that can be developed when carrying them out are described. The way to perform the tasks is illustrated and their objectives are mentioned. Variants and possible modifications of the tasks are included. The results of the experiences applying the tasks are presented and what was observed during those applications is discussed, so there is a foresight and a point of comparison for those who wish to use them in the future.

1 Introduction

As is well known, volume is a mathematical concept included in the primary and secondary school curricula of many countries. In our experience as teachers' educators, we have found that school primary teachers pointed out volume as a difficult concept to teach and to learn, together with fractions and division. One reason of

M. Sáiz
Professor, Learning and Teaching of sciences, humanities and arts, Universidad Pedagógica Nacional Mexico City, Mexico

O. Figueras
Researcher, Mathematics Education Department of the Center for Research and Advanced Studies of the National Poly-technique Institute (Cinvestav), Mexico

B. Clarke, B. Grevholm, and R. Millman (eds.), *Tasks in Primary Mathematics Teacher Education: Purpose, Use and Exemplars,* Mathematics Teacher Education 4,

the complexity of the concept of volume is its several meanings; Piaget, Inhelder, and Szeminska (1970) found three different meanings assigned by children to the term *volume*. The first one is interior volume, for which these researchers use two definitions that they consider equivalent: "the number of unit bricks in the construction" (p. 360) and "the amount of matter which is contained within the boundary surfaces" (p. 359). The second meaning of volume is as occupied space that is "the amount of space occupied by the object as a whole in relation to other objects round about" (p. 360) and the third one is complementary volume, which refers to the volume of the water displaced when a body is submerged. From our research experience, other meanings were found: volume as a number and volume as a quality "associated with the bodies' characteristic of having three dimensions" (Sáiz, 2003).

Another difficulty with the teaching and learning of volume is a tendency to use this term as a synonym for capacity and the lack of relationship between the two concepts except for that given at school by the equivalence between the measurement units of capacity and volume. Further complexities of this mathematical concept are linked to its physical nature that relates it with other properties of bodies such as surface area, weight, and mass and the Archimedean principle.

From a solely mathematical point of view, the concept of volume entails a lot of complications besides the difficulties related to any type of magnitude such as length, area, capacity or weight; for example the effect on the volume by enlarging or diminishing a body's linear dimensions and others that will be mentioned later on.

In this chapter three tasks related to the concept of volume that are suggested as appropriate for teachers attending basic training and upgrading courses are described. The tasks have been proved effective in several workshops for inservice teachers carried out in different places in Mexico. These tasks are also suited for future teachers as will be discuss throughout this chapter.

When the tasks were designed or selected, the first objective was to obtain information for a research study about primary school teachers' conceptions related to the concept of volume. One aim at that moment was to make teachers "think aloud" about volume's features and properties. In the context of our professional duties and commitment to give quality mathematics courses for inservice teachers, a workshop about volume for inservice primary school teachers was offered. Information obtained during the building up of the theoretical framework developed for the aforementioned research was taken into account for the selection of tasks, activities and problems that were to be included in the workshop.

In order to develop that framework, the phenomenological analysis applied by Freudenthal (1983) to the concept of volume was considered and a review of literature about the teaching and learning of the concept of volume regarding children and adults was carried out. In this process the more common errors and misconceptions related to this concept were identified. Some of these are:

- Children have difficulties with two-dimensional representations of bodies; specifically with counting cubes that are not visible (Battista & Clements, 1996; Figueras & Waldegg, 1986; Hart, Brown, Kerslake, Küchemann, & Ruddock, 1985)
- Children do not distinguish between weight and volume (Potari & Spiliotopoulou, 1996; Ricco & Vergnaud, 1983).

- Children believe that enlarging k-times the linear magnitudes of a body enlarges k-times its volume (Hart et al., 1985; Ricco & Vergnaud, 1983).
- Children and teachers do not distinguish between volume and capacity (Janvier, 1994; Potari & Spiliotopoulou, 1996; Sáiz, 2002, 2005).
- Children and teachers do not distinguish between surface area and volume (Enochs and Gabel, 1984; Janvier, 1997; Ricco & Vergnaud, 1983).
- Children and teachers believe that two bodies with equal surface area have the same volume (Janvier, 1994, 1997; Sáiz & Figueras, 2000).
- Children and teachers relate the rise of liquid to weight rather than to volume (Freudenthal, 1983; Potari & Spiliotopoulou, 1996; Sáiz & Figueras, 2000).
- Teachers have difficulties obtaining a body's volume if it does not have a regular form (Enochs and Gabel, 1984; Sáiz, 2003).
- Teachers have difficulties working with volume units and relating units of volume and capacity (Enochs and Gabel, 1984; Sáiz, 2002, 2005).

In the course of selecting and designing the tasks, we noticed that a task suitable for making teachers "think aloud" was compatible with making them reason, reconsider their ideas, and look at an old concept from a new point of view. We considered that this approach, together with the fact that the tasks were organized in a workshop (where the dynamic was based on working in teams, discussing ideas with peers and so on) would make teachers participating in the experience build up a new and/or richer conceptualization of the concept of volume.

As previously mentioned, the first time the tasks were applied we also had a research agenda. Therefore it was decided to video and audio record the workshop sessions in order to have some evidence of the tasks' effectiveness, strengths, weaknesses and possibilities. In subsequent applications of the tasks there has been no systematic data collection; nevertheless it has been observed that many of the results obtained in the first application occur.

2 General Aspects of the Workshop

In our experience, organizing participants in teams of three or four inservice teachers works well. At the same time, when a problem or task is first introduced to the students we consider it important that all participants first read the problem or instructions silently. For some of the tasks posed, it's important to request an initial intuitive answer. Afterwards, participants are invited to discuss how to solve the problem or carry out the activity with their team partners and together come up with a conclusion that satisfies all participants. Once team members have reached an internal agreement about how to solve the problem, a final discussion is held in which the diverse approaches applied by the members of all teams are shared and all participants comment about their thoughts, strategies, answers and conclusions. After a general agreement is reached regarding the solution(s) of the problem or task performed, it's interesting to promote a discussion about the relation between the problem just solved and teachers' professional practice.

Some questions that may be posed to initiate such a discussion are: Do you think this task is applicable to your present or future pupils? How would you modify this task or problem to fit into your regular practice? Do you think that it's not possible to incorporate this problem into your daily practice? What do you think will be the principal difficulties that children confront when solving this task? How will you help children solve the problem?

3 The Tasks

For each one of the tasks described in the following sections:

1. An explanation of the activity and how to implement it is given; providing when necessary its potential variants and possible courses of action to follow depending on the events taking place during its presentation.
2. A description of the errors or misconceptions that the activity is designed to make participants confront is made, mentioning the published source or experience in which a difficulty was first reported.
3. Tasks' objectives are mentioned.
4. Comments about the application of the activity and the various experiences that it promoted are included, and
5. The results of analyses of previous information are given.

3.1 Task One: The Cylinders

The following problem is posed to the workshop participants:

> A factory produces tanks made of rectangular metal sheets. The tanks have no top and the bottom is made with other material, so the rectangular metal sheets are only used for the cylinder's contour. If we want the tanks to have the largest capacity possible, and if we consider that length is the longest side of the rectangle and width the shortest one, answer the following questions: Is it more convenient to roll the sheets lengthwise or width-wise? Is the result the same? Justify or explain your answer.

Before performing any calculation it's a good idea to ask participants to give a first intuitive answer and to register on the blackboard:

1. How many of the participants think that the first cylinder will have the largest volume?
2. How many teachers think that the second cylinder have the largest volume?
3. How many think that both will have the same volume?

In each case it's important that participants explain their responses.

4 Why did the Cylinder Task was Included in the Workshop?

At the time the first workshop was set up, one of the few published results concerning teachers' conceptions about volume was Enochs and Gabel's report (1984) about the confusion teachers participating in their study had with volume and surface area. The common belief: "As the surface area of a body increases, so does its volume", has also been observed by Ricco & Vergnaud (1983) who carried out their study with children.

More recently, Merseth (2003) describes a case related to this conception, involving this task, which she called "Slippery Cylinders". Although Merseth's work is not a research report, the cases discussed in her book are results of her work as an instructor of teachers, so the situation and the examples presented in the cases reflect a real experience. The actors in that case were future teachers, and the problem was proposed in almost the same way as the one we posed to the inservice teachers – one difference being that participants were also asked to obtain the lateral surface area. As in our study, Merseth (2003) also asked for a first intuitive answer finding that the larger part of participants believed that both cylinders would have the same volume. After they were given the chance to perform calculations they couldn't trust their result: the two cylinders had different volume. Merseth mentions that even three students who had correctly solved the problem eagerly checked their calculations; they were sure that cylinders had equal volumes and thought this incredible outcome was due to a numerical mistake.

5 Objectives of the Task

As it has been said, it is important to ask teachers for a first intuitive response because they acquire awareness of the beliefs they have regarding the topic.

The main objective of the activity is to make future teachers consider the truth of the statement: If bodies have equal lateral surface areas (not including the lids) then they have equal volumes. However, the activity involves other knowledge or skills such as the application of the formula to obtain the volume of a cylinder and the development of competencies related to spatial imagination, among others.

6 Experiences Applying the Cylinder Task

1. Most of the teachers when reading the problem thought that both cylinders have the same volume.
2. Some teachers solve the problem making two cylinders like those described in the problem using sheets of paper and filling them with seeds to compare their volumes. With only these outcomes, of a particular case, which were what they expected, they generalize the results. Most of the teams used a letter-sized sheet

of paper. In some cases, teachers constructed two paper rectangles, more often than not their dimensions were 5 cm by 10 cm.

3. Teachers who solve the problem using an arithmetical approach assigned a given value to the dimensions of the rectangle, frequently, the length and width of a letter-size sheet of paper, and applied the formula $V = \pi r^2 h$. The result they obtained with this single example was enough for them to reach a general result: "it is better to roll lengthwise".

4. After the experience, some teachers, insisted that as surface area increases so does the volume, reasoning that the area of the contour of both cylinders is the same, but not that of the lids.

7 Analysis

From point 1 above, it can be observed that the belief that the same surface area gives place to the same volume is a common misconception. There are teachers that doubt or disagree with this response; however, in the majority of cases this is due to a suspicion that in this kind of workshop the questions always have a surprising answer. Merseth (2003) also mentions this behaviour in her experience.

In several occasions we found that primary school teachers were reluctant to deal with problems in which no numerical data is provided. It is relevant to recall that Ricco & Vergnaud (1983) observed that children showed the same type of resistance to begin a reasoning process when they were confronted with a problem lacking numbers.

As was mentioned before, spatial imagination is needed for solving the problem: for some teachers it's not clear that the perimeter of the cylinders' base corresponds to the length of the sheet's side, so dividing by 2π they will obtain the radius of the basis which is needed to calculate its area and then the cylinder's volume. That is why they prefer to construct the cylinders and compare their volume using seeds. A similar difficulty is also mentioned by Merseth (2003): a student peeled off the tape she had used to attach the sides of the paper to form a cylinder in order to understand how to calculate the lateral surface area.

During Merseth's experience some future teachers insisted that the volumes were the same because they believed that volume is "perimeter times height". This confusion was not perceived in our experiences.

On various occasions the cylinder task has been posed to groups of primary school teachers; the use of literals or algebraic methods to solve the problem has not been observed. Although, as pointed out in point 3 (see previous section), teachers generalize their results taking into account the outcomes of one single example. In some cases, suggestions have been made to teachers for trying to generalize their results using algebra, and with a good deal of assistance they were able to find a general response.

As may be concluded from point 4, the cylinder problem is not ideal for the activity's objective, which is to make teachers observe that some bodies with the same surface area may have different volumes, because, in the case of the cylinders, despite the contour being the same, the lid of the cylinder with a smaller volume will always have a lesser surface area than the lid of the cylinder with a larger volume; thus, teachers may persist in their idea. Nevertheless, the problem must not be discarded because it generates insights concerning the surface area-volume relationship.

When teachers argue that the smallest surface area is the one with the smaller volume, it is useful to pose other problems. A simple one is to construct different structures with six cubes and calculate the total surface area for each one, and then focus the attention of teachers on structures that have different surface areas although their volume is fixed. A more complicated problem is the following: a box with a square base is going to be constructed out of a piece of cardboard that has a side measuring 60 cm. To do so, small squares of length c will be cut from the corners of the original cardboard and then the sides will be folded up by the dot line. How long must c be in order to make a box with the largest volume possible? (Janvier, 1994).

This problem reveals that while c increases, making surface area smaller, volume increases to a maximum and then decreases.

7.1 Task 2: The Eiffel Tower

The following problem was proposed to teams of teachers in workshops:

> The height of the Eiffel Tower is 300 m; it is made of iron and it weighs 8,000 tons. A reproduction of the tower is going to be made. If we want to make a model of iron that weighs one kilogram, how tall must it be? Before doing any calculations try to guess: will it be taller than, smaller than, or as tall as a one litre bottle of milk? (Balbuena et al., 1995).

8 Why was the "Eiffel Tower" Task Included in the Workshop?

The effect on volume of enlarging or reducing the dimensions of a body is an important fact, as Freudenthal (1983) states: "Understanding that the multiplication of length by d, areas by d^2, volumes by d^3 go together with the geometrical multiplication by d, is mathematically so fundamental, that, phenomenologically and didactically it should be put first and foremost" (p. 267).

Ricco and Vergnaud (1983) named this idea "homothecy" and they mentioned its significance in the conceptualization of volume's formula. They also mentioned the difficulties homothecy carries for children. In Hart et al. (1985) we found that in the test they applied to secondary school pupils, a problem that involves this kind of relation is one with a lesser percentage of success. Also we have found in the course of our experience, that some teachers share the belief that doubling the linear magnitudes of a body doubles its volume.

9 Objectives and Goals of the Task

One of the main objectives of the Eiffel Tower task is that teachers use the homothecy relationship. A related goal of this objective is to focus the attention of teachers at the relationship between weight and volume. The fact that the problem states that the original tower and the model are made out of the same material is important. At a later stage of the workshop, it results interesting to ask the teachers what could be said if the model is made with a different material. To promote the use of tables to register the results of calculations, that is, to organize data is another goal that could be pursued. Other principal objectives of the Eiffel Tower task are to encourage teachers to search for a proper strategy to solve the problem and to obtain a general procedure to solve similar problems.

10 Experiences Applying the Task

1. Most of the teachers, when they tried to guess the height of the model, thought that it will be as tall as a bottle of milk (almost 30 cm, while the correct answer is 1.5 m).
2. The majority of the teachers use a linear proportionality to solve the problem; they calculated 300/8,000,000. Before they did the division, they suspected something was wrong and when they obtained the result they were sure they were mistaken.
3. Some of the participants recognize that the answer obtained (with the procedure explained in point 2) was incorrect but could not explain why that was wrong.
4. More often than not, in order for teachers to find the solution to the problem it was necessary to solve similar – but easier – problems first. Examples are doubling the linear magnitudes of a box or a rectangular prism made of cubes and observing what happens to its volume.
5. In a workshop session with five primary school teachers who were trying to solve this task, after constructing several prisms and doubling their linear magnitudes, they discovered that the volume is multiplied by eight always. One of the teachers asked: "Where does this eight come from?" That comment provided an invaluable opportunity to invite them to think about the general case of a prism with length a, width b and height c. One of the students went to the blackboard and drew the "doubled prism" at the same time that she wrote the new dimensions:

2a, 2b, and 2c. The *eight* appeared in a natural way: $2 \times 2 \times 2$. Then the question: "What happens if the linear magnitudes are all multiplied by three?" was posed smoothly. After two or three examples teachers referred to the general case and found out that one needs to multiply the former volume by 27. They realized that multiplication by 27 is the same as: $3 \times 3 \times 3$. Continuing in that way for 4 and 5 and carrying out the necessary computations the teachers found out that enlarging the linear dimensions by k causes the volume to increase by k^3.

11 Analysis

As was stated in point 1, the most common guess is that the model will measure about 30 cm. Perhaps this is so because in Mexico 1-litre milk bottles are approximately that height and a litre of milk weighs almost 1 kg.

People do not compensate in order to distribute the weight from the rectangular prism to the slender and graceful form of the Eiffel Tower. Nevertheless, this first approximation to the real answer is helpful because it provokes a conflict with the response obtained by applying a linear model to the relation between height and volume (a fact established in point 2 regarding the applications of the Eiffel Tower task).

Using a linear relation is a response that has also been observed in the case of some secondary school mathematics teachers. In Mexico, secondary school mathematics teachers have a stronger mathematical background than primary teachers and must have mastered algebraic procedures. Nevertheless, their first attempt to solve the problem was of the same type as that made by primary school teachers.

Regarding this behaviour Owens and Outhred (2006) have said: "Research on proportional and non-proportional reasoning related to area and volume tasks indicate how powerful an impact the linear model has on student reasoning" (p. 104). This coincides with our own experiences working with volume.

The Eiffel Tower problem is suitable for the task's objective because the answer obtained by using the erroneous procedure is absurd (as mentioned in point 2), so teachers become eager to understand what is going on and are favourably disposed to work with the homothecy relation.

Another important feature is highlighted in point 4: a very simple procedure is obtained when using a convenient factorization of 8,000,000 (once 8,000 tons have been converted to kilograms). When teachers solved other easier, but similar problems, they found out that when dividing the height by 2, the weight has to be divided by 8. In this way, they apply this procedure sequentially and arrive at an approximation of 3.8 kg. If they divide again by 8 they arrive at an answer of $\sim$0.48 kg. At this point some of them paralyzed – they did not know how to obtain a better approximation. Others began again: this time they first divided the length by 3 and the volume by 27 and continued dividing length by 2 and weight by 8, obtaining a better approximation: 1.13 kg and 1.56 m tall.

As has been pointed out, this problem has been posed to secondary school mathematics' teachers and they also answered as mentioned in points 1 and 2. When making secondary school teachers reflect about the relation between doubling the linear magnitudes of a body and the effect of this transformation on its volume they hastily became aware of their misconception and rapidly found the exact answer considering the cubic root of 8,000,000, that is 200, and then dividing 300 by 200.

When the secondary school teachers' procedure was shown to the primary school teachers, they said they understood better the method of dividing the height by k and the volume by k^3. Nevertheless, in all the sessions with secondary and primary teachers where the Eiffel Tower problem has been used, the strategy that takes you directly to an exact answer, that is divide the tower's height, 2 times by 10 and then by 2 and consequently, divide its volume, 2 times by 1,000 and then by 8, has not been discovered by any of the participants.

11.1 Task 3: Clay Figures

Teams of teachers are asked to mould a clay model of a dove whose volume will be $130\,cm^3$. Each team is given a bar of modelling clay weighing $\sim 250\,g$ and the following instructions: they may use only this material and the instruments given to them to solve the problem. The instructor gave to some teams a ruler with a centimetre measuring scale. Other teams got a 1-L transparent container that has ten marks spaced at equal distance. (It is important that the container is not graduated nor has other marks, except for those that indicate the equipartition of the container's height). When the container is given to the teachers they should be told that it has a capacity of 1 L and that the marks divide it into ten equal parts. Finally, the rest of the teams were given a beam scale and a ruler; the teachers were told that they could use the ruler as a secondary aid but that the beam scale should be the primary instrument employed.

When the teams had finished making their doves, they were asked to put the figures aside and to refrain from using them in the activities to follow. The teams then exchange instruments and were asked to use the new ones to make another clay figure of $130\,cm^3$ (or another quantity), and so on, until each team has used the three types of instruments.

Once the teams have all their clay animals they were asked to share with the others how they made each figure. In the first place, they should comment and discuss the use of the ruler for solving the problem; afterwards each team should describe how the container was used, and finally the members of the teams discussed the use of the beam scale. If the explanation implicitly included a demonstration that the volume of the model at hand was the requested one (i.e. $130\,cm^3$, or a good approximation), the discussion was passed over to the next team. If not, the members of the team were asked to demonstrate that their model had the requested volume.

12 Why was Clay Figures Task included in the Workshop?

During the research carried out we could verify that some teachers think that the difference in the level of a liquid that occurs when an object is submerged in it is due to the weight of the submerged object and not to its volume (Sáiz & Figueras, 2000). It was also found that some teachers did not know how the volume of an object is related to its weight, according to the material it is made of (Sáiz, 2004). Likewise, evidence was obtained regarding teachers' difficulties when making conversions between units of volume and units of capacity; Enochs and Gabel (1984) also have reported this fact. Finally, we know that some teachers think that it is not possible to calculate the volume of irregular bodies, that is, bodies that do not have the shape of the geometric bodies commonly used in schools (Sáiz, 2003) or that the calculations for obtaining the volumes of irregular bodies are very difficult for them (Enochs and Gabel, 1984).

13 Objectives and Goals of the Task

The first objective of this task is that teachers experience different ways to measure the volume of a body (immersion, measurement of linear dimensions, weight). A second objective is that teachers find a geometric solid that has dimensions such that its volume is $130\,cm^3$. The third objective is that teachers work with equivalencies between units of capacity (litres, decilitres) and units of volume (cubic decimetres, cubic centimetres).

14 Experiences Applying the Task

1. In general, teachers who were given only a ruler made a model of a rectangular prism, measure its linear dimensions and calculate the volume. On this basis, they use trial and error as they continue modifying the prism and calculating its volume until they reach the desired volume; after that, they model the dove.
2. The teachers that have worked first with the container and water made a model of the figure, measure it by immersion and then continue modifying and measuring until they reach the requested volume.
3. Some teachers did not believe that the volume could be measured using immersion.
4. Some teachers did not know the relationship between the marks in the transparent container and the units of volume that they represent (cubic decimetres, cubic centimetres).
5. The teachers who work with the beam scale took the longest period of time to solve the problem. They did not understand how this instrument could help them

in the task that they were asked to do. Based on the fact that $1\,dm^3$ of water weighs $1\,kg$ they supposed that $1\,dm^3$ of modelling clay also weighs $1\,kg$ and therefore used the proportionality to obtain the weight of water corresponding to $130\,cm^3$ and then measured a piece of modelling clay of that weight.

15 Analysis

Usually, the study of volume has been reduced to the study of formulas and of measuring systems (Del Olmo, Moreno & Gil, 1993; Enochs & Gabel, 1984; Janvier, 1994, 1997; Ricco & Vergnaud, 1983). The initial idea of the task is that the first thing that each team does is to obtain a piece of modelling clay of the appropriate size and then mould it as a dove. However, this idea is not always the first thought that members of the teams have (see points 1 and 2 above). The idea of first measuring a piece of clay of the desired volume and then moulding does not occur spontaneously; this could be attributed to a behaviour linked to diverse aspects of non-conservation of volume (Piaget, Inhelder, & Szeminska, 1970), that is, thinking that its not worthy obtaining the correct piece of clay since moulding it into another figure will change its volume, but for adults this is not likely to be the case, maybe they don't know how to obtain a prism with the required volume.

The experience students have with the study of the concept of volume at school is limited to the application of formulas. More frequent than not, the problems they have to solve are those where the linear dimensions are given and the computation of the volume is demanded.

The inverse problem, that is, finding the linear magnitudes of a body based on a given volume, surprised the teachers (points 1 and 2). The instruction in arithmetic that they have had, did not helped them much: to solve the problem one has to find three numbers that when multiplied together come to 130 – for some teachers this problem was not so simple.

With respect to point 4, it is a well-known fact that one litre of water weighs $1\,kg$. When teachers have not thought enough about the problem, they conclude that $1\,L$ (or cubic decimetre) of any material weighs $1\,kg$. However, it does not require much effort or discussion for teachers to realize that the weight of an object and its volume are related according to the type of material the object is made of; for example, ask teachers to think about the volume that $1\,kg$ of lead occupies in comparison to the volume that $1\,kg$ of cotton occupies. For some teachers, going from these ideas to the idea of specific weight is not a big problem. In the task discussed here, using this knowledge is not really necessary but it can be interesting for them to discuss.

The beam scale and the ruler can be used to construct any rectangular clay prism, measure its length, width and height, obtain its volume and finally weigh it. Subsequently, by using proportionality the weight corresponding to the required volume ($130\,cm^3$) is obtained, so a piece of moulding clay with that weight can easily be obtained and then moulded as a dove.

This procedure can make some teachers wonder how it is possible that a linear proportional relationship can be used to solve the problem, when in the Eiffel Tower task this was not the case. This confusion may be resolved after a profound discussion or after experiencing weighing and obtaining the volume of bodies made of different materials. However, for many teachers the workshop will be the first time that they can reflect about the different aspects that the study of the concept of volume involves.

During the development of the research project carried out, in one of the workshop's sessions, stones were measured using immersion. At first, many teachers thought that immersion measured the weight. After various experiments they realized that the weight did not affect the change in the water level. In the subsequent workshop session they were asked to compare the volumes of some geometric solids, all of them made of the same kind of wood, using weight. The result obtained in the previous session totally confused them. What they remember was that weight and volume were not related in any way and therefore they did not understand how it was expected that they use weight to solve a volume problem (Sáiz, 2004). Only after much discussion some of the teachers were convinced that it is indeed possible to compare volumes using weight when the bodies to be compared are made of the same material, but some other teachers remained confused.

16 Final Reflections

Although teachers have problems with different aspects of the concept of volume, we believe that the majority of these difficulties are easily overcome with relatively simple problems and tasks. However, this is not the case regarding the difficulties and erroneous conceptions involved in the tasks that were chosen; the evidence collected in the studies carried out sustain this statement.

The tasks exhibited put into play many properties of the concept of volume, some of them fundamental. While it is not expected that those tasks are enough for helping teachers constitute a strong volume mental object (in the sense of Freudenthal, 1983), we do believe that they are essential to improve teachers' competencies when faced with tasks and problems related to volume.

Although there are few references about teachers' conceptions regarding the concept of volume, there are many studies that show that primary school teachers have not mastered the concepts that they have to teach. For example, related to measurement topics, the work of Menon (1998) and Reinke (1997) can be mentioned. Since volume is a complicated notion due to its conceptual richness, it is possible that many mathematics teacher educators could find that the students in their courses have the same difficulties we have indicated here or other similar ones. If for some future or inservice teachers these tasks are easy to solve, it is possible to use them as a base and adjust them taking into account the mathematical knowledge of the workshops' participants.

References

Balbuena, H., Block, D., Dávila, M., Schulmaister, M., García, V., & Moreno, E. (1995). *La enseñanza de las matemáticas en la escuela primaria* (The teaching of mathematics in primary school). Mexico: Pronap SEP.

Battista, M. T., & Clements, D. (1996). Students' understanding of three dimensional arrays. *Journal for the Research in Mathematics Education, 27*(3), 258–292.

Del Olmo, M. A., Moreno, M. F., & Gil, F. (1993). *Superficie y volumen. Algo más que el trabajo con fórmulas?* (Surface and area. Something more than working with formulae?). Spain: Síntesis.

Enochs L. G., & Gabel, L. D. (1984). Preservice elementary teachers' conceptions of volume. *School Science and Mathematics, 84*(8), 670–680.

Figueras, O., & Waldegg, G. (1986). *La medición en la escuela secundaria.* (Measuring in secondary school). Cuadernos de Investigación 2. Mexico: SME Cinvestav.

Freudenthal, H. (1983). *Didactical phenomenology of mathematical structures.* The Netherlands: Reidel Pub. Co.

Hart, K., Brown M., Kerslake D., Küchemann D., & Ruddock, G. (1985). *Teacher's guide. Chelsea diagnostic mathematics test.* London: NFER-Nelson.

Janvier, C. (1994). *Le volume. mais où sont les formulas?* Quebec: Modulo Editeur.

Janvier, C. (1997). Grandeur et mesure: la place des formules a partir de l'exemple du volume. *Bulletin AMQ, 37*(3), 28–41.

Menon, R. (1998). Preservice teachers' understanding of perimeter and area. *School, Science and Mathematics, 98*(7), 361–368.

Merseth, K. (Ed.). (2003). *Windows in teaching math. Cases of middle and secondary classrooms.* New York: Teachers College Press.

Owens, K., & Outhred, L. (2006). The learning of geometry and measurement. In Angel Gutierrez and P. Boero (Eds.), *Handbook of research on the psychology of mathematics education. Past, present and future* (pp. 83–116). The Netherlands: Sense Publishers.

Piaget, J., Inhelder, B., & Szeminska, A. (1970). *The child's conception of geometry.* London: Routledge & Kegan Paul.

Potari, D., & Spiliotopoulou, V. (1996). Children's approaches to the concept of volume. *Science Education, 80*(3), 341–360.

Reinke, K. (1997). Area and perimeter: Preservice teachers' confusion. *School, Science and Mathematics, 97*(2), 75–77.

Ricco, G., & Vergnaud, G. (1983). Représentation du volume et arithmétisation. Entretiens individuels avec des élèves de 11 a 15 ans. *Recherches en Didactique des Mathématiques, 4*(1), 27–69.

Sáiz, M. (2002). El pensamiento del maestro de primaria acerca del concepto matemático de volumen y su enseñanza. (Primary school teachers' thinking about the mathematical concept of volume and its teaching). PhD Dissertation, Cinvestav, DF, México.

Sáiz, M. (2003). Primary teachers' conceptions about the concept of volume: The case of volume measurable objects. In N. A. Pateman, B. J. Dougherty, and J. T. Zilliox (Eds), *Proceedings of the 27thPME International Conference* (Vol. 4, pp. 95–102).

Sáiz, M. (2004). *Some primary teachers' conceptions about the relations between volume and weight.* Paper presented at ICME 10, TSG 10. Available from ICME web site: http://www.icme10.dk/.

Sáiz, M. (2005). An approach to teachers' knowledge about the mathematical concept of volume. *Proceedings of the 25th Conference of the PME* (Vol. 1, p. 363).

Sáiz, M., & Figueras, O. (2000). Some primary teachers' conceptions on the mathematical notion of volume. *Proceedings of the 22nd Annual Meeting of the PME-NA* (Vol. 2, pp. 491–497).

Task-Based Lessons: The Central Focus of a Mathematics Content Course for Future Elementary Teachers

Anne R. Teppo

A task-based lesson serves as the organizing principle for a university mathematics content course for future elementary teachers. The course, which provides the first semester of a year-long sequence, covers the arithmetic of numbers. The daily classroom activities follow a Japanese-style lesson plan and use tasks developed through a didactical phenomenological analysis. A situated learning perspective frames an understanding of the classroom activity. The goals for using and the criteria for developing task-based lesson materials are discussed and an example of an actual classroom lesson is provided to illustrate the power of this instructional approach.

1 Introduction

> Mathematics and education are peculiar subjects, but even more peculiar bedfellows. ... for whereas mathematics develops by reducing the problematic and creative to establish procedures and techniques, effective education enables students to reconstruct and regenerate those procedures from their own understanding. (Mason, 1997, p. 377)

This chapter describes an effort to address the "tensions" identified by Mason (1997) through the use of task-based lessons in a mathematics content course. While the course is intended to fulfill the future elementary teachers' mathematics requirement, it is designed to reflect the special needs of the students it serves. The topics are unpacked, and the classroom activities carefully structured, not only to deepen the students' conceptual understanding of the subject matter, but also to purposefully address *how* the future teachers come to know this mathematics. The task-based lessons provide students opportunities to engage in what Ball (2003) characterizes as the *mathematical work* that teaching involves. "Teaching requires justifying, explaining, analyzing errors, generalizing, and defining. It requires knowing ideas and procedures in detail, and knowing them well

A.R. Teppo
Independent scholar who collaborates with other mathematics educators around the world

B. Clarke, B. Grevholm, and R. Millman (eds.), *Tasks in Primary Mathematics Teacher Education:*
Purpose, Use and Exemplars, Mathematics Teacher Education 4,
© Springer Science+Business Media LLC 2009

enough to represent and explain them skillfully in more than one way. This is *mathematics*" (p. 4).

The course engages students in active learning in ways that they may not have previously experienced, having learned the subject in more traditional K-12 mathematics programs. For such students, mathematics is perceived to be "rule-based, where problems are solved and exercises completed by applying memorized formulas and algorithms" (Teppo, 2001, p. 4). The challenge of the course is to enable such students to build conceptual understandings for ideas that they had formerly assimilated only procedurally (Hiebert, 1999). As Ball (2003, p. 9) notes, "Teachers cannot be expected to know or do what they have not had opportunities to learn."

A set of carefully sequenced task-based lessons, rather than a textbook, serves as the focus and primary learning resource. A typical class period, which involves small group work followed by whole-class discussion, is centered on a particular task that embodies the mathematics under study. As they process the task, students are encouraged to use manipulatives, common sense, and experiential knowledge rather than memorized rules and algorithms. The instructor then selects a range of student strategies, which makes use of different components of the mathematics under study, to be written on the board. These strategies are compared and contrasted to focus attention on underlying structure and help the students begin to unpack arithmetical processes and make mathematical connections. Experiencing, and the explicit study of and reflection on, such tasks extend the students' understanding of what it means to learn mathematics deeply, as well as provide pedagogical examples of reform-based classroom practices.

The classroom tasks were adapted from research reports, National Council of Teachers of Mathematics Standards documents, reformed curricula material, and journal publications, and were tested through 3 years of a multi-sectioned, classroom implementation. They typically involve open-process situations that allow students to enter into the problem from different ability levels and utilize multiple solution strategies. The classroom activity illustrates how mathematics is used to represent, organize, and think about everyday, real-world situations. The mathematical structures underlying the tasks are drawn out of the relationships and processes used by the students. The study of this structure also leads to the development of rich concept images encompassing conceptual understanding, specific procedures, algorithms, formal definitions, and mathematical connections.

2 Theoretical Framework

2.1 Situated Learning

The task-based lesson follows an elementary school, Japanese-style lesson plan, which places the *processes* of problem-solving at the center of activity and utilizes student *productions* as the primary medium for learning (Becker & Shimada, 1997; Peterson, 2005; Shimizu 1999; Stigler, Fernandez, & Yoshida, 1996). This type of classroom organization is in sharp contrast to that of a typical American school mathematics lesson. Here, a framework of *situated learning* is a useful lens for considering the nature of the classroom learning. "How a person learns a particular set of knowledge and skills, and the situation in which a person learns, are a fundamental part of what is learned" (Peressini, Borko, Romagnano, Knuth, & Willis, 2004, p. 68).

A situated learning perspective focuses on practices. Knowledge is viewed as "embodied, or as located in activity, where activity is broadly construed and includes perceiving, reasoning, and talking" (Cobb & Bowers, 1999, p. 11). Learning is characterized as an individual's reorganization of his or her (in this case) mathematical activity. It develops through participation in the context of particular activity and is evidenced by changes in the nature of this participation (Greeno, 1998).

2.2 Japanese-Style Mathematics Lessons

A Japanese-style classroom like those described by Shimada (1997) and Sawada (1997) uses an "open-ended approach." Students are presented a "small-scale" problem and asked to develop different methods or ways to arrive at a solution. During the whole-class discussion that follows, the emphasis is not on the answer to this problem, but on the variety of solution strategies that the students develop. The teacher carefully orchestrates this discussion by selecting solutions, to be written on the board, that exhibit a range of mathematical approaches. The students' explanations of their selected methods and the teacher's synthesis of these methods encourage students to reflect on and make connections among mathematical operations and relations. Because the students generate solutions that are based on their present levels of mathematical understanding and skills, they provide familiar platforms from which to develop new mathematical understanding.

Although the students' productions influence the direction of the lesson, reflective planning prior to the lesson prepares the teacher for the range of expected solution methods. In a typical teacher's lesson plan, he or she organizes a list of anticipated solutions, arranged according to their mathematical features (Sawada, 1997). This pre-planning is facilitated by Japanese reference books and publications that have assembled student's ways of thinking about topics in the mathematics curriculum (Stigler, Fernandez, & Yoshida, 1996). The inclusion in the lesson plan of expected student solutions is a key element of the success of this approach to classroom instruction. Knowledge of potential student solutions has also been found to be an effective component for American elementary teachers who use the program of Cognitively Guided Instruction (Fennema et al., 1996; Fennema, Franke, & Carpenter, 1993; Knapp, & Peterson, 1995).

The effectiveness of a Japanese-style lesson can be understood in terms of its *coherence*, characterized by four aspects of the teacher's classroom discourse management (Sekiguchi, 2006). "Rhetorical" management, or coherence between goals and discourse production, is organized by the lesson's "four-phase script," comprising the introduction, student work, student explanations, and teacher summary. "Thematic" management, related to content, coordinates the related topics within and across lessons that comprise a particular mathematical theme. "Referential" management refers to the ways that discourse participants in the classroom keep track of referents through the teacher's deliberate use of processes such as naming, symbolizing, using blackboards, and homework problems. "Focus" management deals with strategies that center students' attention on the "point" of the lesson, including the use of comparison and contrast, discussion, and summary. Taken together, these four aspects of classroom discourse management provide a useful lens for analyzing the components of an effective mathematics lesson.

2.3 Didactical Phenomenological Analysis

Task selection is a critical component in any classroom in which students' productions form the generative source of learning. In particular, the premises of mathematics education, articulated by Freudenthal (1983) and amplified in the Dutch instructional theory of Realistic Mathematics Education, inform the selection and sequencing of the task-based lesson (de Lange, 1987; Gravemeijer, van Galen & Keijzer, 2005; van den Heuvel-Panhuizen, 2003). A key aspect of Freudenthal's approach to education is that mathematics is not regarded as a body of knowledge but as a human activity, and that mathematics is learned by *doing*. Learning comes about as students are guided through the processes of "re-invention." Knowledge is constructed both through "horizontal mathematizing" – organizing and solving everyday experiences, and "vertical mathematizing" – re-organizing and operating within mathematics itself (Gravemeijer, van Galen & Keijzer, 2005; van den Heuvel-Panhuizen, 2003).

Appropriate tasks that promote mathematization are identified through "didactical phenomenological analyses" (Freudenthal, 1983). "These analyses reveal what kind of mathematics is worthwhile to learn, and which actual phenomena can offer possibilities for developing the intended mathematical knowledge and understanding" (van den Heuvel-Panhuizen, 2005, p. 39). Tasks are derived from situations that "reflect the essentials of the concepts that are to be embodied [and] from those phenomena that beg to be organized" by the mathematics under study (Freudenthal, 1983, p. 32).

Tasks are not developed as isolated activities. Their design should reflect a carefully sequenced instructional trajectory based on a didactical phenomenological analysis of the mathematical concepts, skills, knowledge, and connections underlying the course content. Each task should be coherent with those that come before and after it, and making mathematical connections should be an integral part of task design. As Ball (2003) suggests, "seeing the mathematical horizon [and] ... knowing how particular ideas anticipate later ones" (pp. 4, 6).

3 The Task-Based Lesson

3.1 Future Teachers' and Instructors' Responsibilities

A situated learning perspective and the Japanese approach to instruction, including the notion of coherence, provide the framework for the design of the future teachers' mathematics content course and, in particular, the task-based lesson. The lesson is purposefully organized to optimize the mathematical and pedagogical richness of the classroom activity. However, it is not enough to simply turn the students loose on the task – the instructor must carefully orchestrate how the students' work is processed to draw out and reflect upon the intended focus of the lesson. Both the future teachers and the instructor have important roles to play within the lesson.

The future teachers are responsible for devising solutions to the given problem, using their small groups as thinking/doing resources. They are encouraged to use basic processes of arithmetic rather learned algorithms, and model these processes using manipulatives or drawings. Their solutions must be fully written down and the students should be able to interpret their numerical answers within the context of the given problem. During the whole-class discussion they should be prepared to write their solutions on the chalk board or demonstrate their manipulations to the class. They are expected to listen carefully to others' explanations and ask clarifying questions.

The class instructor is responsible for understanding the mathematical richness embedded in the given task, the learning potential of the particular activity, and its execution. She or he identifies the individual student solutions, to be used in the whole-class discussion, that emphasize particular aspects of the mathematics under study, asks probing questions of students to elicit full explanations of their presented strategies, compares, contrasts, and synthesizes these strategies to construct new knowledge, and uses appropriate mathematical vocabulary to name new concepts, procedures, and operations.

In the implemented course a set of *Teacher Notes* (Teppo, 2001) was used to manage the classroom complexity. These notes contain examples of strategies typically used by future teachers; interpretations of the mathematics embodied in each strategy; a discussion of the mathematical construct under study – including connections to other mathematical ideas and related vocabulary; and suggestions for maximizing the instructional impact of the lesson. (The level of detail contained in the *Teacher Notes* was important for successfully conducting the course, where the majority of the instructors were graduate student Teaching Assistants, rather than Teacher Educators.)

3.2 Characteristics of an Effective Task

A successful instructional task should be a contextualized "problem" that is open-entry and open-process. The nature of the students' engagement is based on the assumption that the future teachers have been exposed to the mathematics under study but have, for the most part, internalized information previously only in the form of memorized algorithms about isolated topics. While the task is real-world based, the particulars of the context must invite, rather than divert attention, from the mathematization of the problem. The problem should elicit a range of strategies that unpacks key aspects of the mathematical construct. It should be possible to find solutions and conduct a follow-up discussion of these processes during a single class period.

The task-based lessons within each unit are carefully sequenced to move from informal experiences with particular constructs, through explorations of the structure underlying particular processes, to formal considerations of mathematical concepts and their connections to the big ideas of the arithmetic of numbers. (In the implemented course, the task, rather than a text, is the primary source of learning. A text is available as a resource only – it is recognized that mathematics is learned by *doing*, not by reading.)

Participation in the task-based lesson not only facilitates the students' construction of mathematical knowledge, it also impacts their beliefs about the nature of mathematics and what it means to learn the subject. As these students gain practice in mathematical discourse, they experience the central role that student thinking has both for their own learning and for that of their prospective students.

4 Task-Based Lesson: Introduction to Proportion

Excerpts from a typical task-based lesson, in this case covering an introduction to proportional reasoning, is presented to illustrate how the underlying instructional frameworks and principles of task design are operationalized. This lesson is the third in a sequence of five class-long activities that introduces students to the concept of multiplicative structures. The sequence begins with an activity that compares additive and multiplicative structures. A second activity introduces students intuitively to the concept of ratio. In the activity described below, students begin to explore the meaning of proportional relationships. A fourth activity decompresses the cross multiplication algorithm and ties this procedure to the underlying mathematical structure explored in the preceding lessons.

The example comprises a selection of actual students' strategies from the implemented course for a set of six proportional word problems. Summaries from the *Teacher Notes* (Teppo, 2001) identify how these procedures embody important aspects of the underlying mathematics and facilitate student learning.

4.1 Task: Proportion Word Problems

The goal of the activity is to develop an understanding of the mathematical structure of proportional relationships before introducing the standard solution method (i.e., set up the proportion and use algebra (or cross multiplication) to solve for the missing number). Students work in small groups to solve the six word problems, shown below (taken from Kaput, & West, 1994, pp. 267–268). They are requested to use common sense and intuitive reasoning about the mathematical relationships given in each problem to reach a solution. They must not use algorithms such as cross multiplication to find the answer.

1. Simon worked 3 h and earned US $12. How long does it take him to earn US $36?
2. In a certain school there are three boys to every seven girls in every class. How many girls are there in a classroom with nine boys?
3. A large restaurant sets tables by setting 7 pieces of silverware and 4 pieces of china on each place mat. If it used 392 pieces of silverware on its table settings last night, how many pieces of china did it use?
4. A printing press takes exactly 12 min to print 14 dictionaries. How many dictionaries can it print in 30 min?
5. To bake donuts, Jerome needs exactly 8 cups of flour to make 14 donuts. How many donuts can he make with 12 cups of flour?
6. To make Italian dressing, you need 4 parts vinegar for 9 parts oil. How much oil do you need for 828 oz of vinegar?

4.2 Explanation of Student Solutions

When the students are required to use a method other than cross multiplication for their solutions, they intuitively use processes that rely on either the scalar multiplier or the functional rule (see below). The whole-class discussion of these strategies provides an explicit focus on the nature of a proportion's multiplicative relationships. An understanding of this mathematical structure provides the foundation upon which algorithmic approaches can be constructed.

The following student solutions (shown as "Sa)," "Sb)," etc.) illustrate the range of approaches that can be used to solve the problems. The notes attached to each solution include the student's interpretations of the contextualized numbers, as well as a brief discussion of the underlying mathematics. This commentary (included in the *Teacher Notes*) informs the course instructor as to how she or he can draw contextual and mathematical meaning out of the solution process. (Interpretations of these meanings are informed by Kaput and West's (1994) analyses of "competent, but informal proportional reasoning patterns.")

#1. Simon worked 3 h and earned US $12. How long does it take him to earn US $36?

Sa) $12 \div 3 = 4$ and $36 \div 4 = 9$

Interpretation: The "4" is the rate – US $4 per h. Dividing this into US $36 gives the number of hours Simon worked.

Sb)   h   h   h   = US $12   (This strategy can also be
       h   h   h   = US $12   displayed in a table.)
       h   h   h   = US $12

Hours	3	6	9
9 h = US$36	Earnings	12	24	36

Interpretation: Groups of 3 h and US $12 each are added until a total of US $36 is reached. This gives a total of 9 h. This strategy involves a *building-up* process that coordinates the incrementation of each quantity.

#2.A printing press takes exactly 12 min to print 14 dictionaries. How many dictionaries can it print in 30 min?

Sc) $14 \div 12 = 1.1667$ dictionaries per min
$1.1667 \times 30 = 35$ dictionaries

Interpretation: A unit rate is found and multiplied by the total time of production

Sd) $12 : 14 = 6 : 7$, $30 \div 6 = 5$, and $5 \times 7 = 35$

Interpretation: The "unit" sizes of "12 minutes" and "14 dictionaries" are correspondingly reduced to produce a unit size that divides evenly into the known final quantity. Thus, "5" is the number of groups of seven dictionaries each that are produced in 30 min, and 35 dictionaries are made in all.

Se) $\dfrac{12 \times 2}{14 \times 2} = \dfrac{24}{28}$ and $\dfrac{24+6}{28+7} = \dfrac{30}{35}$

Interpretation: The ratio is first expressed in fractional form. Equivalent fractions are then produced by a combination of multiplication and building-up addition. The student recognized that the ratio was preserved by multiplying each part by the same amount and then adding 6 to the numerator for every 7 added to the denominator.

#3. To bake donuts, Jerome needs exactly 8 cups of flour to make 14 donuts. How many donuts can he make with 12 cups of flour?

Sf) 8 cups are changed to 12 cups. This is an increase of 4 cups or $1/2$ of the original quantity. To preserve the ratio, the number of donuts would also be increased by $1/2$ of the original amount or by 7 more donuts. Thus, 12 cups of flour would make 21 donuts.

Interpretation: This strategy uses a building-up process with the increase formulated as a fractional amount. The proportional nature of the relationship is recognized by the fact that both amounts increase by $1/2$ their original number. (This particular strategy may have been adopted because of the "friendly" nature of the numbers involved.)

Note: Several students tended to see the creation of different pairs of numbers that exhibited the same ratio as an additive rather than a multiplicative event. Using a building-up process, they increased each number in the pair by repeatedly adding to it the appropriate part of the given ratio – a kind of double skip counting.

#4. To make Italian dressing you need 4 parts vinegar for 9 parts oil. How much oil do you need for 828 oz of vinegar?

Sg) $828 \div 4 = 207$ and $207 \times 9 = 1863$

Interpretation: The 207 represents the number of times 4 is multiplied to produce 828. Therefore, to preserve the ratio, 9 must also be multiplied by 207. It was difficult for students to provide a contextual meaning for 207. Here "207" represents the number of groups of related parts needed to constitute the total amount of Italian dressing.

Several students had difficulty with the units in this problem, claiming that because the original ratio was given in parts and the final amount in ounces, they couldn't complete the problem. A discussion of the different units involved in the problem brings out a property of ratio – when quantities have the same units, the units are not important in stating the ratio, only the multiplicative relationship between the two numbers matters. (Here the ratio is "4 parts to 9 parts," irrespective of the units of measurement for the two liquids. It could equally have been "4 ounces to 9 ounces.")

Sh) $9 \div 4 = 2.25$

$828 \times 2.25 = 1863$

Interpretation: The amount of oil is always 2.25 times the amount of vinegar in the dressing. (This number is the unit ratio of oil to vinegar, or 2.25:1.)

4.3 Mathematics Underlying the Activity

During the whole class discussion, it is the instructor's job to highlight various aspects of the proportional structure implicit in the students' solutions. While the notion of *proportion* as the equality of two ratios is not explicit in this work, it forms part of the underlying mathematical activity. However, the *multiplicative relationships* of proportional situations are evident in many of the solutions.

The solutions Sg) and Sh) to problem #4 are a good example of this mathematical structure. The within- and across-quantity natures of the multiplicative relationships are shown in Fig. 1.

In 4g), "207" is the *scalar multiplier*. This number is a *within*-quantity multiplier. It represents the factor by which each quantity must be multiplied to change its value while maintaining the original ratio. This number can be interpreted in the context of each problem as the number of "groups" of each quantity that are required to constitute the larger related amounts.

In 4h) "multiply by 2.25" is the *functional rule*. This rule indicates the multiplicative relationship *across* the different quantities. To maintain the same ratio, pairs of quantities must maintain the same functional rule between them. This rule may be stated as a *unit rate*. For example, in #1, Simon earns US \$4 per h and in #4, the press produces 1.1667 dictionaries per min.

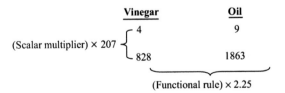

Fig. 1 Multiplicative structure of proportional relationships

5 Discussion

As the above examples illustrate, the task that forms the basis for the classroom learning activity need not be an elaborate problem situation. A good source for material is research reports that design tasks for teaching experiments with elementary school students. Such activities have been carefully developed to elicit student responses related to the mathematical constructs under study. In particular, the six proportion problems (taken from a larger set of 15) were constructed based on the researchers' knowledge of school students' informal proportional reasoning patterns (Kaput, & West, 1994). When these problems were used in the future teacher course, it was found that many of the students' solutions paralleled the processes observed by the researchers.

Standard homework problems, found in mathematics texts for future teachers, are also a good source for tasks. For example, towards the end of an earlier unit on operations with whole numbers, students were assigned a set of four such problems that used the lattice method of multiplication, the scaffold method of division, and the Russian peasant method of multiplication. The techniques for using each method were given in the problem set. During the subsequent class, these methods were unpacked and the underlying structures of multiplication and division were examined. The purpose of the activity was to provide the students opportunities to unpack unfamiliar mathematical procedures and create clear explanations of underlying structures. (See Simonsen, & Teppo, 1999, for a discussion of this activity and selected students' responses.)

Of course, a key to the successful implementation of any task is a knowledge of the mathematics implicit in the future teachers' solution strategies. If a task-based lesson approach is adopted for a particular course, several iterations of the sequence of lessons may be required to assemble an effective set of "teacher notes." [The first several offerings of the course described here involved a great deal of work in between each lesson to understand the mathematics implicit in the students' methods. This process, while time consuming, was also an incredible learning experience for the Teacher Educators (Teppo, & Simonsen, 1997).]

The task-based lesson responds to Ball's (2003, p. 1) challenge for teacher preparation in the United States. "[U]sing curriculum effectively and working responsibly with standards depend on understanding the subject matter. How teachers know mathematics is central to their capacity to use instructional materials wisely, to assess students' progress, and to make sound judgments about presentation, emphasis, and sequencing." The task-based lesson, with its focus on learning through activity attends to the *how* of Ball's statement. The careful selection and structuring of these activities enables future teachers to deepen their understanding of the subject matter they will someday teach, in ways that go well beyond simply knowing it for themselves. They become, along with their course instructor, participants in a rich culture of mathematical activity.

While no formal research study was conducted to investigate the impact of the task-based lesson approach on its participants, copies of students' work and journal responses were collected throughout the 3 years of the course's implementation.

Based on this anecdotal evidence, I end the chapter with a comment written by one of the future teachers in the assigned mid-term autobiography.

> Math is not simply about doing problems and punching the calculator. This course has prompted me to ask why? Instead of blindly accepting the functions of certain operations and calculations, I have been motivated to learn why these operations work the way they do. I have learned how they can be done differently with the same results. I have learned to question and truly understand the relationships and procedures of mathematical operations. (Teppo, 2001, p. 12)

References

Ball, D. L. (2003, February 6). What mathematical knowledge is needed for teaching mathematics? *Secretary's Summit on Mathematics, US Department of Education*. Washington, DC. Retrieved May 11, 2006, from http://www-personal.umich.edu/~dball.

Becker, J. P., & Shimada, S. (1997). *The open-ended approach: A new proposal for teaching mathematics*. Reston, VA: National Council of Teachers of Mathematics.

Cobb, P., & Bowers, J. (1999). Cognitive and situated learning: Perspectives in theory and practice. *Educational Researcher, 28*(2), 4–15.

de Lange, J. (1987). *Mathematics, insight and meaning*. Utrecht: OWandOC, Utrecht University.

Fennema, E., Franke, M. L., & Carpenter, T. P. (1993). Using children's mathematical knowledge in instruction. *American Educational Research Journal, 30*(3), 555–583.

Fennema, E., Carpenter, T., Franke, M. L., Levi, L., Jacobs, V. R., & Empson, S. B. (1996). A longitudinal study of learning to use children's mathematical thinking in mathematics instruction. *Journal for Research in Mathematics Education, 27*(4), 430–434.

Freudenthal, H. (1983). *Didactical phenomenology of mathematical structures*. Dordrecht: D. Ridel Publishing.

Gravemeijer, K., van Galen, F., & Keijzer, R. (2005). Designing instruction on proportional reasoning with average speed. In H. L. Chick and J. L. Vincent (Eds.), *Proceedings of the 29th Conference of the International Group for the Psychology of Mathematics Education* (Vol. 1, pp. 93–122). Melbourne: PME.

Greeno, J. G., Middle School Mathematics Through Applications Project Group. (1998). The situativity of knowing, learning, and research. *American Psychologist, 53*(1), 5–26.

Heibert, J. (1999). Relationships between research and the NCTM standards. *Journal for Research in Mathematics Education, 30*(1), 3–19.

Kaput, J. J., & West, M. M. (1994). Missing-value proportional reasoning problems: Factors affecting informal reasoning patterns. In G. Harel and J. Confrey (Eds.), *The development of multiplicative reasoning in the learning of mathematics* (pp. 237–292). Albany, NY: State University of New York Press.

Knapp, N. F., & Peterson, P.L. (1995). Teachers' interpretations of "CGI" after four years: Meanings and practices. *Journal for Research in Mathematics Education, 26*(1), 40–65.

Mason, J. (1997). Describing the elephant: Seeking structure in mathematical thinking. *Journal for Research in Mathematics Education, 28*(3), 377–382.

Peressini, D., Borko, H., Romagnano, L., Knuth, E., & Willis, C. (2004). A conceptual framework for learning to teach secondary mathematics: A situative perspective. *Educational Studies in Mathematics, 56*, 67–96.

Peterson, B. E. (2005). Student teaching in Japan: The lesson. *Journal of Mathematics Teacher Education, 8*(1), 61–74.

Sawada, T. (1997). Developing lesson plans. In J. P. Becker & S. Shimada (Eds.), *The open-ended approach: A new proposal for teaching mathematics* (pp. 23–35). Reston, VA: National Council of Teachers of Mathematics.

Sekiguchi, Y. (2006). Coherence of mathematics lessons in Japanese eighth-grade classrooms. In J. Novotiná, H. Moraová, M. Krátká, & N. Stehliková (Eds.), *Proceedings of the 30th Conference of the International Group for the Psychology of Mathematics Education* (Vol. 5, pp. 81–88). Prague: PME.

Shimada, S. (1997). The significance of an open-ended approach. In J. P. Becker and S. Shimada (Eds.), *The open-ended approach: A new proposal for teaching mathematics* (pp. 1–9). Reston, VA: National Council of Teachers of Mathematics.

Shimizu, Y. (1999). Aspects of mathematics teacher education in Japan: Focusing on teachers' roles. *Journal of Mathematics Teacher Education, 2*(1), 107–116.

Simonsen, L. M., & Teppo, A. R. (1999). Using alternative algorithms with preservice teachers. *Teaching Children Mathematics, 5*(9), 516–519.

Stigler, J. W., Fernandez, C., & Yoshida, M. (1996). Traditions of school mathematics in Japanese and American elementary classrooms. In L. P. Steffe, P. Nesher, P. Cobb, & B. Grier (Eds.), *Theories of mathematical learning* (pp. 149–175). Mahwah, NJ: Erlbaum.

Teppo, A. R. (2001) Teacher notes for mathematics for elementary school teachers: The arithmetic of numbers. Published by the author.

Teppo, A. R., & Simonsen, L. (1997). Collaborative action research across multiple sections of a preservice elementary mathematics course. In V. Zack, J. Mousley, & C. Breen (Eds.), *Developing practice: Teachers' inquiry and educational change* (pp. 75–85). Geelong, Victoria: Centre for Studies in Mathematics, Science and Environmental Education, Deakin University.

van den Heuvel-Panhuizen, M. (2003). The didactic use of models in Realistic Mathematics Education: An example from a longitudinal trajectory of percentages. *Educational Studies in Mathematics, 54*(1), 9–35.

van den Heuvel-Panhuizen, M. (2005). Can research answer the 'what' question of mathematics education? *Cambridge Journal of Education, 35*, 35–53.

Section C
Tasks as a Tool for Developing Knowledge through and for Practice

Barbara Clarke

Many of us who work in teacher professional development lament the focus of some teachers on the need to provide activities they can use "in the classroom tomorrow". The expectation for "tricks and tips" as the sign of a good session and the associated critique that there is too much theory and not enough practice happens too often. The chapters in this section provide some exemplars of how the vital links with practice can be made while developing robust and important knowledge for prospective and practising teachers. These exemplars have the potential to help us to understand and focus on issues around the link between the practice of teacher education and the practice of teaching. Some focus explicitly on teachers as mathematics learners and then link to student learning while others focus on classroom situations and provide opportunity for teachers to explore their own learning and that of their students.

Amato focuses on the need for children to develop relational understanding rather than instrumental understanding. She acknowledges that this can be a challenge for many teachers as they generally learned in an instrumental way during their own school experience. She argues that this has also led to a negative attitude to mathematics on the part of many primary teachers and so the discussion highlights the importance of teacher attitudes in helping to facilitate their own and their students' mathematical development. She shares her research on the use of classroom tasks in the context of teacher education as a way of re-learning the mathematics in relational forms that will assist them in their future teaching careers. The specific tasks involved rational number games and the use of representations. The outcomes included the development of deeper understanding of the mathematical needs of primary school children, a more positive view of their ability to teach mathematics, and strategies for teaching in a more relational manner. Most of the trainee teachers said that they enjoyed experiencing children's tasks. These results triangulated with

B. Clarke
Associate Professor and Associate Dean of Staff, Faculty of Education, Monash University, Australia

B. Clarke, B. Grevholm, and R. Millman (eds.), *Tasks in Primary Mathematics Teacher Education: Purpose, Use and Exemplars,* Mathematics Teacher Education 4,

the results from practising teachers, arguably in part due to the interactive nature of the activities but also the explicit link to the classroom.

One of the disturbing observations of Amato's research is that anecdotal evidence of the lack of confidence of some of the teachers in the teaching of mathematics results in a reduction in the time that they give to it in the curriculum, thereby avoiding the teaching of mathematics. While there is no data on how wide spread this problem is, even single anecdotes are disturbing. The reader is also reminded of the challenges that are faced in many developing countries with limited resources and large class sizes but are encouraged by constructive ways to manage these challenges.

Next, Ashline and Quinn present a series of tasks based on Pythagoras' theorem that are intended to develop practising teacher's content knowledge. The authors share the experiences of a group of teachers in a school as they work through these tasks and provide some insight into the impact these experiences have on the teachers' practice, While the study of Pythagoras is beyond the typical curriculum of the primary school, it does represent a development of their personal mathematical knowledge for many of the teachers and an example of how the structuring and sequencing of the tasks provided insights and developed knowledge for the primary classroom. The modelling of an exploratory teaching approach was intended to provide the teachers with the experience of learning mathematics as well as an opportunity to reflect on the process for use in their own classrooms. A powerful model is presented through the use of a carefully constructed sequence of mathematically rich tasks which begin with content and the use of tools focusing on children's development of mathematical understanding and move to a point where the teachers are the learners.

Carillo and Climent make an explicit link between the practice of teacher education and the practice of teaching through the use of videos of classroom situations. The specific video clip involves a series of episodes in a grade 5 lesson where the children are exploring folding shapes to create halves and quarters. Focused questions are provided to facilitate an analysis and critique of the lesson. Through implementing the task with both student and practising teachers, the authors explore issues around the differences between the notions, processes, tools and contexts for each group. There is a clear link between the mathematical knowledge, pedagogical knowledge and practices highlighted through the analysis. The authors argue for the importance of this linking and comment that, for the teachers, "doing mathematics or doing mathematics problem solving for its own sake does not interest the teachers"; however, the task provides for both the doing of the mathematics and the reflecting on the practice of teaching to be accomplished. Clearly the success of the video as a tool is dependant on the appropriate choice of mathematical task, the implementing teacher and the questions asked. Video clips in teacher education are also used as a tool in the chapter of Gadanidis and Namukasa and the chapter of Millman, Svec, and Williams in Section B.

With a similar emphasis, Malara and Navarra bring the classroom into teacher education through the use of classroom scenes or scenarios. Their particular focus was on developing understanding and awareness of the role and extent of early algebra. A simulation was designed specifically to facilitate discussion and to elicit specific aspects of learning and teaching early algebra. Quite detailed analysis of their theoretical basis as well as the implementation is included and provides important insights in to some useful tools for future and practising primary teachers.

Moss, in her chapter on outdoor mathematical experiences, makes an argument for the value of outdoor activities for children's mathematical development. She presents a range of tasks and ideas for many mathematical concepts in the elementary classroom. Powerful ideas such as large scale Cartesian graphs and number lines where the scale or physical engagement has the potential to enhance mental models as well as more traditional tasks that link the mathematics to realistic and multidisciplinary contexts are shared. She uses these tasks in teacher education and argues that teachers are more likely to implement outdoor activities with their own classes if they have had positive experiences in their own learning using this type of activity. Through the engagement and practice of these tasks in the preservice setting, the potential and possibilities are more obvious.

Finally, Palhares, Gomes, Carvalho and Cebolo discuss the implementation of a task exploring polyminoes with teachers in a professional development setting. The task was an investigation that made visible both traditional mathematical content and more process oriented reasoning and strategies. A further implementation by these teachers in the school classroom highlighted a number of differences or contrasts from observing their teaching. The authors argue that these reflect the contrasting traditional and constructivist approaches to teaching. There was evidence of a loss of some of the mathematical power of the task – more telling by the teacher than exploring by the children.

The mathematical and pedagogical knowledge demanded for the successful implementation of current models of teaching mathematics is significant for prospective and practising teachers. These chapters represent some promising practices that explicitly link the school classroom with teacher education settings.

The Use of Relational Games in Initial Teacher Education: Bringing the Classroom into the Lecture Theatre

Solange Amorim Amato

The research results presented in this chapter are only a small part of action research performed with the aims of improving Brazilian primary school teacher trainees' understanding of, and attitudes to, mathematics. The teaching strategies were similar to those suggested for their future use in teaching children. They involved the use of multiple modes of representation for communicating the concepts, operations and relationships in the primary school curriculum. One of the most interesting children's tasks performed by the trainees was trading games which clearly expose relationships among two or more number concepts. The data collected indicated that playing these games was an important strategy to improve trainees' understanding of, and attitudes to, fractions. Teacher educators in developing countries who face similar problems to the ones presented here may find the tasks in this chapter useful for training primary school teachers.

1 Introduction

For Skemp (1976) relational understanding involves knowing both what to do and why it works, while instrumental understanding involves knowing only what to do, the procedure, but not the reason why it works. My initial experiences as a novice mathematics school teacher in Brazil and much later my experiences as a teacher educator led me to think that both mathematics teacher trainees and primary school teacher trainees do not have an appropriate relational understanding of the mathematics content they are supposed to teach. It did not take long, after I started teaching at schools, to notice that I did not have enough mathematics understanding to teach even the most basic curriculum contents to my first class of 11-year-olds (5th graders). I could present my students with correct procedures, but could not answer most of their questions concerning the reasons for using certain steps in the procedures (Amato, 2004a).

S.A. Amato
Lecturer, Faculty of Education, University of Brasília, Brasil

B. Clarke, B. Grevholm, and R. Millman (eds.), *Tasks in Primary Mathematics Teacher Education: Purpose, Use and Exemplars,* Mathematics Teacher Education 4,
© Springer Science+Business Media LLC 2009

Later in my work as a teacher educator, I could hear primary school teachers and trainees express their feelings about their instrumental understanding of, and dislike for, mathematics. Although their understanding of, and attitudes to, mathematics were not probed in any systematic way, during workshops and inservice courses they would spontaneously make comments such as "I had never realized that was the reason for writing a zero in the remainder, I just did it," or "not fractions, I hate them." These experiences led me to undertake a research project with the main aim of investigating ways of helping primary school trainees to improve their understanding of, and attitudes to, mathematics in preservice teacher education.

Similar problems seem to exist in developed countries and have been discussed in the literature about teacher education. It is widely recognized that primary school teachers and trainees' knowledge of mathematics is, on the average, insufficient (e.g., Ball & McDiarmid, 1990; Goulding, Rowland & Barber, 2002; Southwell & Penglase, 2005). Research has also revealed that some primary school teachers and trainees demonstrate negative attitudes toward mathematics (e.g., Ball & McDiarmid, 1990; Hannula, Kaasila, Laine, & Pehkonen, 2005; Philippou & Christou, 1998). Yet Ball and McDiarmid (1990) argue that continued documentation about teachers and trainees' insufficient knowledge of mathematics will not contribute much to ameliorate the problems encountered in teacher education and teaching. The implication is that research-based methods of tackling the problem are required. Improving trainees' understanding involves "working with what they bring [to teacher education] and helping them to move toward the kinds of mathematical understanding needed in order to teach mathematics well" (Ball, 1990, p. 465).

2 Some Background Literature

Shulman (1986) identified several knowledge components which teachers may use in order to make decisions for the purpose of teaching and to help them promote understanding on the part of their students. One of these components is subject matter knowledge (SMK) which includes both the substantive and syntactic structures of the discipline. The focus of this study was on teachers and trainees' acquisition of substantive understanding of the mathematics they are supposed to teach. However, pedagogical content knowledge (PCK) which includes "the ways of representing and formulating the subject that make it comprehensible to others and ... an understanding of what makes the learning of specific topics easy or difficult" (Shulman 1986, p. 9) and general pedagogic knowledge or "knowledge of generic principles of classroom organization and management" (Shulman, 1986, p. 14) are also mentioned.

Wilson, Shulman and Richert (1987) suggest that attitudes and beliefs are outcomes of subject matter learning. Teachers' attitudes to mathematics are said to affect the way they will teach in the future (Ball, 1988) and the classroom ethos (Ernest, 1989). Yet the literature provides little discussion about the particular ways in which teachers' attitudes to mathematics may affect their teaching practices and classroom ethos. One exception is Bromme and Brophy (1986) who think that teachers model their attitudes and beliefs during their teaching. In most cases messages are conveyed without teachers' awareness. The most direct influence of primary school teachers' negative attitudes to mathematics on their students' learning appears to be time allocation. Bromme and Brophy point out that "such teachers have been found to allocate more instruction time to subject-matter areas that they enjoy, and less to areas that they dislike" (p. 122).

Time allocation has been found to be a very important aspect in improving mathematics learning (Brophy, 1986; Fisher, 1995), since for many students the construction of mathematical knowledge is a slow process. Research also tends to show that adults with a degree in other subjects (e.g., Quilter & Harper, 1988) and primary school trainees and teachers (e.g., Brown, Askew, Rhodes, William, & Johnson, 1997; Haylock, 1995) tend to blame instrumental teaching for their negative attitudes to mathematics. So the main research questions of the present study were

- In what ways can primary school trainees be helped to improve their relational understanding of the mathematical content they will be expected to teach?
- Can trainees improve their liking for mathematics as a by-product of the efforts to improve their understanding of the subject?

There are some suggestions in the literature about how to improve trainees' and teachers' relational understanding of mathematics. Most of these involve helping them re-learn mathematics in teacher education. Simon (1993), for example, recommends that the mathematics education of primary school trainees should focus more in helping them to understand, construct connections and organize the knowledge they will have to teach than in teaching additional content (vertical coverage). In the literature about trainees' SMK, there are also a few results of teacher educators' efforts to improve trainees' knowledge of particular mathematics content. In the intervention carried out by Stoddart, Connell, Stofflett, & Peck, (1993), concrete materials and iconic representations were used in an attempt to reconstruct trainees' understanding of rational number concepts. Many other teacher educators probably attempted to improve their trainees' SMK because it is implicit in what they wrote (e.g., Sowder, Bezuk, & Sowder, 1993) but not many seem to have reported the results achieved.

Previous attempts to improve trainees' attitudes to mathematics in teacher education also involve improving their understanding of the subject (e.g., Haylock, 1995; Philippou & Christou, 1998). The integration between the re-teaching of mathematics (SMK) and the teaching of mathematics pedagogy (PCK) is said to be a way of improving trainees' understanding (e.g., Bezuk & Gawronski, 2003) and attitudes to mathematics (e.g., Weissglass, 1983). Teacher educators often suggest that such integration involves re-teaching mathematics to teachers and trainees by using the same tasks that could be used to teach mathematics in a relational way to school students. According to Weissglass (1983), to develop positive attitudes to mathematics in children, future primary school teachers must learn how to set up learning experiences that are enjoyable, interesting and give the learner a sense of accomplishment. In order to be able to do this, the teachers must have had such experiences themselves.

Some teacher educators also argue that the integration between the teaching of mathematical content and pedagogy is beneficial to trainees' acquisition of PCK (e.g., Ball & Bass, 2000; Polya, 1981; Sernadini, 1983; Sowder et al., 1993) This is probably because they think that PCK is dependent on SMK. Trainees "should understand the subject in sufficient depth to be able to represent it appropriately and in multiple ways" (Ball, 1990, p. 458). Learning some initial ideas about PCK was thought to be more easily achieved from trainees' efforts to re-learn mathematical content through tasks which were new to them and from trying to understand how those tasks have helped them to acquire a more relational mathematical knowledge (Sowder et al., 1993). In teacher education it does not seem to be a good idea to tell trainees that their conceptions about teaching acquired during their long experiences in learning mathematics at school are inappropriate. They must be provided with new experiences to be able to form their own opinions about what may be better. So using children's tasks was thought to help trainees acquire some PCK in an experiential or tacit way (Sotto, 1994) in initial teacher education.

The ability to translate SMK into representations is considered a fundamental part of teachers' PCK (Shulman, 1986). Yet there is also some research evidence which shows that some teachers, especially novice primary school teachers, do not have a good knowledge of mathematical representations (e.g., Ball, 1990). Teachers have the social responsibility of helping students learn mathematics. So they must develop the ability to work backwards from their symbolic ways of representing mathematics to more informal ways of representing the subject (Ball & Bass, 2000). Otherwise they may lose precious opportunities of using representations in unpredicted moments and helping students construct further relationships. According to Rowland, Huckstep and Thwaites (2005), it is part of a teacher's job to execute "*contingent actions.*" This means that they must be ready to "respond to children's ideas ... and to deviate from an agenda set out when the lesson was prepared" (p. 7). Acquiring a repertoire of representations and tasks that can be transformed by the teacher for classroom use seems to be an adequate and initial form of PCK for a course component about mathematics teaching in preservice teacher education. Although it is a very basic form of PCK, knowledge of representations was also thought to be the most appropriate knowledge about teaching in order to foster trainees' initial feelings of success that would be needed to continue their learning from teaching mathematics.

Bromme and Brophy (1986) argue that it is not enough for trainees to become confident about their mathematical knowledge; they must also become confident that they can teach the subject effectively to their students. Therefore, I had to select the most basic children's tasks in order to help novice teachers start teaching in a more relational way. I also had to consider the short time available in Brazilian teacher education for course components about mathematics teaching and trainees' instrumental understanding to deal with certain teaching strategies. Another issue related to PCK which I had to consider was the viability of certain tasks with large classes of primary school children which is the usual situation in Brazil. Making the decision was further complicated by the fact that there have always been different perspectives and no general consensus on what constitutes good teaching (Stones, 1994). So for the purpose of this study, good children's mathematics tasks for initial teacher education courses were defined as those which

- have the potential to help trainees develop a strong relational understanding of the mathematics they are supposed to teach in the future (SMK);
- improve their liking for the subject;
- help trainees to acquire a repertoire of representations (PCK); and
- can be adopted and sustained with large classes.

One of the most interesting forms of children's tasks that can be performed with trainees is games adapted for large classes. Ernest (1987) presents the rationale for the use of games in the teaching of mathematics. He argues that games provide active learning, enjoyment, co-operation and discussion. The enjoyment generated may result in an improvement in attitudes toward mathematics after a period of time. According to Orton (1994), through playing games students have mental practice which "is not forced and it takes place in a natural and enjoyable way" (p. 47). Play does not finish with childhood. Even adults cannot maintain themselves on a task for long periods if the work involved is not done in a way that is amusing or engaging. It is very common to see adults enjoying themselves while playing with cards, dominoes and even 22 mature men happily chasing a ball in a football game.

Games which clearly expose important relationships among two or more mathematical concepts can be called 'relational games' because they have the potential to develop students' relational understanding of mathematics. They were thought to be particularly important in re-teaching rational numbers to trainees. Research has shown that many school students' (e.g., Ni & Zhou, 2005; Stafylidou & Vosniadou, 2004) and even trainees (e.g., Domoney, 2002) see fractions as two separate natural numbers and not a single number and develop a conception of number that is restricted to natural numbers. Ni and Zhou (2005) suggest that the teaching of fraction concepts should start earlier than is it is often recommended by curriculum developers in order to avoid the development of what they call 'whole number bias. Yet if teachers have not themselves developed an understanding that fractions are numbers, they cannot help school students' to avoid the development of such bias. Teachers must develop a strong understanding of rational numbers which, among many other things, involves the ability to distinguish between natural numbers and fractions.

3 Methodology

I carried out action research (Amato, 2001) with the aim of improving primary school trainees' understanding of mathematics. McTaggart and Kemmis (1982, p.5) emphasize the knowledge which must be sought through the action research method "trying out ideas in practice as a means of improvement and as a means of increasing knowledge about the curriculum, teaching and learning." According to McTaggart and Kemmis (1982, p. 21) one of the aims of the reconnaissance stage is to answer questions such as "What is happening already? What is the rationale for what is happening already?" In a first phase of the reconnaissance stage, trainees' liking for and understanding of mathematics were investigated empirically through two small questionnaires that were administered to two different samples of trainees ($n_1 = 224$ and $n_2 = 184$, respectively). In a second phase of the reconnaissance stage seven primary school teachers were interviewed in the hope that their answers and suggestions would provide more information in order to clarify the two research problems and to improve the plan for the first action step. As this action research was concerned with my teaching practice as a teacher educator, they were teachers whom I had taught in inservice courses with similar content to the course component I would be teaching in the action steps of the research. Those teachers had also completed a similar course component at preservice teacher education and had experience in teaching mathematics to children, so they were thought to be more able to provide information about novice teachers' initial difficulties in the teaching of mathematics than trainees or teacher educators. They could also reveal their opinions about how their preservice teacher education could have been different and prevent them from having some of those difficulties. So they could provide useful suggestions for the action steps of this research.

The action steps of the research were performed at University of Brasília, Brazil, through a mathematics teaching course component (MTCC) in preservice teacher education. This component consists of a semester with about 80 h of lectures in which both theories related to the teaching of mathematics and strategies for teaching the content in the primary school curriculum must be discussed. So the previous MTCC teaching program was mainly related to trainees' acquisition of PCK. This is the only compulsory component related to mathematics offered to primary school trainees at University of Brasília. There is an optional course component about mathematics teaching (MTCC2), but it is offered infrequently because of a shortage of mathematics teacher educators. There were two main action steps and each had the duration of one semester. Thus each action step took place with a different cohort of trainees. As the third and subsequent action steps were less formal in nature and involved less data collection, limited results will be reported from this.

In the action steps of the research, the re-teaching of mathematics (SMK) was integrated with the teaching of pedagogical content knowledge (PCK) by asking the trainees to perform children's tasks which have the potential to develop relational understanding for most of the contents in the primary school curriculum. A new teaching program was designed with two other aims in mind:

- To improve trainees' relational understanding of the content they would be expected to teach in the future; and
- To improve their liking for mathematics.

The tasks performed by the trainees had four more specific aims in mind:

- To promote trainees' familiarity with multiple modes of representation for most concepts and operations in the primary school curriculum;
- To expose trainees to several ways of performing operations with concrete materials;

- To help trainees to construct relationships among concepts and operations through the use of versatile representations; and
- To facilitate trainees' transition from concrete to symbolic mathematics.

Versatile representations such as straws, part-whole diagrams, and number lines (English & Halford, 1995) were often used in practical and written tasks in an attempt to help trainees relate natural numbers to fractions, decimals and percentages. The idea is to represent together two or more related concepts in order to make their relationships clear (e.g., 35 whole straws and 3 pieces of $1/4$ to represent the mixed number $35 \, 3/4$). A summary of the main tasks in the teaching program can be found in Amato (2004b).

In my previous courses, tasks involving translations among and within multiple modes of representation and the use of versatile representations were being advocated to help children construct relationships among mathematical concepts and operations, but they were not being used with the teachers and trainees often enough. As trainees needed to improve their relational understanding of the content in the primary school curriculum, they also needed to be treated as learners of mathematics. Therefore, about 90% of the new teaching program became children's classroom tasks.

Teaching time was anticipated to be the greatest problem in this research as all teaching strategies I am familiar with to help children acquire relational understanding require a certain amount of time to be put into practice. The problem was aggravated by my decision to re-teach the trainees most of the primary school curriculum and not just a sample of it. So an analysis of the MTCC syllabus was performed in order to reduce or exclude certain items and increase the time devoted to the teaching of more complex mathematical content. I decided to reduce the theoretical content of the syllabus and to exclude from the program a few mathematical contents such as the teaching of small numbers (zero to 9) and measurement of capacity, mass and time. Providing examples of the theories in practice was thought to be more profitable than asking the trainees to read books and articles about them.

Four data collection instruments were used to monitor the effects of the strategic actions in the action steps of the research: researcher's daily diary; middle and end of semester interviews; beginning, middle and end of semester questionnaires; and pre- and post-tests. The daily diary was a way of keeping a record of my own thinking and of observations made inside and outside the classroom concerning the research questions, the strategic actions and the problems encountered during the action steps of the research. The questions in the questionnaires and interviews focused on trainees' perceptions about their own understanding of mathematics and their attitudes toward mathematics before and after experiencing the tasks in the teaching program. They also focused on an evaluation of the tasks in the teaching program. The tests involved open-ended questions in such a way that relational understanding could be probed through a context of teaching children. For example, "How would you help your students to understand the reason for the result of $3/4 \times 1/2$?" The data analysis was mostly qualitative, but a simple quantitative analysis (frequency and percentages) was also used to describe some of the results. Much information was produced by the data collection instruments administered in the two phases of the reconnaissance stage and in the two main action steps of the research but, because of the limitations of space, only some teachers and trainees' responses related to their use of children's tasks and relational games will be presented here.

According to Thompson and Walle (1980, 1981), teachers can help students to translate from concrete to symbolic modes of representation by asking them to simultaneously manipulate concrete materials and digits to solve word problems on a Place Value Board (PVB). Orton and Frobisher (1996) also argue that students should not be asked to write symbols at a distance from the operations performed with concrete materials and propose similar association of concrete materials and symbols on a PVB. The PVB I use with Brazilian teachers, trainees, and school students (Fig. 1) is a cheaper version of the PVB proposed by Thompson and Walle. It consists of a sheet of white A3 paper (or 2 sheets of A4 paper glued together) folded into four equal lines and three unequal columns: large, medium, and small columns which can be used to represent either

- natural numbers with three digits such as 215 and 134 (First PVB, Fig. 2);
- mixed numbers such as 15 $\frac{3}{5}$ and 34 $\frac{4}{5}$ (Second PVB, Fig. 2) and decimals such as 27.8; or
- decimals with three digits such as 1.56 and 3.48 using paper strips (Third PVB, Fig. 2).

I also use a bigger teachers' version of the PVB made with transparent plastic pockets for displaying concrete materials and digits during whole classroom discussions (Fig. 3).

Pair work is used during the games and other tasks with the students' PVB (Fig. 1) to encourage trainees' interaction and sharing of ideas. The pairs also interact among themselves if they get stuck. Some of the representations used for natural numbers were extended to fractions, mixed numbers and decimals in order

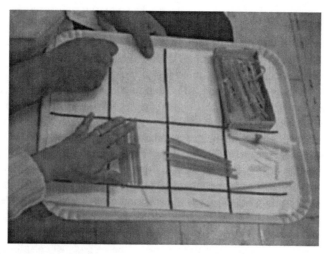

Fig. 1 Students' Place Value Board

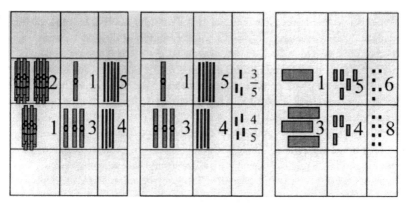

Fig. 2 Three Place Value Boards with concrete materials for representing natural numbers, mixed numbers and decimals, respectively

Fig. 3 Teachers' Place Value Board

to help school students develop the concept of rational numbers as an extension to the number system (Amato, 2005). Versatile representations such as straws, part-whole diagrams, and number lines are often used in practical and written tasks in an attempt to help trainees relate natural numbers to fractions and decimals. The PVB is used to represent place value concepts and the four basic operations with natural numbers, proper fractions, mixed numbers and decimals. Therefore, the use of these versatile representations is a way of developing trainees' learning of rational numbers in a meaningful way by relating rational numbers to their prior learning of natural numbers (Ausubel, 2000). The idea is to represent natural numbers and fractions together in order to make their relationships clear. For example, I use 15 whole straws and 3 pieces of $1/5$ to represent the mixed number 15 $3/5$ (Second PVB, Fig. 2). Natural numbers (First PVB, Fig. 2) and fractions (Second PVB, Fig. 2) are represented together with plastic drinking straws as follows:

- units = loose whole plastic straws of any color;
- tens = bunches of ten straws gathered with a rubber band;
- hundreds = bunches of ten tens gathered with a rubber band; and
- several pieces of straws: halves (red pieces), quarters (yellow pieces), fifths (green pieces), eighths (blue pieces) and tenths and hundredths (purple or pink pieces).

3.1 The Forward and Backward Trading Games

The forward and backward 'trading games' suggested by Thompson & Walle (1980; 1981) to help students develop the concepts of place value with natural numbers were extended to fractions and mixed numbers. These are games that can be played in pairs and that are orchestrated by the teacher. If the class is small, the pairs are responsible for rolling a spinner. If the class is large, the teacher rolls a giant spinner (Fig. 4) for all the pairs. In the forward version of the trading game for mixed numbers, the pair of players select the materials needed for the game (a box with 40 divisible units such as colored drinking straws, 20 fifths, and 4 rubber bands). Each player chooses one of the lines of the PVB to play the game and rolls a spinner with numbers such as $5/5$, 1, $1/5$, 2 $1/5$, $2/5$, 1 $4/5$, $3/5$ and 2 $3/5$ (for the version of game with fifths) written on it. The player who gets the bigger number starts the game. If both players score the same number, each player must roll the spinner again. Each player in his/her turn

- rolls the spinner and gets as many units and pieces as indicated by the spinner;
- places the units and the pieces in the correct places in his line of the PVB (i.e., units in the medium column and pieces in the small column); and
- changes 5 fifths for one unit and places the new unit in medium column (the units' place) of the board. Players continue accumulating units and fifths until they get ten units. Then the units are joined together with a rubber band forming a ten which should be placed in the large column (the tens' place). The winner is the player who first gets two tens.

Fig. 4 Teacher's spinner

In the backward version of the trading game for mixed numbers, the materials needed, and the way of deciding who starts the game, are the same for the forward version of the game. Each player places the number defined by the teacher (e.g., 2 tens, 4 units and 3 fifths) in the correct places in his/her line of the PVB. Each player in his/her turn, rolls the spinner and removes as many units and pieces as indicated by the spinner. Players continue removing units and fifths from the PVB. If the player does not have enough units to remove the amount of units indicated by the spinner, he/she removes one ten from the tens' place and takes the rubber band from the ten to get more loose units. If the player does not have enough fifths to remove the amount of fifths indicated by the spinner, he/she removes one straw from the units' place of the PVB, and changes the straw for 5 fifths to get more fifths. The winner is the player who first removes all his/her whole straws and pieces from the PVB. When played with fractions and mixed numbers the trading games can help school students and trainees visualize the relationship between fractions of the type n/n, $n \neq 0$ (e.g., 5/5) and the natural number one (e.g., 5/5 = 1) (Amato, 2005).

Other versions of the forward and backward trading games with rational numbers were also used with the trainees. The rules were the same as described above, only the symbols written on the spinner varied. In the second version, the spinner had improper fractions such as $6/5$, $7/5$, $8/5$, $9/5$, $10/5$, $11/5$ and $12/5$ (for the version of game with fifths) written on it. In this version, the trainees had first to convert the improper fractions to mixed numbers mentally and then play the forward and backward trading games as before. In the third version, the spinner had decimals such as 0.1, 0.2, 0.3, 0.4, 0.5, 0.6, 0.7, 0.8, 0.9, and 1 (for the version of game with tenths) written on it. In the fourth version, the spinner had decimals such as 0.01, 0.02, 0.03, 0.04, 0.05, 0.06, 0.07, 0.08, 0.09, and 0.1 (for the version of game with hundredths and played with paper strips) written on it. In this last case, the winner is the player who first gets three units in the forward trading game (Third PVB, Fig. 2).

Apart from playing the trading games with straws for base 10 with whole numbers (First PVB, Fig. 2) and later their extensions for rational numbers (Second and third PVB, Fig. 2), the trainees were initially asked to play the games for smaller bases than 10 with whole numbers (e.g., base 3, 5, or 4) as proposed by Thompson & Walle (1980, 1981). Both Polya (1981) and Sernadini (1983) recommend the inclusion of trainees' reflection after performing similar actions to those proposed for school students. So after performing the trading games, I often invited trainees to participate in short methodological discussions. I usually start the discussions with questions such as "How can this game be adapted to younger children?" or "Which relationships can this game help children construct?"

4 Some Results of the Second Phase of Reconnaissance Stage

In the second phase of the reconnaissance stage I did not ask the teachers about their attitudes to mathematics. This was done in the first phase of the reconnaissance stage with primary school trainees. The focus of the interviews with the teachers (second phase) was on their initial experiences in teaching mathematics and on the inservice courses. However, some teachers revealed how their negative attitudes to mathematics and/or their weak PCK had affected their initial teaching (Amato, 2004a). These teachers said that, at the beginning of their careers, they avoided teaching mathematics when possible. One example was "We spend more time on teaching the subject which we feel better. We often make students dislike mathematics because we [teachers] do not identify ourselves with the subject."

Another teacher expressed her perceptions about her colleagues' feelings toward mathematics and how this appeared to affect their teaching in terms of time allocation: "I hear my own school colleagues saying that they emphasize something else because they do not like mathematics. Then they do not teach much mathematics to their students." In this action research, similar to the findings reviewed by Bromme & Brophy (1986), low time allocation to the teaching of mathematics seemed to be related to teachers' negative attitudes and instrumental understanding. Avoiding the teaching of certain content could be even more damaging to children's learning than only teaching them instrumentally. As a low time allocation restricts students' opportunities to learn, teachers need to be aware of the benefits of increased teaching time particularly focusing on tasks that have the potential to develop relational understanding.

In the inservice courses a few tasks were undertaken by the teachers pretending they were children. After the first interview it was decided to ask the rest of the teachers what they felt when they were asked to participate in this way. All six teachers said that they found the idea valid, as they were being prepared to teach children. It was interesting to note that one of the teachers spontaneously mentioned the idea before being asked specifically about the theme:

> It was also important for me to place myself in the role of the student and experience some of the tasks in the inservice course. When I went to the classroom I could see a lot of things

I could do with my students. My lessons became richer and the students became more involved.

All the teachers interviewed said that they enjoyed the more practical aspect of the inservice course (Amato, 2004a). They said that learning how to use the concrete materials improved their own understanding of mathematics and their teaching practice. One of the teachers also mentioned the role of the children's classroom tasks with concrete materials in improving her attitude to mathematics: "I started liking mathematics together with my students. I noticed that, when you lean on something concrete and when you see the "whys," mathematics is not a monster with seven heads." Yet most of the time in the inservice courses, the teachers only saw examples of children's tasks and the manipulation of concrete materials by a pair of colleagues who volunteered to play the game or perform the actions to the whole group on the teacher's PVB. However, it seems that just seeing other teachers play the game or use concrete materials helped them in gaining some confidence in teaching mathematics.

The teachers also said that everything in the inservice course had been very helpful to their work. However, with the exception of one of the teachers, they complained that the inservice course had been too short to discuss the teaching of certain mathematical contents in greater detail (Amato, 2004a). Their main suggestion was to increase the duration of the inservice courses. In the past I had opted for teaching less content, to be able to do it in a more detailed way. After the reconnaissance interviews, it became clear that teachers should be asked to perform children's tasks and games much more often than it had been done in previous courses. Such decision could be even more appropriate in the case of trainees who may not have had much experience in teaching and who needed to improve their understanding of, and/or liking for, mathematics. Besides, as many trainees would be teaching any primary school grade in the very near future, they needed to perceive the curriculum as a more coherent and organic whole. Therefore, I decided to help them acquire some relational understanding of a wide range of mathematical content in the primary school curriculum.

5 Some Results of the Action Steps

Only a few trainees presented some relational understanding in the pre-tests, mainly concerning addition and subtraction of natural numbers and a few fraction concepts. The pre-test median mark was 10% and the post-test median mark was 70%. The difference in the two medians indicates a considerable improvement in understanding, as judged by the tests. Using children's tasks proved to be an appropriate strategy to improve trainees' relational understanding of mathematics since the majority of trainees said, and many indicated in the post-tests, that their understanding had improved. Some also said that they had improved their liking for the subject and their remarks clearly demonstrated a connection between the affective and cognitive domains (Amato, 2004c). However, one of my main worries about the new teaching program for initial teacher education was the effect on the trainees of asking them, as adults, to perform many children's tasks for one whole semester. The data tended to show that most of the trainees did not mind experiencing children's tasks. They appeared to accept it as a normal strategy in a course component about teaching children. On the contrary, many trainees mentioned that experiencing children's tasks had been a positive aspect of the program and had improved their understanding of, and liking for, mathematics (Amato, 2004b).

Especially during the trading games, the classes of trainees were as noisy as any children's class. After playing them, it was common to hear comments such as "It was very good" or "The children will love it." It was also common to hear one or more of the trainees asking "Are we not playing a game today?" when they noticed that the lecture was finishing and no games were played on that day. One of the questions on a questionnaire administered at the end of the semester asked the trainees to evaluate the tasks in the teaching program: "Write if you liked or didn't like participating in the tasks listed below. Tick your answer in the appropriate column according to the following code: (a) Strongly Disliked; (b) Disliked; (c) Indifferent; (d) Liked; and (e) Strongly Liked." Item (9) of the list of tasks was "to play the trading games with concrete materials on the PVB." In the first semester, 100% of the trainees who answered the questionnaire said that they liked (marked either liked or strongly liked) to play these games. In the second semester, 8% answered that they were indifferent and 92% answered that they liked to play these games.

There were also many remarks (12 trainees and 18 remarks in the first semester and 20 trainees and 45 remarks in the second semester) in several of the open-ended questions of the interviews and questionnaires about their enjoyment of the games. Those responses were considered more valid as they were not prompted by the wording of the question. The number of remarks about "playing tasks" which included games was even greater (17 trainees and 29 remarks in the first semester and 26 trainees and 69 remarks in the second semester). Some of these trainees (3 trainees and 3 remarks in the first semester and 5 trainees and 8 remarks in the second semester) suggested the inclusion of even more games in the program. The trainees commented that the games improved their understanding of, and liking for, mathematics and was one of the aspects they enjoyed in the MTCC. For example, Maria explained that the games affected her understanding by helping her to relax, and Ana said that they helped to change her attitude to teaching mathematics in the future:

Maria (Interview): Games are great. They represent relaxing moments. When you relax it seems you broaden your insight. You say: Ah! I understood. It is nice to say: 'I understood'. They are not a useless task. Have you noticed how the child inside you teaches you about life? What does a child like to do? They like to play.

Ana (post-questionnaire about the tasks in the teaching program): I would like only to emphasize the great consolidating power that the games in the classroom and the tasks involving identifying misconceptions in children's exercises. They definitely belong to this course component.

Ana (Interview): My attitude to mathematics changed for the better.... There are so many games and ways to teach the students. Now I know how to enter a classroom and talk about something. Of course I will have to prepare the lessons, but not with so much fear and lack of confidence.

One of the problems I have to face every semester is the number of trainees enrolled in each teaching group (for example, there were 42 in the first semester and 44 trainees in the second semester). I explain that their classes are a similar size to those they will be facing in the future. It is not easy to convince teachers that these teaching strategies are possible with classes of 35 to 45 primary school students, which is the usual situation in Brazil. Some adaptations and extra energy from the teacher are certainly needed, but strategies like practical work and games can still be used. Experiencing, observing and reflecting about some of the adaptations I made while using practical work and playing games was thought to help trainees see the possibilities and limitations presented by large classes. It was also thought to help them implement these tasks in their future teaching.

Games are difficult to implement even in small classes. There are always some students complaining that their partners are cheating while rolling the spinner. My previous experiences has showed me that the best way to avoid classroom management problems when playing games with large classes is to have the teacher (or teacher educator in the case of playing them in teacher education) orchestrating the game. The class is divided into pairs and I roll a giant spinner (Fig. 4) for all the pairs. In this way, all the pairs have the same scores at any given time. This allows me to ask quick short questions during the game in order to check if the pairs understand well the rules of the game and if they are doing the trades appropriately. For example, "How many straws does the left hand side (All students sitting on the left hand side of the pair) have?" and "How many straws does the right hand side (All students sitting on the right hand side of the pair) still need in order to win?" I think these adaptations are a very important form of PCK to teachers who face similar problems of large class sizes.

Apart from helping trainees relate fractions to natural numbers (e.g., $5/5 = 1$) (Amato, 2005), other important connections were facilitated by the use of the trading games on the PVB, especially the connections between the fraction and decimal notations. During a whole classroom discussion after a trading game was played with quarters, I asked how many units we had in the number $3/4$. Several trainees said "none." Then I asked the class what digit I could write in the units' place in order to say more clearly that there were no units in the number $3/4$. A trainee replied that I could write a large zero in front of the fraction. Then I wrote on the blackboard a zero in front of the fraction (i.e., $0\,3/4$) and asked the class what was the difference between the number written with the zero and the one written before without the zero. Most trainees replied none, but one trainee said jokingly that I was "wasting chalk." In other classes the trainees enjoyed the idea of writing a zero in the units' place and "wasting ink on paper" to transform a proper fraction in a mixed number with zero units. Writing a zero in the units' place became an important link between the notations for fractions and decimals, because the two notations become visually more similar (i.e., $0\,7/10 = 0.7$).

Some trainees suggested the inclusion of even more playing tasks in the program. The trading games were the main games played in the first two action steps. Yet more relational games and other children's tasks involving rational numbers concepts and operations were included in the third and subsequent semesters and also in recent inservice courses and workshops for teachers. These changes proved to be quite effective in helping other classes of teachers and trainees overcome their difficulties with, and dislike for, fractions. Relational games also proved to be a way of motivating adult learners, such as teachers and trainees, to manipulate concrete materials which become the materials used in a game, and not a tool used only by young children to help them understand mathematics.

6 Some Conclusions

Most trainees said that they enjoyed experiencing children's tasks. These results triangulated with the results obtained in the reconnaissance stage with the practicing teachers. Those teachers and the trainees in the action steps appeared to accept the main teaching strategy; that is, the use of children's tasks, as normal in a course component about teaching children. Part of trainees' dislike for mathematics was perceived as related to their instrumental understanding of the subject. Along the action steps of this research, the use of relational games proved to be one of the most effective children's tasks to improve their understanding of, and liking for, mathematics in initial teacher education.

Although my belief that instrumental teaching was going on in schools in Brasília was confirmed by what the teachers said in interviews and by trainees' instrumental understanding demonstrated in the pre-tests, I was not expecting primary school teachers to allocate less teaching time to mathematics than to other subjects. More research is certainly needed in order to investigate the extent of this "avoidance" problem and how it can be prevented. Taking into consideration that the teachers who participated in the reconnaissance stage of this research all had done a teacher education course at tertiary level and that the avoidance problem has already been mentioned in the literature in English language (e.g., Bromme & Brophy, 1986), it seems appropriate to suggest that teacher educators and researchers from developed countries should also investigate its existence and ways of ameliorating the problem.

Some teacher educators seem to believe that working toward developing teachers who are autonomous, and who seek study groups and other means of learning and growth, is incompatible with the idea of learning about SMK and PCK through formal instruction in preservice teacher education. On the contrary, my own experiences as a novice mathematics teacher and the ideas about the relationships between knowledge, democracy and autonomy elaborated by social theorists such as Antonio Gramsci (Gramsci, 1998) led me to think that trainees' acquisition of SMK and PCK in preservice teacher education is an important precondition for their future autonomy as teachers. My professional autonomy as a novice mathematics teacher was, in many moments, hindered by my instrumental understanding and by my insufficient knowledge of appropriate representations to deal with my students' difficulties.

Novice teachers have to face many constraints and challenges at the beginning of their careers (e.g., Sullivan, 2004). Natural classroom settings can be quite stressful for novice teachers whose pedagogical thinking appears to be dominated by concerns of classroom management. I think that artificially constructed environments in teacher education may help trainees focus more on learning SMK and PCK by avoiding the complexity and stress associated with whole classes. Acquiring some SMK and PCK from my own teaching experiences proved to be a very slow process. It took me a long time and a great effort to acquire some relational understanding and PCK while teaching several large classes every day. Learning mathematics from teaching also seems to be a slow process for primary school teachers, as they have to teach several subjects to the same class.

I think that trainees must acquire in preservice teacher education SMK and PCK of an adequate level to face the responsibility of providing effective learning experiences to all school students since the beginning of their teaching careers. When teachers find the time to work together in study groups, they should be discussing complex problems related to their practice and not dedicate their time trying to acquire SMK of the mathematics they teach, which I consider a basic part of their professional knowledge and so the responsibility of preservice teacher education. An initial knowledge base, which is a combination of a strong relational understanding of mathematics (SMK) and knowledge of a repertoire of representations (PCK), must be available to trainees in preservice teacher education when they are supposed to have the time to dedicate themselves to such learning. Otherwise their first students may well be led to think that mathematics is a complicated and unreachable form of knowledge because teachers have not yet learned ways of communicating the subject in a relational way. Students' learning may also be greatly harmed by their novice teachers' low time allocation to the teaching of mathematics.

Increasing general theoretical knowledge has been the main focus of teacher education courses at University of Brasília. The discussion of teaching strategies such as games and practical work and discussions about representations for the teaching of particular mathematical content, may be interpreted by some academics in a negative way and as providing trainees with recipes or procedures. These are indeed very simple forms of teachers' knowledge, but also a very basic form of pedagogical content knowledge. I think that novice teachers' reflections on what happened in the classroom as a result of their actions are much more important than where the ideas they have used in their teaching planning have come from. Slowly they can start combining the ideas gathered from textbooks, from other more mature teachers and from teacher educators with their own ideas. Teachers need to be creative, but it is important to know some of the teaching alternatives developed in the past in order to make useful adaptations and informed choices while planning and teaching particular mathematical content. Hart (1993) believes that students benefit from a sense of confidence on the part of the novice teacher: "Remember, if you are being fed by a 'plain cook' it might be best to have the food he can cook, everyday, rather than starve until he is able to produce a single gourmet dinner" (p. 30). With time and teaching experience trainees will certainly be more able to use such basic knowledge in combination with more sophisticated teaching strategies.

Acknowledgments This work benefited extensively from the insights and support of the late Mr. John Backhouse, the supervisor of my Doctorate thesis. I am also very grateful to Dr Anne Watson who supervised the thesis after his death. Acknowledgements are also due to the teachers and trainees who provided valuable information for this research.

References

Amato, S. A. (2001). *Brazilian primary school student teachers' understanding of, and attitudes to, mathematics*. Thesis submitted for the Degree of Doctor of Philosophy, Linacre College, University of Oxford, England.

Amato, S. A. (2004a). *Primary school teachers' perceptions about their needs concerning mathematics teacher education*. In Proceedings of the 10th International Congress on Mathematical Education, Copenhagen, Denmark.

Amato, S. A. (2004b). *Improving student teachers' mathematical knowledge*. In Proceedings of the 10th International Congress on Mathematical Education, Copenhagen, Denmark.

Amato, S. A. (2004c). Improving student teachers' attitudes to mathematics. In *Proceedings of the 28th International Conference for the Psychology of Mathematics Education* (Vol. 2, pp. 25–32). Bergen, Norway.

Amato, S. A. (2005). Developing students' understanding of the concept of fractions as numbers. In *Proceedings of the 29th International Conference for the Psychology of Mathematics Education* (Vol. 2, pp. 49–56). Melbourne, Australia.

Ausubel, D. P. (2000). *The acquisition and retention of knowledge: A cognitive view*. The Netherlands: Kluwer.

Ball, D. (1988). Unlearning to teach mathematics. *For the Learning of Mathematics, 8*(1), 40–48.

Ball, D. (1990). The mathematical understanding that prospective teachers bring to teacher education. *Elementary School Journal, 90*(4), 449–466.

Ball, D., & Bass, H. (2000). Interweaving content and pedagogy in teaching and learning to teach: knowing and using mathematics. In J. Boaler (Ed.), *Multiple perspectives on mathematics teaching and learning*. Westport, CT: Ablex.

Ball, D., & McDiarmid, G. W. (1990). The subject-matter preparation of teachers. In W. R. Houston (Ed.), *Handbook of research on teacher education* (pp. 437–449). New York: Macmillan.

Bezuk, N., & Gawronski, J. (2003). Increasing content and pedagogical knowledge of practicing elementary teachers. In *Proceedings of the 27th International Conference for the Psychology of Mathematics Education* (Vol. 1, p. 206). Honolulu, USA.

Bromme, R., & Brophy, J. (1986). Teachers' cognitive activities. In B. Christiansen, A. G. Howson, & M. Otte (Eds.), *Perspectives on mathematics education*. Dordrecht, Holland: D. Reidel.

Brophy, J. (1986). Teacher influences on student achievement. *American Psychologist, 41*(10), 1069–1077.

Brown, M., Askew, M., Rhodes, V., William, D., & Johnson, D. (1997). Effective teachers of numeracy in UK primary schools: Teachers' content knowledge and pupils' learning. In *Proceedings of the 21st International Conference for the Psychology of Mathematics Education* (pp. 121–128). Lahti, Finland.

Domoney, B. (2002). Student teachers' understanding of rational number: Part-whole and numerical constructs. In J. Winter & S. Pope (Eds.), *Research in mathematics education: Papers of the British Society for Research into Learning Mathematics* (Vol. 4, pp. 53–67).. London: British Society for Research into Learning Mathematics.

English, L. D., & Halford, G. S. (1995). *Mathematics education models and processes*. Mahwah, NJ: Erlbaum.

Ernest, P. (1987). Games: A rationale for their use in the teaching of mathematics in school. In R. Fisher (Ed.), *Problem solving in primary school* (pp. 202–231). Oxford: Basil Blackwell.

Ernest, P. (1989). The knowledge, beliefs and attitudes of the mathematics teacher: A model. *Journal of Education for Teaching, 15*(1), 13–33.

Fisher, C. W. (1995). Academic learning time. In L. W. Anderson (Ed.), *International encyclopedia of teaching and teacher education*. Cambridge, UK: Cambridge University Press.

Goulding, M., Rowland, T., & Barber, P. (2002). Does it matter? Primary teacher trainees' subject matter knowledge in mathematics. *British Educational Research Journal, 28*(5), 689–704.

Gramsci, A. (1998). *Selections from the prison notebooks*. London: Lawrence and Wishart.

Hannula, M. S., Kaasila, R., Laine, A., & Pehkonen, E. (2005). Structure and typical profiles of elementary teacher students' view of mathematics. In *Proceedings of the 29th International Conference for the Psychology of Mathematics Education* (Vol. 3, pp. 89–96). Melbourne, Australia.

Hart, K. M. (1993). Confidence in success. In *Proceedings of the 17th International Conference for the Psychology of Mathematics Education* (pp. 117–131). Tsukuba, Japan.

Haylock, D. (1995). *Mathematics explained for primary teachers*. London: Paul Chapman.

McTaggart, R., & Kemmis, S. (1982). *The action research planner*. Geelong, Victoria: Deakin University Press.

Ni, Y., & Zhou, K. Y. (2005). Teaching and learning fraction and rational numbers: The origins and implications of whole number bias. *Educational Psychologist, 40*(1), 27–52.

Orton, A. (1994). Learning mathematics: Implications for teaching. In A. Orton & G. Wain (Eds.), *Issues in teaching mathematics*. London: Cassel.

Orton, A., & Frobisher, L. (1996). *Insights into teaching mathematics*. London: Cassell.

Philippou, G. N., & Christou, C. (1998). The effects of a preparatory mathematics program in changing prospective teachers' attitudes towards mathematics. *Educational Studies in Mathematics, 35*(2), 189–206.

Polya, G. (1981). *Mathematical discovery*. New York: John Wiley & Sons.

Quilter, D., & Harper, E. (1988). Why we didn't like mathematics and why we can't do it. *Educational Research, 30*(2), 121–134.

Rowland, T., Huckstep, P., & Thwaites, A. (2005). Elementary teachers' mathematics subject knowledge: The knowledge quartet and the case of Naomi. *Journal of Mathematics Teacher Education, 8*(3), 255–281.

Sernadini, Z. (1983). Integration of content and pedagogy in preservice training of mathematics teachers. In M. Zweng, T. Green, J. Kilpatrick, H. Pollak., & M. Suydam (Eds.), *Proceedings of the 4th International Congress on Mathematical Education* (pp. 96–98). Berkeley, USA.

Shulman, L. S. (1986). Those who understand: Knowledge growth in teaching. *Educational Researcher, 15*(2), 4–14.

Simon, M. A. (1993). Prospective elementary teachers' knowledge of division. *Journal for Research in Mathematics Education, 24*(3), 233–254.

Skemp, R. R. (1976). Relational understanding and instrumental understanding. *Mathematics Teaching, 77*, 20–26.

Sotto, E. (1994). *When teaching becomes learning: A theory and practice of teaching*. London: Cassell.

Southwell, B., & Penglase, M. (2005). Mathematical knowledge of preservice primary teachers. In *Proceedings of the 29th International Conference for the Psychology of Mathematics Education* (Vol. 4, pp. 209–216). Melbourne, Australia.

Sowder, J. T., Bezuk, N., & Sowder, L. K. (1993). Using principles from cognitive psychology to guide rational number instruction for prospective teachers. In T. P. Carpenter, E. Fennema, & T. A. Romberg (Eds.), *Rational numbers: An integration of research*. Hillsdale, NJ: Erlbaum.

Stafylidou, S., & Vosniadou, S. (2004). The development of students' understanding of the numerical value of fractions. *Learning and Instruction, 14*(5), 503–518.

Stoddart, T., Connell, M., Stofflett, R., & Peck, D. (1993). Reconstructing elementary teacher candidates' understanding of mathematics and science content. *Teaching and Teacher Education, 9*(3), 229–241.

Stones, E. (1994). *Quality of teaching: A sample of cases*. London: Routledge.

Sullivan, P. (2004). A reaction to the background document: Recognising and addressing constraints on teachers realizing their altruistic goals. In R. Strasser, G. Brandell, B. Grevholm, & O. Helenius (Eds.), *Educating for the future. Proceedings of an international symposium on mathematics teacher education* (pp. 69–75). Sweden: The Royal Swedish Academy of Sciences.

Thompson, C. S., & Walle, J. V. (1980). Transition boards: Moving from materials to symbols in addition. *Arithmetic Teacher, 28*(4), 4–8.

Thompson, C. S., & Walle, J. V. (1981). Transition boards: Moving from materials to symbols in subtraction. *Arithmetic Teacher, 28*(5), 4–6.

Weissglass, J. (1983). Introducing pedagogy informally into a preservice mathematics course for elementary teachers. In M. Zweng, T. Green, J. Kilpatrick, H. Pollak, & M. Suydam (Eds.), *Proceedings of the 4th International Congress on Mathematical Education* (pp. 98–100). Berkeley, CA: Birkhäuser.

Wilson, S. M., Shulman, L. S., & Richert, A. E. (1987). 150 different ways of knowing: Representations of knowledge in teaching. In J. Calderhead (Ed.), *Exploring teachers' thinking.* Eastbourne: Cassell.

Using Mathematically Rich Tasks to Deepen the Pedagogical Content Knowledge of Primary Teachers

George Ashline and Regina Quinn

Professional development experiences for elementary educators in the United States are often of insufficient depth, duration or relevance to have an impact on teaching (Bransford, Brown, & Cocking, 1999). To counter this prevailing norm, mathematics and education faculty involved in the Vermont Mathematics Partnership (VMP) design courses and series of workshops for inservice and preservice elementary teachers to help them more deeply understand mathematics and the critical role of the primary curriculum in building young students' foundation for learning complex mathematics.

This chapter describes primary grade teacher professional development sessions which focused on mathematically rich tasks that featured:

- adult exploration of significant mathematical content,
- engaging activities designed and carefully sequenced to build conceptual understanding of mathematics that most educators have previously learned as simple rote procedures,
- open-ended design so that challenging tasks were accessible to all participants – regardless of their prior learning, and
- mathematical content that, although not directly transferable to the primary classroom, was clearly linked to the fundamental roots that develop in the early grades.

The tasks included in these sessions were one feature of the Vermont Mathematics Partnership, a comprehensive initiative to improve mathematics teaching and learning in schools across the state of Vermont.

G. Ashline
Professor of Mathematics, Saint Michaels College, Vermont, USA

R. Quinn
Project Director and co-PI of the Vermont Mathematics Partnership, USA

B. Clarke, B. Grevholm, and R. Millman (eds.), *Tasks in Primary Mathematics Teacher Education: Purpose, Use and Exemplars,* Mathematics Teacher Education 4,
© Springer Science+Business Media LLC 2009

1 Introduction

Primary teachers in the United States face significant challenges in preparing all of their students for success in mathematics. Since the publication of standards by the National Council of Teachers of Mathematics in 1989 and subsequent updates (National Council of Teachers of Mathematics, 2000), the expectations for student learning have expanded in scope and in depth to encompass more mathematical topics and to place a greater emphasis on conceptual understanding and complex problem solving, beginning in the earliest grades. During the 1990s, curriculum researchers, developers and publishers produced materials designed to address the increased scope and depth of the standards; however, few primary grade teachers have had adequate preparation to use those materials effectively or to plan instruction that fosters deep mathematical understanding.

Over the past decade, nearly all Vermont elementary schools adopted these curricula, yet most struggled with implementation. When teachers, administrators, and higher education faculty were asked to identify the challenges and the priorities for professional development, three themes, consistent with current research, emerged: **deeper content knowledge** (Conference Board of the Mathematical Sciences, 2001; Darling-Hammond & Sykes, 1999), experience with **instructional practices that build conceptual understanding** of that content in the primary grades (Kilpatrick, Swafford, & Findell, 2001), and assistance with lesson-design that encourages young students to make **connections and generalizations** (Weiss, Pasley, Smith, & Heck, 2003).

Teachers of mathematics at all grade levels require significant expertise in mathematics content and instruction; however, primary grade teachers face unique challenges that require specialized knowledge. Teachers of young children need to recognize the very early roots of abstract mathematical concepts in the primary grade curriculum, to discern the mathematical significance of deceptively simple primary grade activities, and to elicit mathematical conjectures, connections, and generalizations from their young students. This is particularly difficult if teachers know mathematics simply as a set of rules and procedures to be memorized.

In response to these challenges and needs, the Vermont Mathematics Partnership was established in 2002. Funded by the National Science Foundation (NSF) and the U.S. Department of Education, the VMP builds upon more than a decade of successful, statewide efforts to improve mathematics teaching and learning. VMP's core partners include mathematicians from public and private institutions of higher education, educational leaders and researchers, assessment specialists, and K–12 educators dedicated to achieving equity and excellence in mathematics education. The VMP founding partners share a history of substantive collaboration, such as through the Vermont Mathematics Initiative (VMI), a three-year, content-focused master's degree program at the University of Vermont that prepares mathematics teacher leaders who work in schools across the state.

The heart of the work of the Vermont Mathematics Partnership is to provide **opportunities for all students to succeed in learning rich, rigorous mathematics.** A fundamental question, *"What will it take to help all of the students in this system* *succeed in mathematics?*" guides every aspect of the VMP –from interactions with individual teachers to major partnerships with state and national organizations and institutions. With this focusing question in mind, VMP works with schools systems to design long-term, comprehensive plans for improving mathematics teaching and learning. A key component of these plans is to strengthen teachers' pedagogical content knowledge, the mathematical knowledge needed to teach all students effectively.

Based on the particular mathematics content knowledge needs of Vermont primary teachers, VMP instructional teams, comprised of mathematicians and educators, develop original tasks and resource materials or modify existing VMI graduate course materials to make them appropriate and accessible to a general audience of inservice and preservice teachers. As teams plan and sequence mathematical tasks, they are faced with a set of opportunities, dilemmas, and questions:

- How to maintain the intellectual rigor of the materials while respecting the immediacy of teacher concerns about classroom applications?
- How to get past the widespread belief that primary grade teachers need to know only rudimentary mathematics?
- How to translate materials that were originally designed for a graduate program for mathematics leaders into a format that is intellectually engaging and relevant to all teachers?
- How to provide ample opportunities for primary teachers to make mathematical generalizations and to see the connections between the mathematics they learn as adults and the mathematics they teach young children?

In this chapter, we provide a detailed description of the tasks designed for a series of three teacher professional development sessions, illustrating one example of how the VMP responds to these questions and challenges. These tasks were implemented in sessions totaling approximately two and a half days over a 5-month period. The tasks were developed for all faculty and support staff from one of Vermont's largest elementary schools with approximately seventy-five K–6 teachers and teacher assistants (also known as "paraeducators") with widely varied backgrounds and levels of confidence in mathematics.

2 Initial Planning

Mathematics instructional leaders at this partner school invited a VMP instructional team, consisting of mathematicians and educators, to design a series of inservice sessions for their faculty. For many participants, these workshops constituted **their first in-depth exploration of mathematics content as adult learners**. Introductory sessions were designed to provide fruitful and enjoyable mathematical explorations, filled with opportunities to understand an important mathematical idea more deeply through a sequence of exploratory tasks. These tasks encouraged primary teachers to recognize connections across branches of mathematics and ways in which their curriculum builds the foundation for more complex mathematics. As instructors, we also intended to provide a comfortable starting point for faculty, who might otherwise feel reticent about voluntarily enrolling in a mathematics course.

Drawing from existing materials designed for VMI graduate courses, we selected an engaging mathematics exploration that allowed teachers to revisit a topic with which they most likely had some familiarity, but not a deep understanding. This task, a hands-on investigation of the Pythagorean Theorem developed by Dr Edwin Marsden (Marsden, 1999), involves physically manipulating a set of right triangles and linking the resulting geometric models to algebraic approaches, ultimately recreating some of the classical proofs of the Theorem. We realized that most faculty members likely had learned the Pythagorean Theorem as a rule to be applied in particular problem situations, without understanding why it works, how it is connected to other mathematics they know, or how it relates to the mathematics they teach in the early grades.

In designing the inservice sessions, two overarching questions that guided our planning emerged: "How can we design these inservice sessions so that participants develop a conceptual understanding of a theorem they may have only memorized in high school?" and "How can we design tasks and sessions to foster teachers' ability to apply their conceptual understanding of mathematical ideas to the primary level curriculum they teach?"

As we analyzed the original Pythagorean Theorem task, we considered the question: *"What will teachers need to understand so that they will be able to get the most out of this activity?"* We knew that if we moved directly from the manipulation of a concrete model to its algebraic representation, we risked leaving participants with the same kind of superficial understanding retained from their initial high school exposure to the Pythagorean Theorem. Based on several years of experience designing content-rich professional development, we knew that it would be important to take time to build deep understandings of basic mathematical ideas, described by Liping Ma as "profound understanding of fundamental mathematics" (Ma, 1999). Another important guiding principle was to base instruction on current research on how people learn new material – anticipating, eliciting and working with partial understandings and misconceptions (Bransford et al., 1999).

3 Organizing a Series of Tasks to Deepen Content Understanding

3.1 Building Conceptual Understanding and Establishing the Culture for Conjecture

Participating teachers from this school use the Everyday Mathematics Program, developed by the University of Chicago School Mathematics Project (UCSMP, 2004). Like other curricula founded on current U.S.-based mathematics standards, this program emphasizes solving problems, formulating conjectures, evaluating arguments, testing hypotheses, and making generalizations. While educators may acknowledge the importance of establishing this kind of culture, few have had the opportunity to learn mathematics in such an environment.

To help establish an environment that encourages mathematical reasoning, we began our initial inservice session with a quote from the Scarecrow at the end of the *Wizard of Oz* movie (LeRoy, 1939). Endowed by the Wizard with certification that he had a brain, the Scarecrow quipped, "The sum of the square roots of any two sides of an isosceles triangle is equal to the square root of the remaining side." To the casual listener, this mathematical proposition, filled with technical jargon, may sound reasonable. We decided to use this familiar quote to engage teachers in thinking critically about an erroneous conjecture and in generating arguments, based on their evolving understanding of related mathematical principles.

As groups completed tasks, they explored conjectures and solved problems building toward a proof of the Pythagorean Theorem. We circulated, observed, and carefully monitored progress, noting specific problems with which participants struggled, made errors, or demonstrated misconceptions. Participants were encouraged to construct mathematical arguments to defend their solutions and to evaluate conflicting ideas. The ensuing discussion shed light on numerous partial understandings, worthy of further exploration.

3.2 Explorations in Geometry

Based on our earlier experiences of using these tasks with teachers, we determined that it would be most useful to build foundational understandings in geometry in advance of more direct explorations of the Pythagorean Theorem. Highlighting several geometrical concepts, these initial tasks helped to provide the language needed for later proof investigation. We developed explorations on the classification and properties of basic geometric shapes, the concept of area and how formulas for finding the area of various polygons are generated, the area model for multiplication and a concrete, physical basis for algebra and geometry. These exploratory tasks were designed to assist teachers in making connections across branches of mathematics and in developing vocabulary needed for deeper mathematical analysis and proof.

During the first inservice session, teachers investigated the characteristics of parallelograms and triangles and generated rules for measuring areas, considering initial examples of rectangular area as the product of the length and width:

> A room that is 5 m by 9 m requires 45 m^2 of carpet to cover the floor.
> A base-ten block that is 10 cm long and 10 cm wide has an area of 100 cm^2.

Groups of teachers worked together to use that basic knowledge to determine the areas of a variety of triangular and quadrilateral regions, such as those illustrated in Fig. 1.

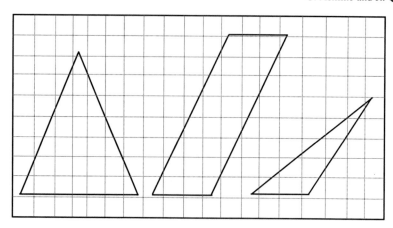

Fig. 1 Examples of geometric figures included in initial explorations

As groups shared their work, we stressed the importance of their precise use of mathematical terminology when communicating in mathematics. Teachers were asked to formulate definitions for the *base* and *height* of a triangle and parallelogram and to use their definitions to find the areas of any right triangle, generic triangle, and parallelogram. Whereas a number of the teachers had memorized the formulas for the areas of a parallelogram as the product of *base* and *height* and a triangle as half the product of *base* and *height*, teachers better understood the origins of these results through this investigation.

During the second inservice session, fundamental concepts that had been explored during the first session were highlighted, reinforced and extended to include other properties of triangles. Teachers were encouraged to conjecture and generalize about properties of various types of triangles. Some noted that right triangles can have side lengths which are multiples of 3, 4, and 5 units. Others stated that it is impossible for the longer side length to equal or surpass the sum of the two smaller side lengths. These insights led to the conclusion that, to form a triangle, the sum of any two side lengths of a triangle must be greater than that of the third. By starting with concrete examples, teachers were able to reach more general conclusions, and ultimately predict whether or not a given set of three numbers represents the side lengths of a triangle. By providing time to rediscover formulas and revisit fundamental ideas, the stage was set for the challenging task of proving the Pythagorean Theorem in the final session, which will be detailed in a later section of this chapter.

3.3 Working Toward a Proof with the Tri-square Rug Activity

To facilitate a deeper understanding of the relationships between initial geometric explorations and the Pythagorean Theorem, we used the "tri-square rug activity," adapted from the Integrated Mathematics Program (Fendel & Resek, 1999),

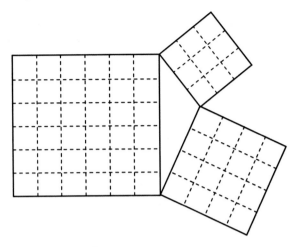

Fig. 2 Example of a "tri-square rug"

in which teachers rediscovered the statement and meaning of the Pythagorean Theorem. In this task, Al and Betty have designed a game using a "tri-square rug" that is made by sewing three separate square rugs together at their corners, with an empty triangular space resulting, as illustrated in Fig. 2.

In Al and Betty's game, a dart falls randomly on the rug, with three possible outcomes:

- If the dart hits the largest of the three squares, Al wins.
- If the dart hits either of the other two smaller squares, Betty wins.
- If the dart misses the rug, they just let another dart fall.

The goal of this task was for teachers to find tri-square rug configurations ultimately yielding fair games or wins for Al or Betty. Listing several examples for each category, teachers noticed patterns and were able to efficiently predict the long term outcome by carefully looking at a tri-square rug (See Picture 1 on p. 206.).

Through this task, teachers reinforced their understanding of the types of triangles discussed in the first inservice session. Given a particular tri-square rug, they recognized that by measuring the largest angle C of its middle triangle T, they could find the winner by determining if the triangle was obtuse, acute, or right. Furthermore, in subsequent discussion, teachers connected this with the relationships among the middle triangular side lengths of a, b, and c (the longest side of T). A summary of their conclusions is given in Table 1.

Table 1 Tri-square rug activity conclusions

Al wins	Betty wins	Fair game
T is obtuse	T is acute	T is right
$C > 90°$	$C < 90°$	$C = 90°$
$a^2 + b^2 < c^2$	$a^2 + b^2 > c^2$	$a^2 + b^2 = c^2$

Picture 1 Teachers engaging in tri-square rug activity

Discussion also ensued on the need to carefully measure triangular angles and side lengths and to recognize precision limitations of common measuring devices such as compasses and rulers.

This task offered insight into a concrete model for the Pythagorean Theorem. The squares of the side lengths of the triangle are actually areas of square regions.

3.4 The Area Model for Multiplication

The goal of the final inservice session was to provide teachers with the opportunity to discover a proof of the Pythagorean Theorem. As a prelude to the hands-on proof of the Theorem, we designed a task to introduce the area model for multiplication. This task also provided an opportunity for primary teachers to understand connections between algebraic and geometric approaches. We knew that this was an important focal point because we have found that most teachers have had limited opportunities to understand and appreciate the intimate linkages between algebra and geometry, although current standards and curricula emphasize the importance of building young students' understanding of these connections.

Teachers began their exploration of the area model for multiplication with a concrete application, multiplying two-digit numbers. This model builds upon teachers' knowledge of multiplication algorithms, such as the partial product and lattice methods, and connects to algebraic and geometric representations. For example, consider the area model for 24 × 37, depicted in Fig. 3.

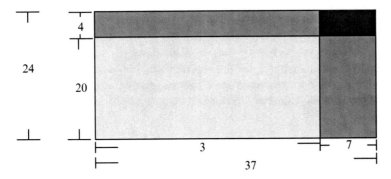

Fig. 3 Example of a specific application of the area model for multiplication

Herein, teachers envisioned the area of the entire region in terms of its four decomposed subregions as follows:

$$\begin{aligned} 24 \times 37 &= (20+4) \times (30+7) \\ &= (20 \times 30) + (20 \times 7) + (4 \times 30) + (4 \times 7) \\ &= 600 + 140 + 120 + 28 \\ &= 888 \end{aligned}$$

Building from this relevant example, teachers then investigated the algebraic representation of general area models for multiplication, namely,

$$\begin{aligned} (x+y)^2 &= x^2 + 2xy + y^2 \text{ and} \\ (x+y)(z+w) &= xz + xw + yz + yw \end{aligned}$$

These equations can be represented and verified using the models in Fig. 4.

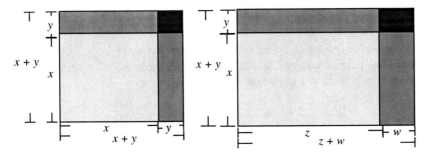

Fig. 4 Generalized area models for multiplication

The total area of the square on the left of Fig. 4 with side length $x+y$ is $(x+y)^2$. It is also the sum of the areas of its four pieces: one square with side x (and area x^2), one square with side y (and area y^2), and two rectangles with side lengths x and y (and areas $x \cdot y = y \cdot x$). In the more general setting, the total area of the rectangle on the right with side lengths $x+y$ and $z+w$ is $(x+y)(z+w)$, but its total area is also the sum of the areas of its four rectangular pieces, namely (taken from bottom to top) $xz+xw+yz+yw$. As teachers analyzed the illustrative models in this task, they better understood and appreciated the rule of "FOIL," in which the area of the four rectangular pieces corresponds to the algebraic product of the First, Outer, Inner, and Last terms of the binomial product $(x+y)(z+w)$.

3.5 Framing the Pythagorean Theorem

After recognizing rich connections between algebra and geometry and discussing area model results, teachers were prepared to work cooperatively on the culminating task – a proof of the Pythagorean Theorem. More specifically, for the right triangle pictured in Fig. 5 with leg lengths a units and b units and hypotenuse length c units, teachers worked toward a proof that $a^2 + b^2 = c^2$.

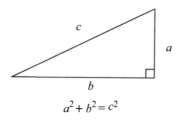

$$a^2 + b^2 = c^2.$$

Fig. 5 The Pythagorean Theorem

    To help them focus their efforts, we encouraged teachers to create a "picture frame" region with the four congruent triangular regions pictured in Fig. 6. (This "picture frame" would be shaped less like something purchased in an art supply store, and more like something constructed by a math teacher!) Each group of teachers was supplied with four large, labeled, congruent right triangles like the ones in Fig. 6, as well as poster paper on which to arrange them. This paper also provided space to record observations, ideas and conjectures about the relationships between geometric and algebraic representations.

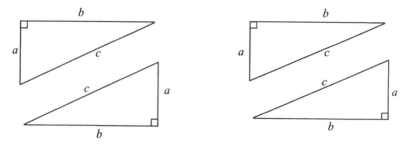

Fig. 6 Set of right triangles used in the culminating task – "Framing the Pythagorean Theorem"

Viewing these triangles as "picture frame components" and applying area model results, teachers strove toward a proof of the Pythagorean Theorem. This process was challenging for many. Some groups struggled to find a configuration connecting the side lengths of the four right triangles; others began by forming frames with irregular areas or containing no space for an enclosed "picture." With encouragement and minimal assistance by instructors, groups persevered through this task and found geometric representations leading to a proof of the Theorem. Most frequently, they created two types of frames: a "Small Frame" or a "Large Frame."

While building their physical models, teams spontaneously began to represent their work algebraically. After numerous false starts and refinements, they were ultimately able to translate from physical to algebraic models to prove the Pythagorean Theorem.

Groups that created a *Small Frame*, as in Fig. 7, represented the total model area as the sum of the areas of the inner square "picture" and the four congruent "framing" triangles, as in Fig. 8.

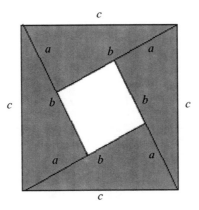

Fig. 7 Small Frame model for the Pythagorean Theorem

$$c^2 = (b-a)^2 + 4\left(\frac{1}{2}ab\right)$$

$$c^2 = (b-a)^2 + 2ab$$

$$c^2 = (b^2 - 2ab + a^2) + 2ab$$

$$c^2 = b^2 + a^2 - 2ab + 2ab$$

$$c^2 = a^2 + b^2$$

Fig. 8 Algebraic equations for the Small Frame model

Another way teachers envisioned the connection between the physical model of the *Small Frame* and its related algebraic expressions was to rearrange or decompose the model into its components, depicted in Fig. 9.

Other teams formed a *Large Frame*, as in Fig. 10, and algebraically represented the total area as the sum of the areas of the inner square "picture" and the four congruent "framing" triangles, as in Fig. 11.

As shown in Fig. 12, the sections of the *Large Frame* can be rearranged into component parts to clarify the algebraic progression in Fig. 11.

Using either approach to this task, teachers "framed" the proof of the Pythagorean Theorem. For some teachers, this was the first proof they had ever created, and hence represented a significant accomplishment. Despite the challenge of working concurrently in an algebraic and geometric fashion, collaboration on this proof enhanced teachers' understanding and sense of ownership of these concepts. (See Picture 2 on p. 209).

This hands-on task and resulting proof techniques offered an opportunity for teachers to reflect upon contributions of various cultures in the history of

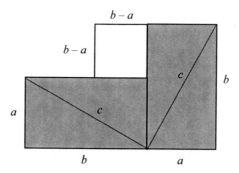

Fig. 9 Rearrangement of the Small Frame

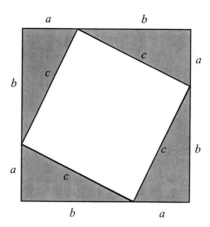

Fig. 10 Large Frame model for the Pythagorean Theorem

$$(a+b)^2 = c^2 + 4\left(\frac{1}{2}ab\right)$$

$\updownarrow$

$$a^2 + 2ab + b^2 = c^2 + 2ab$$

$\updownarrow$

$$a^2 + b^2 = c^2$$

Fig. 11 Algebraic equations for the Large Frame model

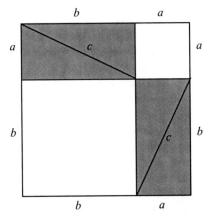

Fig. 12 Rearrangement of the Large Frame

Picture 2 Teachers discovering Large Frame proof

mathematics. The *Small Frame* idea was used by the 12th century Indian mathematician Bhaskara (Weisstein, 2004), and the *Large Frame* idea can be traced back to the ancient Chinese (University of South Australia, UNISA, 1996). These references deepen discussion of the proof and illustrate ways to connect mathematics to its rich history.

3.6 Building Pedagogical Content Knowledge

"Most of us encountered the geometry of Euclid with its axioms and theorems in high school. And for many this was a mystifying experience. One reason is the inappropriate structure and content of many of these geometry courses – a situation that is slowly changing as new approaches to secondary school geometry instruction are being developed. *But an equally compelling reason is that many students have little or no formal experience with geometry prior to their high school courses. The Everyday Mathematics curriculum places significant emphasis on this part of mathematics, beginning in Kindergarten.*" (EDM Grades 4–6 Teacher's Reference Manual [UCSMP, 2004, pp. 160–161])

As we planned workshop sessions, we reviewed K–6 lessons from the Everyday Mathematics program. Keeping in mind the importance of geometry in the curriculum, we selected tasks across grade levels that build student experience with fundamental mathematics related to the Pythagorean Theorem to help teachers connect their explorations of the Theorem to the elementary curriculum they teach. Throughout the sessions, we provided opportunities for teachers to review lessons and tasks at each grade level related to area, perimeter, properties of triangles and squares, linear versus square units of measure, area models for multiplication, and algebraic modelling.

Although the verification and application of the Pythagorean Theorem begins in the sixth grade Everyday Mathematics program, there are many preliminary underlying concepts that are developed in earlier grades. Groups of kindergarteners explore perimeter and properties of triangles, squares and other shapes by using a large loop of rope to make polygons with the same perimeter. Across the primary grades, students encounter the concept of area through several "tiling" activities, in which they cover surfaces with various objects such as pattern blocks or paper squares. During the early grades, students use models to explore square numbers, find areas of regular and irregular shapes, and solve multiplication problems by building arrays. By sixth grade, students are expected to identify two-dimensional shapes and the base and height of triangles and parallelograms and to generate formulas for finding the area of those figures. Fifth and sixth graders play games to estimate the square root of a number.

As teachers deepened their mathematical understanding and studied related K–6 lessons and tasks, they began to see their own curricular materials "with new eyes" and considered questions such as those in Fig. 13.

- *How will the deeper understanding you have developed during these sessions inform the way you do this lesson?*
- *What is important mathematically about this task?*
- *How will you guide your students to think about this mathematics?*
- *What questions could you pose that will help your students make mathematically significant observations?*
- *In what way does this lesson or task relate to the Pythagorean Theorem?*

Fig. 13 Questions to guide analysis of primary grade curriculum materials

They began to recognize that improving their understanding of mathematics and of curricula across grade levels can positively impact their own instruction. As further described below, teachers at the school participated in grade-level teams, and the mathematics teacher leaders for those teams helped to facilitate some discussions after our sessions and collect some of this feedback. As informally shared in conversations and team meetings after our sessions, teachers reported the experience of being midway into a lesson and suddenly struck by a new connection between long-taught material and a new mathematical insight developed through our sessions. Although making these connections takes time (sometimes days or even longer), we were intentional about creating tasks to provide opportunities for teachers to transfer their learning and to connect adult-level content with primary-level teaching. Making these links explicit is neither straightforward nor simple. Even with strong mathematics content knowledge, it is not always easy to see how a simple kindergarten activity lays the foundation for more sophisticated mathematics. Exploring mathematics concepts in-depth and tracing back the roots to the earliest grade levels helps teachers recognize the importance of understanding mathematics content that is well beyond the grade levels they teach – a recurring theme of our initiative.

Teachers who participated in these sessions weekly met in grade-level teams, to review upcoming units of study and to discuss the important mathematical ideas and strategies for helping their students learn that content. Having a common experience in learning mathematics as adults, these teachers were better able to selectively use or modify their own curriculum materials to focus on the significant mathematics that underlies primary grade tasks and lessons.

4 Conclusion

We returned to the Scarecrow's quote (LeRoy, 1939) during our final session after spending significant time formulating and testing mathematics conjectures as outlined above. The Scarecrow, surprised by the words that came out of his mouth, exclaimed, "Oh joy! Rapture! I've got a brain!" Teachers at our sessions experienced their own excitement as they became more adept at finding the fallacy in the

Scarecrow's statement and generating their own proof of the Pythagorean Theorem, the culmination of these carefully sequenced tasks.

The sessions described in this chapter comprise one small part of a multiyear comprehensive plan for strengthening mathematics teaching and learning at this school. Other activities include on-site graduate courses, the formation of a team of mathematics teacher leaders from each grade level, training for administrators, technical assistance in the use of assessment to inform and improve instruction, and classroom modelling and coaching by outstanding mathematics teachers. Midway into this project, students at this school have demonstrated significantly improved scores in mathematical problem solving and conceptual understanding on statewide mathematics assessments. Teachers have demonstrated deeper content knowledge, improvements in instructional practices, and greater confidence in their ability to understand and teach challenging mathematics. Administrators report changes in the quality of instruction they observe and the enthusiasm with which teachers and students engage in mathematics.

In addition to this school, six other VMP partner school systems across the state have implemented their own comprehensive plans for improving mathematics teaching and learning. These plans are tailored to each school systems' unique assets and needs. Although models vary considerably, each plan maintains focus on the essential question, *"What will it take to help all of the students in this system succeed in mathematics?"*

Through work at these seven partner systems during the first 4 years of the VMP, project leaders and evaluators have found that primary teachers change and improve their practice as they

- deepen their mathematics content knowledge,
- have multiple opportunities to link that knowledge to their curriculum,
- systematically use ongoing, formative assessment to collect evidence of student understanding, and use that evidence to guide their instruction,
- engage in and learn about mathematics education research findings, and
- have direct experiences, such as observing master teachers, that demonstrate that students are capable of learning more complex mathematics than previously believed.

The kind of learning described in this chapter ideally commences during initial teacher preparation; however, sustained work in mathematics professional development for primary teachers, throughout their careers, is critical in the current climate of high expectations and increasing demands on educators and students. To have a lasting, positive impact upon a school, it takes an in-depth, comprehensive approach and commitment on the part of teachers, administrators and professional developers. To be effective, such professional development should offer many entry points, including workshop sessions designed to stimulate interest in learning mathematics, such as those detailed in this chapter.

It is essential for mathematicians and educators to collaborate and contribute their expertise, in planning and creating the materials and services necessary for the success of such endeavors. When mathematicians and educators work closely on all aspects of planning and development, the resulting professional development can result in powerful and engaging learning for participants and instructors. This approach to professional development contrasts sharply with approaches that relegate the mathematics content to the mathematicians and the educational content to the educators.

Finally, it is important to keep in mind the nature of elementary mathematics in which this development is embedded. As Liping Ma points out (Ma, 1999, p. 116),

> ... elementary mathematics is not a simple collection of disconnected number facts and calculational algorithms. Rather it is an intellectually demanding, challenging, and exciting field – a foundation on which much can be built. Elementary mathematics is fundamental mathematics.

In her conclusion, Ma argues (Ma, 1999, p. 153) that

> The real mathematical thinking going on in a classroom ... depends heavily on the teacher's understanding of mathematics .... If a teacher's own knowledge of the mathematics taught in elementary school is limited to procedures, how could we expect his or her classroom to have a tradition of inquiry mathematics? The change that we are expecting can occur only if we work on changing teachers' knowledge of mathematics.

We heartily agree and feel that the implementation of professional development opportunities, like the one described in this chapter, will allow primary teachers to more deeply understand the mathematics they teach.

Acknowledgments The VMP is funded by a grant provided by the US Department of Education (Award Number S366A020002) and the National Science Foundation (Award Number EHR-0227057). (http://www.vermontmathematics.org).

The authors of this chapter have collaborated for several years on initiatives to improve mathematics teaching and learning: the Vermont Mathematics Initiative, a content-intensive, graduate program for teacher leaders and the Vermont Mathematics Partnership (VMP), a project funded by the National Science Foundation and US Department of Education to work with school systems to improve mathematics learning for all students.

References

Bransford, J., Brown, A., & Cocking, R. (Eds.). (1999). *How people learn: Brain, mind, experience, and school*. Washington, DC: National Academy Press.

Conference Board of the Mathematical Sciences. (2001). *The Mathematical education of teachers*. Washington DC: American Mathematical Society and Mathematical Association of America.

Darling-Hammond, L., & Sykes, G. (Eds.). (1999). *Teaching as the learning profession: Handbook of policy and practice*. San Francisco, CA: Jossey-Bass.

Fendel, D., & Resek D. (with Alper, L., & Fraser, S.). (1999). *Interactive mathematics program year 2* (p. 226). Emeryville, CA: Key Curriculum Press.

Kilpatrick, J., Swafford, J., & Findell B. (Eds.). (2001). *Adding it up: Helping children learn mathematics*. Washington, DC: National Academy Press.

LeRoy, M. (Producer), & Fleming, V. (Director). (1939). *The Wizard of Oz* [Film], [Videocassette]. MGM (distributor).

Ma, L. (1999). *Knowing and teaching elementary mathematics*. Mahwah, NJ: Erlbaum.

Marsden, E. (1999). *The Pythagorean Theorem: A proof based on geometry.* Activity created for Vermont Mathematics Initiative.

National Council of Teachers of Mathematics (NCTM). (2000). *Principles and standards of school mathematics.* Reston, VA: NCTM.

University of Chicago School Mathematics Project (UCSMP). (2004). *Everyday mathematics program (EDM).* Chicago, IL: Wright Group/McGraw-Hill.

University of South Australia (UNISA). (1996) *History of mathematics.* Retreived from UNISA Web site homepage: http://www.roma.unisa.edu.au/07305/pythag.htm (Retrieved August 25, 2008).

Weiss, I. R., Pasley, J. D., Smith, P. S., & Heck, D. J. (2003). *Looking inside the classroom: A study of K–12 mathematics and science education in the United States.* Chapel Hill, NC: Horizon Research, Inc.

Weisstein, E. (2004). *MathWorld: The web's most extensive mathematical resource.* Retreived from Wolfram Research, Inc. Web site: http://mathworld.wolfram.com/PythagoreanTheorem.html (Retrieved August 25, 2008).

From Professional Tasks in Collaborative Environments to Educational Tasks in Mathematics Teacher Education

José Carrillo and Nuria Climent

This chapter concerns the work of a group of primary teachers and teacher educators-researchers in the field of Mathematics Education within a project of collaborative research (PIC), which is aimed at promoting primary teachers' professional development as well as investigating such development. In the sessions of PIC we have set some professional tasks, analysed how they promote professional development and modified them according to our reflections. At the same time, as primary teachers' educators, we have adapted these tasks in order to use them in preservice teacher education. The findings from the PIC have illuminated both our and the student teachers' decision-making concerning these tasks. In this chapter we present an overview of these tasks and deal with actual examples concerning their implementation in both preservice and inservice teacher education within the collaborative environment of the PIC.

1 Context

In Spanish Primary Education today, teachers act as class tutors to their pupils, and teach mathematics, society and nature studies, language, and art education. The training they will have received depends largely on the syllabus they followed and when they undertook their university studies, although in general, practising primary teachers with children aged between 6 and 12 are not specialised in mathematics, as is the case with the teachers we refer to in this chapter. Current student teachers receive little teaching in mathematics, with few significant differences, in the main, between one university and another. Specifically, at the University of Huelva, from a total of 2,060 h, future primary teachers follow just one 45-h course dedicated

J. Carrillo
Assistant Professor, Faculty of Educational Sciences, University of Huelva, Spain

N. Climent
University of Huelva, Spain

B. Clarke, B. Grevholm, and R. Millman (eds.), *Tasks in Primary Mathematics Teacher Education: Purpose, Use and Exemplars,* Mathematics Teacher Education 4,
© Springer Science+Business Media LLC 2009

exclusively to mathematics, along with another of 120 h which jointly covers mathematics and pedagogical issues. It is within this latter course, which takes place in the third and last year of the degree, that the class-based task with the trainees that we present here is undertaken.

Since 1999 a group of primary teachers and teacher educators-researchers have been working together in the field of Mathematics Education within a project of collaborative research (PIC, *Proyecto de Investigación Colaborativa*) at the University of Huelva. The PIC is currently composed of three primary teachers, two teacher educators-researchers and two young researchers. There are three features which have characterised and enriched the group throughout its existence: the importance of reflection as a catalyst for professional development, collaboration – the design process is collaborative as against cooperative, where the researchers design activities and schemes of work for the teachers' use, and actual classroom practice as the backdrop against which all group discussions are put to the test.

2 Theoretical background

The work described here is consistent with our perspective of professional development as a continuum that includes pre- and inservice teacher education (Carrillo, Coriat, & Oliveira, 1999). From our perspective, it is crucial that student teachers begin to conceptualise practice in a way that promotes their professional development. For that purpose, in both pre- and inservice teacher education (as teacher educators and researchers) we use various theoretical notions as analytical conceptual tools.

Our notion of mathematics teacher development (Climent & Carrillo, 2002), in which reflection plays a major role, has been influenced chiefly by Cooney and Shealy's (1997) autonomy and permeability of conceptions, on Krainer's (2001) understanding of practice and Jaworski's (1998) reflective practice. In PIC we specially deal with Krainer's (2001) reflection and networking. Also useful in describing the context of the PIC is Jaworski's (1992, 1994) teaching triad and the notion of the *educational triangle*. Zaslavsky and Leikin (2004) make an interesting extension to Jaworski's triad into the context of mathematics teacher education. In this case, the vertices of the mathematics teacher educator triad are *Jaworski's triad, management of mathematics teachers' learning*, and *sensitivity to mathematics teachers*. This is similar to the amplification we present from the educational triangle (Fig. 1) to the professional development triangle (Fig. 2), although it foregrounds the learning content and professional knowledge more than the participants themselves, who receive greater attention in the educational triangle.

The educational triangle comprises tree vertices: teacher, pupils and content (Fig. 1).

This triangle, which can be considered as a specific case of one in which the vertices are organiser, participants and content, has various expansions, in such a way that we can design triangles that represent the context of professional development.

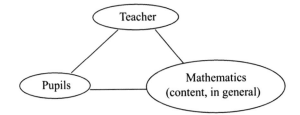

Fig. 1 The educational triangle

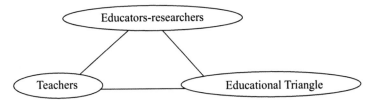

Fig. 2 Professional development triangle

We present the extension of the educational triangle to professional development associated with the PIC (Fig. 2).

The educators-researchers vertex indicates the main activity of the researchers involved in the PIC, but their role as co-learners in the environment of the PIC should not be forgotten (Jaworski, 2001). We agree with Lesh and Lovitts (2000) when they say,

> To develop more productive links between theory and practice, it is naïve to think in terms of a one-way process in which practitioners present problems and researchers provide answers that are distributed through external agents (p. 52).

Collaborative environments have been proven to promote links between theory and practice, teachers and researchers (Climent & Carrillo, 2002, 2003). It is in this spirit that Jaworski (2004), due to the complexity of mathematics teaching, proposes joint research between teachers and teacher educators as a means of promoting deeper forms of understanding in the teacher development community.

In both the PIC and our preservice courses we use video recordings of real classroom situations. They are a powerful tool allowing close examination of many aspects of teaching which can be returned to whenever required (Lampert & Ball, 1998). In the group analysis, the (student) teachers learn to establish ways of professional networking with their colleagues and ways of development. We do not think the notions, processes, tools and contexts for preservice teacher education and for inservice teacher education are the same. What we have learned from our experience is that the development of trainee mathematics teachers is fostered through a variety of means, chief amongst which are reflection, classroom-based activities, and opportunities to ask real questions. Llinares and Krainer (2006), viewing this development from the perspective of learning-to-teach, suggest that for student teachers,

One way of coordinating messages produced by different contexts in which learning-to-
teach takes place is by incorporating teaching analysis in teacher education programs"
(p. 434).

Concerning the teachers participating in the PIC, we consider our analytical focus on teaching as a means of entering theoretical loops (from practice to theory
to practice) (Skott, 2004) that should be interpreted not as prescriptions for performance, but as issues relevant to the teacher's reflective activity.

Many authors have highlighted the importance of analysing classroom situations
(Moje & Wade, 1997; Shulman, 1992). We believe it is important to capture as full
a picture as possible (whole lessons, including students' reactions and their interactions with each other and with the teacher). Our goal is not only to draw theoretical
principles from practice, or to see how practice confirms these principles; rather, we
attempt to present a realistic situation as fully as possible, with its complexity and
richness of interpretations and its inherently interconnected theoretical principles.
We also share the philosophy of projects like MILE (Goffree & Oonk, 1999) with
respect to the relevance of the concepts of the reflective practitioner and practical
knowledge, and the principle of investigating real practice as a means of development (Goffree & Oonk, 2001). What we contribute here is the simultaneity of both
scenarios: the PIC deals with real classroom situations and these situations (nurtured
by the discussions in the PIC) are subsequently transferred to the initial training programme.

The aim is, therefore, to gather theoretical knowledge from actual situations,
and from this to develop a theoretical understanding of practice (Krainer, 2001),
learning to use theory to interpret practice. It is very important that theories are
seen as useful by teachers and prospective teachers, because they often put up a
barrier between theory (linked to initial education) and practice (primary schools).
In this sense, Goffree (1999) speaks about *theoretical reflection*, in which the teacher
educator analyses a concrete situation based on his/her experience and knowledge,
and emphasises how the theory may help understand the practice and, sometimes,
help make predictions. In our case, the tasks set for the (prospective) teachers are
mathematics-revealing:

> There has been a deliberate and unmistakable shift in mathematics education away from a
> focus on students and their learning to teachers, their mathematically-related knowledge and
> the relationships of their mathematical knowledge to their teaching (Wood, 2005, p. 193).

We attempt to find an integrated way of building knowledge by the (prospective)
teachers through both the specific content of mathematics teaching and its pedagogical content, promoting its functionality and the perception of this functionality. We
agree with Cooney (2001), and extend his conclusion to inservice teachers, when
he says:

> The best entry into their [preservice teachers'] belief systems about mathematics and the
> teaching of mathematics is through the study of school mathematics. It is here that reflection
> can become commonplace with respect to both mathematics and pedagogy. Consequently,
> I submit that the integration of content and pedagogy is a strategic site for encouraging
> reflection and the consequences of that reflective thinking (pp. 26–27).

It is a question of learning to reflect on mathematics teaching and learning situations, of being aware of the major role of mathematics (Jaworski, 1999).

Summarising, the key points of our approach to professional development are:

- The conception of the student teacher as a teacher in progress. Real practice situations and emerging issues in the PIC: transference to the initial teacher education.
- Collaboration (shared goals) between teachers and educators-researchers as a means to go deeper in our understanding of teaching and learning mathematics (Fig. 1) and teacher learning (Fig. 2).
- Classroom-based reflection, with special attention to the role that mathematics plays in the process of teaching and learning mathematics.
- Reflection as a means of entering theoretical loops (that comprises theory and practice). Theoretical reasoning about practice.

3 The Professional Task and its Role in Teacher Training for Mathematics

We consider three main types of task:

1. Mathematics tasks. These deal with mathematics content, frequently problematic for trainee and teacher alike, acting them as an apprentice. The objective is its solution from the content perspective.
2. Classroom situations. These are presented on video for analysis. In this case, the teacher or future teacher acts as a professional critically observing the practice of a colleague in a real world classroom session.
3. The design, simulation and/or practice of classroom situations. The teacher tackles the problem of how to present specific content in given conditions (real or fictitious), designing a solution and putting this into practice. In some cases a group of student teachers might replace the school classroom.

The approach described here, used with both students in their initial training and teachers participating in the PIC, involves a series of two or three of the task types above in no particular order, but always interrelated. The following paragraphs offer some specific examples of these tasks and the relations between them.

4 An Example from the PIC Inservice Training Context

The example outlined below is a series of tasks which arose from the PIC and were then adapted for use during the initial training course.

The first task of the sequence is to view and analyse a real class session of one of the teachers in the project (type B task). The analysis includes a discussion of the teacher's lesson plan, and moves onto consideration of an individual case arising from the lesson in question (a variation of a type B task). This particular case was selected by the teacher trainers for its pedagogical and mathematical interest, and discussing it from a mathematical perspective naturally leads into the formulation of problematic mathematical issue for the teachers (type A task), exemplifying a form of mathematical reasoning which is useful for solving mathematical questions such as the particular case mentioned above.

4.1 Task 1: Analysis of a Classroom

One of the activities that the PIC carries out is recording lessons given by the participating teachers and analysing them afterwards. One such recording concerned the introduction of the notion of fraction in 5th grade. We viewed the video in a PIC meeting. The teacher trainers had watched it beforehand and divided the lesson into different parts (which we termed episodes), selecting the most interesting for viewing in the project. Accompanying notes were also prepared to guide viewers through the structure of the lesson. Using this guide the selected episodes were watched, with pauses for comments to be made and observations to be noted down for discussion at the end of the viewing. The aim of the group analysis is to discuss the lesson from the perspective of teaching the planned material, focusing on the teacher, Ana's, performance. In this case we will not go deeply into task design (type C task), although the objectives which the teacher set in this session and the adaptation of the task are considered.

The mathematical task that Ana sets to her pupils is "to fold as many ways as possible a rectangle, a circle and a square to make halves and quarters". The students work in small groups and afterwards a plenary is carried out. Before reading further, we suggest reading the appendix to get a clearer picture of the lesson. In what follows we focus on those aspects of the discussion which are most relevant to the possibilities of this task from the point of view of the teachers' professional development (as well as those of great interest for their contrast with the analysis of the student teachers – see section "Initial Teacher Training").

Present during the video discussions in the PIC were Ana, another of the teachers involved in the project (Pilar), and the two trainers. Pilar shows her enthusiasm for Ana's performance including making comments such as, "You come across as a researcher!" In the face of this, Ana confesses that her impatience sometimes gets the better of her and she doesn't wait long enough for the students to give her their ideas.

What follows are the most salient points of the discussion:

1. Ana clarifies why she explicitly proposed doing the divisions in all ways possible – that she wanted the pupils to see that there is no single solution

On being asked about her interest in this, she places the emphasis on providing mathematical tasks with more than one solution, and on emphasising not sticking with the first solution that presents itself. This also values different solutions and other ways of thinking. The emphasis is not placed, therefore, on representations of the concept of fractions and on the limitations imposed on the concept by a weak conceptual image. Ana believes that unless she asks the pupils to do so explicitly, they will not attempt to find more than one solution.

2. Both teachers underline the richness of the resulting representations

They question some of the solutions obtained and the possible number. Ana asks whether there is an infinite number of ways to divide the square in half; Pilar questions solution 1.3.

3. Ana provides information about her pupils

It helps us to understand the lesson better and to understand her decisions.

4. They discuss the suitability of the task to group work and how effective it is

Their conclusion is that by working with classmates the task is really more productive than individual work as a result of the help that these can bring (making reference to the children's *zone of proximal development*), as well as different ideas. This leads on to the conditions that Ana asks of the pupils. They discuss whether it might have been more appropriate in this sense to have given a single shape to each group. They also discuss whether it would have better to have put a short period of individual work before the group work so that the more able pupils would not get too far ahead.

5. They discuss the task features in terms of a problem solving task for the pupils

They should be more open to its possible advantages and disadvantages. They show some anxiety with respect to getting the most out of the time spent on it. In this vein they discuss the roles of the teacher and pupils, and the necessary balance for the former to direct things and the latter to discover things for themselves. Besides timing, they wonder about controlling the lesson. Ana shows insecurity towards this way of working (the tasks more open-ended than those she would normally set, and the pupils in small groups).

6. They discuss the consequences of unexpected students' ideas

Relating to the above, Ana states that this type of task causes ideas to arise during the lesson which she had not previously considered and for which she did not have an answer. Such is the case in episode 8. This causes her some anxiety.

7. We discuss whether this way of working in class is especially appropriate for introducing new material

The teachers are agreed on the value of introducing the topic this way as it is worth spending more time on it. When the time comes to go more deeply into it, they see an advantage to moving onto individual work, using exercises taken from the textbook.

8. Is the activity basically concerned with geometric concepts or is it focussed on the concept of fraction? (Question thrown out by the teacher trainers)

Ana's intention was not to focus attention on the geometric aspects of the activity (the different ways of dividing the shapes), but when she decided that it should best be done through physically manipulating things, this lead her to present it in this way. They question whether the geometric element has been emphasised over the numerical, hiding the objective of the activity – the concept of fraction itself – from the pupils. Ana expresses her disappointment because despite believing that the lesson was fruitful, there was no confirmation afterwards that it had helped to clarify the concept of fraction for the pupils. Ana finds this interpretation logical, indicating that instead of noting the number of pieces obtained in their notebooks, they noted that "I've done six different ways" (of dividing the rectangle in half).

4.2 Task 2: A True Incident

During discussion of the video (task 1), the validity of the division in 3.2 arises, along with the conjecture expressed by Miguel in episode 8 (the bigger the circle, the more ways there are to divide it in half). In both cases the teachers are in agreement that both are wrong. Once the discussion of the lesson is concluded, the trainers come back to these cases, this time as an excerpt of a teaching-learning situation (Climent & Carrillo, 2002). Summarising the discussion, and focusing on *Miguel's conjecture*, Ana admits to not having dealt with it in class because she didn't know if he was right or not. "At moments like those," she says, "you realise you need to know more about mathematics because you find yourself without the background." She feels that as a result it is not possible to pick up on interesting ideas from the pupils for fear of giving them false information.

Initially, their intuition leads them to see the problem in much the same way as the children. But then, in contrast, they make the supposition that the solution is infinite, by which each circle would then have the same number of possibilities. Although they find this reasoning logical, they find it difficult to believe. When we illustrate the situation by drawing two concentric circles they see that any diameter we draw for one is equally a diameter for the other. We mention other conceptual problems similar to this (the different magnitudes of infinity, and the fact that there is an infinite number of points along any line of finite length).

With respect to the folds suggested in answer 3.2, they believe that the folding strategy used in class shows that it is wrong. They also believe that no folds done in this way can be correct, as the two outer parts with circular borders would never coincide with the central area. For this problem, we suggest considering the function f given by the difference in area of both parts. If we accept that it should be a continuous function and that it clearly has cases where it is greater than 0 and others where it is less than 0, then at some point it must actually be equal to 0, or put another way, both parts coincide (as halves) (Fig. 3).

Challenges like this have helped to change the thinking of the teachers in the PIC about what knowledge of mathematics is needed by primary teachers. At the start of the project they thought that not much more was needed than what is specified for

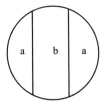

Fig. 3 Assuming equal segments on diametrically opposite sides of the circle, the difference in area of parts b and $a[S(b) - 2S(a)]$ can be written as $f(x)$, x being the distance between the centre of the circle and one of those segments $(0 \leq x \leq r)$. As f is a continuous function and $f(0) < 0 < f(r)$, at least a number x_0 exists $(0 < x_0 < r)$ so that $f(x_0) = 0$, that is to say: $S(b) = 2S(a)$ in this case

the pupils at that level. The teachers were not sure how much more they needed, but they recognise the need to know more so as to "see where the item you are working on is going, so that you can get the most out of the pupils" ideas without letting them fall into error.' However, doing mathematics or doing mathematical problem-solving for its own sake does not interest the teachers.

4.3 Task 3: A Mathematical Problem

In addition to gaps in their knowledge *of* mathematics (Ball, 1990), another difficulty facing the teachers in problems such as those in task 2 is their lack of strategies and resources to tackle mathematical problems and evaluate possible solutions. So as to highlight the importance of this knowledge *about* mathematics the teacher trainers presented them with a problem whose solution required the use of the same method that was brought to bear on Miguel's conjecture – the study of polar cases. The proposed problem was:

> Given a square with 8 unit sides, will it be possible to make another square inscribed within this in such a way that the area of the inner square is half that of the outer?

(Climent & Carrillo, 2003).

We clarify that the inner square should not be limited to integer units sides and the teachers set about working out the possibilities. After several attempts they hit on a solution (Fig. 4). Beyond this, though, they were unable to find another solution nor did they know whether this is the only possibility. We observe that each vertex of the inner square necessarily divides the side of the outer square into two segments,

Fig. 4 Teachers' solution

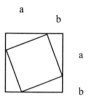

Fig. 5 General solution

a and b, in such a way that the segments on one side are equal in length to the corresponding segments on the othe cited figures ther sides (Fig. 5).

The study of polar cases can be usefully applied here. Given that the problem remains the same whatever the point along the edges of the outer square the vertices of the inner square are positioned, then we need only consider the cases that we consider polar extremes (with respect to the range of possibilities). In this case these will be the instances where the vertices of the inner square are exactly halfway along the edges of the outer square, and where the vertices of both squares coincide. Given that in the first instance the area of the inner square is half that of the outer, and in the second instance the areas are identical, then, following the same kind of reasoning used in the discussion of Miguel's conjecture, there can only be one instance in which the outcome is half, as in all others it will be greater than half.

The research developed in the PIC with respect to professional development in the teaching of mathematics has allowed us to verify how, with tasks like the above, teachers re-examine their vision of school mathematics, finding it making more sense than their initial preservice training. They come to value the importance of specific subject knowledge and they re-examine their own professional necessities and their commitment to meeting them. They are more prepared to enter into theoretical considerations of their practice via reflection, and to widen their didactic knowledge of the content. They question their conceptions about how to teach mathematics and how it is learnt, and they evaluate the importance of using professional tasks (such as the analysis of classroom situations) with colleagues.

5 Initial Teacher Training

In our initial teacher training courses we have implemented sequences of tasks inspired and extracted from the examples of the PIC, collecting at the same time information about this implementation. In keeping with this policy, we asked some trainee teachers[1] to watch and analyse the video of Ana's lesson introducing fractions. We prefaced the viewing with some brief background information on the school, the teacher and her group of pupils, the year they were in and stage they

---

[1] We focus on five, all women, who represent a varied sample of the viewpoints taken in the analysis, and of the attitudes and abilities with respect to mathematics.

were at in the school year. We also explained that the lesson had been divided into episodes to make viewing and discussion easier. The trainees were first asked to analyse the video individually. This they did using a sheet of chapter divided into columns, writing a summary of what went on in the class in the first, and any comments that occurred to them about this in the second. This way they were required to be a little more analytical and systematic, and to appreciate the details and get beyond a simple descriptive account of what they were watching. When this had been completed we conducted a feedback session to share observations[2].

The following comments represent the issues and foci identified from their notes and the feedback session which was recorded. First are those coinciding with aspects which had been commented on by the teachers (1–4):

5.1 The Task as an Open-Ended Problem (Relating to i – All Possible Divisions, and v Problem Solving)

They discuss the features of the task as a problem-solving situation for the pupils. Is it really a problem for them? Is it within the scope of everybody? What underlies this methodology as against the teacher explaining and giving the representations? Many find the video confirms the advantages of setting tasks with more than one solution and encouraging the pupils to think in various different ways (Marta: "She shows them that they can fold the chapter in more than one way, so they don't follow just one route and I think that's very positive" [M7]).

5.2 Representations of Fractions (Relating to ii – Representations)

They are surprised by the ideas that the pupils come up with and by the sophistication of their contributions. The reiterated comments of Marta set the tone: "The pupils can see that 1.6 and 2 are the same, just in a different position" [M9], "They are able to see halves that are not the typical ones you'd expect" [M11]. Some note the role of the social construction of knowledge in the course of the exchange (Inma says that the idea that there are millions of solutions for the halves of the circle arises "after seeing all the different folds that their classmates had done. It is necessary to follow these steps to reach that conclusion" [I22]).

They appreciate the pupils' solutions not only for their sophistication and variety, but also for what they represent with respect to the concept of fractions. They are not the standard ones [M11 above], and the pupils do not associate them with the orientation of the shape [M9]. In this sense, some of the trainee teachers make more conceptual observations than the primary teachers, taking into account the mathematical

---

[2] The aim here was that each trainee should make explicit their thinking about this particular situation and about mathematics teaching in general, without feeling inhibited by other opinions.

subject content in question and its construction (delving into the area of pedagogical content knowledge). Teresa's comments are worth reproducing (from discussion of the children in 3.1 and their confusion with thirds) when she notes that "one important thing is that [...] the concept of denominator and the equality of the parts in the fraction is introduced". The fact that they work on this particular division is seen as a potential obstacle to the pupils' learning for many of them:

"When they divide the shape into three parts first they talk about thirds, but later they reach the conclusion that they are halves (the middle piece is the same size as the other two together, says one child!). I think this can confuse the class. I think it should have been limited to talking about two equal halves given that this was the aim, instead of mixing up the halves themselves. Being the first time they've seen halves, this doesn't strike me as right." [Carmen, C14–15].

In the discussion with the trainee teachers the idea of representations of fractions in continuous and discrete contexts is introduced, as all these are continuous, and they consider the suitability of working on both types of representation. Some of the trainees attribute the sophistication of the pupils' ideas to the features of the task and also to the teacher's management of it (C33, relating to the millions of possibilities with the circle: "I think that the children are the ones who have reached this conclusion thanks to the teacher asking them for different possibilities"). They give a positive evaluation to solutions which are discounted as wrong as these are counterexamples to the concept of fractions (C12).

5.3 Group Work Issues (Related to iv – Group Work)

The appropriateness of putting the pupils into groups. There is almost unanimous approval as they associate this with increased motivation on the part of the pupils. Ana's organising of the group work such that they are all working on the same thing at the same time is positively viewed by most of them; according to Inma it allows "the pupils to help each other". For others, however, this can also affect the rhythm of work as the faster pupils will be those that do the bulk of the work. This leads them to consider how best to distribute the load in group work.

5.4 Methodological Issues (Related to v – Problem Solving)

The general methodology of the class attracted many comments. Many trainees go no deeper than superficial observations (without entering into specific issues of teaching and learning mathematical subject content). In general they are surprised by what they see. "It really strikes me that a discussion starts and everyone can stand up and give their opinion, and even draw what they think on the board" (I15), and classify it as non-traditional. Some amplify this impression, noting several variables including use of pupils' previous knowledge, use of textbook, the teacher's and pupils' roles, material, and activity type. As a result during the discussion of the lesson these variables inevitably come up in the teacher training class. Some of these concrete questions lead to more general questions such as other possibilities or advantages and disadvantages of each option. In their contributions about the lesson observed from a methodological point of view many trainees used fixed terminological expressions from their early training such as:

"The teacher [...] is not a transmitter of conceptual subject content, but instead tries to make the pupils themselves develop the concepts" [M5].

For some, the video supports their belief that this type of methodology has advantages for the pupils' mathematical learning:

"As it's clear to see, this type of activity encourages the pupils' creativity and motivation, as well as promoting their logico-mathematical knowledge." [T26, relating to the debate about halves in episode 5].

Other trainees express their reservations, showing a concern for the less able pupils:

"As for the pieces of the shapes divided into three, they find it difficult to see that there are two the same and a third which is double the size of the other two. I think that when this part is explained to them they are tending to repeat it without really understanding" [Laura, L12].

On the other hand, there are aspects which were highlighted by the prospective teachers but not by the teachers. We present them next.

5.5 Observations on Pedagogical Content Knowledge

Some trainees are able to make fairly conceptual observations, linked to pedagogical content knowledge, as mentioned above with respect to the children's shapes representing halves. Teresa's comments are particularly noteworthy here. She analyses the ideas arising in the class and Ana's performance from this perspective, along with the set task:

"The shapes selected are suitable because they are an everyday means of representing fractions and because they offer a variety of possibilities" [T10].

"Suggesting that they number each part is useful for working on the concept of numerator" [T11].

"It's an introductory activity on the concept of fractions, and more importantly, on part and unity" [T8]).

In contrast to many of her peers, a good ability in mathematics and a positive attitude towards the subject coincide in this particular student.

5.6 Criticism on the Teacher's Needs and Performance

Some trainees are highly critical of Ana's performance, suggesting not only what questions they would modify, but also what the teacher needs to be able to solve the problems they detect. For example, in the debate, both Teresa and Inma underline the need to plan the activity very carefully, giving substantial consideration to its possibilities and what might arise.

In summary, through the analysis of real cases and videos of lessons during the initial teacher training stage we have seen how this kind of activity encourages trainees to articulate and to contrast their thinking on teaching and learning mathematics, to draw on alternative examples of classroom performance which are under-represented in the primary classroom, to appreciate pupils' learning traits in a real classroom context, to recognise and establish relations between analysis and their theoretical knowledge as analytical tools, to acquire the habit of reflecting on the teaching and learning of the subject, taking key issues on board and thinking about the importance of specific aspects of the teaching of mathematical subject content, to reflect on what knowledge and skills future primary teachers need, to assimilate key questions relating to pedagogical content knowledge in a natural context (where they will have to apply it), and experience the advantages of sharing this analysis with peers and professionals within teaching.

With respect to the specific case presented in the PIC (task 2 in section "An Example from the PIC Inservice Training Context"), the trainee teachers tend to locate themselves in positions that are very similar to those described by the primary teachers, with scant mathematical resources to evaluate the pupils' conjectures and wrong conceptions on the topic. In this instance they also discussed the appropriateness of dealing with such conjectures in the primary classroom (when they come up, as in Ana's class) and what the teacher needs to know in order to do so.

6 Final Remarks

With these tasks we have tried to deal with various aspects which, in our experience with the teachers in the PIC, have proved complex however the process suggests that the tasks are effective: how to approach tasks in mathematics, driving home the teacher's need for subject matter knowledge, articulating opinions on mathematics teaching models and how learning takes place, exploring questions related to pedagogical content knowledge, and assimilating the culture of sharing educational tasks with colleagues. These aspects continue to be at the core of research on mathematics teacher's knowledge.

Although the types of task are the same and the tasks themselves can be very similar (in relation to initial and continuous training), the two groups treated them in different ways. Hence, regarding the analysis of the lesson which we used as an exemplification, surprisingly, some of the trainee primary teachers were more critical of what they saw than the PIC teachers. Among the reasons we can find for this difference is that in the case of the teachers, it is a question of analysing the classroom performance of their peers (although they have shown themselves to be fairly critical in this respect on other occasions), and so they come at it from a class-based perspective, giving considerable credit to the teacher's efforts to incorporate an innovative methodology. They empathise with the role of the teacher, intuitively understanding the classroom management issues incurred by the methodological model being used, and so take a sympathetic attitude. Their positive responses make them more tolerant and even lead them to miss possible areas for improvement. In contrast, the teacher trainees take up a position from within the theoretical sphere, applying expectations from what they have learned in their course as to the non-traditional elements and their advantages. This results in them being harsher critics and they focus more on the things that do not work out. On the other hand, the teachers enjoy a fuller knowledge of the context, of the pupils' difficulties with this material, of the representations and activities for introducing the subject content suggested in the textbooks and even by the pupils themselves in the observed class. This leads them to understand aspects which remain unclear to the trainees. For example, some of the latter doubt whether all, or the majority, of the pupils in the class are following the matter arising, while the teachers are all convinced that such is the case and that the set task is consequently more appropriate than another which places the emphasis on working on previously studied elements.

The perspectives from which the trainee teachers analyse the video are varied. While some centre on the less able pupils, others compare the teacher's performance with what typically happens in the primary classroom, and others compare this with what they consider the ideal. We can discuss these differences on the initial teacher training course and try to approach more complex perspectives. Such reflexive processes will improve their interpretation of teaching incidents (Sullivan & Mousley, 1998).

In other series of tasks that have been implemented, in both contexts (PIC and initial primary training), we have found significant differences regarding the potential of the tasks. For example, we have observed that while the trainee teachers seem happy to deal with mathematical tasks for their own sake (that is, independently of classroom considerations), tackling them initially as learners and only later considering the issues of taking them into the primary classroom, the teachers in the PIC were resistant to doing mathematical tasks in this way, unless they were firmly rooted in classroom practice. Considering the learning cycles which Simon (1994) proposes, our investigation suggests that in the case of the practising teachers the first cycle should move from the *experiencing of mathematical situations* to the *experiencing of mathematical teaching and learning situations*, leading in a later cycle to the development of knowledge of and about mathematics.

We consider that in both contexts the role of the group (of trainee teachers and of teachers and teacher trainers) is fundamental for the sharing and comparing of ideas, for taking a more critical stance of one's own beliefs, for considering other perspectives, and in the case of serving teachers, for tackling tasks which would be unmanageable on one's own.

Finally, we have shown a story of effective tasks, which is linked to our perspective of teacher's professional development starting from initial teacher education. These tasks provide opportunity for improving our understanding of teaching and learning mathematics, and teacher learning. Reflection and collaboration have proved their potential being central parts of the rich learning environments in which these tasks are dealt with.

7 Appendix: Introduction to Fractions in Primary Year 5 (Ana's Class)

It is the first hour of lessons of the day, so the children and their teacher have just arrived at school. Ana has planned to begin the topic of fractions. The children's tables are arranged in the shape of a "U" so that everyone can see each other and the teacher when she sits in front of them.

1st Episode

Ana introduces the activity. The children are sitting in their places and she stands in front of the group. She tells them that are not going to work with the book, but are going to work in groups, "the way they like" – she notes. She explains the task:

"Each child is going to get a rectangle, a circle and a square (showing them cut out of paper). What you have to do is to fold them to find different ways to make halves and afterwards quarters. You have to do it as many ways as possible."

Ana informs them that there is not just one way of doing it, and reiterates that the important thing is to find more. She tells them that when a pupil finds one way, they should show it to the rest of their group, who should then copy it (folding their shapes the same way) and everybody draw it in their notebooks. By this means, all the ways that the group discovers should end up drawn in their notebooks. She underlines that they should make halves, so that one part must be the same as the other.

When they have completed this part of the task, they then have to number each one of the parts that they have differentiated. In response to a doubt raised by a child, she says that if they can't do it with numbers they can do it another way, not using numbers.

The pupils form groups of 3 or 4 children and Ana distributes the paper shapes.

2nd Episode

Ana tells them that they must agree about which shape they will start with, so that all the children in the group are working on the same one. She asks them first to copy the order that she writes on the board. She writes the following order and the children copy it into their notebooks:

Fold your chapter in half in different ways. Now draw the results.

How many pieces did you get in each case?

3rd Episode

The children get down to work and Ana circulates around the groups (the pupils' group work and the teacher's monitoring of them constitute the 3rd episode).

4th Episode

The group work finishes. Various children put their hands up. Ana invites a group of three girls to come to the front and asks them to draw their solutions to halves on the board. She asks the rest to pay attention to see if they have really made halves and if they have any other ways of doing it. The girls draw their solutions (1.1–1.6 of the shapes at the end of the 6th episode).

5th Episode

Various children put their hands up to contribute. The teacher asks for different shapes and invites those with their hands up to respond. Several possibilities are dealt with in this way.

1. One group says that it has a different fold for the squares (2). Although some children say that it is the same as 1.2, they decide to consider it a different way.
2. A group of girls adds the suggestions for folding in half 3.1, 3.2 and 3.3.

Other children point out that these are "thirds" because there are three parts.

Ana: "Because there are three parts. And when we make three parts ... are they always thirds? ... And so ... whenever we make two parts are they halves ...?" [José says yes]. "Yes. In other words, if I take the same square" [goes to the board and draws: ▢], "and I fold it here in two ... they are halves ..." [David says that they have to be the same and José repeats it]. "Ah, so, I repeat, I ask you again, are these thirds?" [José says no]. "Why not?" ["Because they are not the same", says José]. "Because they are not the same! It's true that there are three parts, that much is true, but are they thirds?" [José says no]. "No! For them to be thirds ..." [looking at José for him to complete the sentence, who replies that they have to be the same]. "And they have to be the same. The girls have said that they have made halves here. Now you have to decide why or why not".

The children discuss this possibility. Some say yes it is because the centre is the same as the two outer parts together (referring to rectangle 3.1). Others say the centre is larger. Ana asks those who say yes to demonstrate to the others that it is. One of the girls in the group that came up with this solution shows that by folding the two outer parts along the lines of division, the central part is exactly covered. Everybody is then convinced of the equality.

Ana asks if any other group has more folds and various children come up to the board, adding drawings 4, 5 and 6.

1. Ana draws their attention to drawing 1.3. "I wanted everyone to see clearly that these lines go from here to here, and not from corner to corner". She asks them if it is halved or not. There are disagreements again so she asks those who say yes that they convince the others. One girl from the group that came up with the solution explains: "like that it's not halved [folded, because they do not coincide]

but like this it is", [as she opens it out, showing the two parts]. Some remain un-
convinced, so the teacher herself takes some scissors, cuts both halves and places
one on top of the other, stating that this is the only way that she thinks it will be
possible to see it. She asks the children why they have had to cut it in this case
to see that the parts coincided. Some children point out that "here it's the wrong
way round". Ana reminds them of an activity that they did in the art education
class where they drew symmetrical shapes about a vertical axis (without making reference to the concept of symmetry, just indicating the positioning of the
drawings).

2. They move on to see how many pieces they have made in each case. In the case
   of the three pieces, Ana pushes them to be more specific, so that they conclude
   that in the other cases there are "two equal parts" and in these "three parts, two
   equal pieces and one which is double the size of one of the other two". This last
   expression takes a long time for the pupils to be more precise, pushed by the
   teacher.

It is now break-time and they have to finish. Ana suggests that after break, they
note down all the drawings that their group didn't have in their notebooks, along
with the number of pieces that they have made in each case.

6th Episode
How the board was completed:

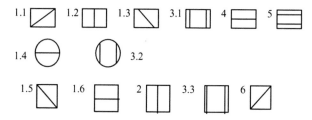

7th Episode
They talk about cases 3.2 and 3.3, on Ana's request. Some pupils object that the
problem with 3.2 is that it is badly drawn, as a result of which the girl who gave
this solution rubs out the lines of division and redraws them closer to the centre of
the circumference. As there is some disagreement, Ana asks those who say yes to
demonstrate it to the others. When they do the folding as in the case of the rectangle,
they have two circular sectors left over at the edges. Consequently, they eliminate
this one. However, case 3.3 works out.

8th Episode
Ana then points out that they have just one way for the circles. Other children
come to the front and give new ways in the following order: with the diameter placed
vertically (there was already one placed horizontally), with the diameter inclined to
the right, with the diameter inclined to the left. All the children see these possibilities
clearly. Miguel draws another case where he slightly moves one of the previously
inclined diameters (turning it on the centre). A lot of pupils say that it is the same.

Miguel conjectures that there must be "millions" of such diameters, as "you can do it like this, like this, and like this ... A centimetre more this way, a centimetre more that way ..." Miguel says that the number of halves that you can get depends on how big the circle is, because "if it's a small circle we can make fewer halves than if it's a big circle ..." (as there will be less centimetres or millimetres to consider). Another girl believes that it should come out the same, but cannot argue her case. Ana decides to leave this topic and focus on what she had planned.

[The lesson ends with the children working on how to name each part and a feedback session].

References

Ball, D. L. (1990). The mathematical understanding that prospective teachers bring to teacher education. *Elementary School Journal, 90*(4), 446–449.

Carrillo, J., Coriat, M., & Oliveira, H. (1999). Teacher education and investigations into teacher's knowledge. In K. Krainer, F. Goffree, & P. Berger (Eds.), *European Research in mathematics education I.III. On Research in Mathematics Teacher Education* (pp. 99–145). Osnabrück: University of Osnabrück.

Climent, N., & Carrillo, J. (2002). Developing and researching professional knowledge with primary teachers. In J. Novotná (Ed.), *European Research in Mathematics Education II* (Vol. 1, pp. 269–280). Praga: Charles University.

Climent, N., & Carrillo, J. (2003). El dominio compartido de la investigación y el desarrollo profesional. *Una experiencia en matemáticas con maestras, Enseñanza de las Ciencias, 21*(3), 387–404.

Cooney, T. J. (2001). Considering the paradoxes, perils, and purposes of conceptualizing teacher development. In F.-L. Lin & T. J. Cooney (Eds.), *Making sense of mathematics teacher education* (pp. 9–31). Dordrecht, The Netherlands: Kluwer Academic Publishers.

Cooney, T. J., & Shealy, B. E. (1997). On understanding the structure of teachers' beliefs and their relationship to change. In E. Fennema & B. S. Nelson (Eds.), *Mathematics teachers in transition* (pp. 87–109). New Jersey: Erlbaum.

Goffree, F. (1999). Standards for primary mathematics teacher education. Madrid: Academia de las Ciencias (http://www.mat.ucm.es/deptos/am/guzman/guzman.htm).

Goffree, F., & Oonk, W. (1999). Educating primary school mathematics teachers in the Netherlands: back to the classroom. *Journal of Mathematics Teacher Education, 2*(2), 207–214.

Goffree, F., & Oonk, W. (2001). Digitizing real teaching practice for teacher education programmes: The MILE project. In F.-L. Lin & T. J. Cooney (Eds.), *Making sense of mathematics teacher education* (pp. 111–145). Dordrecht, the Netherlands: Kluwer Academic Publishers.

Jaworski, B. (1992). Mathematics teaching: What is it? *For the Learning of Mathematics, 12*(1), 8–14.

Jaworski, B. (1994). *Investigating mathematics teaching: A constructivist enquiry.* London: Falmer Press.

Jaworski, B. (1998). Mathematics teacher research: Process, practice and the development of teaching. *Journal of Mathematics Teacher Education, 1*(1), 3–31.

Jaworski, B. (1999). Teacher education through teachers' investigation into their own practice. In K. Krainer; F. Goffree, & P. Berger (Eds.), *European research in mathematics education I.III. On research in mathematics teacher education* (pp. 201–221). Osnabrück: University of Osnabrück.

Jaworski, B. (2001). Developing mathematics teaching: Teachers, teacher educators, and researchers as co-learners. In F.-L. Lin & T. J. Cooney (Eds.), *Making sense of mathematics teacher education* (pp. 295–320). Dordrecht, the Netherlands: Kluwer Academic Publishers.

Jaworski, B. (2004). Grappling with complexity: Co-learning in inquiry communities in mathematics teaching development. In M. J. Høines & A. B. Fuglestad (Eds.), *Proceedings of the 28th Conference of the International Group for the Psychology of Mathematics Education* (Vol. 1, pp. 17–36). Bergen, Norway: Bergen University College.

Krainer, K. (2001). Investigations into practice as a powerful means of promoting (student) teachers' professional growth. In J. Novotná (Ed.), *European research in mathematics education II* (Vol. 1, pp. 269–280). Praga: Charles University.

Lampert, M., & Ball, D. (1998). *Teaching, multimedia, and mathematics: Investigations of real practice*. New York: Teachers College Press.

Lesh, R., & Lovitts, B. (2000). Research agendas: Identifying priority problems and developing useful theoretical perspectives. In A. E. Kelly & R. A. Lesh (Eds.), *Handbook of research design in mathematics and science education* (Chap. 3, pp. 45–71). Mahwah, NJ: Erlbaum.

Llinares, S., & Krainer, K. (2006). Mathematics (student) teachers and teacher educators as learners. In A. Gutiérrez & P. Boero (Eds.), *Handbook of research on the psychology of mathematics education. Past, present and future* (pp. 429–459). Rotterdam: Sense Publishers.

Moje, E. B., & Wade, S. E. (1997). What case discussion reveal about teacher thinking. *Teaching and Teacher Education, 13*(7), 691–712.

Shulman, L. S. (1992). Toward a pedagogy of cases. In J. Shulman (Ed.), *Case methods in teacher education* (pp. 1–30). New York: Teachers College Press.

Simon, M. A. (1994). Learning mathematics and learning to teach: Learning cycles in mathematics teacher education, *Educational Studies in Mathematics, 26*(1), 71–94.

Skott, J. (2004). The forced autonomy of mathematics teachers. *Educational Studies in Mathematics Education, 55*(1–3), 227–257.

Sullivan, P., & Mousley, J. (1998). Conceptualising mathematics teaching: The role of autonomy in stimulating teacher reflection. In A. Olivier & K. Newstead (Eds.), *Proceedings of the 22nd PME International Conference* (Vol. 4, pp. 105–112). Stellenbosch, South Africa: University of Stellenbosch.

Wood, T. (2005). Editorial. Understanding mathematics teaching: Where we began and where we are going. *Journal of Mathematics Teacher Education, 8*(3), 193–195.

Zaslavsky, O., & Leikin, R. (2004). Professional development of mathematics teacher educators: Growth through practice. *Journal of Mathematics Teacher Education, 7*(1), 5–32.

The Analysis of Classroom-Based Processes as a Key Task in Teacher Training for the Approach to Early Algebra

Nicolina A. Malara and Giancarlo Navarra

We synthesise here a theoretical framework outlined for the renewal of the teaching of algebra, giving a prominent role to a linguistic approach to the discipline starting from primary school. We tackle the issue of how teachers can be led to acquire conceptions and models of behaviour suitable to foster such a view of algebra among pupils and, in particular, to develop in them modelling, interpretation and thought production skills. For this we propose a model of task addressed to teachers and devoted to the analysis of activities and pupils' productions, as well as on the design of classroom discussions. The task is aimed at favouring the development of predictive and interpretative thinking by teachers as to pupils' behaviour. The structure, made of enchained scenes, induces teachers to question and review their convictions about their own role in the classroom and to become aware of the dynamic processes involved in the social construction of knowledge.

1 Introduction

Everyday teaching and learning practice is very often characterised by mere transmission of mathematical facts and application of rules, thus neglecting the conquest of the underlying sense. It is extremely rare to find a *teaching practice based on the exploration of problems*, in which focus is shifted *from results to processes*. Such a shift in perspective would give the opportunity to build in pupils – and hence to disseminate in the social context – an image of mathematics more in accordance with its real nature: that of a discipline born *from and for the study of problems*.

N.A. Malara
Department of Mathematics, Faculty of Science, University of Modena & Reggio Emilia, Italy

G. Navarra
Department of Mathematics, University of Modena & Reggio E, Italy

B. Clarke, B. Grevholm, and R. Millman (eds.), *Tasks in Primary Mathematics Teacher Education: Purpose, Use and Exemplars,* Mathematics Teacher Education 4,

Current research points to the *socio-constructivist* approach as the most suitable to raise pupils' interest in mathematics and foster in them a *meaningful* conception of the discipline. This approach is based on a theory according to which the mind constructs schemes through which knowledge develops by selection, organisation and continuous *re-structuring* of facts and relationships, drawing on the richness of sensations and stimuli that come from the environment and from social interactions.

This has notable implications for teaching and learning: the teachers' role acquires different and more complex features. The teacher cannot be a simple knowledge conveyor any longer: he/she rather becomes a person in charge of creating an environment that enables pupils to construct their own mathematical knowledge.

It is significant that, in recent years, research studies have been dedicated more and more to the teacher, as underlined at the recent ICME-10 congress (Copenhagen, 2004).[1] In particular, a model of teacher was outlined as a *reflexive and critical* decision maker (Jaworski, 1998, 2003; Malara & Zan, 2002; Mason 1998, 2002; Peter-Koop, 2001; Ponte, 2004; Schoenfeld 1998), pedagogically sensitive,[2] able to observe him/herself analytically in the moment he/she acts and to consciously make decisions in real time.

Teacher training according to such a model is necessary to obtain a socio-constructivist teaching practice based on the mastering of meaning as a prerequisite for the growth of the pupils' competencies. The challenge is thus in leading teachers to reflect on both the discipline and the model of teacher they have and apply. Training must be, therefore, an important time for reflection about central questions such as: *What mathematics do we need to teach? How can we do this? What should I refine, modify or reconstitute in myself in order to fit in the current trends of teaching?*

In this perspective, on one hand teachers need to be offered chances, through both individual study and suitable experimental activities, to revise their knowledge and beliefs about the discipline and its teaching, in order to overcome possible stereotypes and misconceptions. On the other hand, they need to become aware that their main task is to make students able to give *sense and substance* to their experience and construct new knowledge by exploring situations and making links with familiar concepts.

---

[1] In her plenary lecture, Anna Sfard pointed out the features of research in mathematics education in the last 50 years: from the *'programs' era* in years 1960s–1970s there was a shift to the *'students' era'* in years 1980s–1990s, to get on the way of the *'teachers' era'* at the beginning of years 2000. In brief: 'good practices' characterising the *'programs' era'*, or knowledge of students' cognitive styles and related changes, typical of the *'students' era'* are necessary but not sufficient for a renewal of teaching if teachers are not given opportunities to refine their mathematical and educational knowledge, to discuss and reflect upon their individual beliefs.

[2] With this term we mean what Jaworski, (2003) calls 'sensitivity to the students' and concerns: how the teacher knows pupils, his/her attention to their needs; his/her interaction with individuals and ability of guiding group interactions.

The actual attainment of these goals is strictly related to the type of mathematical content at stake, as well as to teaching traditions and educational policies in the different countries. This is extremely complex in the case of classical thematic areas, such as arithmetic and algebra, which suffer from their antiquity, and the teaching of which is affected by the way they historically developed.

Teacher training referring to *early algebra* currently is of great research interest: this disciplinary area became increasingly important in the last decade, as an answer to issues related to the teaching and learning of algebra. The work we present here concerns this content area and deals with methods and educational processes for teachers, aiming at a renewal of the teaching of arithmetic and algebra in a socio-constructive perspective, developed in co-operation of researchers and teachers.

2 Why Early Algebra

One of the most heartfelt problems for secondary school teachers concerns the difficulties that students have in their approach to algebra. The main reasons for these difficulties essentially lie in the heavy loss of meaning felt by students about the objects of study.

Since the 1980s, research has pointed to a way to modify this situation, underlying the need to promote, since primary school, a pre-algebraic teaching of arithmetic. This type of teaching would cast toward the observation of numerical regularities, the recognition of analogies, generalisation and an early use of letters to represent observed facts (Davis 1985; Linchevski 1995).

Starting from the second half of the 1990s, many theoretical and experimental studies were carried out on these aspects, mainly addressing 11–13-year-olds. Some of these studies stand out due to a theorisation of socio-constructive models of conceptual development; they emphasise the influence of the class environment on learning and promote the use of physical instruments as means of semeiotic mediation, in the frame of a view of algebra as a language (Da Rocha Falcão,1995; Meira, 1990, 1996; Radford, 2000; Radford & Grenier, 1996).

Since 2000, broad studies concerning teaching experiments, carried out at primary school level in relation to algebraic contents, appear: resolution of simple equations through problems with the introduction of unknowns; study of relations, functions and sequences; introduction to proof (see for instance Carraher, Brizuela, & Schliemann 2000, or Carpenter & Franke, 2001). Some of these studies also concern the setting up of projects aimed at training primary school teachers on these issues (Blanton & Kaput, 2001; Brown & Coles, 1999; Dougherty, 2001; Menzel, 2001). Our *ArAl Project, paths in arithmetic to favour pre-algebraic thinking* locates within this frame (Malara & Navarra, 2003), and is a project that merges teacher training and innovation in the classroom.

3 Our Hypotheses and Basic Theoretical Elements in the Approach to Early Algebra

Algebra is usually introduced as a study of algebraic forms, privileging syntactic aspects, as if formal manipulation preceded meaning understanding. As a consequence, algebraic language comes to lose some of its essential features: that of being a suitable language for describing reality, by coding knowledge or making hypotheses about phenomena; that of being a powerful reasoning and predicting instrument, that enables the individual to derive new pieces of knowledge about phenomena, by means of transformations allowed by arithmetic-algebraic formalism.

Our fundamental hypothesis is that one cannot focus exclusively on syntax and leave semantics aside, but rather that there is a need to start from the latter, taking an approach to the teaching of algebraic language in analogy with the learning modalities of natural language. We make use of the babbling metaphor to explain this perspective.

3.1 Algebraic Babbling

In their early years children learn a language gradually, appropriating its terms in relation to the meanings they associate with them, and develop rules gradually, through imitation and adjustments, up to the school age, when they will learn to read and reflect on grammatical and syntactic aspects of language.

Our hypothesis is that the mental models that characterise algebraic thinking must be constructed since the early years of primary school, when children approach arithmetical thinking: this is the time to teach them to think about arithmetic algebraically. In other words, algebraic thinking should be built up in children progressively, in a rigorous interrelation with arithmetic, starting from the meanings of the latter. Meanwhile, one should pursue the construction of an environment which can informally stimulate the autonomous processing of what we call algebraic babbling, i.e. the experimental and continuously redefined mastering of a new language, in which the rules can gradually find their place within a teaching situation which is tolerant of initial, syntactically "shaky" moments. In this process, a crucial point is represented by understanding the difference between the concepts of representing and solving.

3.2 Representing and Solving: Process and Product

A very common pupils' belief is that the solution to a verbal problem is essentially the statement of a result. This naturally implies that attention is focused on what produces that result: operations. Let us consider the following problem that poses a classical question: *There are 13 crows perched on a branch; another 9 crows arrive at the tree while 6 of the previous ones fly away. How many crows are now on the tree?*

Now let us modify the question: *'Represent in mathematical language the situation so that we can find the total number of crows'*. Where is the difference between the two formulations?

In the first case, the focus is on the identification of the *product* (16), whereas the second concentrates on the identification of the *process (13 + 9 – 6)*, that is, the representation of the relationships among the elements in play.

This difference is linked with one of the most important aspects of the *epistemological gap* between arithmetic and algebra: whilst arithmetic requires an *immediate* search of a solution, on the contrary algebra *postpones* the search of a solution and begins with a formal trans-positioning from the dominion of a natural language to a specific system of *representation*. If guided to overcome the worry of the result, each pupil reaches an upper level of thinking, substituting the calculations with the observation of him/herself reasoning. He/she passes to a meta-cognitive level, interpreting the *structure* of the problem.

3.3 Canonical or Non-Canonical Representation of a Natural Number

Among the infinite representations of a number, the *canonical* one is obviously the most popular. Thinking of a number means for anyone thinking of the *cardinality it represents*. But the canonical representation is *meaning-wise opaque*, as *it says little about itself* to the pupil. For instance: the writing '12' suggests a certain 'number of things', or at most the idea of 'evenness'. Other representations – always suiting pupils' age – may broaden the field of information about the number itself: '3 × 4' points out that it is a multiple of both 3 and 4; '$2^2 \times 3$', that it is also a multiple of 2; '2 × 2 × 3' leads to '2 × 6' and therefore to the multiple of 6; 36/3 or 60/5 that it is sub-multiple of other numbers and so forth.

We can say that each possible connotation of a number adds information to get to a deeper knowledge of it, as it happens with people: there are the first and family name, opaque if compared to other more expressive connotations of the subject, for instance with reference to other individuals he or she is linked to by social or family relationships (father of …, teacher of …, brother of somebody's husband …). It is extremely important that pupils learn to see as appropriate the canonical representation of a number as well as any other arithmetical expression of which such number is the result (non-canonical representation of the number). In the case of twelve, appropriate and acceptable representations besides '12' are also '9 + 3' or '$2^2 \times 3$'. This is done not only to favour acceptance and understanding of algebraic written expressions like 'a + b' or 'x^2y', but mainly to facilitate the identification of numerical relationships and their representation in general terms.

In relation to this, there is a significant conceptual challenge, e.g.: in $1 \times (4 + 2) = 90$ a pupil, operating a reading left/right 'sees' $15 \times (4 + 2)$ as an 'operation' and '90' as its 'result'. But he/she has to be educated to 'see' the sentence as an equality between two representations of the same number. The following section is devoted to this aspect.

3.4 The Equal Sign

In primary-school teaching of arithmetic, the equal sign essentially takes up the meaning of *directional operator*: $4 + 6 = 10$ means to a pupil 'I add 4 and 6 and I find 10'. This is a dominant conception in the first seven or eight school years during which the equal sign is mainly characterised by a *space-time* connotation: it marks the steps of an operative simplification or reduction path (operations are carried out sequentially) which must be read from left to right up to its end (i.e. the reaching of the result). Later, when the pupil meets algebra, the equal sign suddenly takes up a totally different, *relational* meaning. In a written expression like $(a + 1)^2 = a^2 + 2a + 1$ it carries the idea of a symmetry between the expressions: it points to the fact that they represent the same number, whatever the value given to a, and the two expressions are said to be equal (in fact, they identify because they are equivalent with respect to the relation 'representing the same number, as a varies'). Again, in the writing '$8 + x = 2x - 5$' the equal sign points to the (*still unverified*) hypothesis about the equivalence of the two writings for some value of the variable x. Although nobody told him about this broader meaning, the student must now move into a completely different conceptual universe, where it is necessary to go *beyond* the familiar space-time connotation. But if the student thinks that 'the number after the equal sign is the *result*' he or she will be lost and will probably attach little meaning to a writing like '$11 = n$', although he/she might be able to solve the linear equation leading to it.

This reasoning shows an evident correlation to *linguistic* aspects such as the concepts of *interpretation, translation,* comparison of *paraphrases* and *conscious respect of rules*. In order to make pupils get aware of the role of such aspects, we introduced a fictional character called Brioshi.

3.5 Brioshi and the Algebraic Code

Brioshi is a *virtual* Japanese pupil, aged variably depending on his interlocutors' age. He does not speak any other language except Japanese, but he knows how to use the mathematical language. Brioshi loves to find non-Japanese peers for an exchange of mathematical problems via e-mail. He was introduced in order to help pupils grasp the problem of the algebraic representation of relations or procedures expressed verbally and, above all, in order to convey the idea (difficult for pupils aged 8–14) that on using a language it is necessary to *respect its rules*, which is an even stronger need when the language is formalised, owing to the synthetic nature of the symbols used. Brioshi was introduced along with structured activities: an exchange of messages to be translated into mathematical language or natural language; where the 'expert' Japanese friend plays the role of controller of the translation. If Brioshi cannot understand the translation, this must be revised through collective discussion. Such 'role-play' works with all pupils, regardless of their age, and Brioshi's arbitral role as a call to correctness and transparency brings about very positive results (for further details see Malara & Navarra, 2001).

So far we have reflected on mathematical and linguistic questions about early algebra, now we shall analyse the elements which are at the basis of its methodological approach.

4 Relevant Methodological Aspects in Our Approach to Early Algebra

The didactical situations we propose are born within stimulating teaching and learning environments, but they are not easily manageable by teachers. As a consequence, those who wish to undertake innovative educational practices need to deal with a set of relevant methodological and organisational aspects that actively support a *culture of change*. We shall now discuss some of these aspects.

4.1 The Didactical Contract

The didactical contract is a theoretical construct (Brousseau, 1988) which indicates the set of relationships, mainly implicit, that govern the pupil-teacher relationship when they face the development of knowledge concerning a particular mathematical content. These relationships make up a system of obligations, involving both the teacher and his/her pupils within the teaching and learning process, which should be fulfilled and for which each of them is responsible.

In the case of early algebra, with pupils aged 6–14, the contract concentrates on the construction of mathematical conceptions rather than on technical competencies. Pupils must be brought to an awareness of the essence of the contract: they are protagonists in the collective construction of algebraic babbling. This means they should be educated to gradually become sensitive towards complex forms of a new language, through a reflection on differences between and equivalences of meanings of mathematical written expressions, a gradual discovery of the use of letters instead of numbers, an understanding of the different meanings of the "equal sign", the infinite representations of a number, the meaningful identification of arithmetic properties and so forth. In this case, the didactical contract concerns the solution of algebraic problems and is characterised by the fundamental principle '*first* represent and *then* solve'. This seems to be a promising perspective when we need to face one of the most important key points of the conceptual field of algebra: the transposition in terms of representations, from natural language (in which problems are formulated or described) to formal-algebraic language (in which the relationships they contain are translated).

4.2 The Interpretation of Protocols

Protocols are written productions made by individuals or groups with reference to a task given by the teacher. In the case of activities aimed at the enactment of algebraic babbling, constructing competencies for the interpretation of protocols and a classification of translations made by pupils implies that the teacher has to face a variety of mathematical writings, often elaborated through a mixed and personal use of languages and symbols, linked to one another in more or less appropriate ways.

Such a variety develops when the teacher stimulates, through reflection, creativity. When the pupils realise that they are producing mathematical thinking and contributing to a collective construction of knowledge and languages, they make a variety of mostly interesting and non-trivial proposals, which altogether represent a common legacy for the whole class. The collective analysis of the protocols is sharply intertwined with the practices of discussion in the classroom.

4.3 Discussion on Mathematical Themes

By 'mathematical discussion' we mean the net of interventions occurring in a class with reference to a certain situation on which pupils are requested by the teacher to express their thinking and argue in relation to what other classmates expressed as well. Through this net of interventions, the situation is analysed and debated from different points of view, until shared solutions are obtained.

The enactment of a collective discussion on mathematical themes stresses metacognitive and metalinguistic aspects: pupils are guided through a reflection on language, knowledge and processes (like solving a problem, analysing a procedure), to relate to classmates' hypotheses and proposals, to compare and classify translations, evaluate their own beliefs, make motivated choices. In this context, the teacher should be aware of the risks and peculiarities of this teaching and learning mode.

The teacher plays a delicate role in orchestrating discussions. First, he/she must be clear about the constructive path along which pupils should be guided, and about the cognitive or psychological difficulties they might encounter. From a methodological point of view, he/she must try to harmonise the various voices in the class, inviting usually silent pupils to intervene, avoiding that leaders and their followers prevail and that rivalries between groups arise. Finally, he/she must help the class recognise what has been achieved as a result of a collective work involving everybody. He/she must learn to act as a participant-observer, that is to keep his/her own decisions under control during the discussion, trying to be neutral and proposing hypotheses, reasoning paths and deductions produced by either individuals or small groups. He/she must learn to predict pupils' reactions to the proposed situations and capture significant unpredicted interventions to open up new perspectives in the development of the ongoing construction.

This is a hard-to-achieve collection of skills and a careful analysis of class processes is needed if a teacher wants to engage productively with pupils. We will shortly come back to this point, after lingering on a theoretical instrument, the glossary, which is progressively developed along with the various themes faced with teachers. Our aim is to use this instrument in order to make teachers deepen their reflection on important aspects of their action in class and to become aware that, in order to achieve good practice, they should acknowledge the value of theoretical knowledge (not only in the aspects attaining the discipline or its epistemology, but also in linguistic, psycho-pedagogical and social aspects).

4.4 The Glossary

Early algebra is a *polycentric* set of themes. When dealing with it, there is no predefined path leading to a *goal*. This can puzzle teachers, also because it is rather difficult to insert these activities in their everyday work. We believe it is necessary to outline a reference system that might help the teacher gradually achieve, through a revision of his/her knowledge, a global view of early algebra that merges *theory* and *practice*, in which *connections existing between mathematics and linguistics* are considered, in order to get closer to a conception of *mathematics as a language.*

The hypothesis is that the exploration of the glossary which is undertaken by the student teachers is an individual adventure that *depends on the way in which the teacher decides to interact with it.* Our intention is to make teachers find out a *reading key* that can promote a reflection on the *grammar* needed to explore it. Through the application of this grammar, everyone can get to know *everything they will be capable of* in that particular moment, as well as move within the polarity *local/global* along two directions: (1) within the single *local*; (2) in the *map of possible connections between the various locals.*

If we see early algebra as a *machine the functioning of which must be understood* through the re-construction of the relationships among its mechanisms, the *glossary* is its core, the constitution of which is based on the assumption that: (a) one's own knowledge is constructed by organizing exploration *in a personal way*; (b) the process of knowledge acquisition is a *constructive act* itself.

The glossary can be seen as constituted by five categories which reflect our approach to early algebra. Here are some examples (Table 1).

Each term is described by a text containing other terms in the glossary, to which it cross-refers for a wider and deeper analysis. For example, the term *Arguing* leads to

Table 1 Five categories of an approach to early algebra

Categories	General	Pre-algebraic thinking, relational thinking, process/product, metacognitive/metalinguistic, Brioshi, representation, represent/solve, opaque/transparent representations, mediation tools ...
	Mathematical	Formal coding, additive/multiplicative form, mathematical sentence, unknown, regularity, relation, structure, equal, variable, ...
	Linguistic	Arguing, algebraic babbling, canonical/non canonical form, letter, language, metaphor, paraphrase, semantics/syntax, translate, ...
	Social-educational	Collective (exchange, ...), sharing, didactical contract, discussion, social mediation, negotiation, ...
	Psychological	Perception, emotional interference, semantic persistence, ...

Collective, Process/product, Representation, Relation, Semantics/syntax. We conventionally name this set of terms *the Net* of the term *Arguing.* Generalising, a Net of a term is 'the set of cross-references that link the term with other terms of the glossary'. So the Glossary can be seen as a matrix of Nets.

General, psychological and social questions represent a *methodological support* to mathematical and linguistic questions. Although early algebra concerns *mathematics* education, it is certainly true that the importance of the three 'supportive' components is fundamental. The approach to arithmetic in an algebraic perspective is based on a strong basis of *social* and *psychological* assumptions and on a set of *general* basic concepts that the teacher should learn to promote and manage.

In order to carry out mathematical activities, teachers cannot forget that (a) the construction of knowledge occurs through promotion of *social dynamics* that favour *exchange* and *verbalisation* in the classroom; (b) the identification of suitable *didactical mediators* (such as Brioshi) is crucial to a stable acquisition of *meanings*; (c) it is necessary to promote activities highlighting *metacognitive* and *metalinguistic* aspects.

All these interrelationships are highlighted in the glossary by the nets of its terms and by numerousness of the occurrence of each term in the nets.

5 The Present Study and Its Methodology

Our research experience with the teachers made us aware of their difficulties in designing and managing classroom discussions (Malara 2003, 2005). This persuaded us about the importance of the analysis of classroom processes in order to help teachers acquire the necessary competencies for the orchestration of discussions. For this reason, in these past few years we have addressed our research towards the individuation of methodologies and tools aimed at producing in teachers the mathematical/pedagogical competencies necessary to approach early algebra in a socio-constructivistic way.

Our research methodology is based on: (1) planning didactical classroom routes with the teachers; (2) teachers' production of *diaries*, i.e., transcripts of audio-recordings of the classroom activities intertwined with their comments and re-flections); (3) joint (researcher & teacher) analysis of diaries; (4) sharing of the diaries among the teachers involved, writing of meta-comments, discussions and reflections.

Documenting the classroom episodes analysis – paradigmatic in highlighting the sharp correlation between the students' mathematical constructions and the teacher's sensitiveness in the discussion – brought us to elaborate the model of task we focus on in the following paragraphs.

6 A Model of Task for Teachers: The Analysis of Classroom Scenes in Sequence

Our model of task gives teachers the chance to deal with the practice of constructive teaching 'theoretically', forcing them to focus on provisional and reflection-related aspects. The task develops along *5 or 6 Scenes*, structured as a 'connected set of issues', and a *Final Reflection*. The scenes are based on excerpts of transcripts of one of our experimentations. Each scene is composed of two sections: the first concerns the presentation of a classroom situation, and the second focuses on questions for the teacher.

Teachers are sequentially proposed scenes at regular time intervals (of about 20–30 min): while they are working on the first scene they do not know the second yet; when they work on the second one they do not know the third one yet and so forth up to the conclusion. After analysing the input proposed in the first part of the scene, the teacher makes hypotheses about the class' reaction. In the sub-sequent scene these hypotheses are compared with what actually happened and so forth up to the last scene. At the end, a global review of the work carried out is formulated.

This kind of task has developed with time and can be seen as the result of a research process. The first idea was born of producing interconnected e-learning worksheets for teachers in order to promote a constructive and linguistic approach to algebra, to which a transposition of these materials in a first version of the task for teacher workshops followed. The present version of the task has been used in workshops for teacher-trainees of junior secondary school since 2005. The example we report was given to 45 teachers as the final test of a 40 hour course on didactics of early algebra. Here, 20 hours were devoted to workshops dealing with similar tasks together with the analysis of excerpts from classroom discussions.

6.1 An Example of Task in Early Algebra

The First Scene

The class teacher presents the situation:
Ann likes chocolate cookies ★ and finger biscuits ◊, which she eats for breakfast every school day. She eats different quantities every day, but follows a rule she set.

Then she shows a drawing with two ice cream spots which are hiding only the finger biscuits Ann ate on Friday and the chocolate cookies she ate on Saturday.

Monday	Tuesday	Wednesday	Thursday	Friday	Saturday

At this moment the teacher gives a first task: Write down Ann's rule in natural language.

Task for teachers:

1. Carry out the task.
2. Give a short explanation of why it is important to search for regularities in mathematics.
3. Discuss the instruments and/or strategies you view as the most effective to identify regularities.

One initial goal is to make teachers identify possible difficulties pupils might encounter and think about instruments and strategies that can be used to solve the task. By examining the drawing, pupils must find a link between the number of biscuits and that of cookies. This is not a difficult task if one tries to express the number of biscuits as a function of that of cookies; much more difficult is to express the relationship in the inverse way. Other two aspects, that should not be underestimated, concern the issues of the interval in which each quantity may vary and the generalisation of the law (the situation might induce a cyclic view of the law and inhibit its view in general terms).

Saturday is problematic because, once identified the law in the formulation 'the number of finger biscuits is one more than twice the number of chocolate cookies', the solution is that Ann does not eat any chocolate cookie on that day. From a psychological point of view, this brings about a conflict with the implicit hypothesis that Ann always eats both types of biscuits, since one can infer that she loves both. From a mathematical point of view, this entails the acceptance of zero as a number (since zero is an indicator of absence of quantities).

More in general, we aim at verifying the impact of theoretical studies developed during the course and the use of specific constructs, either of mathematical character, such as 'canonical and non canonical form of a number', 'procedural-relational polarity', or of educational-methodological character such as 'didactical mediator' or 'didactical contract'.

The Second Scene

Pupils' sentences are classified by the class teacher and the most representative ones are written on the blackboard. Then the teacher opens up the discussion with the purpose of making the class decide what sentence best represents the rule followed by Ann.

(a) Ann takes from finger biscuits the same number of chocolate cookies, she multiplies it by 2 and adds 1.
(b) She eats an odd number of finger biscuits and from 1 to 5 chocolate cookies.
(c) Chocolate cookies are always one more.
(d) One day she eats more and one day she eats less

Task for teachers:

4. Comment upon each of the four sentences written on the board concerning their consistency, completeness and efficacy with respect to the formulation of the regularity.
5. Imagine a plot for a discussion: opening, key steps and end.

This scene makes teachers face the task of first analysing prototypes of pupils' productions, trying to trace back the mental views that produced them and interpret unexpressed intuitions; and second imagining the development of a possible class discussion aimed at sharing results and constructing a clear proposition expressing the law, so that the subsequent task of translating it into algebraic language becomes easier.

The Third Scene

After a collective discussion, pupils agree on the choice of (a).
The class teacher proposes '*Each of you may try to write (a) in other ways*'
After a while some significant expressions written by pupils are reported on the blackboard:

(a_1) The number of finger biscuits is 1 more than twice the number of chocolate cookies.
(a_2) The number of finger biscuits is twice plus 1 the number of chocolate cookies.
(a_3) The number of chocolate cookies multiplied by 2, adding 1 equals the number of finger biscuits.

Based on these sentences the teacher opens up a new discussion.

Task for teachers:

6. Comment the choice made by the class to propose sentence (a).
7. Analyse the last three sentences, highlighting any possible difference with reference to the relational-procedural polarity.
8. Figure out a plot for a possible classroom discussion.

The aim is to lead teachers to refine their interpretative skills in the case of verbal expressions produced by pupils in order to guide them to identify differences, by making them clear: (a) in which sentences the time dimension of the counting act (procedural view) prevails over those in which the relationship between the two quantities is objectified; (b) how the interaction of these two views induces a verbal formulation of the law in which the predicate 'to be', typical of relational formulations, is re-formulated in terms of equality ('to be equal to').

The Fourth Scene

At the end of the discussion the class chooses sentence (a_1); the remaining two are erased.
The teacher gives a second task: Translate Ann's law for Brioshi in algebraic language.

Task for teachers:

9. Translate Ann's law in more than one way.
10. Predict the possible translations by pupils.

The goal of this task is twofold: first it is to evaluate teachers' abilities in finding algebraic formulations equivalent to the literal translation of the sentence; second, and this is more delicate, to predict pupils' translations, including the naive or incorrect ones.

The Fifth Scene

After an individual work, sentences are written on the blackboard (pupils' legend in brackets):

1) 1×2 2) $a + 1 \times 2$ (a = number of finger biscuits)
3) $fb + 1 \times 2$ 4) $a \times 2 + 1$
5) $fb + 1 \times 2 = a$ 6) $b = c + 1 \times 2$
7) $a \times +1 = b$ (a = number of chocolate cookies)
8) $a = b \times 2 + 1$ 9) $(a - 1) \times 2$

A discussion is enacted to choose the sentence that should be sent to Brioshi.

Task for teachers:

11. Comment upon each translation of Ann's law, underlining their correctness/incorrectness, consistency, possible redundancies etc.
12. Predict what the class will possibly choose and the related argumentation about the sentence they will send to Brioshi.

A delicate issue in this scene is the comparison between the expressions: '$a = b \times 2 + 1$' and '$a \times 2 + 1 = b$ (a = number of chocolate cookies)': the same letters represent different variables and it would be appropriate to predict pupils' behaviour on facing this fact.

The Sixth Scene

At the end of the discussion about the sentence to be sent to Brioshi, the following rule is chosen: $b = a \times 2 + 1$. The class teacher poses the problem *Are we able to understand what happens on Friday and Saturday even if ice cream spots hide part of the drawings?* Some pupils almost immediately use the formula correctly, but other pupils are initially puzzled. This difficulty is overcome during the discussion.

Task for teachers:

13. Is the rule sent out by the class the same you predicted at the end of the Fifth Scene? Is it different? Write down your comments on this.
14. Identify what the spots hide in the table illustrating the biscuits Ann eats.
15. With relation to the question posed by the teacher, interpret the reasons underlying the widespread confusion in the class.

This scene is a chance to test teachers' abilities on both the didactical and the mathematical side: teachers are expected to argue about mental and operative processes that pupils need to enact and about difficulties brought about by the Saturday situation, linked to the interpretation of zero as the solution to the equation 'a $\times 2 + 1 = 1$'.

Concluding Reflections

16. Write down a short reflection on the didactical situation you were asked to comment upon, also referring to a possibility of reproducing it in a hypothetical class of yours.
17. Write down a short concluding reflection on the structure of the whole set of tasks, mainly referring to its significance as model of task that may help trainee teachers explore what they learned both at mathematical and pedagogical level.

This is a task where teachers are expected to express themselves about the reproducibility of the didactical situation and, more generally, on the global value of the task they just carried out, with reference to their culture as to 'pedagogical content knowledge' (Shulman, 1986).

7 Analysis of Teachers' Protocols

7.1 Study of the First Scene

Question 1. *Carry out the task*

Eighty percent of the teachers easily identify the correspondence law. Two different kinds of behaviour arise: some identify the law by analysing numerical cases following the days' order; others feel the need to rank data according to the increasing number of chocolate cookies. In both categories there are some who make comments that highlight their view on the situation:

> Day by day Ann eats a number of finger biscuits which is twice the number of chocolate cookies plus one finger biscuit more. There does not seem to be a 'defined' number, expressing a certain 'rule' for the choice of chocolate cookies[3] (I can only see that chocolate cookies increase from 0 to 11). The relationship between finger biscuits and chocolate cookies only links the number of finger biscuits to twice plus 1 the number of chocolate cookies. Moreover, I observe that the numbers of finger biscuits are all odd.

---

[3] Our underlining.

The underlined sentence reveals the fact that the author sees the relationship as limited to the examined cases and not as a general one. In the latter case, in fact, the set of natural numbers would be seen as the domain in which the number of chocolate cookies varies (this is highlighted by other protocols). Though an acknowledgment of a realistic limit to the number of cookies that can be eaten might be reasonable.

Finally, about 20% do not interrelate the two variables but consider them separately:

> On each day Ann eats 1 chocolate cookie more than two days earlier and two finger biscuits more than two days earlier.

The difficulties met by these teachers show their little familiarity with the identification of correspondence laws, and, at the same time, how complex it is for inexperienced subjects to work in the 'search for regularities' environment.

Question 2. *Give a short explanation of why it is important to search for regularities in mathematics*

Teachers did not always express their ideas relevantly:

> Searching for regularities is important because it makes order arise from an apparently chaotic set, thus giving opportunities to find the relationship between entities of the set itself.

Many underline the importance of searching for regularities in order to favour the transition from the particular to the general, or sometimes of determining laws that can be adapted to other contexts or situations. A minority underlines the predictive power of laws with relation to the studied phenomenon. Some others highlight the educational value: through this activity pupils can be led to understand how mathematical laws originate:

> Searching for regularities is important because it enables us: to make the process leading to the formulation of any mathematical law more transparent; to help pupils to develop the metacognitive thinking which enables them to abstract and generalise.

Question 3. *Discuss the instruments and/or strategies you view as the most effective to identify regularities*

Many teachers refer to the rewriting of the table according to increasing values of the number of chocolate cookies as a helpful strategy for the identification of the law and its generalisation. Few teachers mention the class discussion as a strategy that may favour a sharing of the law's verbal formulation (a step we consider important towards its algebraic coding). Often, notions learned during the course emerge, for instance, the reference to non-canonical representation as a tool to make the correspondence between pairs transparent and to get to the generalisation of the law. An example:

The situation is suitable to a collective discussion in class. After listening to pupils' descriptions in natural language, I would propose them to construct a table at the blackboard in order to report numerical values in an organised way:

No. of chocolate cookies	2	4	3	5
No. of finger biscuits	5	9	7	11

At this point it would be important to invite pupils (even after they understood the relationship between the number of finger biscuits and that of chocolate cookies) to "paraphrase" the <u>canonical form</u> of the number of finger biscuits into the <u>non-canonical form</u>, i.e. to see it in a less <u>opaque</u> form. In fact, the number of finger biscuits might be seen in this way, n. finger biscuits:

$$5 = \underline{2} \times 2 + \underline{1}; 9 = \underline{2} \times 4 + \underline{1}; 7 = \underline{2} \times 3 + \underline{1}$$

So pupils might be able to identify "blocked" numbers ($\underline{2}$ and $\underline{1}$). The last step would be getting to the generalisation: $m = 2 \times n + 1$ *with m = number of biscuits and n = number of cookies.*[4]

8 Study of the Second and Third Scene

The two scenes highlight the educational importance of the verbal formulation of the observed regularities. Teachers often underestimate it, not grasping its impact on the algebraic formulation of a law. This often happens because teachers do not have a linguistic view of the approach to algebra.

Question 4. *Comment upon each of the four sentences written on the board as to their consistency, completeness and efficacy with reference to the formulation of the regularity.*

Question 6. *Comment upon the choice made by the class to propose sentence (a).*

Question 7. *Analyse the last three sentences, highlighting any possible difference with reference to the relational-procedural polarity.*

Some protocols mainly highlight the comparison of 'relational representations' and 'procedural representations': sentences a_1 and a_2 are identified as relationships, whereas a_3 is seen as strictly procedural. Some others reveal sensitivity towards important but barely noticed aspects, possible outcome of what has been done during the course:

> I would say that from a_1 to a_3 we can notice an increasing 'unclearness of thinking' and a use of natural language that hides a more and more elementary mathematical thinking. a_3 denotes a clear 'arithmetic[5]' approach by the pupil; it may be translated into a classical operation read from left to right with the result on the right, after the equal sign.

In other ones, we find explicitly stated difficulties met by the teacher or his/her beliefs translated as 'pupils' inclinations or difficulties':

---

[4] The underlined words reflect the study of theory: each of them is a specific item of the Glossary.

[5] Several students use the term 'arithmetic' with the meaning of procedural.

I think that I would hardly convince pupils that sentence a_1 is better than a_3 because a_3 is the most simple to be translated and I think it is more transparent and clear to them because it carried inside the exact procedure they should apply.

Many analyse sentences referring to the difficulties inherent in their algebraic formulation:

The source sentence 'a', although correct, is not very clear but was helpful for pupils in order to elaborate more transparent sentences: a_1) 'The number of finger biscuits is 1 more than twice the number of chocolate cookies' can be translated by following the sequential nature of the sentence into: $m = 1 + 2n$; a_2) 'The number of finger biscuits is twice plus 1 the number of chocolate cookies' can be translated into: $m = 2n + 1$.; a_3) 'The number of chocolate cookies multiplied by 2, adding 1 equals the number of finger biscuits' is translated into: $2n + 1 = m$.

Question 5 *Imagine a plot for a discussion: opening, key steps and end*

Question 8 *Figure out a plot for a discussion*

In these situations teachers have great difficulties; besides those who ignore the request or simulate scarcely constructive excerpts of discussions, teachers' behaviour can be grouped into four categories. Teachers:

(a) simplify the task restricting it to a generic talk about what needs to be done:[6]

The discussion starts from the analysis of the four proposed sentences; the goal will be to identify the most transparent one, the one which better describes the situation by means of arguments produced by each pupil (each will possibly provide arguments supporting their own sentence). The outcome should be the choice of the first sentence (a), as the one which best reflects Ann's law.

(b) only figure out the opening of the discussion:

the first situation might be analysed asking pupils to represent it and then making them reflect on the meaning of 'multiplying by 2' and 'adding'

(c) sketch out the discussion's structure, focusing on themselves as teacher:

I would start from (c) and I would remark that what the pupil says is not true. To get to an organised analysis I would suggest the construction of a table (key step). I would say the same in the case of (b) and say that to be sure that finger biscuits are always odd we must find a rule that enables us to calculate them every time, then I would point out that sentence (a) generalises what happens every day and it is the only one which enables us to see what happens on Friday and Saturday.

(d) sketch out the discussion's structure, focusing on students:

In a hypothetical discussion pupils might be led to reflect starting from sentence (c); they would notice that not chocolate cookies but finger biscuits are one more. Once this point is made clear, the reflection might shift on (b), pointing out that it is not sure that on days like Friday, Saturday and Sunday Ann eats a number of c. cookies between 1 and 5, keeping the fact that the number of f. biscuits is odd. Next, sentence (d) might be analysed, highlighting that it is not a rule that clarifies the relationship between the number of sweets (c. cookies and f. biscuits). Finally I would focus on (a) and analyse it from the point of view of meaning, also using additional strategies (e.g. graphical, like a table) making pupils get, through an argument-supported progressive reflection, to say that (a) is the one that best expresses Ann's law.

---

[6] All protocols in this paragraph refer to the second scene, except where differently specified.

9 Study of the Fourth Scene

In this scene the central problem is the formal translation of the relationship 'the number of finger biscuits is 1 more than twice the number of chocolate cookies'. The task for teachers is twofold:

Question 9. *Translate Ann's law in more than one way*

Question 10. *Predict the possible translations by pupils*

Behavioural categories emerged can be classified as follows:

(a) Poor productions: teachers do not distinguish the different levels in the two tasks and simply produce the translations '$2 \times c + 1 = f$' and '$f = 1 + 2 \times c$' ('f' representing the number of finger biscuits and 'c' that of chocolate cookies) and declare for example:

> The first one can be the most frequent among pupils because the equal sign is at the end.

(b) Rich productions, centred on teachers only: teachers translate the relationship also in the implicit form, or taking the number of chocolate cookies as subject (a translation that pupils can hardly make in this phase); they do not put themselves in pupils' shoes and are not able to predict possible translations;

(c) Rich productions, centred on teachers and pupils: teachers provide a wide range of translations and at the same time analyse them in terms of possible pupils' translations. As to this, teachers' hypotheses differ considerably. They maintain that:

(c_1) the most probable translation is the one that represents the calculation process to get the number of finger biscuits ($2 \times c + 1 = b$);

(c_2) the most probable translation is the literal one ($b = 2 \times c + 1$);

(c_3) both can be chosen, as the following protocol claims:

$u = n.$ chocolate cookies; $v = n.$ finger biscuits: (1) $u \times 2 + 1 = v$; (2) $v = 1 + u \times 2 \ldots$

> I think that among the possible translations the first one would be the most popular because it puts equal at the end, but also the second one could be very spread because it follows the literal and sequential translation of the sentence in natural language.

As to Question 10 in particular, '*Predict pupils' possible translations*', almost all teachers suppose that pupils:

– in translating the term 'twice', would make explicit use of the multiplication sign '$\times$' and that weaker pupils would use the additive representation;

– would use writings referring to the semantics of the situation, such as '$nb = 1 + 2 \times nc$'

– omit the explanatory key to the meaning attached to each letter used.

One controversial point concerns the possible making of 'twin' representations such as '$b = 1 + 2 \times c$' and '$b = 2 \times c + 1$'; the commutative law is intuitive to some teachers but not to others. Few teachers reflect on the possible wrong or incomplete translations.

10 Study of the Fifth Scene

Question 11. *Comment upon each translation of Ann's law, underlying their correctness/incorrectness, consistency, possible redundancies etc.*

Almost all teachers carried out a careful analysis of the sentences, justifying also the possible reasons that led to them. What comes out is a 'cultured' reading, making reference to theory. Terms like 'adulterate' or 'unfaithful' translation which were introduced at a theoretical level during the course, drawing on linguistics[7], were used.

Question 12. *Predict what the class will possibly choose and the related argumentation about the sentence they will send to Brioshi.*

As usual, this is the most problematic task. Not all teachers carried it out successfully; on the basis of the analysis, many of them only indicate the following sentences as the one that will be chosen by the class: '$a = b \times 2 + 1$' and '$a \times 2 + 1 = b$, a = number of chocolate cookies'. In the first translation, more faithful to the text, the meanings of the used letters are not expressed; in the second one the problem is to lead pupils to reflect upon the symmetrical use of the equal sign. There are also teachers who express these concepts by making up brilliant excerpts of possible conversations in the classroom.

The effects of training can be seen in those who tackle the problem of the collective analysis of the various translations: the courses they followed highlighted the importance of making pupils interpret 'unclear' sentences in order to get to a reasoned choice of the correct ones, appreciating everybody's contributions. About this, a teacher writes:

> ... We might also point out that all sentences are not wrong 'per se', as they indicate something anyway, but they do not reflect the presented situation.

Somebody conjectures that initially some pupils may make 'easy' choices because they are semantically more expressive:

> Initially some might be 'attracted' by sentences that make use of abbreviations because they are more 'pleasant' from the symbolic point of view, and exclude them only later.

Another important emerging aspect concerns teacher's conception of their own role in the development of a class discussion:

---

[7] For a deeper discussion about these aspects see Malara and Navarra (2001).

(a) some view the management of the activity as giving room to pupils' interventions:

> The class might initially take into consideration sentences between the fifth and the eighth, because only in them is the number of finger biscuits compared to the number of chocolate cookies. By substituting numbers in each translation[8] the class soon realises that only the seventh and the eighth translations are valid. Perhaps in the end the class would choose to send the seventh sentence because it best translates the starting verbal expression.

(b) some put themselves at the centre and view the class in a listening attitude:

> I think that after listening to the various translations, the class needs to decide between '$a = b \times 2 + 1$' and '$a \times 2 + 1 = b$. (a = number of chocolate cookies)'. Both are written in correct mathematical language and represent the situation consistently. Nevertheless, I believe that $a = b \times 2 + 1$ is more precise, because it respects the sequence and order in which the law is expressed.

11 Study of the Sixth Scene

In this scene, teachers face the following questions:

Question 13. *Is the rule sent out by the class the same you predicted at the end of the Fifth Scene? Is it different? Write down your comments on this.*

Question 14. *Identify what the spots hide in the table illustrating the biscuits Ann eats.*

Question 15. *With reference to the question posed by the teacher, interpret the reasons underlying the widespread confusion in the class.*

Puzzlement refers to the study of Friday and Saturday cases, in which it is necessary to substitute the known value of the variable in the given law and solve the resulting equation. In order to do this, teachers must re-examine the initial situation and highlight that the Saturday case concerns the inverse relationship and that an equation is needed to solve it. Teachers mainly give correct interpretations:

> One common difficulty may be linked to Saturday, because it is difficult to accept that Ann does not eat any chocolate cookie on that day. Another possible reason may attain to Saturday from an operational viewpoint: pupils have the number corresponding to 'b' available and must find 'a', and this is a non trivial task for grade-6 pupils.

Some interpretations are particularly meaningful, as they are conducted in the line of a co-ordination of cognitive and psychological aspects. For example:

> I think the difficulty was ... also to accept the idea that in the graphical representation the ice cream spot did not cover anything!

---

[8] The teacher thinks of the number substitution as a suitable strategy to verify the correctness of formal translations.

12 Study of the 'Concluding Reflection'

Question 16. *Write down a short reflection on the didactical situation you were asked to comment upon, also referring to a possibility of reproducing it in a hypothetical class of yours.*

Question 17. *Write down a short concluding reflection on the structure of the whole set of tasks, mainly referring to its significance as model of task that may help trainee teachers explore what they learned both at mathematical and pedagogical level.*

The productive presentation of the activity as a playful challenge is underlined and the general educational value of the game is analysed. Teachers also point out how attractive the game can be, due to the arguments solicited and to the mediation towards algebraic language by means of natural language:

> This is certainly a didactical situation that will be fun for the class, also because it leaves pupils free to express themselves and the "heaviness" of reasoning in algebraic terms does not come up immediately. Playing games is always helpful.

Generally positive opinions are expressed about the reproducibility of the proposed situation, even though some envisage an unsuccessful management of the class:

> I would certainly propose this kind of situation (I believe this teaching approach is very good and for sure to be preferred to traditional teaching); my fear, perhaps due to lack of experience, is to be unable to deal with unexpected situations which come out in the class' dynamic processes.

Reflections gather around two aspects, often interwoven: (a) value of the task as guiding instrument for the teacher; (b) complexity of the task, difficulties and fears this generated. We deal with the two aspects separately.

(a) *Value of the task as guiding instrument for the teacher*

It is generally acknowledged that the task is a valid instrument to lead teachers, and especially those who do not have class teaching experience, to approach issues that characterise the teaching activity such as predicting pupils' behaviour, interpreting their productions and setting up discussions.

> The type of task is very positive. Not knowing what happened next, I was forced to think more and examine all the possibilities I could think about. The subsequent scenes can be used to confirm or refute reasoning and permit a meta-analysis of what we developed and appropriated as ours in the previous scene.

The fact that the task forces the teacher to predict pupils' behaviour is highlighted:

> This test can be helpful to put ourselves in pupils' shoes, to consider aspects that are usually taken for granted and predict 'unusual' developments (often pupils react in ways we did not expect).

Several teachers underline that the task is presented in a very stimulating and attractive form:

> I never entered a school as a teacher and my memory as student focused on a traditional school made of rules and definitions given from above! Anyway, I believe that dialogue and discussion are the foundations of learning and engaging with this didactical situation was very instructive and amusing.

Others recommend that this kind of tasks be proposed more often:

> I think that in the professional training of teachers, situations of this kind should be proposed very often during the course in the form of laboratories.

(b) *Difficulties met and fears raised*

Some teachers underline the complexity of the test, highlight difficulties and most of all express their fears about their own abilities to carry out constructive teaching in the future. The difficulties teachers express are grouped as follows:

(1) Difficulties met in carrying out the task (trainee's point of view about the task)

> As you might have observed I found it difficult to find the rule. .... I must say that I would probably not have obtained good results after proposing classes in this way, because, as we said during the lessons, it is up to pupils to propose the various ways of translating a sentence and moreover they all must be ready to acquire this type of language.

(2) Wrong perception of the situation's impact on pupils

Teachers coming from background studies in physics or mathematics underestimate the difficulties that students may encounter:

> The search for regularities may be used because it enables an easy transition from a concrete example to its abstraction and because it allows for simple translations in mathematical language, thus allowing the subject to grasp relationships between elements.

(3) Difficulties in predicting one's own actions towards students (trainee's point of view as to students)

> The main difficulty comes up when pupils propose their situations in symbolic terms. If their answers are partially predictable, it is sometimes difficult to get into their reasoning and understand which thought led them to elaborate certain pseudo-equations.

(4) Difficulties due to the intersection of the role of teacher and that of trainee

Trainees often are temporary teachers, this double role becomes an object of reflection:

> I start with this self-critical reflection. I admit I misread the expression reported on sheet 1 '... two ice cream spots hide finger biscuits on Friday and c. cookies on Saturday' and therefore I ignored its meaning (I believed that biscuits outside the spot were not relevant). ... I suppose at this point I transmitted the original text of the problem in a wrong way to the class, making pupils puzzled and misleading their understanding. In the case none of them would have asked for explanations we would have naturally reached the sixth scene with puzzlement and incapacity of completing the tasks, as it actually happened. ... Nevertheless I fell into this trap because today I suffered the 'test' almost like a pupil and that probably would not have happened if I had studied and proposed it as a teacher.

(5) The key point for the management of a class discussion

Protocols clearly show that letting pupils discuss is a source of worries for teachers, especially due to their lack of expertise:

> ... What worries me more (and I scarcely analysed it in this test) is how a collective discussion should be managed and how it is possible to lead the class to share correct meanings. I feel that the goal of each proposed phase is rather clear to me; what is difficult is to actually lead the class to that, by guiding the discussion in a constructive way, without harsh criticisms or forcing.

One problem concerns the impact of the primitive model of teacher in the classroom as far as the management of the discussion is concerned. Sometimes teachers, although agreeing to tackle a discussion, figure out a directive way of piloting it:

> I would set up the discussion starting from the last sentence back to the first one, trying to make pupils understand that the last two ones are useless to our aims, that the second one only expresses a partial truth and that the first one is the only one that expresses a useful regularity.

13 Concluding Remarks

In this chapter we sketched a synthesis of our theoretical framework aimed at an early and linguistic approach to algebra, to be carried out constructively. We recalled some of our theoretical constructs, including 'algebraic babbling', which reflects our conception of algebraic language learning. We underlined how valuable for teacher education are the study of theory and the reference to a glossary, instrument which comes to fulfil the constantly increasing intellectual need (Harel, 1998) felt by teachers.

We tackled the issue of how teachers can be led to acquire conceptions and behavioural models that may foster among pupils a view of algebra as a representation system, and in particular develop in pupils skills related to modelling, interpretation and production of thinking.

For this reason we proposed here our model of task, specifically designed so as to give teachers the chance to deal with the practice of constructive teaching 'theoretically'.

The structure of the task, divided into scenes, is considered an effective classroom simulation to guide the teacher in a step-by-step involvement with the teaching sequence. Hypotheses about classroom-based actions are seen as very demanding tasks, still it is highlighted that the task is a powerful means to force the teacher to compare predictions with the actual development of the class activity.

Protocols show teachers' difficulties and fears concerning their own future abilities to implement constructive teaching. Difficulties mainly concern the design of discussion plots, the interpretation of and comment on formal written expressions, identification with students.Other fears concern not being able to understand pupils, confusing them, not being able to make them actually discuss, and implementing a directive way of piloting the class due to an unconscious stereotyped model of teacher.

The protocols also highlight remarks about teachers' awareness of how culturally important it is to make their own development as teachers explicit and open to collective sharing. Processes in which new knowledge and new meanings are shared, come to be enacted at three different levels:

- with oneself, leading to reflections on the courses and the tasks impact on ones own professional development and, more generally, on the 'renewed' relationship between theory and practice;
- with colleagues, by means of a peer to peer comparison of things learned during the course and the explicit statement of underlying beliefs, this leads teachers to become aware of the features of their own beliefs as well as of their way of living the classroom activity (the latter is a fundamental step for a review of one's own attitudes and a change of unsuitable ones);
- with pupils, maybe the most stimulating and innovative aspect- as it induces teachers to set up a didactical contract based on constant explicit claims about the reasons underlying the teaching activities they propose to pupils. This way, they get used to seeing themselves as active participants in the construction of knowledge.

References

Blanton, M., & Kaput, J. (2001). Algebrafying the elementary mathematics experience: Part II. Transforming practice on a district-wide scale. In K. Stacey, H. Chick, & M. Kendall (Eds.), *The future of the teaching and learning of Algebra: Proceedings of the 12th ICMI Study* (Vol. 1, pp. 87–95). Melbourne.

Brousseau, G. (1988). Le contrat didactique: Le milieu. *Recherches en didactique des mathématiques, 9*(3), 309–336.

Brown, L., & Coles, A. (1999). Needing to use algebras: A case study. In *Proceedings of PME 23* (Vol. 2, pp. 153–160).

Carpenter, T., & Franke, M. L. (2001) Developing algebraic reasoning in the elementary school: Generalization and proof. In K. Stacey, H. Chick, & M. Kendall (Eds.), *The future of the teaching and learning of Algebra: Proceedings of the 12th ICMI Study* (Vol. 1. 155–162). Melbourne.

Carraher, D., Brizuela, B., & Schliemann, A. (2000). Bringing out the algebraic character of arithmetic: Instantiating variables in addition and subtraction. In *Proceedings of PME 24* (Vol. 2, pp. 145–152).

Davis, R. B. (1985). ICME-5 report: Algebraic thinking in early grades. *Journal of Mathematical Behaviour, 4*, 195–208.

Da Rocha Falcão, J. T. (1995). A case study of Algebraic Scaffolding: From balance to algebraic notation. In *Proceedings of PME 19* (Vol. 2, pp. 66–73).

Dougherty, B. (2001). Access to algebra: A process approach. In K. Stacey, H. Chick, & M. Kendall (Eds.), *The future of the teaching and learning of Algebra: Proceeding of the 12th ICMI Study* (Vol. 1, pp. 344–353, 87–95). Melbourne.

Harel, G. (1998). The dual assertion: The first on learning the second on teaching (or vice versa). *The American Mathematical Monthly, 105*, 497–507.

Jaworski, B. (1998). Mathematics teacher research: process, practice and the development of teaching. *Journal of Mathematics Teacher Education, 1*, 3–31

Jaworski, B. (2003). Research practice into/influencing mathematics teaching and learning development: Towards a theoretical framework based on co-learning partnerships. *Educational Studies in Mathematics, 54,* 249–282.

Linchevski, L. (1995). Algebra with numbers and arithmetic with letters: A definition of pre-algebra. *Journal of Mathematical Behaviour, 14,* 113–120.

Malara, N. A. (2003). Dialectics between theory and practice: Theoretical issues and aspects of practice from an early algebra project, plenary lecture. In *Proceedings of PME 27* (Vol. 1, pp. 33–48).

Malara, N. A. (2005). Leading in-service teachers to approach early algebra. In L. Santos, A. P. Canavarro, & J. Brocardo (Eds.), *Mathematics education: Paths and crossroads: international meeting in honour of Paulo Abrantes* (pp. 285–304). Lisbon: Etigrafe.

Malara, N. A., & Navarra, G. (2001). "Brioshi" and other mediation tools employed in a teaching of arithmetic with the aim of approaching algebra as a language. In K. Stacey, H. Chick, & M. Kendall (Eds.), *The future of the teaching and learning of Algebra: Proceeding of the 12*th *ICMI Study* (Vol. 2, pp. 412–419). Melbourne.

Malara, N. A., & Navarra, G. (2003). *ArAl project: Arithmetic pathways towards favouring pre-algebraic thinking.* Bologna: Pitagora.

Malara, N. A., & Zan, R. (2002). The problematic relationship between theory and practice. In L. English (Ed.), *Handbook of international research in mathematics education* (pp. 553–580). NJ: Erlbaum.

Mason, J. (1998). Enabling teachers to be real teachers: Necessary levels of awareness and structure of attention. *Journal of Mathematics Teacher Education, 1,* 243–267.

Mason, J. (2002). *Researching your own practice: The discipline of noticing.* London: The Falmer Press.

Meira, L. (1990). Developing knowledge of functions through manipulation of a physical device. In *Proceedings of PME 14* (Vol. 2, pp. 101–108).

Meira, L. (1996). Students' early algebraic activity: Sense making and production of meanings in mathematics. In *Proceedings of PME 20* (Vol. 3, pp. 377–384).

Menzel, B. (2001) Language conceptions of algebra are idiosyncratic. In K. Stacey, H. Chick, & M. Kendall (Eds.), *The future of the teaching and learning of Algebra: Proceeding of the 12*th *ICMI Study* (Vol. 2, pp. 446–453). Melbourne.

Peter-Koop, A. (2001). From "Teacher Researchers" to "Student Teacher Researchers": Diagnostically enriched didactics. In *Proceedings of PME 25* (Vol. 1, pp. 72–79). Utrecht.

Ponte, J. P. (2004). Investigar a nossa própria prática: una stratégia de formaçáo e de construçáo de conhecimento professional. In E. Castro & E. De la Torre, (Eds.), *Investigación en educación matemática.* Spain: University of Coruña.

Radford, L. (2000). Signs and meanings in students' emergent algebraic thinking: A semiotic analysis. *Educational Studies in Mathematics, 42*(3), 237–268.

Radford, L., & Grenier, M. (1996). On dialectical relationship between signs and algebraic ideas. In *Proceedings of PME 20* (Vol. 4, pp. 179–186).

Schoenfeld, A. (1998). Toward a theory of teaching in context. *Issues in Education, 4*(1), 1–94.

Shulman, L. S. (1986). Those who understand: Knowledge growth in teaching. *Educational Researcher, 15,* 4–14.

Outdoor Mathematical Experiences: Constructivism, Connections, and Health

Meg Moss

Outdoor mathematics activities in both preservice teacher education and in elementary schools can help teachers and children connect with the world we live in. Children are naturally curious about the world around them, and enjoy using mathematics to help them understand their world. Through this natural curiosity, they are able to construct mathematical knowledge using both a psychological and socio-cultural perspective of constructivism. Outdoor mathematics experiences not only help learners to see connections between mathematics and other disciplines, but also can help learners feel more connected to their natural world. This chapter will define outdoor mathematics, lay a theoretical framework of why it is important, and then provide specific examples of outdoor mathematics tasks that can be used in primary teacher education.

> If a child is to keep alive his inborn sense of wonder, he needs the companionship of at least one adult who can share it, rediscovering with him the joy, excitement, and mystery of the world we live in. (Carson, 1956, p. 45)

Preservice teachers must rediscover and build on a sense of wonder about the world we live in during their training if they are to become that one adult that can share this excitement with children. Outdoor mathematics activities in both teacher education and primary schools can help teachers and children rediscover the joy, excitement, and mystery of the world we live in. Children are naturally curious about the world around them, and enjoy using mathematics to help them understand their world. From measuring their height, dividing cookies, and games they play; mathematics is a natural part of their world. This natural curiosity enables them to construct mathematical knowledge through the perspective of both psychological and socio-cultural constructivism. Outdoor mathematics experiences not only help learners to see connections between mathematics and other disciplines, but also can help learners feel more connected to their natural world. In a society where physical outside activity is becoming scarce, reconnecting to the natural world and becoming

M. Moss
Associate Professor of Mathematics and Teacher Education Coordinator, Pellissippi State Technical Community College in Knoxville, TN, USA

B. Clarke, B. Grevholm, and R. Millman (eds.), *Tasks in Primary Mathematics Teacher Education: Purpose, Use and Exemplars,* Mathematics Teacher Education 4,

more active is critical. Outdoor mathematics in elementary schools is now required or at least encouraged in several countries (Bones & Gravanes, 2004). Responsibility for implementing an outdoor mathematics approach in the elementary mathematics curriculum lies with the teacher who needs to experience and understand this approach in teacher education.

1 What Is Meant by Outdoor Mathematics?

Several types of outdoor mathematics activities can help children and teachers to experience and connect to the world outside of the classroom walls. Some of these activities are necessarily done outside to help learners to explore and understand the world around them, such as a bird inventory of the neighborhood, exploring geometric figures in both the natural world and the human created world of automobiles and buildings, or observing the stars in the sky. Some outdoor activities may require a large space that most indoor facilities do not have. Examples of this type of activity include creating a full size model of different types of whales and sharks, estimating and walking a kilometer or graphing on a grid large enough for people to be the points. Lastly, some mathematics activities can be fun to do outside as a change of pace and of scenery such as practicing mathematical computations with sidewalk chalk instead of at a desk with pencil or paper, or having mathematical discussions outside in the sunshine.

2 Why Outdoor Mathematics?

On that beautiful spring day, many teachers have heard from their students at the beginning of class, "Can we go outside today?" Besides enjoying a lovely spring day, there are many reasons to take students outside to explore mathematics and the natural world. Outdoor mathematics can help students to explore mathematics consistent with constructivist approaches to teaching. In a world of technology, shopping malls, and drive through restaurants, people need to be encouraged to get outside more often both to reconnect with the world as well as to promote better health. Learning mathematics outside of the classroom can help to make easier connections between mathematics and other subjects. When teachers experience outdoor mathematics in their teacher training, it increases the likelihood that they will be able to use these methods with their students.

2.1 Constructivist Perspective

Constructivist learning theories have been widely interpreted and analyzed and have helped mathematics educators to better appreciate how mathematical understanding can be developed. Practical methods of implementing constructivism in both teacher education and elementary schools are important in making the theory applicable to practice. Outdoor mathematics activities are a practical way to implement constructivist learning through both a psychological learning philosophy and a socio-cultural perspective.

Psychological learning theory aspects of constructivism include the concept that learners construct new knowledge based on previous experiences and understanding. Young children are very connected to the world around them since much of their early learning is based on experiencing their world. Prospective teachers can also learn mathematics by constructing new knowledge based on their world. By learning mathematics in connection to the outside world, teachers are better able to help their students use mathematics to connect and build upon their previous knowledge.

A socio-cultural perspective of constructivism is that learners construct new knowledge through engagement in activities and mathematical reasoning within a community (Ball & Bass, 2000). The outdoor activities suggested in this chapter create community outside of the classroom walls and provide opportunities for sharing and communicating about mathematics. A collaborative activity in a natural setting helps build a community of learners in a unique way.

2.2 Kids and Adults Need to be Outside More

Mental, physical, and psychological benefits are gained from spending time outdoors. Unfortunately, people tend to be spending increasing time indoors. With more television channels, more video games, internet surfing, and controlled climates, most of us spend more time exploring these than exploring what is in our back yard. Outdoor mathematics activities in teacher education and in elementary schools can help people to reconnect and be more active.

Connection to the world around them and gaining a sense of joy, excitement, and mystery about the environment is important for young students and teachers. Education should provide both teachers and students the opportunity to discover a sense of place (Louv, 2005). All of life is interconnected, but it seems that the more we get connected to the internet and cable television, the less we are connected to the trees and stars and animals.

The World Health Organization (2006) states that reduced physical activity in today's society is a major cause for the global obesity epidemic. More technology and leisurely hobbies have contributed to less physical activity. It is imperative that teachers and their students get out of the classroom desks and into a more active lifestyle. Simply going outside for a mathematics activity is not going to cure the obesity epidemic, but getting out of a classroom desk for any reason is a start to becoming more active.

2.3 Connections to Other Subjects

Outdoor mathematics is a natural way to connect mathematics to other subjects and help students see that mathematics is not just something that happens only in the classroom and textbooks. Science, literature, art and physical fitness are connected easily to mathematics through outdoor experiences. Children, adults, and especially teachers need to see mathematics outside, in the woods, on the sports fields, even in the busy streets. Collaboration between mathematics educators and teachers from other disciplines can help both teacher and students to make these connections. In Fig. 1 student teachers are outside combining mathematics and science through an exploration of the environment.

2.4 Outdoor Mathematics in Teacher Education

Teachers need to experience mathematics in ways that they are expected to teach it. Some countries are expecting or at least encouraging teachers to implement outdoor mathematics activities in the classroom (Bones & Gravanes, 2004). Teachers are encouraged to teach mathematics in a connected way that helps students to construct mathematical understanding. Outdoor mathematics activities can create these types of learning opportunities as they provide opportunities to experience mathematics in the natural world. Teachers are more likely to implement outdoor activities in their own classes if they have had positive experiences in their own learning with this type of activity.

Fig. 1 Teacher education students exploring both math and science

3 Outdoor Mathematics Tasks for Prospective Elementary Teachers

There are clearly some strong arguments for including outdoor mathematics tasks in the school curriculum but what tasks might be appropriate in the context of teacher education and how might they be used? While it is acknowledged that these activities may take some extra time, the benefits in the potential construction of knowledge, in the potential connections with other disciplines, and for the health of students are well worth the time. Implementing even one of these activities can open up the idea and possibilities of outdoor mathematics to prospective elementary teachers. Each of the following outdoor mathematical tasks can be done in courses that focus on either the development of mathematical knowledge or with a mathematics pedagogy focus. Readers are encouraged to look around their own settings and be creative in adapting these tasks to meet their needs and those of their communities. Following are some examples of tasks that the author has found successful in elementary teacher training.

3.1 Geometer's Scavenger Hunt

Seeing the geometry in the world around us can not only help us to connect to the natural world, but can also help us to understand geometric ideas better (Fig. 2). Several adaptations can be made to this activity depending on your location and what technology you have available. Collecting examples of the geometric items can be done with a digital camera, Polaroid or film camera, drawings, or discussions. This activity is a good one to do with groups of three or four people working together.

Provide the students with a list of geometric terms a few days before the activity so that they have time to look up any terms and sketch each one. This can be a great review of the terms, and it may be beneficial to have the students draw them on the board to make sure everyone knows what they look like. On the day of the activity,

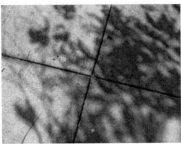

Fig. 2 Pictures submitted for this project include a leaf showing symmetry and perpendicular line segments in a sidewalk

send them out with either a camera or a sketchpad and have them find the items. Encourage them to find as many things as possible in the natural world, as well as the human created world. A point system can also be utilized if the teacher educator would like to make a game out of it where they get extra points for finding harder items, and extra points for finding natural objects.

The final product to this activity can take on many forms. If the students have digital cameras to capture the images, then these can be used to create a power point, website or other electronic medium to display their findings. Whether sketches or digital images are used, the prospective teachers can display their findings through a scrap book, poster board, or other creative mediums. Whatever the display, the prospective teacher hopefully creates a product that may be useful in future teaching.

Prospective teachers often remark that this is their favorite activity of the semester. After this activity, they report that they begin to truly see the geometry all around them. They also report that it helps them to understand the geometric terms better. This activity also helps the teacher educator to better assess what understandings and misunderstandings that prospective teachers possess. Through this project in one class, it became evident that some of the students had a misconception that a diameter must touch two opposite sides of the circle, but not necessarily go through the center. This created an opportunity to become aware of and therefore immediately clarify this misconception.

3.2 Designing and Creating Models

One of the many places that mathematics is used every day is in designing and creating models such as a parking lot or playground. Being aware of upcoming projects on your campus and getting your students involved in the planning can provide additional relevance to the task. For example, if your college or university has a particular area to build a parking lot, how should the parking spaces be arranged to maximize the number of cars that it can hold? Perhaps a park in your community, or an elementary school, is planning to build a new playground. Visit the area and have the students create a scale model of how to best design the playground given the space constraints. Designing a community garden, an obstacle course or labyrinth, and perhaps even building one of the designs as a community service project, could be a great community building idea.

At a previous college, the maintenance crew installed large flower pots around campus. Some of them were rectangular prisms, some were cylindrical, and others were cubes. A favorite activity in the prospective teacher mathematics content courses was to design how these should be planted. Given specifications on gravel and soil mixtures, they first figured out how much topsoil and gravel was needed for their chosen planter. They then created a design for arranging the flowers, and then created a model of it using *Geometer's Sketchpad* software. The maintenance people at the college would choose their favorite designs and actually create some of the student's designs in the planters. By engaging in a realistic outdoor mathematics task that involved looking around the campus, and working with colleagues, the prospective teachers not only became more connected to nature and geometry, but also the college community.

3.3 Measuring Heights with Clinometer, Mirror, or Similar Triangles

Another task which provides outdoor activities for prospective elementary teachers as well as giving meaning to mathematics involves using geometry and/or trigonometry to measure heights of trees. First have the students estimate the height of a tree on campus (or flagpole or telephone pole or building), as experiences in estimating distances are important in developing this skill. From there several methods exist to find the height. If given time to communicate in groups and to explore, and if given a variety of tools, the students can usually come up with a method, or the professor can guide them to use a particular method if appropriate.

If it is a sunny day, then shadows can help create similar triangles. Experiencing similar triangles this way is much more dynamic than similar triangles drawn in a textbook. Many mathematics textbooks have problems in the similar triangle section about shadows and heights, but it is much more meaningful and fun for the prospective teachers to actually experience this. The students measure their height, the length of their shadow, and the length of the tree's shadow and create similar triangles which then enable them to use proportionality to find the height of the tree.

Another method is using a mirror and similar triangles. Draw a line segment across the center of a small mirror and lay the mirror on the ground with this line segment perpendicular to the tree. The student then walks away from the mirror, in the opposite direction from the tree, until the top of the tree can be seen in the mirror lined up with the perpendicular line segment. Because the angles of reflections are congruent, this again creates two similar triangles. The person, the distance from the person to the mirror along the ground, and the line of sight distance is one triangle and the second is the tree, the distance from the base of the tree to the mirror, and the distance from the top of the tree to the mirror. Using proportional reasoning, the height of the tree can be found.

Two other methods using the angle of elevation can also be explored. A handmade clinometer can easily be made with a protractor, a piece of string, and a paperclip by tying the string on at the vertex point, and putting the paperclip on the other end as a weight. This handmade clinometer can then be used to measure the angle of elevation to the top of the tree. If the student then carefully draws an angle of the same size on a piece of paper, and completes the right triangle, then no matter what size the sides are, this will be a similar triangle to the one created by the tree and the distance from the base of the tree when measuring the angle of elevation. Using the angle of elevation and the distance from the base of the tree, trigonometry ratios can also be used to find the height, although this might not be included in the curriculum of many content courses for prospective elementary teachers.

3.4 Outdoor Graphing

Outdoor graphing, both linear and Cartesian, is a great way to get students outside, moving, and learning in a very kinesthetic way. A life size number line can be easily created using sidewalk chalk, or a piece of string taped to the ground, or perhaps a long seam or line in a sidewalk. People can then serve as the points and easily illustrate ordering and operations. For example, three times four could be illustrated by a person starting at zero and moving four spaces 3 times and noting the results. Representing fractions and operations of fractions with this large number line can also give a meaningful visual image to prospective teachers. For example, modelling one half times one third on this large number line by taking one half of the one third and seeing that the answer is one sixth and why is very powerful and memorable, perhaps more memorable than seeing it drawn on the board.

A Cartesian grid can easily be made by taping two pieces of string to the ground, perpendicular to each other, to form the x and y axes. Pieces of tape can be put on the axes to show the x and y values. For graphing functions, pair up the students so one person is the point and the other helps them figure out where to be. Give each "point" person an x value, and then given some rule (e.g., $y = 2x + 3$). They start on the x axis, walk to the y position based on the rule, and together form a line. Concepts such as slope and distance formula can be easily developed at this time.

A quick and fun related activity is to create a variety of statistical graphs using people and a life size grid rather than the more abstract paper and pencil. For example, make a human bar graph of the number of siblings they have, with each person standing in the correct spot. Other statistical graphs, such as line plots or scatter plots, can be created similarly in the outdoors on a large interactive scale.

3.5 Orienteering and Angle Understanding

The concept of angles can seem very abstract to students. The rotation and size of angles often is not evident in the representations of angles that are usually drawn on paper. Therefore, providing opportunities for prospective teachers to experience angles can be important for them to construct an understanding. This activity can be teacher directed or student created. Actual compasses can be used if available, or a protractor.

The professor can create a set of "directions" to guide the students from the classroom to a special tree, for example. The students would then take turns, perhaps working in small groups, to follow these directions to the secret place. The directions would include things such as, facing the elevator doors, turn 90 degrees to the left and walk 15 paces, or 15 metres. Then turn 20 degrees to the right and walk 10 paces, or metres. If they follow these directions, then they all should end up in the same secret place.

An alternate way to implement this activity is to have the students create a set of directions for another student. Starting from any place, they pair up and trade directions and see where they end up. If one student ends up in a different position from where the other student was trying to get them, then encourage a dialogue about where the directions were unclear or misinterpreted. This discussion can help to clarify their thinking and mathematical communication.

3.6 Large Numbers, Estimation, and Proportionality

Several outdoor tasks can help prospective elementary teachers to better understand large numbers and relationships. Large distances and sizes can be difficult for people to comprehend. For example, the distances between the orbits of the planets are so large that they are difficult if not impossible to visualize. Making a scale model of these distances, with students holding a string and standing at a point on the string that represents the position of the planet can help students to grasp and see these large numbers. Also, understanding the relative size of a whale to other animals can be constructed by drawing a full scale model of a whale with sidewalk chalk in the parking lot, and then a full scale model of perhaps a dolphin and land animals to understand the relative size of these creatures.

Visual images and reference points of measurements are an important skill for prospective teachers to enable them to understand and estimate size. A prospective teacher must have a sense of what a kilometre is if they are to understand distances. In order to develop this, experiences with estimating and measuring distances is important. Stand outside looking down a straight pathway (perhaps a road, sidewalk or walking path). Ask the students where they estimate they would be on this pathway after walking a kilometre. Then, using a measuring wheel, pedometer or even a tape measure, walk the distance until half a kilometre has been reached. The students can then adjust their initial estimate of how far the kilometre is. Once the kilometre has been walked, the students then have a visual and experiential image of a kilometer and better understand what this unit means. For a twist, on the walk back, make a game of finding the most numerals (such as on street signs) or look for different geometric shapes in the buildings and natural objects. A similar but quicker activity is to do the same thing but with only a decametre or hectometre.

Another activity involving estimation, large numbers, and measurements is in estimating large quantities such as the blades of grass in the field beside campus, or the number of gravel rocks in the gravel parking lot, or the number of grains of sand in the beach near campus. Estimating the number of blades of grass, for example, can help students to understand this large number, and develop techniques of estimation. With this, the professor and prospective teachers can design a method to determine an estimate. First ask the prospective teachers to make an estimate of this, with no other information. Then have a discussion of methods that can be used to get a better estimate. The concept of solving a simpler problem can be developed here as often the method that develops is to count the number of blades of grass in a square unit (the class can decide whether a square decimetre or a square centimetre is more appropriate) and then extending this to create an estimate for the entire field. The concept of square units is easily developed through this as well as a better understanding of large numbers.

3.7 Perimeter, Area, and Volume

Leaves and rocks can help prospective teachers to better understand the concepts of perimeter, area and volume. As a means of getting the prospective teachers outside noticing leaves, ask them to bring two or three different types of leaves in to class. Then working in groups of three or four people, ask the prospective teachers to first line up the leaves in order of which they think has the greatest area to the least area. By drawing the leaves on graph paper the prospective teachers can then get an estimate of the areas and test their conjectures of which had the largest area. Secondly, ask that they arrange them in order by perimeter. This helps develop the concept that even if the area of one leaf is larger, that does not mean that the perimeter is always going to be larger. By tracing the perimeter of the leaf with string or a tape measure, the prospective teachers can gain a measurement to test their conjectures. The uses and differences of linear and square units are enhanced through this activity.

A similar activity involving rocks can help develop the concepts of surface area and volume and their relationships and units. Ask the prospective teachers to bring in two rocks with varying surface areas and volumes. Considering surface area, arrange the rocks in the estimated order, then measure the surface area by covering the rock with aluminum foil, laying the foil flat, and then tracing this on graph paper to get an estimate of the surface area with appropriate units. Then with volume, have them estimate the order of the rocks according to volume and then measure the volume by water displacement in a graduated cylinder. This part of the activity can reinforce the concept that one milliliter is equivalent to one cubic centimetre in size.

3.8 Looking to the Stars

What do people see when they look at the stars? How often do people even look up at the stars anymore? In a big city where stars are not very visible, perhaps a visit to the planetarium is in order. Humans have seen the geometric shapes that the stars create since the beginning of history. Helping prospective teachers to see geometry in the stars is important. This can be developed through a couple of activities involving finding geometric figures in general and finding constellations, which is a nice connection to astronomy. When the prospective teachers are studying quadrilaterals or triangles, assign them the task that evening of finding stars that are the vertices of the different types of quadrilaterals or triangles. The prospective teachers can draw a scale model of the quadrilaterals or triangles by holding a ruler and protractor at arms length and looking to the stars. Similarly, they can draw scale models of the constellations which can also help them to identify and better understand the constellations that they study in science class.

4 Conclusion

Prospective teachers need experiences to reconnect with the natural world so that they can help their future students to make similar connections. Primary age children have a great opportunity to gain knowledge through their environment through actively exploring their world (Kellert & Westervelt, 1983). Mathematics tasks outside of the classroom can help students to construct mathematical understanding by connecting to the real world and providing social interactions. Helping people to get outside, reconnect and be more active is a necessary goal of education, especially in our current technological society.

Science educators argue that outdoor learning experiences can result in greater gains in knowledge and understanding than traditional indoor classroom instruction (Harvey, 1990). There is evidence that outdoor learning experiences can be attributed to better academic achievement (Louv, 2005). A need exists for research on how outdoor mathematics experiences affect mathematical understanding specifically.

Prospective teachers and mathematics educators should be encouraged to walk around their own campus and community with the idea of mathematics in their minds. This chapter provides examples of outdoor mathematics tasks that the author has found worthwhile in preparing primary mathematics teachers. Many of these ideas developed through observing the community. Whether in an urban setting, rural setting, forests, or desert, these tasks can be adapted to your setting and others developed using the natural setting as a guide.

References

Ball, D. L., & Bass, H. (2000). Making believe: The collective construction of public mathematical knowledge in the elementary classroom. In D. C. Phillips (Ed.), *Constructivism in education*. Chicago: The University of Chicago Press.

Bones, G., & Gravanes, A. (2004). Outdoor mathematics activities–experience–activity–knowledge! Presentation at the 10th International Congress on Mathematics Education, July 4–11, 2004, Copenhagen, Denmark.

Carson, R. (1956). *The sense of wonder*. New York: Harper and Row.

Harvey, M. R. (1990). The relationship between children's experiences with vegetation on school grounds and their environmental attitudes. *Journal of Environmental Education, 21*(2), 9–15.

Kellert, S. R., & Westervelt, M. O. (1983). Children's attitudes, knowledge, and behaviors towards animals (Report No. #024-010-00641-2). Washington, DC: US Government Printing Office.

Louv, R. (2005). *Last child in the woods: Saving our children from nature-deficit disorder*. Chapel Hill, NC: Algonquin Books.

World Health Organization. (2006). Global strategy on diet, physical activity and health: Obesity and overweight. Retrieved January 18, 2006, from http://www.who.int/dietphysicalactivity/publications/facts/obesity/en/.

From Teacher Education to Teacher Practice: A Gap Affecting the Implementation of Tasks

Pedro Palhares, Alexandra Gomes, Paulo Carvalho, and Valter Cebolo

A new inservice mathematical training programme was launched by the Ministry of Education in Portugal. It has been developed and implemented in each district by different educational institutions. In the district of Braga, the programme is being developed and implemented by our institution, Institute of Child Studies, University of Minho, with direct involvement as teacher trainers. During the time we were working with the teachers, we have exchanged and discussed information. We have found some differences between the way we conceive teacher training and the teachers involved in implementation. We have also found differences in the approach teachers have towards the implementation of mathematical tasks. These differences are discussed in this chapter, trying to connect with the possible subsequent effect on student learning.

1 Introduction

Elementary mathematics represents, both scientifically and pedagogically, a complex structure composed of entangled branches that can hardly be classified as "easy" or simple to teach. It constitutes the foundation of future mathematical knowledge containing the rudiments of many important concepts of more advanced stages of the discipline. In this sense, primary school teachers play a crucial role in introducing children to basic but fundamental mathematical ideas and initiating a process of mathematical learning, with every stage highly dependent on the previous.

P. Palhares
Assistant Professor, Institute of Child Studies, University of Minho, Portugal

A. Gomes
Assistant Professor, Institute of Child Studies, University of Minho, Portugal

P. Carvalho
Institute of Child Studies, University of Minho, Portugal

V. Cebolo
Institute of Child Studies, University of Minho, Portugal

B. Clarke, B. Grevholm, and R. Millman (eds.), *Tasks in Primary Mathematics Teacher Education: Purpose, Use and Exemplars,* Mathematics Teacher Education 4,
© Springer Science+Business Media LLC 2009

2 In-service Mathematical Training: A New Programme Under Development

The mathematical training of primary school teachers deserves careful attention. In spite of this, in Portugal, the mathematical training of these teachers has been neglected for an extensive time by the scientific community. More recently, and particularly due to the persistently poor results in mathematics achieved by Portuguese students in either international studies (PISA and TIMSS) or national tests, not only the scientific community but also the government have began to show some concern about the mathematical training of teachers, especially, primary school teachers.

In particular, the Ministry of Education decided to promote an in-service mathematical training programme with the following main goals:

- To deepen primary school teachers mathematical, pedagogical and curricular knowledge;
- To promote experiences of curricular development;
- To develop a positive attitude towards mathematics;
- To create the dynamics of collaborative work in schools.

This is a 2-year programme that involves all public higher education institutions (universities and polytechnics) responsible for training primary school teachers. The programme is not compulsory but teachers were encouraged to enrol. A national commission was set up to develop core guidelines of the "curriculum" for this programme and to determine the way it should be structured and organised.

2.1 Curricular Features

The themes that should be approached in the training are organized the same way as in the primary school curriculum, that is, number and operations; shape and space; measurement and data analysis.

2.2 Organizational Features

1. Once a week, the *trainer team* meets to discuss difficulties/progress and to organize tasks.
2. Once a fortnight, each trainer has a 3h training session with a group of 8–12 teachers.
3. For each teacher, the trainer goes to his/her classroom to observe/participate, at least 3 times a year.
4. At the end of each year, each *trainer team* has to organize a large meeting, meant for all participants of each institution.

Based on these common features, each institution developed its own programme. This implies that one might find very different approaches to this same "programme", depending on the institution and on the vision it has of mathematics education.

3 Visions of Mathematics Education

We can consider two opposing views concerning mathematics education, the traditional, which is the one prevailing for the teachers at the start of the initial training (Brown & Borko, 1992), and the constructivist view. We shall present them and state our own position.

3.1 Concerning the Acquisition of Knowledge

The first distinction within the two visions of mathematics education has to do with how we consider acquisition of knowledge.

On the one hand, Thorndyke's connectionism theory, which later was reinforced by Skinner's behaviourism, followed the principle of the *tabulae rasae*, which implies transmission of knowledge from the teacher (Orton, 1992).

On the other hand, constructivism defends a different perspective: Every learner constructs his/her knowledge. However, it is widely assumed that even in mathematics there is knowledge of a social origin and knowledge of a logical type (Nunes & Bryant, 1996). Nevertheless, it is possible to consider extreme versions of constructivism that take this division as artificial. For them all knowledge is socially originated leading theoretically to the conclusion that all knowledge can be constructed in the classroom (Ernest, 1991).

Hewitt (1999) makes a distinction between those things that are arbitrary (and therefore students must be informed) and those necessary (and students must construct them, otherwise they will memorize without understanding) and defends the need for both in the curriculum.

This is also our opinion: mathematics curriculum should be divided between those things that have to be transmitted by the teacher (e.g. number names or algorithms) and those that have to be constructed by the students.

3.2 Concerning Mathematical Tasks

In the beginning of the twentieth century Thorndyke stipulated that exercises were the central part of mathematics teaching. For a considerable number of years exercises and the practice of routines were so valued that even nowadays it is hard to find classes where they are not present (Kilpatrick, 1992).

It is with Pólya (1957) that problem solving arose. Today it is included in many curricula around the world. However, as Schoenfeld (1992) warns, it is necessary to exercise some caution because much intended problem solving is actually exercise solving. Many people have just changed the name but not the nature of the tasks they propose.

In a so-called traditional view, exercise solving is the fundamental component, however, we argue that, even though exercises have a place in mathematics teaching, it is problem solving that should be the fundamental component.

3.3 Concerning Products/Processes

The traditional view on mathematics education stresses the correctness of solutions, achieved rapidly and with a unique procedure, the one considered to be the easiest and the fastest. In the constructivist view we value the creation of varied and personal procedures, even if not so fast or easy.

3.4 Concerning Silence/Activity

The main concern teachers have, in a traditional classroom, is to maintain order and control. For instance the use of manipulative materials is allowed as long as students do not exceed the usual levels of noise and movement. In a constructivist view the main priority is that students are active even if they are moving more or making more noise. We consider that students should be active but, of course, we should interpret being active as being intellectually active (Ball, 2000).

3.5 Concerning Learning Supports

The traditional view builds on the abstract. But it is Freudenthal that recommends the modification of teaching from the abstractions to the abstracting (Becker & Selter, 1996). This is also our position, rejecting both an exclusive work on the abstract field and on the concrete field. The concrete environment should be a means and not an end in itself. However, concreteness may refer to a previous mathematical system. For example, an equation may be abstracted from a series of number sentences.

4 The Task

Bearing this framework in mind, our group developed a series of tasks to share with the teachers in the training sessions. In what follows, we describe one of those tasks and analyse different approaches made by trainers and by teachers.

This particular task consisted of an investigation involving polyminoes. This subject is not familiar to teachers in the district. They all know dominoes but see them just as a game with different pieces. They do not look at each piece in a "geometric" way, that is, even though they recognize that each piece has a shape of a rectangle divided into two congruent squares they do not use that knowledge to explore shapes. Therefore, it was our intention to present an investigation task that allowed teachers to look at a known concept – dominoes – in an entirely new way and make further explorations.

Exploring polyminoes

Definition of polyminoes
Polyminoes are shapes obtained by juxtaposition of congruent squares.

Examples of polyminoes: Not polyminoes:

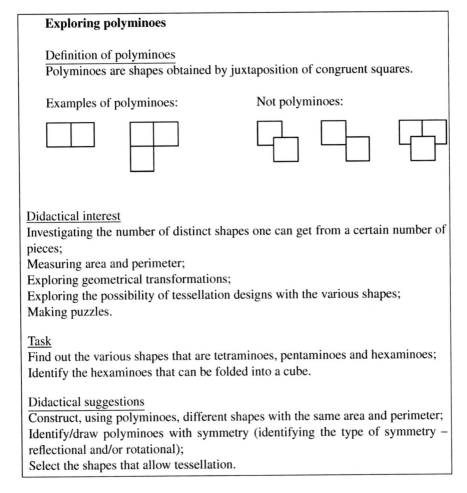

Didactical interest
Investigating the number of distinct shapes one can get from a certain number of pieces;
Measuring area and perimeter;
Exploring geometrical transformations;
Exploring the possibility of tessellation designs with the various shapes;
Making puzzles.

Task
Find out the various shapes that are tetraminoes, pentaminoes and hexaminoes;
Identify the hexaminoes that can be folded into a cube.

Didactical suggestions
Construct, using polyminoes, different shapes with the same area and perimeter;
Identify/draw polyminoes with symmetry (identifying the type of symmetry – reflectional and/or rotational);
Select the shapes that allow tessellation.

---

5 Differences and Similarities Among Those Involved

During the exploration of the task, we have noted some aspects that induced us to engage in deeper reflection. They are explored below.

5.1 Teacher Trainers: Professional Experiences and Scientific Background

The teacher trainers who were involved in this training programme had different professional backgrounds and experiences. On one hand there were some teacher trainers who teach at a university that offers preservice primary teacher training. These had a deeper scientific formation in mathematics but no experience in teaching at primary level. On the other hand there were teacher trainers who were practising school teachers who had undertaken further professional development. These trainers have a higher level of scientific formation than the teachers who were participating in the programme. Despite the differences previously mentioned, the teacher trainers have in common the constructivist view on mathematics education.

Thus, we can see in this training programme, a privileged opportunity for introducing a kind of task that most primary school teachers (and students), in Portugal, are not used to developing and using. Investigation tasks enable the constructing of mathematics. They allow exploring, formulating and examining conjectures, generalizing, problem posing and solving, pattern recognition. Above all, they can influence the understanding of the nature of mathematics and optimize mathematical development of each student, taking account of their different levels and limitations.

However, despite their common conceptions, in relation to mathematics education and investigation tasks in particular, it has been noticed, in the reflections the teacher trainers made after the training sessions, that there were different views of professional development among the primary school teachers which matched, in some aspects, those two profiles of teacher trainers identified above.

In fact, teacher trainers whose professional experience had been in primary education had the tendency to put more emphasis on the mathematical content of the curriculum. This emphasis seems to be based on their professional experience. As referred by Papert (1980), teachers are highly influenced by a culture of curriculum restricted to the development of content. This may come from the pressure that teachers feel for completing "the programme" which, for most teachers, is a synonym of "textbook". This pressure may be the result of several factors, some external and some internal.

Even though, it was not a purpose of these teacher trainers to give much significance to content, but to give meaning to the mathematical activity, they finally developed this activity task focusing on the exploration of several content areas. This way, they seemed to be validating, to the teachers, the task as part of the curriculum they are required to develop for students. Therefore, this activity served mainly as a context for the exploration of themes as spatial reasoning, symmetry, area, and perimeter, with the goal of later convincing teachers that it is the mathematical activity that should give meaning to content.

As far as the other type of teacher trainers is concerned (university teachers), they focused above all on the development of cognitive skills such as to structure forms of reasoning without worrying (too much) about specific (traditional) mathematical content. Even though it was not a purpose of these teacher trainers to avoid content, they tried to empower teachers and therefore convince them to empower their students.

This teaching programme raised the following questions:

- Which of the two approaches will be the most effective way of guiding teachers away from the traditional vision of mathematics education?
- Will it be the first approach to have better results in changing teachers' practices? Or will it risk being transformed in a series of unconnected exercises with the exploration and reasoning disappearing?
- Will the second approach be the best way of breaking teachers' restrictive vision of curriculum? Or will it lead to teachers disregarding investigation tasks due to not considering them connected to the curriculum?

We do not have complete answers to all these questions yet, but it seems to us, that this kind of reflection in a team composed by different experiences and professional formation may bring new and richer perspectives about the theme.

5.2 From the Trainer to the Teacher

As we have already said, teachers are not familiar with the concept of polyminoes, and they are not used to implementing investigations. Therefore, it was very exciting for them to try to find all the possible shapes even though some difficulties arose in finding the pentaminoes and especially the hexaminoes. On the one hand, they had problems in identifying symmetrical shapes and most of them did not follow any structured path or systematic process that enabled them to see if all the shapes had been found.

During the activity, the trainers gave different suggestions like cutting off the shapes, making several squares to construct the polyminoes, or rotating the sheet of paper.

Some differences were found when we compared the task implementation in the training sessions by the trainer with the subsequent implementation in the classroom by the teachers. First of all it is important to note that teachers' low expectations relating to their students' performance on this task were strongly countered during the classroom implementation.

Despite the broad nature of the training session approach, we found a narrowing of the task in the classroom. Desired goals and instructions (by the teachers) were

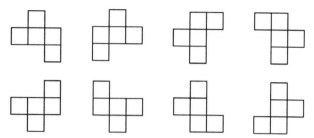

Fig. 1 Pentominoes

too explicit, either at the beginning or along the way to find the solution. For example, giving the students the number of shapes of each polymino type that they required to find rather than this being part of the challenge.

Other important finding is a loss of mathematical power from the training session to the classroom. We conceived the polymino task as requiring relevant spatial reasoning. Many of the polyminoes, when displayed on different positions, or on different angle orientations, tend to stir up the wrong expectation that they are different shapes. For example: shapes without symmetry allow eight possibilities of representation, using horizontal and vertical lines only, as we can observe about this pentomino (Fig. 1).

In the classroom, the tendency to repeat shapes in this way was common probably due to the absence of a spatial reasoning focus by the teacher.

In the training sessions the trainers focused on aspects like symmetry, reasoning strategies, perimeter and folding into a cube. However, in the classroom the task often involved free exploration of shapes, without (in many cases) self regulation concerns. In part, the explanation of this fact may be related to the following: the training sessions had been developed without manipulative materials. This support could have helped teachers understand symmetries embodied in the task. We presume that this absence indicated some lack of knowledge about spatial reasoning, because in many cases teachers did not offer manipulatives to children, who had major difficulties especially when they were faced with the need to perform reflections.

Hewitt's (1999) perspective of mathematical knowledge, lead us to another kind of analysis: on the training sessions the cognitive focus was directed to the *necessary knowledge*, but in the classroom we found some cases in which the teacher contemplated essentially the *arbitrary knowledge*. Despite the fact that this task can be presented and developed without any references to the correct terminology, this aspect became the main source of the student's labour due to the significance their teacher attributed to it. In some cases a large part of the time was ocused on the naming of the polyminoes, and children got involved in transcribing that information from the blackboard to their notebooks.

Finally we report some tendency for management aspects to impact the use of the task in the classroom: some teachers imposed time limits and restricted the possibilities of searching, raised by the students. We think that those teachers ascribe greater importance to strictly following the plan, despite the low concern related to this aspect in the training sessions.

5.3 Differences Among Teachers

Several differences or contrasts were observed among teachers when they were teaching their classes using this particular task. Some of these differences, we think, are explained by our analytic framework:

— One difference observed concerns the use of group work in the classroom.

- Some teachers organized their students in groups. Each group would have a group speaker, but all children were encouraged to participate within the group, giving opinions and offering paths to the solution.
- Other teachers organized their students for individual work. This could happen either by students being placed isolated from the others or being physically placed as groups but with clear instructions to work alone.

— A second difference, which is clearly connected with the previous one, concerns the representation teachers have of mathematical activity.

- For some teachers, students must be engaged and motivated, even if they are noisy;
- For other teachers, students must be in silence in order to be concentrated and be able to learn. Sharing disturbs concentration and so students are better left working alone.

— A third difference that has a slight connection with the previous one, concerns the use of manipulative.

- For some teachers, students must be allowed the use of manipulative (usually for this task, cardboard squares) in order to try shapes and explore the task.
- For other teachers, manipulative would constitute a distraction; they would give their students a pencil and squared paper and that was considered enough support. In some cases, teachers would use manipulative just to show students, that is, it was the teacher who would manipulate the cardboard squares.

— A fourth difference involved the amount of information teachers would give.

- Some teachers would refrain from giving information on how many pentominoes there are or on any method to discover them all and check if all were constructed. Students would have to devise methods and find solutions.
- Some other teachers would give immediately the number of pentominoes and a method to discover them all. This means that students would not require much reasoning to find solutions.

Another difference that we have found concerns the care teachers showed on the planning of the lesson. Some would show ample preparation, some would show scarce preparation. We do not have an explanation from our framework and besides, regardless of the way of teaching, we could find teachers preparing extensively the task and teachers preparing it insufficiently.

6 Conclusion

As general conclusions of our reflection, we think that even when teachers share the same vision of mathematics education, other factors and particularly mathematical knowledge and professional experience play a major role in approaching a task. This task proved to be effective in changing some teachers' practices from their traditional view to a more constructivist one. However, in general terms, it is clear that there was a diminishing of the mathematical power of this activity when passing from the training sessions to the primary school class.

References

Ball, D. L. (2000). Bridging practices: Intertwining content and pedagogy in teaching and learning to teach. *Journal of Teacher Education, 51*(3), 241–247.

Becker, J., & Selter, C. (1996). Elementary school practices. In: A. Bishop, K. Clements, C. Keitel, K. Kilpatrick, & Collette Laborde (Eds.), *International Handbook of Mathematics Education* (Vol. 1, pp. 511–564). Netherlands: Kluwer.

Brown, C., & Borko, H. (1992). Becoming a mathematics teacher. In D. A. Grouws (Ed.), *Handbook of research in mathematics teaching and learning* (pp. 209–239). New York: Macmillan.

Ernest, P. (1991). *Philosophy of mathematics education*. London: Falmer.

Hewitt, D. (1999). Arbitrary and necessary. Part 1: A way of viewing the Mathematics Curriculum. *For the Learning of Mathematics, 19*(3), 2–9.

Kilpatrick, J. (1992). A history of research in mathematics education. In D. A. Grouws (Ed.), *Handbook of research in mathematics teaching and learning* (pp. 3–38). New York: MacMillan.

Nunes, T., & Bryant, P. (1996). *Children doing mathematics*. Oxford: Blackwell.

Orton, A. (1992). *Learning mathematics: Issues, theory and classroom practice*. London: Cassell.

Papert, S. (1980). *Mindstorms: Children, computers, and powerful ideas*. New York: Basic Books, Inc.

Pólya, G. (1957). *How to Solve It*. Princeton, NJ: Princeton University Press.

Schoenfeld, A. (1992). Learning to think mathematically: Problem solving, metacognition, and sensemaking in mathematics. In D. A. Grouws. (Ed), *Handbook of research on mathematics teaching and learning*. New York: MacMillan.

Concluding Remarks

Barbara Clarke, Barbro Grevholm, and Richard Millman

1 Introduction

Watson and Sullivan (2008) suggest that tasks for teachers have multiple purposes in teacher education and that teachers' engagement in such tasks can

- inform them about the range and purpose of possible classroom tasks;
- provide opportunities to learn more about mathematics;
- provide insight into the nature of mathematical activity; and
- stimulate and inform teachers' theorizing about students' learning. (p. 110)

This reminds us of some of the multiple agendas for teacher educators involved in mathematics teacher preparation and development. In the introductory chapter a model was presented illustrating this further (see page 2). What we have read in this volume is a selection of tasks that have been developed, used, improved and in most cases evaluated. They mirror the creative and imaginative work of many devoted teacher educators, who have spent time searching for good ideas, finding supporting artefacts, developing them and trying them out with students. There has been a clear purpose for the development and introduction of these tasks. The aim is to help and support the learning of some important aspects of teachers' professional knowledge and practice and remind future teachers of the importance of mathematical knowledge for teachers.

B. Clarke
Associate Professor and Associate Dean of Staff, Faculty of Education, Monash University, Australia

B. Grevholm
Professor of Mathematics Education, University of Agder, Norway

R. Millman
Director, Center for Education Integrating Science, Mathematics and Computing, and Professor of the Practice of Mathematics, Georgia Institute of Technology, USA

B. Clarke, B. Grevholm, and R. Millman (eds.), *Tasks in Primary Mathematics Teacher Education: Purpose, Use and Exemplars,* Mathematics Teacher Education 4,
© Springer Science+Business Media LLC 2009

One of the strengths of the volume is the range of contexts and perspectives of the authors. It is an international volume, not intended to be an international comparison but instead representing a collective wisdom based on varied experiences. The authors were encouraged to tell the story of the task purpose, design and implementation. As editors, we were reluctant to over prescribe to the authors the nature of the chapters and potentially reducing the richness of the experiences. We acknowledge that the danger in this strategy was less coherence across the stories. In this chapter we have attempted to highlight some of the overall themes, return briefly to the introductory chapter and build on the section overviews.

2 Form, Function and Focus of Tasks

What can we learn from these chapters about the form, function and focus of productive tasks? This is not an easy question to answer. As can be seen from the contents, the form varied across a wide range of pedagogical approaches using a variety of tools. This included modelling classroom games, using video, the study of lessons through to the development of teaching portfolios. As previously mentioned the function and purpose of tasks in teacher education are varied and the authors provide some insights into their individual decision making processes. Amato in Chap. 11 used children's mathematical activities in the context of initial teacher education and looked for tasks which

1. have the potential to help trainees develop a strong relational understanding of the mathematics they are supposed to teach in the future (SMK),
2. improve their liking for the subject,
3. help trainees to acquire a repertoire of representations (PCK); and
4. can be adopted and sustained with large classes.

The mathematical foci of the tasks include many different content areas both within the traditional curriculum of primary schools as well as some higher level content. There was a focus in many tasks on reasoning and argument in mathematics and a range of representations and tools for supporting learning were provided. There is some evidence of the cultural and social variation in teacher education in different countries though the themes that are discussed in the next section seem to cross the boundaries.

3 Themes Emerging from the Task Analyses and Implementation

While clearly a range of issues have emerged from the rich discussion of the tasks, three themes are highlighted: the role of reflection, the value of links between theory and practice and the role of mathematical content knowledge. The first two of these will be discussed briefly but the third was clearly the most powerful theme that emerged.

The first is linked closely to the focus of Section A but is evidenced across many tasks. The use of action research and lesson study cycles provide teachers with opportunities for supported reflection. The co-reflection between the teacher and the teacher educator, provided opportunity for critique but then, importantly, further trial or practice to enable improvement. Such practices enable both prospective and practising teachers to develop as reflective practitioner (Schon, 1983) a clear purpose for many authors. José Carillo and Nuria Climent write of reflection as a means of entering theoretical loops – theoretical reasoning about practice.

Many prospective teachers enter teacher education with a view that there is a recipe for teaching that they will be told how to teach. This makes reflection and critiquing problematic (Loughran, Berry, & Tudball, 2005). The productive tasks involving a cyclic approach to reflection provide an opportunity to challenge these perceptions as well as to develop revised perspectives.

It might be argued that the whole purpose of a task in teacher education is to link theory with practice, the practice of teacher education, and the purpose of the book is to share the implementation of such tasks. However there was clearly a strong focus on the link of both theory and practice in teacher education to practice in the school classroom. This is highlighted explicitly in Section C but also a feature across many chapters and tasks. Watson and Sullivan (2008) argue for the value of reflective engagement with classroom tasks in the context of mathematics teacher education and a similar explicit argument is made by Solange Amato and Meg Moss in their chapters.

4 Mathematical Knowledge for Teaching

There is ambiguous evidence on the relationship between knowledge and teaching. On one hand, Darling-Hammond (1997) summarized research on data from 900 school districts in Texas that found that 40% of the measured variance in student achievement across grades 1 to 11 was due to teacher expertise. Her main measures include students' scores on numeracy and literacy assessments. She argued that, even after controlling for socio-economic status, the large differences in achievement between "black and white were almost entirely accounted for by differences in the qualifications of their teachers" (p. 8). On the other hand, Kilpatrick, Swafford, and Findell (2001) claim that "there seems to be no association, however, between how many advanced mathematics courses a teacher takes and how well that teachers' students achieve overall in mathematics" (p. 324). They go on to suggest that "crude measures of teacher knowledge, such as the number of mathematics courses taken, do not correlate positively with student performance data, supports the need to study more closely the nature of the mathematical knowledge needed to teach and to measure it more sensitively" (p. 375).

It is more productive to focus on forms of knowledge more closely related to teaching, in particular pedagogical content knowledge (Shulman, 1986). There is increasing agreement that the mathematical content knowledge required for teaching is connected to the teaching of particular content, for example, fractions, and that how teachers hold knowledge may matter more than how much knowledge they hold (Hill & Ball, 2004). They argued that teachers need to be able to deconstruct their own mathematics knowledge into less polished and final form, where elemental components are accessible and visible.

> Because teachers must be able to work with content for students in its growing, not finished state, they must be able to do something perverse: work backward from mature and compressed understanding of the content to unpack its constituent elements (Ball & Bass, 2000, p. 98).

A focus on *mathematical knowledge for teaching* is a feature of the tasks highlighted in Section B but also the key theme of the book.

There is still much debate about the extent and form of the mathematical knowledge used and needed for teaching. The Mathematical Education of Teachers (CBMS, 2000) from the USA provides recommendations on the mathematics content requirements for teachers according to the levels at which they are teaching. However, the point is clearly made that:

> This is not to say that prospective teachers will be learning the mathematics as if they were nine-year-olds. The understanding required of them includes acquiring a rich network of concepts extending in to the content of higher grades; a strong facility in making, following, and assessing mathematical argument; and a wide array of mathematical strategies (Chapter 5, p. 3).

Similar arguments are made in preceding chapters as well as evidence of tasks that support development of such knowledge. George Ashline and Regina Quinn found that teachers began to recognize that improving their understanding of mathematics and of curricula across grade levels could positively impact their own instruction.

In discussing teachers' mathematical knowledge it is important to acknowledge the link between knowledge and attitudinal views of teachers and their impacts on students. There is considerable evidence (e.g. Baturo et al., 2004) that the confidence and competence of primary school teachers with mathematics are a cause for concern which is shared in many of the countries and contexts in which the authors are working. Effective strategies again tend to be cyclical in nature. If we can support the mathematical knowledge development that can build the confidence – if we can build the confidence, then they are more likely to take the risk to learn the mathematics. The challenge in teacher education is to know where and when to start the cycle.

The demands on teacher understanding have increased as educational practices change to emphasize the concepts behind content, rather than the earlier focus on procedural knowledge. Brophy (1991) argued in relation to content knowledge that:

> Where teachers' knowledge is more explicit, better connected, and more integrated, they will tend to teach the subject more dynamically, represent it in more varied ways and encourage and respond fully to students' comments and questions. Where their knowledge is limited, they will tend to depend on the text for content, de-emphasize interactive discourse in favor of seatwork assignments, and in general, portray the subject as a collection of static, factual knowledge (p. 352).

5 Implementation of Tasks

Is there a fundamental difference between tasks for teacher education and tasks for teacher professional development? Is the focus of the phase of learning to teach different from those where the process is more a "refining"? It would seem that some tasks are successful across both groups but that we need to acknowledge the differences both in the background and knowledge they have.

Stein, Grover, and Henningsen (1996) argue that the implementation of classroom tasks by teachers proceeds in a sequence of four steps:

1. mathematical task as presented in instructional materials, to
2. mathematical task as set up by the teacher in the classroom, to
3. mathematical task as experienced by students, which creates the potential for
4. student learning.

This clearly links to notions of the intended, implemented and achieved curriculum. It might be argued that the same steps exist in teacher education. While all chapters provide the task there are varying degrees of implementation and evaluation. These provide readers with useful insights but it must also be acknowledged that the context plays an important part in the final achieved task. There is considerable evidence that prospective and practicing teachers have different needs and expectations. However the different beliefs of both teachers and teacher educators can influence strongly the form and focus of the implementation. Nicolina Malara and Giancarlo Navarra provide evidence of these differences and highlight the contrasts in observed practice.

Effective mathematics teaching involves a range of complex factors, and education of the mathematics teacher should ideally prepare teachers for the challenge of managing this complexity (Watson & Sullivan, 2008). The limited time available in most teacher education courses makes the selection of appropriate tasks a challenge. Readers are encouraged to identify tasks that enable connected and integrated learning, stressing the importance of the mathematics content knowledge for teaching and its connection to pedagogical content knowledge.

The intent was not a text book or any comprehensive attempt to map the appropriate area of mathematics teacher education. That role is elsewhere but hopefully this provides some promising and productive practices that can be adapted and used in a range of contexts and the insights provided by the authors help build a picture of effective mathematics teacher education practices.

References

Ball, D. L., & Bass, H. (2000). Interweaving content and pedagogy in teaching and learning to teach: Knowing and using mathematics. In J. Boaler (Ed.), *Multiple perspective on the teaching and learning of mathematics* (pp. 83–103). Greenwich, CT: JAI/Albex.

Baturo, A., Cooper, T., Dietzmann, C., Heirdsfield, A., Kidman, G., Shield, P., Warren, E., Nisbet, S., Klein, M., & Putt, I. (2004). *Teachers enhancing numeracy*. Canberra: Commonwealth of Australia. (http://www.dest.gov.au/sectors/school_education/publications_resources/profiles/teachers_enhancing_numeracy.htm)

Brophy, J. E. (1991). Conclusion to advances in research on teaching, Vol 11: Teachers' knowledge of subject matter as it relates to teaching practice. In J. E. Brophy (Ed.), *Advances in research on teaching: Teachers' subject-matter knowledge and classroom instruction* (Vol. 2, pp. 347–362). Greenwich CT: JAI Press.

CBMS (Conference Board of the Mathematical Sciences) (2000). *The mathematical education of teachers: Issues in mathematics education* (Vol. 2). Washington, DC: Mathematical Association of America.

Darling-Hammond, L. (1997). *Doing what matters most: Investing in quality teaching.* New York: National Commission on Teaching and America's Future. Hill, H., & Ball, D. L. (2004). Learning mathematics for teaching: Results from California's mathematics profession. *Journal for Research in Mathematics Education, 35*(5), 330–351.

Kilpatrick, J., Swafford, J., & Findell, B. (2001). *Adding it up: Helping children learn mathematics.* Washington, DC: National Academy Press.

Loughran, J. J., Berry, A. K., & Tudball, E. J. (2005). Developing a culture of critique in teacher education classes. In Garry F. Hoban (Ed.), *The missing links in teacher education design. Developing a multi-linked conceptual framework* (pp. 193–208). Dordrecht, the Netherlands: Springer.

Schon, D. (1983). *The reflective practitioner: How professionals think in action.* New York: Basic Books.

Shulman, L. (1987). Knowledge and teaching: Foundations of the reform. *Harvard Educational Review, 57*(1), 1–22.

Stein, M. K., Grover, B., & Henningsen, M. (1996). Building students' capacity for mathematical thinking and reasoning: An analysis of mathematical tasks used in reform classrooms. *American Educational Research Journal, 33*(2), 455–488.

Watson, A., & Sullivan, P. (2008). Teachers learning about tasks and lessons. In D. Tirosh, & T. Wood (Eds.), *Tools and resources in mathematics teacher education* (pp. 109–135). Rotterdam: Sense Publishers.

Author Notes

Amato, Solange, a mathematics teacher and a teacher educator since 1983 teaching 11–17-year-olds, has been a teacher educator at the Faculty of Education, University of Brasília, Brazil, where she teaches mainly course components about methods for teaching mathematics to 7–10-year-olds. She also teaches several in-service courses and workshops about mathematics teaching for primary and secondary school teachers. She has a mathematics degree from University of Brasília (1982), and a master's (1989) and a doctorate (2001) degree in Education from Oxford University, England. Email: sraamato@unb.br

Ashline, George, received his BS from Saint Lawrence University, his MS from the University of Notre Dame and his PhD from the University of Notre Dame in 1994 in complex analysis. He has taught at Saint Michael's College for many years. He is a participant in Project NExT, a programme created for new or recent PhDs in the mathematical sciences who are interested in improving the teaching and learning of undergraduate mathematics. He is also actively involved in professional development programmes in mathematics for elementary and middle school teachers. Email: gashline@smcvt.edu

Canada, Dan, a mathematics teacher for over 20 years, has worked with the elementary levels all the way up through college levels. His educational experiences have included substantial time in Africa, Asia and America, and currently he is a mathematics educator at Eastern Washington University. He particularly enjoys finding new ways of helping elementary preservice teachers connect their own understanding of data analysis and probability to the conceptions that children often have. Email: dcanada@mail.ewu.edu

Carrillo, José, is Assistant Professor at the University of Huelva (Spain), receiving a PhD in Mathematics Education in 1996. His fields of expertise are mathematics teacher development (mainly teacher's development in collaborative environments) and mathematical problem solving. University of Huelva (Spain). Email: carrillo@uhu.es

Carvalho, Paulo, is a primary teacher, master in teaching and learning mathematics, instructor in continuing training in mathematics for primary teachers at the Institute of Child Studies of the University of Minho, Portugal, Email: paulojfrcarvalho@net. sapo.pt

Cebolo, Valter, is a mathematics teacher of fifth and sixth grades, master in teaching and learning mathematics, instructor in continuing training in mathematics for teachers at the Institute of Child Studies of the University of Minho, Portugal, Email: valterretlav@gmail.com

Clarke, Barbara, is an associate professor in Mathematics Education and Associate Dean (Staff) in the Faculty of Education, Monash University. The major focus of her writing and research has been concerned with mathematics teachers, their practice and their professional development. Her PhD research related to the challenges for teachers as they implemented an innovative mathematics curriculum and the impact on their practice. Dr Clarke has a research interest in teachers and professional development, and makes regular presentations at professional conferences and teacher professional development sessions. Email: Barbara.Clarke@Education.monash.edu.au

Climent, Nuria, gained her PhD in Mathematics Education in 2002. She works at the University of Huelva (Spain) and her field of expertise is mathematics teacher development, mainly teacher's development in collaborative environments. Email: climent@uhu.es

Figueras, Olimpia, is currently focused on two main areas: Children learning mathematics, particularly, natural and rational numbers, and measurement, and Classroom practices and teacher's professional development. Olimpia earned her doctorate, in 1989, in the Mathematics Education Department of the Center for Research and Advanced Studies of the National Poly-technique Institute (Cinvestav), where she also works as a researcher. She coordinated the national mathematics curriculum change of 1993 for pre-school, primary and secondary education and the set up of a M.Ed study programme for in-service teachers in Cinvestav. She has several contributions published in textbooks, books and proceedings. Email: figuerao@cinvestav.mx

Gadanidis, George, is an associate professor at the Faculty of Education at the University of Western Ontario. His research interests include: the design of mathematics experiences for teachers, students as performance mathematicians (as in the arts) and technology as an co-actor in the learning, teaching and doing of mathematics. Email: ggadanid@uwo.ca. Website: http://publish.edu.uwo.ca/george. gadanidis

García, Mercedes, is a professor at the Department of Didactic of Mathematics at the University of Seville, Spain. In that University, she is developing her work as teacher and researcher. She has taught mathematics teacher education courses and mathematics courses for elementary teachers. She also has taught graduate level courses on research in mathematics education. Her research in mathematics education spreads over several areas: mathematics teacher education, the relation-ship between research and practice in mathematics teacher education, mathemat-ics teacher's knowledge and practice and advanced mathematics thinking. Email: mgblanco@us.es

Gomes, Alexandra, PhD in Child Studies – Elementary Mathematics, assistant pro-fessor in the area of Elementary Mathematics at the Institute of Child Studies of the University of Minho, Portugal. Email: magomes@iec.uminho.pt

Grant, Theresa, is professor in the Department of Mathematics at Western Michigan University. She is interested in the knowledge teachers need in order to base mathematics instruction on student thinking, and the processes by which they come to know and utilize, this information. Her work in this area has three main components: designing professional development for practicing teachers and courses for prospective teachers; researching the impact of these experiences; and studying the impact of implementing standards-based curricula on teachers' efforts to focus on student thinking. Email: terry.grant@wmich.edu

Grevholm, Barbro is professor of mathematics education at University of Agder in Norway. She is the leader of the doctoral programme in didactics of mathematics there and also director of the Nordic Graduate School in Mathematics Education. Her research interests are related to teacher education and mathematical concept development, problem solving, use of ICT, research education and gender aspects. Lately she has been involved in several research projects within communities of didacticians and mathematics teachers. Barbro Grevholm is also professor at Luleå University of Technology, Narvik University College and Kristianstad University College, where she supervises doctoral students. Email: barbro.grevholm@hia.no

Lieberman, Joanne is an assistant professor in the Mathematics and Statistics De-partment at California State University, Monterey Bay. Her major research interests include mathematics education and teacher professional development. Her most re-cent work has been concerned with the relationship between professional learning communities and the lesson study process in mathematics teachers' professional development. Email: Joanne_Lieberman@csumb.edu

Lo, Jane-Jane, is an associate professor in the Department of Mathematics at Western Michigan University. The focus of her research interest is on mathematics learning which encompasses three complementary areas: the development of ratio and proportion concepts, classroom discourse and social norms and mathematics teacher education. She has conducted studies in a variety of settings including k-14 classrooms as well as textbook analysis both within United States and across several Asian regions. Email: jane-jane.lo@wmich.edu

Malara, Nicolina is a professor, Department of Mathematics, Faculty of Science, University of Modena & Reggio Emilia, Italy, where he teaches Didactics of Math-ematics, Foundations of Mathematics for the degree in Mathematics, and Didactics of Mathematics in the post degree schools for education of secondary school teach-ers, He is leader of the Project on Early Algebra (ArAl) in GREM, and author of over 100 papers. Italy. Email: malara@unimore.it

Millman, Richard, received his BS from MIT and PhD in mathematics from Cornell University. He has written extensively in differential geometry and mathematics education. His four co-authored books are *Elements of Differential Geometry, Geometry: A Metric Approach with Models,* and *Calculus: A Practical Approach* (all with G. Parker), and *Mathematical Reasoning for Future Teachers* (fifth edition with C. Long and D. DeTemple). He has been Provost of Whittier College and California State University, San Marcos and President of Knox College in Galesburg, IL. He has taught most recently at the University of Kentucky and is presently Director of the Center for Education Integrating Science, Mathematics and Computing at Georgia Institute of Technology. Email: Richard.Millman@ceismc.gatech.edu

Moss, Meg earned her PhD in Mathematics Education from the University of Tennessee – Knoxville, her MA degree in Mathematics Education at Appalachian State University in Boone, NC, and BA in Mathematics Education from the University of North Carolina – Chapel Hill. She has been an associate professor of Mathematics and Teacher Education Coordinator at Pellissippi State Technical Community College in Knoxville, TN, and before that was a mathematics professor at Treasure Valley Community College in Ontario, OR, for eight years. She has taught mathematics courses for preservice elementary teachers for 16 years, has taught Geometry in secondary schools, and done numerous mathematics activities in her son's primary classrooms. She has been gathering and exploring outdoor mathematics activities for many years. Email: mvmoss@pstcc.edu

Movshovitz-Hadar, Nitsa is professor of mathematics education at Technion – Israel Institute of Technology. Emeritus since 2004. In 2003: Laureate in Residence at La Villa Media, Grenoble France. 1998-2002: Director, Israel National Museum of Science. Since 1975 on the faculty at Technion, sharing her research and development interests combined with 12 years of high school mathematics teaching experiences, with prospective mathematics teachers. She headed major curriculum development projects; Founded in 1986 and since is the head of Kesher-Cham - R&D centre for improving and reviving mathematics education. Published one book (with J. Webb) and many papers (one of which received in 1995 the MAA Lester Ford award with I. Kleiner). Email: nitsa@tx.technion.ac.il

Namukasa, Immaculate Kizito, is an assistant professor at the University of Western Ontario. Her current research interests are students' mathematical thinking, problem solving and mathematics teacher education. Email: inamukas@uwo.ca. Website: http://publish.edu.uwo.ca/ immaculate.namukasa/

Navarra, Giancarlo is engaged in the Project on Early Algebra (ArAl) in GREM, Department of Mathematics, University of Modena & Reggio E, Italy. Email: ginavar@tin.it

Palhares, Pedro, PhD in Child Studies – Elementary Mathematics, assistant professor in the area of Elementary Mathematics at the Institute of Child Studies of the University of Minho, Portugal. Email: palhares@iec.uminho.pt

Peter-Koop, Andrea, is a professor of Mathematics Education at the University of Oldenburg where she is responsible for the preparation and professional development of future primary mathematics teachers. Her research interests include (future) mathematics teachers professional learning processes, the investigation of primary children's modelling strategies, and the development of early mathematical skills and understanding of children in the transition from kindergarten to junior primary school. She is currently one of the editors of the national German journal of mathematics education (*Journal für Mathematikdidaktik*) and also engages in mathematics lectures for primary children during the world mathematics year. Email: andrea.peter.koop@uni-oldenburg.de

Quinn, Regina, is the Project Director and co-PI of the Vermont Mathematics Partnership, an NSF and US DOE-funded initiative aimed at helping schools help all students succeed in mathematics. She received her BA from Trinity College, and her Masters in Curriculum & Instruction with a focus on mathematics professional development from the University of Vermont. Ms. Quinn previously served as Executive Director and instructor for the Vermont Mathematics Initiative, a 3-year graduate programme for elementary mathematics teachers. She has taught mathematics and technology for first- through eighth-grade students. Email: rquinn@cabotschool.org

Sáiz, Mariana is currently focused on the conceptions of primary and secondary school teachers in several topics of mathematics, especially geometry and measurement. Mariana has served as a professor of Statistics and Mathematics Education at the Universidad Pedagógica Nacional in México City. She earned her doctorate degree in Mathematics Education from the Departamento de Matemática Educativa of Cinvestav in 2002. She has several contributions published in the PME and PMENA proceedings and has participated in other mathematics education meetings. She has written mathematics textbooks for secondary pupils with other co-workers. She has also published in Mexican and Spanish journals. Email: saizmar@yahoo.com

Sánchez, Victoria, is a professor at the Department of Didactic of Mathematics at the University of Seville, Spain. In that university, she has developed her work as teacher and researcher in the last two decades. She has taught mathematics teacher education courses and mathematics courses for elementary teachers. She also has taught graduate level courses on research in mathematics education. Her research in mathematics education spreads over several areas: mathematics teacher education, the relationship between research and practice in mathematics teacher education and mathematics teacher's knowledge and practice. Email: vsanchez@us.es

Shriki, Atara is a member of the academic staff at Oranim – Academic College of Education since 2002. Her teaching specialities are mathematics, logic and methods courses. Dr. Shriki is an active member of Kesher-Cham – R&D centre for improving and reviving mathematics education at Technion – Israel Institute of Technology where she studied mathematics and mathematics education and received her D.Sc. in 1996. Her Doctoral dissertation (E. Bar-On supervisor) is a study of the mechanism associated with the ability to retrieve mathematical information from human long-term memory. Her research interest is mainly in the area of mathematics teachers' beliefs and self image and their ability to change their perceptions about learning, as well as their practice of teaching. In addition she is interested in developing creativity of prospective teachers through their engagement in Project-Based-Learning. Email: shriki@tx.technion.ac.il

Spanneberg, Rose, is a Director of the Rhodes University Mathematics Education Project (RUMEP) in South Africa where she works with in-service teachers of mathematics at the undergraduate and graduate levels, respectively. RUMEP strives to find ways of improving mathematics teaching and learning in previously disadvantaged schools in the Eastern Cape. Her research interest is in the professional development of mathematics teachers especially the impact of in-service programmes on teachers' beliefs and classroom practices. She received doctorate degree from Curtin University in Australia. Email: r.spanneberg@ru.ac.za

Svec, Kelly received her BS in Forestry from the University of Kentucky. She is presently working on her certification to teach elementary education from University of Kentucky. She presented at AAMTE (Appalachian Association for Mathematics Teacher Educators) in 2005 where she presented Assessment of IMAP Video Clips of Children for a Content Math Course for Preservice Elementary School Teachers with Dana Williams and Richard Millman. Email: kabone30@yahoo.com

Anne, Teppo, while an Adjunct Instructor at Montana State University, developed and supervised a two-semester mathematics content course for future elementary teachers. She has contributed numerous book chapters and journal articles, including the JRME Monograph *Qualitative Research Methods in Mathematics Education.* She participated in the 12th ICMI Study on the Future of the Teaching and Learning and co-authored the chapter on "Symbols and Language". Although no longer teaching, she remains active in the international mathematics education research community. Email: arteppo@theglobal.net

Williams, Dana graduated from the University of Kentucky in May of 2008. She majored in elementary education and specialized in mathematics. She resides in Austin, Texas with her husband and three children. Dana enjoys teaching and loves to travel around the U.S. with her family. Email: danasw@windstream.net

Author Index

Subject Index

Printed in the United States
127496LV00006B/6/P

9 780387 096681